All Together Different

THE GOLDSTEIN-GOREN SERIES
IN AMERICAN JEWISH HISTORY
General Editor: Hasia R. Diner

*We Remember with Reverence and Love:
American Jews and the Myth of Silence
after the Holocaust, 1945–1962*
Hasia R. Diner

Is Diss a System? A Milt Gross Comic Reader
Edited by Ari Y. Kelman

*All Together Different:
Yiddish Socialists, Garment Workers, and
the Labor Roots of Multiculturalism*
Daniel Katz

All Together Different

Yiddish Socialists, Garment Workers, and the Labor Roots of Multiculturalism

Daniel Katz

NEW YORK UNIVERSITY PRESS
New York and London

For Pat, Christina, and Amanda,
Strong women, all

NEW YORK UNIVERSITY PRESS
New York and London
www.nyupress.org

References to Internet websites (URLs) were accurate at the time of writing.
Neither the author nor New York University Press is responsible for URLs
that may have expired or changed since the manuscript was prepared.

Library of Congress Cataloging-in-Publication Data

Katz, Daniel, 1962–
All together different : Yiddish Socialists, garment workers, and
the Labor roots of multiculturalism / Daniel Katz.
p. cm. — (The Goldstein-Goren Series in American Jewish History)
Includes bibliographical references and index.
ISBN 978–0–8147–4836–7 (cloth : alk. paper) —
ISBN 978–0–8147–6366–7 (ebook) —
ISBN 978–0–8147–6367–4 (ebook)
1. Clothing trade—United States—History—20th century. 2. Collective bargaining—
Clothing industry—United States. 3. Jewish labor unions—United States—History.
4. Working class—Political activity—United States—History—20th century. 5. Jews—
Political activity—United States—History—20th century. 6. Jews—Employment—
United States—History—20th century. 7. Multiculturalism—United States—History—
20th century. 8. International Ladies' Garment Workers' Union. I. Title.
HD6515.C5K38   2011
331.88'18708992407471—dc23   2011028187

New York University Press books are printed on acid-free paper,
and their binding materials are chosen for strength and durability.
We strive to use environmentally responsible suppliers and materials
to the greatest extent possible in publishing our books.

Manufactured in the United States of America

10 9 8 7 6 5 4 3 2 1

Contents

Preface

Some time after the 1991 Crown Heights riots, while riding across the Brooklyn Bridge, my wife and I began a conversation that led me back to graduate school in the mid-1990s. We lived on the border of Crown Heights and both knew Hasidic Jews and Caribbean Blacks from the neighborhood and work. In 1991, Pat was a social worker, and I worked as an organizer for the union of clerical and technical workers at New York University. As awful as the riots were, the popular press inflamed the situation by mischaracterizing the events as part of a historic Black-Jewish conflict. The media's distortions went counter to the complexities of the stories we were hearing and also belied our own family experiences and worldviews. Pat grew up in a working-class African American family in the Bronx, counting Jews among her friends and favorite teachers. Her mother, Frances, grew up in Harlem and has fond memories of her Jewish godmother. My parents were Jewish college professors who encouraged our embrace of civil rights and multiculturalism. Indeed, I grew up feeling that my Jewishness was in part defined by our relationships with other racial-ethnic groups.

In the aftermath of the riots, I wondered about American Jewish identity over time, multiculturalism, working-class life, and Black-Jewish relations. I wanted to understand more about the complexities of these social intersections in New York City. In particular, I began to look for a time when Blacks and Jews, who seemed pitted against one another, had struggled together to advance mutual goals of social justice. I soon found Hasia Diner's *In the Almost Promised Land: American Jews and Blacks, 1915–1935*, which pointed me toward the education programs of the International Ladies' Garment Workers' Union (ILGWU) of the 1930s. With that, I found the moment in time for such an alliance, which also involved other ethnic groups. The ILGWU had it all: Blacks and Jews, immigrants, women, militant local unions, and education. But I was vexed by one question in particular: what made these Jewish union leaders so sensitive to Blacks and others? Was it their long Jewish history, as Diner and others suggested, or was it primarily their socialism? This book argues that their particular socialist worldview was at the root of their multiculturalism.

Ultimately, I discovered even broader implications in this story of multicultural unionism. For the past twenty years, the prevailing wisdom among labor historians has been that the modern industrial labor movement formed in the 1930s because the connections between immigrant workers and ethnic institutions weakened and their connections to each other as workers across ethnic divisions strengthened. But the garment workers' unions dominated by Russian Jewish immigrants had very different relationships to their ethnic institutions and came to the United States after the turn of the twentieth century with well-developed ideas of multiculturalism. Theirs was a different model of unionism that has been ignored or poorly understood by historians, and a model that could inform a contemporary revival of the American labor movement. At the same time, for historians of multiculturalism who rarely look back beyond the 1960s and 1970s, this book highlights an important period to consider. I have identified a very specific form of cultural pluralism that was once well understood by European revolutionaries and informed how most Jews in the decades before World War II came to regard and interact with other racial-ethnic groups in the United States. I think advocates of cultural pluralism, particularly those who find themselves put on the defensive by a new movement of cosmopolitan multiculturalists, will find this story enlightening.

When I look back, I am astonished and humbled by how generous so many people have been with their time, expertise, and, in some cases, their own research. I will undoubtedly neglect to acknowledge some people, for which I apologize in advance. This book began in the fall of 1997 as a graduate research paper in the "Women and Gender History" seminar led by Alice Kessler-Harris and Jennifer Jones at Rutgers University. Over the following thirteen years, I have been reminded daily how very fortunate I have been to be surrounded and nurtured by an extraordinary community of historians, librarians, archivists, activists, university colleagues, editors, neighbors, friends, and family. Alice Kessler-Harris is most responsible for this book coming to fruition. She directed my dissertation and championed the project as it transformed, reading several versions of the manuscript and never for a moment letting me doubt its value. Nor did she ever fail to challenge me to consider more deeply and with greater complexity. My committee members, to whom I am deeply grateful, also shaped the dissertation: David Levering Lewis, Robin D. G. Kelley, and Dorothy Sue Cobble. Sue has continued to support my career in many large and small ways. I owe an enormous debt to Hasia Diner, who embraced me and this book, bringing it to the attention of Eric Zinner at New York University Press. I am honored that this book is being published in the Goldstein-Goren Series in American Jewish History that she edits.

I am extremely lucky to have been part of two exceptional graduate-school experiences, first in the mid-1980s at the University of Wisconsin and second at Rutgers University in the mid– and late 1990s. Brilliant and dynamic faculty and students in both places had a lasting impression on me as a historian and as a political activist. Especially, I want to thank Karen Balcom, Norma Basch, Paul Boyer, Jennifer Brier, William Jelani Cobb, Sara Dubow, Bruce Fehn, Maureen Fitzgerald, Becca Gershenson, Tiffany Gill, Linda Gordon, Sara Gordon, Matt Guterl, Justin Hart, Jennifer Jones, Lisa Kannenberg, Melissa Klapper, Peter Lau, James Levy, Jan Lewis, Nancy MacLean, Tom McCormick, Lucia McMahon, Khalil Muhammad, Lisa Phillips, Mary Poole, Robert Shaffer, Jennifer Tammi, and Chip Young. During the ten-year interregnum between graduate programs, I took David Nasaw's seminar "Culture and Society" at the City University of New York Graduate Center, which had a particularly deep impact on my thinking.

Staff at several archives have gone to extraordinary lengths in assisting my work. At the Kheel Center for Labor-Management Documentation and Archives at Cornell University, I want to thank Melissa Holland, Paulette Manos, Barbara Morley, Hope Nicely, Patrizia Sione, and Richard Strassberg. Richard and Barbara went out of their way to dig through and dig up essential documents. At YIVO, I am grateful to Leo Greenbaum for unfettered access to unprocessed collections, particularly of the Workmen's Circle. The Tamiment Library and Wagner Archives at NYU has been home for me over the years as both a scholar and a union activist. I thank Debra Bernhardt, Rachel Bernstein, Jonathan Bloom, Robert Eberwein, Peter Filardo, Erika Gottfried, Pat Logan, Gail Malmgreen (who pointed me in the right direction more times than I can count), Michael Nash, Arieh Lebowitz of the Jewish Labor Committee, and Nancy Cricco of the NYU Archives. Extremely helpful archivists at the Yale University Library Manuscripts Collection, the New York Public Library (NYPL) Schomburg Center for Research in Black Culture, the NYPL for the Performing Arts at Lincoln Center, and the NYPL Stephen A. Schwarzman Building also assisted me. I wrote the final version of this book as an author in residence at the Frederick Lewis Allen room in the Schwarzman Building. The community of writers and the unrestricted access to the vast materials of the NYPL made the process of finishing both fruitful and joyful. For that privilege, I want to thank David Smith and Jay Barksdale.

Scores of women and men in the ILGWU and UNITE! took me into their confidence and shared unselfishly with me their memories and contacts with others. It was thrilling for me to meet and speak with these life-long fighters for social justice. For opening doors that I did not know existed and for handing me valuable documents, I particularly want to thank Kathy Andrade, Mary Boyer, Amelia Bucchieri, Eliot Eisenbeck, Nettie Harari Shrog, Rubye Jones, Robert Lazar, Walter Menkoff, Jasper Peyton, Saul Salit, Inocencia Chencha Valdez, Leyla Vural, and Paul Zimmerman.

This book has benefited immeasurably from the thoughtful consideration of a number of scholars. For reading entire versions of the manuscript, each contributing important elements to its structure and argument, I am grateful to Jim Barrett, David Browne, Hasia Diner, Will Jones, Laurie Matheson, Randi Storch, and Dan Levinson Wilk. James Levy challenged me on the paddle-ball court and in my theoretical thinking, helping me through that murky process of trying to imagine how to turn a dissertation into a book. Special thanks to Mary Jo Buhle, Anne Enke, Nan Enstad, Katja Esson, Gina Roarke, and Daniel Soyer for their well-considered comments and pointed questions on papers I delivered at the Organization of American Historians, Berkshire Conference on the History of Women, American Studies Association, North American Labor History Conference, YIVO, and New York Public Library. I treasure the conversations I have had with Rich Greenwald, Tony Michels, and Ian Riefowitz, whose own works underpinned various sections of the book. And for sharing their thoughts and insights late into night when they thought they were sleeping for free in my Brooklyn apartment, I thank Jeff Cowie, Jennifer Klein, Nancy MacLean, Laura McEnaney, Mark Soderstrom, and Heather Thompson.

I deeply appreciate the copyediting, editorial support, and commentary of David Browne, Gail Malmgreen, Lisa Philips, Mary Poole, Bob Reynolds, Martha Trachtenberg, and Lauren Yaffe on various aspects of the dissertation, articles, and book chapters. Sylvia Neves, Kendra Tappin, and Yanique Taylor assisted me in finding sources, digitizing images, and transcribing interviews. Collette Hyman, incredibly, gave me a banker's box filled with primary sources she had gathered for her own book on labor theater. Many thanks also to Eric Zinner and Ciara McLaughlin at NYU Press for believing in this project and bringing it to publication. In addition, I want to thank Despina Papazoglou Gimbel and Charles Hames for shepherding this project through production. Also, I want to thank Andrew Katz (no relation) at NYU Press for his meticulous copyediting of the final draft of the book. Especially, I need to give credit to Grey Osterud, who worked with me on the final version of this book. She read and commented on the penultimate manuscript in extraordinary detail, offering me pages and pages of advice on how to make this a leaner, more coherent, and more readable book. No detail was too small for her to consider, and she never lost sight of the big picture. I only regret that I was not able to incorporate all of her wonderful suggestions.

I am also thankful for the material support that allowed me to continue my academic work. It would have been nearly impossible to complete my degree without funding I received from the graduate school and the history department at Rutgers, the YIVO Institute for Jewish Research, and the Joseph Gotteiner fellowship. Steve Diner and Liz Mitchell made it possible for me to finish my dissertation while working in the Rutgers-Newark Honors College. The State University of New York, Empire State College has awarded me several generous grants that have allowed me to continue my research for the book, to transcribe oral-history interviews, and to obtain editorial assistance. I have also been supported by wonderful colleagues and students at Empire State College, many of whom have shown up to my talks and helped me to rally as I struggled to finish.

Many friends have sustained me in the course of writing and rewriting this book. Heartfelt thanks to Sara Elbert, Jennifer Klein and Jim Berger, Bea Rosenberg, Randi Storch, and Meryl Miller, who opened their homes to me and kept me company after the long days at the archives were over. For their love, camaraderie, and good cheer, special thanks go to Beth Barish, Jonathan Best, David Browne, Rich Greenwald, Kim Hewitt, Sid Huang, Tim Kung, James Levy, Mark May, Laura McEnaney, Lucy McLellan, Maggie Murphy, Susan O'Brien, Mary Poole, Kayne Roarke, David Staiger, Ali Stillman, Kendra Tappin, Lisa Van Donsel, Dan Levinson Wilk, Lauren Yaffe, and Chip Young. With affection and unbridled enthusiasm, my brother Fred Katz, sister-in-law Linda Kotis, sister Shira Kirsh, and brother-in-law Izzie Kirsh have looked forward to the publication of this book almost as anxiously as I have. I thank them very much for that support. My parents, Benjamin Joseph Katz and Kaila Goldman Katz, died before this book was conceived. But my sense of their pride in me and the joy they would have felt at its publication has been a constant source of encouragement. Finally, Pat Jerido stood by me and supported this project throughout its long gestation. She believed in it and me, even when I doubted myself. Her sensibilities about race, gender, and social justice are entwined in the narrative and analysis, as I have appropriated many of them for my own. I thank her deeply for her love and friendship and for coproducing the two projects of which I am most proud, our daughters, Christina and Amanda. Together they have been my toughest critics, though not necessarily in regard to scholarship.

Abbreviations

ACWA	Amalgamated Clothing Workers of America
AFL	American Federation of Labor
ALP	American Labor Party
ANLC	American Negro Labor Congress
BSCP	Brotherhood of Sleeping Car Porters
CIO	Congress (Committee) of Industrial Organizations
CP	Communist Party
DSOC	Department Store Organizing Committee
FDR	Franklin Delano Roosevelt
FTP	Federal Theater Project
GEB	General Executive Board
ILGWU	International Ladies' Garment Workers' Union
IWO	International Workers' Order
IWW	Industrial Workers of the World
JAC	Joint Action Committee
JLC	Jewish Labor Committee
MOWM	March on Washington Movement
NAACP	National Association for the Advancement of Colored People
NIRA	National Industrial Recovery Act
NLC	Negro Labor Committee
NRA	National Recovery Administration
NTWIU	Needle Trades Workers' Industrial Union
NYPL	New York Public Library
NYWTUL	New York Women's Trade Union League
SLP	Socialist Labor Party
SR	Socialist Revolutionary Party of Russia
TOA	Theater of Action
TUC	Trade Union Committee for Organizing Colored Workers
TUEL	Trade Union Educational League
TUUL	Trade Union Unity League
UDC	Union Defenders Committee

UHT	United Hebrew Trades
UNITE!	Union of Needletrades Industrial and Textile Employees
WLT	Workers Laboratory Theater
WPA	Works Projects Administration
WTUL	Women's Trade Union League
YMCA	Young Men's Christian Association

Introduction

One April morning in 1999, I sat in Maida Springer-Kemp's Pittsburgh kitchen to talk about her early days as a union activist in the International Ladies' Garment Workers' Union (ILGWU). She served me tea, sat down erect, and began to speak with a highly formal diction. At eighty-nine, her memory was sharp, and she had a warm sense of humor. She delighted in reminiscing about her comrades in the ILGWU and the labor movement she helped to build.[1] But nothing seemed to give her as much pleasure as her realization that I had no idea what she was saying when she sprinkled her stories with Yiddish phrases. For example, in recalling the hostility that erupted during grievance meetings, she remembered one party or the other uttering the curse "Er zol vaksen vi a tsibeleh, mit dem kop in drerd." I looked at her, puzzled. She giggled and translated for me: "He should grow like an onion, with his head in the ground!"[2]

Springer-Kemp immigrated to Harlem with her Panamanian mother and West Indian father in 1917, when she was seven years old. She got her first job in the garment industry in the winter of 1926–1927 and joined the ILGWU in 1933, when it was still a weak remnant of a once powerful union. A few months later, Springer-Kemp was instrumental in organizing the most critical strike in the union's history, in which thousands of Black and Spanish-speaking workers joined for the first time. She stayed active in Local 22's educational department in the 1930s, and during World War II she accepted a job in another local union as education director. She picked up Yiddish phrases in these years through intimate proximity to Jewish co-workers in the shop and while participating in classroom, social, cultural, and recreational activities sponsored by union educational departments. When her local's membership swelled with monolingual Yiddish-speaking refugees after World War II, she took advantage of union-sponsored Yiddish classes to be able to converse with her members. Through formal language training and informal conversations, Springer-Kemp learned a great deal about her fellow unionists' view of the world and how they lived in it.

The union offered Yiddish language instruction, as it did Italian, Spanish, and, later, Chinese classes, in order to demonstrate its respect for ethnic cultures and to help families communicate across generations. But union leaders also recognized the cross-cultural awareness that members developed in programs geared to ethnic groups other than their own. The ILGWU's public celebration of ethnic culture extended to all major racial-ethnic groups in the union as a vehicle to build trust within and among them. When Springer-Kemp joined the union in 1933 as a Spanish speaker and a Black woman, she had numerous opportunities to explore and express the foods, music idioms, languages, and histories of her family. In those venues, members from many backgrounds frequently participated. In time, Springer-Kemp came to see herself as African American after marrying African American men, raising a child, and living most of her adult life in African American communities. While developing her own racial-ethnic identity, she learned to embrace the differences between union members for the sheer joy of it and as a strategic means to a political end.

Springer-Kemp's facility with Yiddish is but one illustration of the multiculturalism that permeated the Jewish labor and socialist movements from the first decade of the twentieth century through the 1930s. Working-class immigrant Jews who formed the ILGWU employed creative strategies to attend to the many gendered, political, generational, religious, and language cultures among their members. In the most highly developed period of racial-ethnic cultural exchange in the ILGWU, from late 1933 to late 1937, tens of thousands of garment workers in several key local unions participated in an extraordinary experiment in multicultural unionism.

The centrality of ethnicity to the formation and operation of unions from 1900 to the late 1930s was not limited to the ILGWU or the Jewish needle trades.[3] What may have been unusual in the Jewish socialist and labor movements was the extent to which Jews were self-conscious about the importance of other ethnic cultures in a multiethnic and interracial movement. Long before multicultural movements emerged in the 1960s and 1970s in the United States, the ILGWU broadcasted the critical significance of its many constituent racial-ethnic groups. The union used the collage "A Union of Many Cultures" in a variety of local and International publications into the late 1930s to reflect the membership's racial as well as cultural diversity.

Jews sought to establish cultural activities and institutions among their own radical coethnics and to encourage those activities and institutions among workers of other ethnic groups as well. Through formal classes, athletic and artistic activities, vacation retreats, and dances, these garment

A UNION OF MANY CULTURES

Figure 1.1. The ILGWU used this collage frequently in the mid-1930s. After the August 1933 strike, Local 22 boasted that it represented workers from thirty-two "nationalities" including Jewish, Italian, Spanish, and Negro. (Ryllis Alexander and Omar Pancoast Goslin, *Growing Up: 21 Years of Education with the I.L.G.W.U., 1917–1938* [New York: H. Wolff, 1938])

workers and their kin wove a chain-mail organization equipped to respond to a complex and rapidly changing industry. In so doing, they pushed the boundaries of interracial socialization and demonstrated an alternative model of unionism that inspired union building throughout the 1930s.

Calling this approach *social unionism*, they implemented it through the most comprehensive worker-education program in American history to that point. Through broadly conceived educational activities, union leaders encouraged workers to explore and express their distinct ethnic and racial identities within the context of a militant union movement.[4] In this way, diverse groups of members developed trust in one another and a fierce loyalty to their union. Social unionism was a radical vision of social organization, a prescription for the political role of unions as well as an organizing strategy. Above all, it was an expression of union culture that intersected with a larger movement for social change. Architects of social unionism saw the union as a mechanism to bring workers, families, and working-class communities into the labor movement through cultural as well as political activism.[5] When it worked, social unionism appealed not only to the material needs of members but to their political hopes and their social and creative desires.

The ILGWU is a fascinating study both for its important position in the American labor movement and because its leaders and activists were connected with the full breadth of social and political movements in the early and mid-twentieth century. Since the 1910s, the ILGWU was a great progenitor of programs and ideas for the American labor movement, and the ideals of social unionism influenced the Congress of Industrial Organizations (CIO) and, through it, the New Deal order.[6] As one of the principal founders of the CIO, the ILGWU helped lead the labor movement in organizing the vast army of industrial workers in dozens of industries.[7] A close look at the people who led the revival of the ILGWU in the 1930s and at the methods they employed reveals an intriguing connection to revolutionary ideas and experiments among Jewish radicals over the preceding forty years. This book puts the spotlight on an alternative vision of unionism that coexisted in the ILGWU along with, and for a while held sway over, the more moderate vision that eventually eclipsed it.

This study highlights a distinct formulation of multiculturalism among Russian Jewish immigrants over half a century. Russian Jewish socialists shared a Jewish national imagination that grew out of their place as permanent foreigners in the Russian Empire. Czarist regimes imposed Russian language and culture on institutions of power and authority throughout the regions under their control. Jews were only the most subdued and marginalized of the scores of national and ethnic groups in the Russian Empire. Socialist movements that opposed the czar, typically led by students, scholars, and artists, formed among many of those national groups. Most radicals worked among their coethnics on the basis of a shared history rooted in territory, countries, or kingdoms that were once autonomous and a source of national cultural pride. But Jews in Russia were among the few ethnic groups, and the largest, to be without any home territory in the empire. As minorities in every region in which they lived, Jews were doubly oppressed by the institutions of the Russian Empire and by locally dominant populations. Jews responded in a multiplicity of ways, but the largest movement was a peculiar form of socialism based on the lives and idiom of the Jewish folk, which began to develop in Russia in the early 1880s, just at the moment when Jews began to emigrate from Russia in massive numbers.[8]

Inspired by Yiddish socialism, Jewish intellectuals labored to recover and elevate their own Yiddish culture and envisioned a class-based revolution in which all workers would be rooted in venerated ethnic folk cultures. Their own revolutionary Jewish identity was tied to the construction of a multicultural movement that encouraged the revolutionary identities of workers from all ethnic groups. The clearest expression of this form of multiculturalism in the United States, which I call *mutual culturalism*, can be seen in a movement of union building in the ILGWU that began in the first decade of the twentieth century, climaxed in the 1930s, and had a far-reaching influence on American social and political culture.

In the United States, ideas and movements for multiculturalism began in the 1910s as social critics grappled with the ramifications of massive immigration, acculturation and assimilation, world war, and nationalism. Randolph Bourne, writing in 1916, was appalled at the ravages of the Great War and blamed European nationalism, which he saw manifest in the United States as well. Americanization efforts failed because they sought to impose Anglo-American culture on other ethnic cultures. He envisioned a "new cosmopolitan idea" in which American nationalism would embrace the "federation of ethnic cultures" that already existed. A radical notion among Anglo-Saxon elites such as himself, Bourne's cosmopolitanism was nevertheless bounded by class and race. He expressly considered only European cultures, and only those "finer forms" of "music, verse, the essay, philosophy."[9] Writing in the 1910s and 1920s, Horace Kallen, who coined the term *cultural pluralism*, argued for the rights of immigrant cultures to resist assimilation.[10] In a 1915 article for the *Nation*, Kallen blamed nationalism for the world war and argued that, since even the working classes had each supported its own nation, the war underscored the weakness of class relative to nationalism. However, Kallen differentiated between negative nationalism based on hate and positive nationalism based on cultural pride and argued for an embrace of diversity within a dominant, though not unitary, American culture. Neither of these models of multiculturalism directly confronts the relationship between class formation and ethnic identity. In all ethnically heterogeneous societies, there are strong correlations between race and ethnicity on the one hand and class, status, and privilege on the other. Writing more recently, James R. Barrett does discuss the prevalent relationships among ethnic groups of workers who create working-class cultures within their ethnic groups, which he calls "ethno-cultural class formation."[11] But the mutual culturalism of Yiddish socialism was predicated on two assumptions that went further than what Barrett has identified: first, in capitalist societies, ethnic identity is a constituent of class; and second, socialism demands mutually venerated ethnic cultures.

Mutual culturalism shares with cultural pluralism a respect for distinct ethnic cultures—including language, religion, and family relationships—and a willingness to tolerate the practice of those cultural forms in society and its institutions. However, mutual culturalism considers ethnic cultural differences in the context of class and the power relations within groups and between the dominant and subordinate ethnic groups. Under state regimes underpinned by capitalism, subordinate ethnic groups struggle for economic and political inclusion as well as cultural expression. For mutual culturalists, the struggle to assert cultural identity is a class struggle as well. The ability for subordinate ethnic groups to coexist is critical to the struggle for social justice and should be encouraged as a central component of movement building. Ethnic cultural coexistence cannot be accomplished through expressions of sympathy or humanitarianism alone but requires a principle of strategic mutual struggle. Among Yiddish socialists, a mutual effort to support the multiplicity of workers' ethnic cultural ties was essential for revolution because it strengthened workers' own ethnic struggle against the dominant culture and made them feel secure that the revolutionary movement was not similarly bent on suppressing their differences. Because the capitalists against whom Jews in Russia and the United States struggled were most often Jewish as well, Yiddish socialism was a class-based ethnic identity.

How did revolutionary Jews imagine and to what extent did they succeed in building a multicultural labor movement in the 1930s? An exploration of these questions offers important insights into the relationship between class and what Benedict Anderson would call the "imagined community" of Jewish nationalists.[12] Not all ILGWU members shared the revolutionary ideas and ethics of Yiddish socialism. But many groups and individuals demanding inclusion readily embraced that worldview. After Jewish immigrant women from the Russian Empire muscled their way into the male-dominated ILGWU, important leaders among them accessed Yiddish socialist ideas and designed educational programs to attract and retain other marginalized workers in the Lower East Side needle trades. These women tapped the revolutionary ideology of Yiddish socialism that framed their ethnic identity to guide them in their relations with workers of other racial-ethnic cultural groups. Just as important, they tapped the extensive resources of the Jewish socialist and labor movements, of which the ILGWU was an integral part.

Separate and interdependent at the same time, various institutions centered in the Jewish Lower East Side of Manhattan cultivated activists, advocates, and leaders. Jews were attracted to the whole panoply of radical movements, including anarchism and, later, communism, and they formed rival institutions. The ideological divide on the Left was very real, but Jewish communists and socialists maintained common tenets that are often overlooked. The Yiddishist methods of transmitting socialist ideas through the experience of ethnic culture were so powerful that they transcended the escalating political schisms in the Jewish socialist movement during the 1920s. Over the course of three decades, Yiddish socialists in the ILGWU and in scores of unions and organizations associated with the Socialist and Communist parties, among other left groups, resisted pressures to conform to a moderate American standard of behavior and thought. Yiddish socialists consistently reached out to make common cause with other racial-ethnic minority groups. In this period, Jewish unionists self-consciously considered and reconsidered their ethnic identities, social visions, and relationships to the American nation.

This book argues for a rehabilitation of multiculturalism to counter the prevalent assumption that ethnic affiliations are inherently incompatible with militant class consciousness. Gary Gerstle and Lizabeth Cohen have contributed to an emerging scholarly debate about the limits of multiculturalism.[13] In both of their studies, the immigrant ethnic community was dominated by cultural, economic, and political elites that stifled working-class militancy. Workers could only become class conscious when ethnicity was tempered and interpreted through exposure to popular culture. According to these authors, unintended consequences in elements of the dominant mass culture, not the multiple ethnic communities from which workers came, were responsible for the success of industrial organizations. By reclaiming a moment when multiculturalism was indistinguishable from the formation of class consciousness and militant union building, I complicate the relationship between ethnicity and class and uncover both the multicultural roots of labor and the labor roots of multiculturalism.

This strategy of multicultural unionism was extraordinarily successful in the 1930s. The character of the ILGWU and conditions in the ladies' garment industry combined to create a fertile bed in which this kind of social and political experimentation could be cultivated. The ILGWU was formed in 1900 with the amalgamation of four previously independent unions representing mostly skilled workers. For the next thirty-five years, local union officers typically resisted the encroachment on their autonomy by International union leaders, who waged a recurring battle to centralize authority. As the union grew to incorporate semiskilled and unskilled workers, a flexible but contentious structure resulted. Members' suspicions of a strong central leadership were coupled with an unpredictable industry dominated by thousands of small, transient manufacturing shops and populated with equally transient union members. At times, shop-level activists, local union leaders, joint board officers, and International union officials all vied with one another for authority through various union functions. Until union power was concentrated firmly on the International level in the late 1930s, individual leaders or small groups were relatively free to innovate with or without cooperation from other groups in the union. Indeed, over a critical period of four years, from 1933 to 1937, local unions could create educational programs without waiting for permission or catering them to more moderate tastes.

Before the Supreme Court in 1937 upheld the Wagner Act, which established the first real mechanism on the federal level to regulate and enforce labor-management contracts in multiple private-sector industries, the union depended on the militancy and activism of union members on the shop floor.[14] Even moderate union leaders, concerned as much with organizational hierarchy and personal authority as with broad social ideals, welcomed any mechanism to foster union loyalty among members. Most union members were young women who sat on the margins of power in their families and communities. Many women craved opportunities to create, lead, and express themselves through these programs. By the mid-1930s, the union confronted the reality of thousands of new members from ethnic and racial groups that had little or no previous representation in the union. Success depended on a strategy that acknowledged that fact. Finally, Jewish leaders with direct links to Yiddish socialism in the first two decades of the twentieth century were well placed on the local and International levels of the union to address changes in the demographics of the garment-industry workforce, and programs that celebrated ethnic and racial difference were familiar options.

Within the ILGWU's diffuse structure, many educational programs both in local unions and the International offices became centers of influence for social unionists and among the greatest sources of the union's power. These centers created conditions under which workers of different racial and ethnic backgrounds forged social bonds in the 1930s. The union marshaled its members through the social and cultural venues it constructed, and it flexed its muscles on the picket line, in the elite cultural venues of the country and in electoral and public-policy campaigns. These exercises of power gave the ILGWU the leverage necessary to build relationships with liberal politicians and to help effect lasting changes.

The rivalry among left factions in the American labor movement at times contributed to greater autonomy for local unions in the ILGWU, often manifested through the proliferation of educational programs. While moderate union leaders may have benefited greatly from the power generated by the turbines of local educational programs, they were often deeply ambivalent about them.[15] Through the 1920s and into the mid-1930s, the International union supported local union programs in part to counter competition from the Communist Party, but educational programing was often the most radicalized part of the ILGWU. In any case, social bonding in local union programs that attracted shopmates was extremely effective. This feeling of camaraderie, simultaneously reinforcing and stretching across racial and ethnic lines, demonstrated the political power inherent in what we now call multiculturalism.

The argument presented here depends on our understanding of how Russian Jewish socialists defined and used the concepts of *culture, nationality,* and *race.* Yiddishists tended to understand all groups in categories of ethnic association.[16] The experience and sensibilities of most immigrant Russian Jews fed a conception of race and nationality that diverged from the constructions forged through federal law and popular culture.[17] Before World War II, they used the terms *nationality* and, alternatively but interchangeably, *culture* to describe all ethnic, racial, language, and national groups. They used *race* less frequently, sometimes when referring to Black people but also interchangeably with culture and nationality, as in "the Jewish race." Though Black, Jewish, and other union leaders spoke about "the Negro race," most often ILGWU leaders placed "Negroes" under the categories of nationality and culture. As late as 1938, Jewish leaders in the ILGWU were counting nationalities in a way that anticipated a late-twentieth-century understanding of ethnicity. A 1934 census of the Dressmakers' Local 22, for example, listed Jewish, Italian, Negro, and Spanish under the category of "nationality."[18] In the census, there was neither a Caucasian nor an Asian category. Along with the major groups, the union identified, for example, German, French, and Irish as well as Hindus, Japanese, and Malayan.

TABLE I.1
Census of the Membership of the Dressmakers' Union Local 22, ILGWU, October 1, 1934

According to Nationalities	Members	Percentage
Jewish	19,842	70.5
Colored	2,569	9.5
Spanish	1,850	6.5
American	1,053	3.7
German	655	2.3
Polish	522	1.8
Greek	278	1.0
British	196	
French	187	
Austrian	185	
Russian	148	
Syrians	150	
Hungarian	100	
Armenians	111	
Irish	99	
Turks	86	
Scandinavian	53	
Roumanian	55	

The ILGWU's use of the terms *nationality* and *culture* fit the revolutionary Russian Jewish worldview in two respects. First, Yiddishists saw culture in the Russian Empire, most often characterized by language rather than territory, as the foundation of nationality. Western European constructs of racial difference did not resonate with Yiddishists' experience of nationality in the Russian Empire, which comprised nearly one hundred ethnic groups spanning northern and eastern Europe, the Middle East, and western, central, and eastern Asia. Second, Russian Jews experienced their culture and their developing nationality as outsiders and minorities within an oppressive dominant culture. Jews, while still in Russia and soon after immigrating

TABLE I.1 (*continued*)
Census of the Membership of the Dressmakers' Union Local 22,
ILGWU, October 1, 1934

According to Nationalities	Members	Percentage
Serbian	35	
Lithuanian	36	
Danish	6	
Mexican	4	
Dutch	3	
Argentine	3	
Czech	3	
Belgium	2	
Ukrainian	2	
Bulgarian	1	
Hindu	1	
Malayan	1	
Chinese	1	
Japanese	1	
Total	28,248	
According to Sex	Members	Percentage
Female	21,808	77.5
Male	6,430	22.5

to the United States, made explicit comparisons between their conditions in czarist Russia and those of Blacks in the American South, referring to lynchings and other white persecution as "pogroms," the Russian-derived Yiddish word that referred to state-sanctioned terror.[19] Many Jews identified themselves as a group in a category equivalent to that of Blacks, who were similarly positioned socially.

Throughout this book, I often link the categories of race and ethnicity, reflecting, in part, how my subjects viewed themselves and each other. I use *ethnicity* to mean the expression of or identification with distinct group cultures that are marked by common language, food, or geographic origin; religious or secular rituals; art, literature, and folklore; and family and gender relations. Ethnicity is, as Kathleen Neils Conzen, David A. Gerber, and colleagues write, "a process of construction or invention which incorporates, adapts, and amplifies preexisting communal solidarities, cultural attributes, and historical memories."[20] Ethnic identities among diasporic people are almost always in a state of flux, especially as people move away from the geographic origin of their cultures. Movement in place and time can weaken some markers of ethnic culture, such as language, or strengthen others, such as identification with the region or nation of family origin, and as David Hollinger points out, individuals may adopt very different cultures, for example, through marriage.[21]

Race has been used to mean many of the same things as ethnicity, particularly before World War II. Before sociologists and politicians settled on five major racial classifications, race often followed specific nationality, language, religious, and geographic designations.[22] And cultural characteristics have always been applied to categories of race.[23] In the United States, race has often determined the choices people made and the choices that were made for them, such as where they could live or work and the eligibility of marriage partners. For migrants and immigrants, those choices contributed to the shape of their ethnic identities. Jewish ILGWU activists in the mid-1930s conflated racial, national, and language categories, reflecting both a radical politics of multiculturalism and what David Roediger and James Barrett call their "inbetweenness."[24] Russian Jews in 1930s America were still heavily accented. Within their families and communities, the second generation had not yet overtaken their parents in social, political, or economic prominence. As a people, Russian Jews in the United States had not yet been assimilated and accepted as white by the dominant culture. In confronting racial injustice by embracing ethnic cultural diversity, these social unionists implicitly acknowledged that race and ethnicity existed as overlapping, if not entirely synonymous, social categories.

Men and women on the margins of the Russian Empire created Yiddish socialism. In New York, Jewish women who found themselves on the margins of their unions accessed Yiddish socialist ideas and conveyed them to racial-ethnic groups of workers who also sat at the margins: Italians first, then Blacks and Puerto Ricans. While some male leaders were sensitive to multiculturalism, women in local unions dominated by militant Jewish women were largely responsible for the institutions and programs of social unionism created in the 1910s and 1920s. Historians have been drawn to the militant feminism of union members during the Progressive Era, especially in the ILGWU. Through women's initiatives, the ILGWU was one of the first unions to establish union health centers, vacation retreats, and educational departments for its members. Some of these studies end in the 1920s at a low point in women's participation and influence in organized labor.[25] Others pick up the story of labor feminism in the 1940s.[26] But as Annelise Orleck and Elizabeth Faue have demonstrated, feminist women played key roles in the resurgence of the ILGWU and the broader labor movement in the 1930s.[27]

Women leaders in the local and International union departments, and in other institutions of the labor movement, marshaled the ranks of the ILGWU and built the structures to maintain militancy. In so doing, they flouted the virulent stereotype that linked working-class manliness and labor militancy.[28] They acted because of their position in the labor force, because of the presence of key leaders in shops and the union, and because they had the support of larger ethnic and political communities. Through education, they created and expanded union venues in which they could experiment with political, social, and cultural ideas. Their youth and their relatively brief time in the workforce contributed to their impatience. But other factors mitigated against women's power. Men, particularly those with more skills, stayed much longer in the workforce and earned higher wages. Through their longevity, men held most leadership positions in the union despite their small numbers. Until the 1930s, women typically worked in the garment shops until they married and began raising children. This pattern began to change during the Great Depression as women stayed in the workforce longer and, increasingly, after they married.[29] But men tended to guard their positions of power jealously and begrudged women leadership posts. The few women who reached high levels of International union authority did so at great personal sacrifice.[30]

This story opens an inquiry into the role of social unionism, as a strategy and as a set of principles rooted in radical ideology, propagated by strong women, and in building a militant union among a multicultural group of workers. The book traces developments across the country but is largely centered in New York City, which was the largest single port of entry for immigrants, including the Jews and Italians discussed in this book. It is also the single largest African American and Caribbean community in the United States outside the South, as well as the largest destination for Puerto Rican migrants. For many of these people, garment manufacturing was a gateway industry. In 1932, 80 percent of all dresses were manufactured in New York. Throughout the 1930s, New York City and the dress industry remained the heart of the ladies' garment industry, the third-largest-grossing industry in New York State. By 1940 the entire ladies' garment industry employed 365,442 people nationwide. Even as manufacturing began a steady migration outside New York, the union's 240,000 members remained concentrated in or near the city. In 1940, 142,589 members belonged to New York City locals, and over 32,000 members belonged to locals in nearby suburbs and small cities.[31]

This book begins by considering the ideological and political origins of revolutionary Jews, with a particular emphasis on the roles of women in the first wave of immigration from Russia to the United States. The climax of the story is reached at the golden moment of social unionism in the 1930s. The educational programs in the ILGWU, particularly those in New York City's Local 22 in the mid-1930s, were an intersection of ideology and cultural practice with routes that extended from Russia, Italy, the American Deep South, the British West Indies, and the Spanish Caribbean.

Social unionism in the ILGWU was spawned and shaped in part by Yiddishism, but it was not interchangeable with Yiddishism. It was a strategy embedded in union members' participation in a twentieth-century American labor movement, and it was put into practice by women of multiple racial-ethnic backgrounds. As workers intermingled, their ethnic cultures changed; in some cases, such as among non–Puerto Rican Hispanics, non-Russian Jews, and British West Indian Blacks, they blended into broader ethnic cultures. But these workers did not choose, nor did the ILGWU leadership immediately encourage them, to subordinate their distinctive cultures to a dominant American monoculture. Rather, union leaders encouraged members to identify with one of many ethnic cultural groups.

The phenomenon of social unionism in the ILGWU in the mid-1930s exposes a wide range of issues historians have grappled with: the roots of contemporary multiculturalism, the genesis of the modern labor movement, race relations, the origins of the New Deal, the character of American radical thought, and women's roles in all these developments. From 1933 to 1937, the ILGWU built a remarkably stable and coherent movement that linked a socialist vision, respect for ethnic and racial cultural difference, and a militant labor movement. Unfortunately, the phenomenon did not last. The male leaders of the International union steadily abandoned their multicultural appeal as they became increasingly linked to the highest echelons of political power in the United States, competition from the Communist Party subsided, and the United States moved closer to war.

This book is divided into three parts. In part 1, I trace the ideological origins of social unionism from the revolutionary philosophies of Jews in the late-nineteenth-century Russian Empire to the fragmented radical-left milieu in New York City of the 1920s and early 1930s. In chapter 1, I discuss the peculiarities of European Jewish nationalisms—both Yiddishism and Zionism—that influenced dominant and subordinate currents of Jewish American thinking in the twentieth century. I follow the immigration of Russian Jews who came to New York in the 1880s and 1890s and founded mutually supporting institutions on Yiddishist principles. In chapter 2, I explain how the experiences of young Jewish women, many of whom fled Russia after the failed 1905 revolution, forged a particularly militant sensibility that led to the surge of union building at the end of the first decade of the twentieth century and through the second. I also explore how the evolving ILGWU union structure provoked competition between local union autonomy and International authority. The tensions generated by these struggles played out along gender lines and involved control over educational and social institutions. Chapters 3 and 4 explore the elements of Yiddishism that underpinned the ideology of Jewish radicalism through World War I and survived the crisis on the Left that was precipitated by the Russian Revolution. I place the educational programs of the ILGWU in the context of the rivalry between radical groups and discuss the significance of women and non-Jews, especially Italians and Blacks, in the battles that took place through the 1920s.

In part 2, I highlight the multicultural phenomenon in the ILGWU during the period 1933–1937. I argue that social unionism as a strategy allowed the ILGWU to hold on to a vastly expanded membership that was more ethnically and racially diverse than ever before. The educational activities of the union functioned as a training ground for rank-and-file leaders and imbued the mostly female membership with a militant union consciousness. In addition, the educational program stabilized the union, allowing its leaders to pursue a newly empowered position in industry and politics. Chapter 5 reveals the complexities of social unionism in the mid-1930s, particularly in the Dressmakers' Local 22. Activities that cultivated and celebrated ethnic and racial differences embodied a vision of unionism and a future society that helped to make the ILGWU a powerful economic and political force. In chapter 6, I look at how multiculturalism intersected with different sectors of power critical to the ILGWU, especially the roles of gender, race, and citizenship in the contexts of the broader Jewish Left, interpersonal politics, contests between sectors of power in the union, and differing visions of state reformation.

In part 3, I explain the decline of social unionism in the ILGWU after 1936 in the context of the union's changing political ideology. Chapter 7 discusses how ILGWU leaders began to assign new meaning to the union's cultural activities as they devoted an enormous portion of educational resources of the union to the Broadway production *Pins and Needles*. I argue that the revue, created at the height of the Popular Front, demonstrates the aspirations of union leaders struggling to come to terms with their new role in the welfare state and as players in helping to shape foreign policy. For ILGWU leaders, *Pins and Needles* became a venue to express their position as political and cultural insiders. The show points to the union's weakening commitment to diverse ethnic and racial cultures and isolates the moment when the ILGWU leadership began to accept a dominant American culture.

PART I

1

"Harmoniously Functioning Nationalities"

Yiddish Socialism in Russia and the United States, 1892–1918

During the Sixth Zionist conference in Basle, Switzerland, in late August 1903, Theodor Herzl, the founder of the modern Zionist movement, asked to speak with Chaim Zhitlowsky, perhaps the most famous philosopher of Yiddish socialism. Though an obscure historical figure today, during the 1890s and 1900s Zhitlowsky commanded the attention of Russian Jewish intellectuals, while Herzl was better known among European heads of state than in the Jewish Diaspora. As a small movement of western European Jews, Zionism was overshadowed by revolutionary movements in the Russian Empire, such as the General Union of Jewish Workers, known as the Bund.

According to Zhitlowsky's account of their August 1903 meeting, Herzl asked him to use his influence in the Bund to halt the revolutionary movement among militant Russian Jews. Herzl had offered him a solution to the Jewish problem in Russia proposed by the Russian interior minister, Vyacheslav Plehve. "I have just come from Plehve. I have his positive, binding promise that in fifteen years, at the maximum, he will effectuate for us a charter for Palestine. But this is tied to one condition: the Jewish revolutionists shall cease their struggle against the Russian government."[1] Zhitlowsky refused on both practical and ideological grounds. He explained,

> We, Jewish revolutionists, even the most national among us, are not Zionists and do not believe that Zionism is able to resolve our problem. To transfer the Jewish people from Russia to *Eretz-Yisroel* [the land of Israel] is, in our eyes, a utopia, and because of a utopia we will not renounce the path upon which we have embarked—the path of the revolutionary struggle against the Russian government, which should also lead to the freedom of the Jewish people.[2]

In the 1880s and 1890s, Zhitlowsky developed his ideas for revolution while living outside Russia, as did many Jewish intellectuals who influenced Russian Yiddishism.[3] In 1891, Zhitlowsky settled in Zurich, where in 1893 he helped to found the Socialist Revolutionary Party (SR), a Jewish revolutionary movement that argued for Jewish agrarian socialism.[4] Agrarian socialism was never more than a marginal philosophy in the urban centers of the Jewish Diaspora, but the SR's vision of a socialist Russia comprising a federation of nations, each exploring and developing its autonomous culture within a socialist context, fired the imagination of other Russian socialists.[5]

Born in 1865 in Vitebsk, Belarus, Zhitlowsky lived with his grandfather, a prosperous merchant and a Lubavitcher Chasid, an ultraorthodox follower of a charismatic teacher.[6] As a teen, Zhitlowsky met Shlomo Ansky, a slightly older man who introduced him to radical Russian and German Enlightenment literature. In 1879, Zhitlowsky entered gymnasium (an elite secondary school) but left before he graduated as he became more radicalized by Russian revolutionary thinkers. Throughout the 1880s, Zhitlowsky found inspiration in articles discussing Jewish nationalism in the Hebrew-language dailies, as well as in his friend Ansky's travels among the poor Jewish shtetlakh (small towns) collecting folk tales.[7] As Zhitlowsky began to write, he urged Jewish intellectuals to adopt a movement of Jewish nationalism built on a foundation of Yiddish culture among working-class Jews in Russia. For Zhitlowsky, the elevation of Yiddish *kultur*, "an all-encompassing, primarily secular civilization in Yiddish" best expressed in literature, was a means to struggle in Russia and throughout the Jewish Diaspora for a socialist society founded on the principles of social justice and human rights.[8]

When Zhitlowsky reflected on his meeting with Herzl years later, he remembered being both astonished and shocked at Herzl's presumptions. First, Herzl misunderstood Zhitlowsky's standing in the Bund, which he had formally left a few months earlier. Though Zhitlowsky still maintained good relations with the revolutionary Jewish organization, he was not its leader, nor was there any singular leader of Jewish revolutionaries. That was a relatively minor point, however. Zhitlowsky was much more disturbed by Herzl's willingness to deal with Minister Plehve, whom Jews regarded as responsible for the Kishinev pogrom that had occurred a few months before, during Easter week of 1903. Hundreds of Jews were beaten, raped, and killed by local mobs whipped up by official anti-Semitic proclamations. Police in the capital city of Bessarabia (now Moldova) watched and did nothing to stop the slaughter. Pogroms—the Russian-derived Yiddish word for state-sponsored or officially tolerated terror visited on Jews—had been a fact of Jewish life in the Russian Pale of Settlement, where Jews had been confined in the far west of the Russian Empire since the 1790s.[9] But the magnitude and viciousness of the attacks in Kishinev, and the widespread belief that the top levels of the Russian government orchestrated the attacks, compelled activists and leaders of almost all Jewish movements to respond.

Plehve, a former director of police, had instituted a series of restrictive and oppressive orders regarding Jews during his tenure as interior minister beginning in April 1902. Police routinely searched houses, fired without warning on suspected meetings of revolutionaries, and developed an intricate spy network. Plehve directed the arrests of nearly forty-five hundred Bundists in the year leading up to his assassination in July 1904.[10] Even Zionists, whose strategy of leaving Russia Plehve favored, were suspect and meetings among them suppressed. As Plehve told Herzl, "We used to be sympathetic toward the Zionist movement, when it confined its aim to emigration. You do not need to expound the movement: you are preaching to the converted."[11] But Plehve worried that the nationalism inherent in Zionism flamed a revolutionary nationalism, which had been building over the preceding several years among some of the movement's followers.

Zhitlowsky decided that Herzl's efforts to seek out a singular leader of the Bund and his willingness to negotiate with perhaps the greatest enemy of the Jewish people stemmed from Herzl's view of the world and his role in it. For Herzl, a Hungarian-born and Austrian-educated journalist turned diplomat, the Kishinev pogrom meant that a Jewish refuge in Palestine had become more critical than ever. Zhitlowsky wrote, "Herzl's 'politics' is built on pure diplomacy, which seriously believes that the political history of humanity is made by a few people, a few leaders, and that what they arrange among themselves becomes the content of political history."[12] Zhitlowsky surmised that in Herzl's mind, the Kishinev pogrom demonstrated that Russia wanted the Jews out, that Plehve "was Russia," and that he, Herzl, was the Jewish people. Zhitlowsky reasoned that only after conversations with Plehve did Herzl look for the leader of the Jewish revolutionaries, which Herzl guessed and hoped would be Zhitlowsky.

In Zhitlowsky's view, Herzl's strategy was deeply flawed. No movement based on the diplomatic meetings of elite leaders could resolve the crisis faced by the Jewish masses. For Zhitlowsky, as for many other revolutionary leaders and philosophers, no Jewish homeland outside Russia could possibly accommodate the five million Jews living in the Pale of Settlement at the beginning of the twentieth century. For the revolutionaries, Kishinev, only the most brutal atrocity among many hundreds of attacks since the early

1880s, forced them to conclude that Jews had to organize for self-defense and to engage in revolutionary activity aimed at overthrowing the czarist regime. Yet, despite these sharp differences, Yiddish socialism and Zionism shared important historical roots, political contexts, and a central concern with the "national question" that was posed by thinkers in many countries in Europe and North America that were confronting a rising number of minority ethnic groups.

Jews and the "National Question"

These two great Jewish nationalist ideologies—Zionism and revolutionary socialism—had evolved in response to massive social and political transformations from the late eighteenth century. Generations of monarchs beginning with Catherine the Great looked on the Jews as obstacles to the state's imperial agenda. Jews doggedly resisted conversion to Russian Orthodox or any other form of Christianity, persisted in speaking a hybrid language of their own, and claimed no territory in the empire. In a state of permanent internal nomadism, Jews threatened the integrity of czarist attempts to forge an empire, which imposed a dominant language, religion, and cultural values. Catherine created the Pale of Settlement to limit that threat. But efforts to contain Jews geographically, politically, and economically chafed against Russia's need to industrialize in the mid-nineteenth century.

During the Crimean War (1853–1856), Russia suffered abject humiliation at the hands of the technologically superior militaries of Great Britain and France. In response, in 1861, Czar Alexander II emancipated the serfs, who were becoming increasingly rebellious, and instituted a series of liberal reforms that affected Jews directly, in spite of the fact that few Jews had been agricultural laborers. Russian officials designed these measures to accelerate the growth of entrepreneurial industrial production. Capitalist industry needed a workforce free to travel to where manufacturing was located, near population centers, energy sources, waterways, and other transportation centers. Wage labor generated some of the internal markets necessary for exchange. In order to cultivate scientific and engineering initiatives that could assist in industrial development, Russia promoted the expansion of professional classes. For a while, an increasing number of Jews were allowed to venture beyond the urban ghettoes and small towns of the Pale of Settlement into the countryside and beyond western Russia to Moscow and other cities. Jews were admitted in larger numbers to Russian gymnasium and universities, which trained them for professions such as medicine, law, architecture, and government service. The reforms were never applied consistently, but enough Jews made it through the Russian education system to create an expanding urban middle class and a small intellectual elite.

These Russian-trained Jewish intellectuals of the 1860s and 1870s formed the backbone of the Haskalah movement, the Jewish Enlightenment. Influenced by scientific advances and modern notions of nation building, rationalist German philosophers such as Immanuel Kant and especially Moses Mendelsohn, and Russian philosophers such as Vissarion Grigoryevich Bielinsky and Alexander Herzen, the Haskalah was the first significant secular movement among eastern European Jews.[13] Like American progressivism several decades later, Haskalah was really multiple movements that shared broad approaches to social problems, such as faith in science and education.

Scholars and activists of the Haskalah, who were known as Maskalim, held many conflicting ideas. One prominent group believed that the czar was fair in offering citizenship to Jews in return for Jewish efforts to acculturate to a modern Russian state. For these Maskalim, Jewish salvation within the empire required Jews to embrace the state as well as the dominant culture, even though both contributed to a weakening of Jewish ethnic identity. These Maskalim stood in direct opposition to orthodox religious cultures, especially the antimodern Chasidic movement. Some leading Haskalah scholars, including a few in the employ of the Russian state, supported autocratic measures by the czar to suppress Jewish religious orthodoxy. One pernicious measure conscripted Jewish children into long periods of military service, during which they would learn to identify with the Russian nation, language, and Orthodox Christianity.[14]

Another noxious policy was the suppression of Jewish schools and the promulgation of Russian-only schools in which Hebrew and Yiddish were forbidden. A few Jews were commissioned by the state to implement education policy among their coethnics. According to one historian, Dr. Max Lilienthal, a Jewish commissioner, helped to implement the educational reforms by recommending "the application of severe police measures against" Jewish dissenters.[15] Reaction to harsh policies associated with some Maskalim bred new ideas that were inspired by Haskalah's powerful secular attractions. Two movements, socialism and Zionism, aimed at combating what they perceived as collaboration between "Russified" Jews and the czarist state. Both appropriated the Enlightenment and asserted their own forms of Jewish nationalism.

For most of the 1880s and 1890s, socialism was made up of small groups of philosophers, students, and other intellectuals who discussed radical liter-

ature in reading groups modeled after Russian reading circles. Jewish socialists participated in ethnically mixed circles and also formed Jewish circles.
While much of the activity in the circles was limited to disseminating literature and to political education and consciousness raising, some participants
were moved to direct action. In 1881, a Polish member of the small radical
socialist group Narodnaia Volia, or the People's Will, assassinated Czar Alexander II. Like Jews, Catholic Poles and other ethnic minorities in the empire
felt their cultures under attack by the czar, particularly through the Russian
education system. The People's Will was composed of young Russian univer-
sity-educated socialists from many ethnic backgrounds, including Jews, who
were impatient with the peaceful methods and poor results of other reform
groups in the empire. They sought to overthrow the regime through violence
as well as through education.

After Alexander's assassination, the period of liberalization, such as it was,
came to an end, and a renewed period of civil restrictions for Jews began. In
1882, Alexander III issued a series of orders, the May Decrees, that reinforced
restrictions on Jewish residence, occupation, education, and movement that
had been relaxed for two decades. With a series of legislative orders, the czarist state forced Jews to move back to the shtetlakh and urban ghettoes within
the Pale of Settlement. The law prohibited Jews from owning land. They
could not vote, sit on a jury, or sue non-Jews for civil damages. State authori-
ties severely curtailed Jewish admission to university and relegated them to
a few spots in Russian gymnasium.[16] State-sponsored schools offered classes
solely in the Russian language as a means to break down ethnic cultural
identity among children. Most Jews refused to send their children to Russian
schools and developed both religious and secular Jewish schools within the
Pale.[17] Educational institutions became arenas of cultural conflict between
czarist efforts to control the economic, political, and social mechanisms of
the empire, on one hand, and Jewish nationalist resistance to those efforts,
on the other. A sharp increase in pogroms, in reprisal for real or perceived
Jewish participation in revolutionary activities, accompanied this period of
state-imposed segregation.

Jewish resistance in the 1890s formed as a direct response to Russian
cultural suppression. Playwrights such as S. Ansky, Sholem Aleichem, and
I. L. Peretz, historian Simon Dubnow, and Zhitlowsky led the movement for
Yiddish-language culture. The radicals among them argued that only a revolutionary movement based on national cultural autonomy could relieve Jewish suffering. Advocates of national autonomy believed that the many diverse
cultures could not be suppressed by the czar, and Jews in particular could

not afford to be assimilated. Zhitlowsky articulated this best in a series of articles he wrote for the Bund journal in 1898 and 1899. He argued that Jews could only effectively struggle for socialism from a position of equality as an autonomous nation within a multinational socialist movement.[18] In "Socialism and the National Question," a paper he wrote in advance of the Austrian Social Democratic Congress in 1899, Zhitlowsky defined what it meant to be a nation.[19] It was a social and cultural construction that precisely fit the Jewish people.

> A nation is a group of people that in the course of many generations has explained for itself all cultural questions common to humanity, and has thereby explained some cultural questions differently from other groups of people . . . and therefore elaborated distinct national forms of creativity, a distinct "national" intellectual/spiritual or physical type that passes from generation to generation.[20]

These ideas were essential materials in constructing a movement to push back against Jewish subordination and cultivate Jewish cultural pride. Without territory of their own, Jews were effectively different from most of the other ethnic groups in the Russian Empire at the turn of the twentieth century. They were a nation without land; they were a people with a religion and language that were treated with contempt by the state, their gentile neighbors, and their own intellectual elite.

By the end of the 1890s, although there were clear differences in ideology and strategy between leaders of Yiddish socialism and Zionism, they shared similar elements of national consciousness. First, Jewish nationalists recognized that they could never achieve full citizenship in the czarist state. Second, they understood that Russians would continue to associate even the most educated and "Russified" Jews—including those who rejected Judaism and converted to Russian Orthodox Christianity—with the Jewish masses. Third, these movements held that there was a larger political bond among Jews, across regional and national boundaries, that extended beyond a common religion, language, and ethnic culture. Finally, Jewish nationalists argued that individual Jews and the collective masses needed to coalesce under a common secular and political goal for self-protection and to secure their economic and cultural emancipation.

Jewish nationalist ideas formed in the 1890s within the currents of international debate over the status of ethnic-minority groups that were migrating by the millions within and between states and empires. Efforts to reconcile the presence of diverse ethnic groups with the construction of a singular state occupied government leaders, philosophers, and political essayists in Europe and the United States from the late 1890s through World War I. Zhitlowsky, while concerned primarily with Russian Jewry, participated in European social-democratic movements and shared key ideas with Austrian Marxists.[21]

Karl Renner, who two decades later assumed the office of the first prime minister of Austria, wrote a seminal essay in 1899 called "State and Nation" in which he proposed one of the innovative reforms embraced by social democrats for the Austro-Hungarian Empire. Renner argued for a form of national-cultural autonomy in which minority ethnic communities within the empire would have proportional representation throughout several levels of government, in addition to territorial representation. Individuals would choose their national affiliation regardless of territory, and an additional legislature would be composed of representatives from national cultures.[22] The proposal sought to ensure that minorities were not overwhelmed by territorial majorities and that such issues as education and cultural affairs would be controlled by national groups. In a later essay, Renner argued that the formal constitution of national groups within the empire was a matter of necessity. "If one wants to make a law for nations, one must first create the nations. . . . Unless nationalities are constituted it is impossible to create national rights and eliminate national dissension."[23] Renner's ideas go well beyond tolerance for ethnic cultural differences. For the integrity of the state, he insisted that national groups form structures for national cultural autonomy, even if people are not demanding it. Renner's contemporary and future deputy, Otto Bauer, expanded on Renner's themes in *The Question of Nationalities and Social Democracy*, published in 1907. Bauer argued that "national autonomy is a necessary goal of the proletarian class struggle."[24] Bauer articulated a view favored by the left wing of European social-democratic parties, in which national cultural autonomy was seen as a function of revolutionary resistance to capitalism.

In the United States, the mass immigration of eastern and southern Europeans that swelled the urban centers contributed to cultural anxieties. In 1893, Frederick Jackson Turner sought to reassure that immigrants had always been absorbed. "In the crucible of the frontier the immigrants were Americanized, liberated, and fused into a mixed race"—a "process" that "has gone on from the early days to our own."[25] Immigrants such as Israel Zangwill also sought to reassure about the capability of Jews and other immigrants to integrate into American society through his play *The Melting Pot*, produced in 1907, though he chafed against the popular interpretation of the title. "The process of Americanization is not assimilation or simple surrender to the dominant type, as is popularly supposed, but an all-round give-and-take by which the final type may be enriched or impoverished."[26] But cultural anxieties were heightened by the nationalisms expressed at home and abroad at the outbreak of World War I. Responses ranged from nativist Americanization campaigns to suppress or purge the national cultures of the recent immigrants to apocryphal progressive pronouncements that the liberal-democratic society of the United States naturally welcomes immigrants. Zangwill's metaphor of the American melting pot was appropriated widely and redefined as a process by which ethnic markers are absorbed in the second and third generations by the dominant, and superior, American national culture. Arguing against the concept of America as a melting pot, Horace Kallen and Randolph Bourne each began to write at the outset of World War I critiquing the nationalisms that, they argued, fueled support for the war on both sides.

Writing in the 1910s and 1920s, Horace Kallen saw a clear link between nationalist, militarist, and assimilationist ideas. He coined the term *cultural pluralism* and supported the right of immigrant cultures to resist assimilation. Kallen, a German-born Jew, envisioned a society that would accept him as a full citizen but also allow for ethnic difference.[27] Kallen's cultural pluralism had political implications, certainly, but it was more of a social critique, responding to Progressive ideas about race and immigration.

Influenced by Kallen, Randolph Bourne deplored the devastating effects of nationalist ideas but favored a cosmopolitan perspective, in which both the American culture and immigrant ethnic cultures are open to change. He emphasized the social advantages of the "dynamic mixing" that goes on when multiple cultures live in the same place.[28] Ideally, he suggested, the dominant culture itself has elements borrowed from the society's major constituent racial-ethnic groups. For cosmopolitans, the acceptance by dominant groups of members of subordinate cultures, in politics and society, was as important as immigrants' willingness to be assimilated. Bourne's ideas were resonant with cosmopolitans from subordinate cultures who urged their own people to adopt dominant cultural norms that included language, political activism, family structures, gender relations, and even religion. But neither Bourne nor Kallen's ideas resonated with Jewish revolutionaries in Russia or in the ghetto of New York's Lower East Side.

The Bund and Yiddish Socialism

The founding of the Bund and the rise of Yiddish socialism overshadowed the Zionist movement for decades. In the Russian Empire, the renewed enforcement of Jewish confinement within the Pale of Settlement and the transformations wrought by capitalism only intensified the marginality of Jews. During the period of liberalization under Czar Alexander II, few Jews were able to accumulate wealth on a large scale. Most Jewish capitalists operated small textile- or tobacco-manufacturing plants within Jewish centers. Overwhelmingly, Jews were relegated by the state and by custom to only a few occupations, as shopkeepers, petty merchants, or industrial workers. Most spoke only Yiddish fluently and maintained Jewish customs, rituals, and dress. Few Russian Jews aspired to or were able to attain urbane middle-class standards of education, language, and taste. By the late 1890s, perhaps six hundred thousand Jews labored in industry under brutal conditions, largely for Jewish employers.[29] So, for the Jewish socialists who came to revolutionary consciousness in the 1880s and 1890s, the czarist state that restricted education, blocked paths to the professions, and relegated Jewish industrial workers to lives of poverty and toil wore a Jewish face.

Advocates of Yiddish socialism, a political current that began in the 1880s in the Lithuanian and Byelorussian provinces, rejected assimilation as unworkable. The Jewish population in these regions came into conflict with Russian, Polish, Lithuanian, and Byelorussian nationals, who considered these territories as their native lands. Spread out as a minority population among many national territories, radical Jews developed sophisticated cultural institutions to combat their isolation. They established schools with curricula taught in their Yiddish vernacular, built a Yiddish theater movement, and founded a variety of Yiddish publications. They were unwilling to abandon these cultural products and institutions to Russian culture, as the few Jewish assimilationists advocated. Rather, they identified themselves as a Jewish working class having common interests with workers throughout the empire. They believed that all workers, regardless of ethnicity or nationality, suffered from a system of capitalist exploitation that was bolstered by Russian cultural domination.

In reality, direct cooperation between distinct ethnic communities was confined to very small groups of revolutionary intellectuals: activists at university; socialist conventiongoers; artists and writers. Nonetheless, the idea of revolutionaries from different ethnic groups encouraging the celebration and elevation of all ethnic folk cultures and engaging in a form of political resistance to cultural domination—what I call *mutual culturalism*—resonated deeply among the leading Jewish revolutionary movements in Russia. Yiddish socialists in the 1890s thought deeply about constructing a new Jewish identity enhanced by a form of secular nationalism and defined by a workers' revolutionary movement. Yiddish socialists regarded the system of capitalism, and the czarist state that supported it, as the root cause of Jewish oppression. The class interests of Jewish capitalists were therefore in direct opposition to the Jewish masses, and a cross-class alliance among Jews was impossible.

In 1897, several Jewish socialist groups gathered to form the Bund as a secret revolutionary organization of Jewish radical intellectuals and workers to struggle for socialism and promote civil rights for Jews within the territories controlled by the Russian czar.[30] The political philosophies of its constituent groups varied widely. Some groups formed under a strictly pragmatic survival-oriented framework, arming for self-defense. Others argued for a form of international socialism and regarded the existence of so many different ethnic cultures in the Russian Empire as enfeebling resistance to the czar. The czar, these internationalists felt, kept the peasantry controlled by exploiting the differences between peoples and provoking ethnic hatred. They worried that, as a dispersed minority group, Jews were particularly vulnerable in these periods of unrest, which might be caused by drought, economic depression, war, or reaction against revolutionary movements. Still, national cultural autonomy attracted the broadest support. Czarist Russia controlled territories comprising more than one hundred national and racial groups, which together constituted more than half of the population of the empire.[31] The Bund sought autonomy for Jewish workers as a national group within Russia and worked to establish associations with other non-Jewish socialist groups of workers organized by nationality.[32] Although the Bund was not founded initially on the principles of Yiddish socialism, Bundist factions began to push for a formal declaration in favor of Jewish national cultural autonomy articulated by Chaim Zhitlowsky.

To achieve the cohesiveness required for revolutionary struggle, Zhitlowsky argued that Jews had to develop a national sense of Jewish pride and that a national identity must emerge out of the Yiddish language.[33] He laid the responsibility for the elevation of the Jewish nation at the feet of Jewish intellectuals and cultural elites. As he put it years later,

> We hope that the Yiddish language, which is to us as dear and holy as German is to the Germans, Russian to the Russians, and Hebrew to the old-fashioned Jews, will become all the richer in words and expressions. It is now still poor, hard, and brittle because the learned Jews, the educated, the poets, and the belletrists, write nothing in Yiddish.[34]

Zhitlowsky advocated an entire cultural reorientation among Jewish intellectuals and workers. Though he wrote about the uplift of the Jewish masses, he wrote and spoke almost exclusively to intellectuals, telling them to write principally in Yiddish. He admired the Yiddish literature of Sholem Aleichem and I. L. Peretz, as well as the Yiddish press in Russia and the United States, including the *Jewish Daily Forward*, to which he contributed articles in the early 1900s.[35] But he found the body of Yiddish literature narrow and sloppy, without substantial contributions from rigorous political thought or science.

> And only when Yiddish literature becomes rich in books and in all branches of science will the new generation not have to look for knowledge among the foreign [non-Jewish] peoples. He [the Jew] will be able to cultivate his human feelings and free thoughts in his home, in his own language. This will bind him even more to his people. Everything he will achieve in art and science will be brought out in Yiddish, and Yiddish culture and Yiddish education will grow continuously and will become a formidable force that will bind together as one not only the educated people with the folk, but also all Jews from all countries.[36]

Having developed his ideas within the context of a political culture resistant to Russian imperialist education, Zhitlowsky argued that the creation of schools and universities in Yiddish, staffed by *secular* intellectuals, was essential to the construction of a revolutionary Jewish national identity.

In a series of declarations, beginning in 1898 when Zhitlowsky formally joined the group, the Bund adopted Yiddishism as the principal idiom of revolutionary Judaism. In so doing, the Bund championed the movement to revive Yiddish as a literary form. Until that point, most Jewish intellectuals regarded Yiddish as a base dialect. But Bundists argued that it was the language spoken by the mass of workers, and there was no better way to communicate ideas of socialism to workers than in their own language.[37] So the Russian Bundists expressed a Yiddishist ideal of constructing a national identity among working-class and revolutionary Jews, celebrating their distinct ethnic culture. In effect, it was an ideology of national identity but not of national supremacy.[38]

Advocates of Yiddish socialism formulated several key principles of the Bundist movement. First, Yiddishists held that the czarist regime served the interest of capitalism through violence and the repression of peasants and workers. Second, they regarded Russian schools and other cultural institutions as arenas of class conflict in which the regime sought to impose controls on ethnic-minority populations. Third, they demanded that all ethnic cultures must be recognized as having equal status. And fourth, they advocated the formation of unions, political parties, and self-defense militias to demand rights, to agitate for social revolution, and to protect the general Jewish population.[39] Bundist men also welcomed women into their ranks, promising a vision of gender equality, though it remained incompletely realized. Women as well as men were encouraged to organize strikes and boycotts, to publish, to speak, to march, and to conspire to overthrow the czarist state. Women did not join as modern feminists but principally to agitate for socialism. Still, as Susan A. Glenn points out, "women derived from the socialist movement a sense of personal dignity and importance available nowhere else in Jewish society."[40] The Bund and associated revolutionary movements afforded young women a new public voice and an entitlement to make demands on employers and the state.

Zhitlowsky joined the Bund because it gave him a forum to express his ideas of socialism and Jewish national cultural autonomy. Those ideas remained a general sentiment among delegates to the Bund conventions until 1901, when Jewish cultural autonomy was formally adopted as a primary tenet of Bund political philosophy.[41] At that time, Zhitlowsky had renewed his activism and leadership in the SR, though the party never formally joined the Bund. These two organizations were now linked not only by the common membership of Zhitlowsky and other activists but also by the common tenet that Jews must create a Yiddish-based political culture. Between 1901 and 1904, the Russian Jewish socialist movements were at their most unified, and they were specifically unified around the concept of national cultural autonomy.

Russian Jewish socialism splintered soon after. A period of intense pogroms that began with the Easter 1903 riots in Kishinev, Bessarabia, began to undermine Zhitlowsky's faith in the Bund. Though the Bund's principal goal was still to achieve civic equality within the Russian Empire and within the Pale of Settlement, through armed revolutionary struggle when necessary, Zhitlowsky criticized what he saw as the Bund's weak response to the anti-Jewish violence.[42] Increasingly, he felt that it was not enough to embrace national cultural autonomy. Regarding the position of Jews in the Pale of Settlement as untenable, he began to explore the idea of establishing a Jewish-controlled territory within Russia.[43] Zhitlowsky argued for a Jewish diasporic nationalism that would support Jewish participation in the Russian revolutionary movements but also struggle for Jewish rights in their newly adopted homelands. He broke with the Bund formally in 1904 and traveled to the United States to build support for the SR Party. Addressing Jewish socialists, he argued against the idea of an American melting pot. Instead, he promoted the idea of supporting a society of "harmoniously functioning nationalities."[44]

After the failure of the 1905 Russian Revolution, retaliation by the czarist state forced Bundists to limit their political and economic activities. The state banned revolutionary unions and political parties, violently broke up rallies and marches, crushed strikes, and jailed movement leaders and activists. So Bundists concentrated the bulk of their efforts on promoting Yiddish culture, which did not directly and publicly challenge the state. They continued to support the publication of Yiddish literature, to found schools and music societies, to offer evening courses, and to develop Yiddish theater, but they abandoned armed resistance and mass strikes.[45] Nonetheless, young Jewish socialist activists of all radical political associations were threatened, beaten, or jailed, resulting in a wave of radical Russian Jewish emigration in the years surrounding the revolution.

Herzl's Zionism

While Yiddish socialism and Bundism were the dominant movements in Russia and the United States around the turn of the twentieth century, Zionism also grew out of Jewish struggles for identity in a world of expanding nationalisms. Since there was no territory anywhere in which Jews formed a majority of the population, all these Jewish national ideologies tended to raise the modern concept of national identity to a new level of abstraction. In 1895, Theodor Herzl published his pamphlet *The Jewish State* and quickly became the most recognized and leading spokesman for the Zionist cause in the world. Like Yiddish socialism, Zionism was a response to violence and hatred aimed at Jews. The anti-Semitism that had intensified in Russia since the early 1880s was evident as well in other major European centers. In one of the most celebrated cases of Jewish persecution, the French army brought a court martial for treason against army captain Alfred Dreyfus, the highest-ranking Jewish military officer in France. At a moment in which French popular and political discourse was rife with open anti-Semitism, Dreyfus was convicted and sentenced to life imprisonment on flimsy evidence. He was publicly humiliated in a dishonorable-discharge ceremony before being sent to Devil's Island.[46] Eventually, Dreyfus was exonerated and reinstated into the military. Jews and non-Jews in France and abroad increasingly criticized the French army and government for what came to be known as the Dreyfus

Affair. Herzl covered the trial and the military discharge as a reporter and later credited the case with his newfound commitment to Zionism.[47]

For Herzl, anti-Semitism was a permanent fixture in every country in which Jews lived. Though hatred of Jews may wax and wane, he argued, "the Jewish Question exists wherever Jews live in perceptible numbers. Where it does not exist, it is carried by Jews in the course of their migrations."[48] Even in France, where Jews had been granted equal rights, Jews faced hatred and discrimination—an opinion that the Dreyfus Affair confirmed in his mind. Herzl's strategy was to secure a Jewish homeland through negotiations with major imperial powers. This approach married several ideas—modern state building, assimilation, internationalism, cosmopolitanism, and cross-class alliance building—that intersected with the questions of Jewish identity, ethnic culture, and the Jewish people's relationship to the state. Many of these ideas were directly opposed both to Yiddish socialism and to the more moderate views of national cultural advocates such as Karl Renner.

In *The Jewish State*, Herzl suggests the radical notion that the world's Jews constituted a separate nation by virtue of their religion and historical circumstances. He argued that Jews remained distinct from the nations in which they lived, in some cases for centuries, because integration and assimilation were all but impossible. Jews would never achieve permanent equal rights in any country, and their only hope was to find a territory in which they could establish an autonomous government. He offered an extraordinary plan to accomplish this goal: the declaration of a Jewish state before settling a territory or even having decided on a territory. "It is true," conceded Herzl, "the Jewish State is conceived as a peculiarly modern structure on unspecified territory. But a State is formed, not by pieces of land, but rather by a number of men united under sovereign rule."[49] It was under this principle that the World Zionist Organization was founded in 1897, elected Herzl as the figurative head of a future state, and gave him the "authority" to meet with European heads of state as a spokesman for the Jewish people.[50]

Herzl's negotiations with European leaders to obtain a territory for Jewish settlement were central to his conception of internationalism. He imagined a European-style Jewish state, particularly if it were established in Palestine, that would be protected by and serve the collective interest of European states. For Herzl, the modern European state was the highest and the most civilized form of government. He admired the coexistence of constitutional law and hereditary rule, suggesting that the Jewish state would ideally include a monarch. Herzl reluctantly concluded that the establishment of a royal family in a Jewish state was impractical, but he continued to espouse the idea of an "aristocratic republic."[51] In return for establishing such a state in Palestine, Herzl assured European leaders that the new state would act as a "guard of honor" to represent and protect European values. "We should there form a portion of a rampart of Europe against Asia, an outpost of civilization as opposed to barbarism. We should as a neutral State remain in contact with all Europe, which would have to guarantee our existence."[52] Herzl was clear: the Jewish state would embody hostility toward, disdain for, and fear of "Oriental" cultures as much as it would serve as a model for European values.

In embracing European government and culture, Herzl privileged the cosmopolitan manners of bourgeois Europe above those of his coreligionists, particularly the overwhelming majority of Jews living in the Pale of Settlement. Herzl saw the Yiddish language as a marker of Jewish poverty and oppression suffered in Russia. He was very open to a multilingual society and pointed to Switzerland as a successful example of a European nation that thrived with "a federation of tongues."[53] But, proclaiming his disdain for Yiddish, he promised, "We shall give up those miserable stunted jargons, those Ghetto languages which we still employ, for these were the stealthy tongues of prisoners."[54] Herzl did not deny the existence of Jewish culture or the importance of religious life in the Jewish community. Indeed, he encouraged the spread of the Zionist message through synagogues, even through rabbis' sermons. But he believed that the Jewish state had to be secular and that, once a state was established, religious clergy would have a cultural, not political, role.

In sum, Herzl conceived of a movement that embraced a modern bourgeois Jewish European identity. For him, the modern European state, framed constitutionally and balanced by the continuity provided by an aristocracy, functioned for those citizens who were granted full civil rights. Jews could enjoy the privileges and protections of the European state only by building their own, with the cooperation and protection of leading European states. To build a modern state, however, Jews would have to reject the culture they developed as second-class citizens or noncitizens of European countries. Herzl's Zionist state was a form of internationalism that would provide for internal autonomy, was predicated on the protection of European powers, accepted the binary oppositional worldview of a civilized Christian Europe and a savage Asia, and relied on a cosmopolitan model of European acculturation.

For a small group of Jewish intellectuals who were influenced by the Haskalah or who were formally educated in Russia and were struggling with various forms of socialism, Herzl's plan included a number of tempting elements. While still a marginal movement, Zionism quickly came to include a broad spectrum of factions, including some socialist trade unionists. Within a decade of the founding of the world Zionist movement, Chaim Zhitlowsky joined the ranks of labor Zionists who saw the potential for a classless society in the process of settling a new territory. Nevertheless, Zionism was dominated and financed by visionaries who intended to perpetuate some form of capitalism in the Jewish state.

Herzl's determination in the 1890s to marry capitalism with Zionism stood in direct opposition to the burgeoning Jewish socialist movements in Europe and the United States. As laid out in *The Jewish State*, Herzl envisioned a cross-class alliance of Jews who would be willing to maintain the social and economic order. He reckoned that the Jewish state would be financed by a "Jewish Company" that would seek investments from wealthy Jews, as well as among Jews of modest means. The company would be responsible for helping to liquidate the assets of wealthy Jews who migrated to the new territory and ensure that they would be able to live in comfort. "For a house it will offer a house in the new country; and for land, land in the new country; everything being, if possible, transferred to the new soil in the same state as it was the old."[55] The poorest Jews would migrate first, to cultivate the soil. They would labor seven hours a day for no wages, except for overtime. In return, they would be provided with the "opportunity to work their way up to private proprietorship."[56] The state would recruit highly skilled labor where needed and provide them with housing. Herzl imagined that the land itself, as well as the national desires of the Jewish settlers, would create a demand in domestic and international markets and offer potential upward mobility for anyone willing to work. Capitalism would be central to Herzl's Jewish state: "Private property, which is the economic basis of independence, shall be developed freely and be respected by us."[57]

Herzl vigorously denied that capitalism per se was the root of Jewish oppression. The Jewish state he proposed could be a model for cross-class cooperation based on a system of fair wages and humane working conditions. Calling on the "richest Jews" to join in this enterprise of a cooperative humane capitalism, he wrote,

> Why do they send men to work underground and to raise coal amid terrible dangers for meager pay? I cannot imagine this to be pleasant, even for the owners of the mines. For I do not believe that capitalists are heartless, and I do not pretend that I believe it. My desire is not to accentuate, but to smooth differences.[58]

To "accentuate" differences meant acknowledging the inequality and oppression inherent in capitalism. To do so would lend legitimacy to the Jewish revolutionary movements that aimed to overthrow the institutions of capitalism and the governments that supported them. Instead, Herzl simply assumed that the shared project of settling Palestine would render class differences unimportant. But for the masses of Jews struggling in Russia and the United States, class conflict was a daily lived experience, and the class harmony inherent to Herzl's Zionism was an impossible dream.

Yiddishism and Bundist Socialism in New York City

From the early 1880s on, Jewish radicals and intellectuals led union movements in New York and other American cities among eastern European Jewish immigrants. Arriving a generation or more later than German Jews, who had immigrated to the United States after 1848, Jews from the Russian Empire came in two huge, swelling waves. During the twenty-three years between 1881 and 1903, approximately 900,000 Jews came through the ports of New York, Philadelphia, and Baltimore. By 1903, 450,000 Jews lived in New York City, out of 4 million residents.[59] Then, in the eleven years from 1904 to 1914, nearly 1.2 million Jews were recorded entering the United States.[60] By 1912, 975,000 Jews lived in New York. Most of them came from Russia, where they left behind a brutal system of terror and segregation, and entered a political, social, and economic fray that was oppressive but dramatically different from conditions back home. Jewish immigrants found themselves living and working in appalling circumstances in the needle trades of the Lower East Side, the largest concentration of Jews in the world outside the Pale of Settlement.[61]

The mass production of the sewing machine during the decades after the Civil War made it possible for a significant number of skilled Jewish tailors to open workshops, often in the overcrowded apartments in which they lived. Typically, these petty entrepreneurs employed a few workers, including family members and boarders. Large manufacturers employed jobbers, or middlemen, to parcel out bundles of clothes, dividing various stages of garment production among several tenement workshops. The sheer number of immigrants, coupled with the deskilling created by the division of labor, meant that jobbers forced sweatshop bosses to compete with one another. The "cutthroat capitalism" that characterized the sweatshops created tremendous instability in the industry and misery among the workforce. The system drove wages down to starvation levels, demanded that workers and owners alike work long hours, employed children, fed a myriad of diseases, and forced workers to fend for themselves during prolonged periods of unemployment.

After the turn of the twentieth century, spurred by municipal electricity infrastructure and innovations in electric sewing-machine technology, industrialists began to build modern garment factories to take advantage of the massive influx of cheap Jewish and Italian labor. Reformers hailed the better lighting and ventilation in what seemed to be far more humane workplaces than the sweatshops, but the young women who constituted the factory workforce experienced speedups facilitated by modern machinery and suffered numerous managerial abuses, including sexual harassment. In New York City, as in Russia, the face of the oppressor in the sweatshop and the modern factory was most often another Jew, sometimes a *landsman* (countryman). Again Russian Jews found themselves in a ghetto. But their concentration in the Lower East Side allowed Jews to form labor unions, fraternal societies, newspapers, and political organizations that were mutually supportive and bound together by the growing socialist movement.

The United Hebrew Trades (UHT) was an important early pillar of the Jewish labor and socialist movements. Organized in New York in 1888 as a Jewish outgrowth of the socialist United German Trades, the UHT was not a union per se.[62] It was an organization of Jewish socialist workers that promoted the formation of unions among those trades in which Jews worked, for example, the Hebrew Choirists and the Hebrew Typographical Union. They organized workers, raised money, supported strikes and boycotts by coordinating and providing mutual aid among the affiliated unions, and agitated for socialism. But once a union was established, the UHT let workers create their own autonomous governing bodies.[63]

Typically, the largely Jewish unions organized under the auspices of the UHT presented themselves for membership in the American Federation of Labor (AFL), which accepted them reluctantly. Led by Samuel Gompers from 1886 to 1924, the AFL viewed the UHT with suspicion, regarding the immigrant associations as potential rival organizations, although the UHT never sought to undermine the AFL.[64] Leaders of the UHT intended the organization to serve as a means for Jews to organize in trades that the AFL had overlooked. Although Gompers was Jewish, he was a member of the highly skilled cigar makers' trade, and he expended little effort to organize unskilled labor in industries with high turnover. The needle trades, in which Jewish immigrants were concentrated, employed workers with little or no previous training. The industry was highly seasonal and unstable and paid low wages, making it difficult to organize within the AFL's trade-union model based on skilled workers who exercised control over their craft. In 1900, several independent unions affiliated with the UHT in the garment industries of New York, Newark, Philadelphia, and Baltimore merged to form the International Ladies' Garment Workers' Union (ILGWU).[65] The Jewish trade federation continued to support the unions it helped to form, especially during periods of crisis. Some of the most important leaders of the Jewish labor and socialist movements in New York began their careers in UHT unions. Members of the Shirt Makers' Union included Morris Hillquit, the prominent Socialist lawyer who helped to found the UHT, and Abraham Cahan, the founder and editor of the *Jewish Daily Forward*, the Jewish community's most popular newspaper.

Like the United Hebrew Trades and the *Jewish Daily Forward*, the Arbiter Ring, or (in English) the Workmen's Circle, had as its mission the support of the Jewish labor and socialist movements. New York Jews organized the Workmen's Circle in 1892 as a fraternal organization to provide sick and burial benefits to members and their families. Though the founders were not political revolutionaries, they were stridently anticapitalist. Indeed, an in-house history of the Workmen's Circle cited an instance during the early years of the association when a member was expelled for working for the Republican Party.[66] An anniversary journal of one branch of the fraternal association that had been organized by Bundists noted,

> Among the rules laid down at the very beginning was that no strikebreaker was eligible for membership, and that no man supporting any of the political parties of Capitalism could belong to it. That is, no one was forced to be a Socialist Party supporter, no one was obliged to vote at all. But those members who did vote were required to vote against the present capitalist system.[67]

The fledgling group made modest efforts to expand the work of the organization into a broader political movement by developing educational programs and organizing cooperative ventures. From the beginning, Workmen's Circle branches sponsored lectures on a wide range of subjects. The first recorded lecture, given on July 8, 1892, by Dr. Zolotaroff, was on Darwinism. The group also sponsored some cooperative enterprises; from 1894 to 1896, the Workmen's Circle ran a cooperative barbershop.[68] After seeking a charter from New York State, the Workmen's Circle organized as a formal order at the end of 1900 with less than one thousand members.

Workmen's Circle members raised money for organizing drives and strikes, staffed picket lines, advertised boycotts, and proselytized for the union movement throughout the membership. Many Jewish garment workers belonged to Workmen's Circle groups, drawing much-needed financial assistance during hard times and particularly during strikes. The Workmen's Circle, like other institutions in the Jewish labor and socialist movements, was limited in funds, lacked a critical mass of members, and most important, did not share a militant revolutionary consciousness. Then the founding of the Bund, events in Russia, and the second wave of Jewish immigration enabled the Workmen's Circle to become a more firmly established institution, multiplied its membership, and pushed it to engage in more militant activities.

Crushing poverty, intensified pogroms, and the outbreak of the Russo-Japanese War in 1904 contributed to the abortive Russian Revolution in 1905. Though these events were wrenching for the Jewish revolutionary movement, young men and women cut their political teeth on organizing in Russia. Sympathetic Jewish socialists began to organize Bundist clubs in the United States around 1900 to support the efforts of radical Jews in the Pale.[69] Many of the radical Jews who came in the later period, particularly the young people who were fresh from revolutionary struggle, joined left-wing political and cultural organizations. In the United States, especially in the Jewish enclave of New York's Lower East Side, the "1905 generation" injected their energies, their socialist ideas, and their militant zeal into the political and cultural organizations of working-class immigrant Jews. Bundists became active in the predominantly Jewish unions such as the ILGWU, the United Garment Workers, and, later, the Amalgamated Clothing Workers of America. They founded their own journals and newspapers, and they increasingly influenced the articles in the *Jewish Daily Forward*. Bundist clubs continued to grow until 1908, when they voted to join the Jewish socialist fraternal organization, the Workmen's Circle, "en masse."[70] As a result, from 1908 to 1909, the membership of the Workmen's Circle jumped 60 percent, from 19,324 to 31,581.[71]

The Bundists' radicalizing effect on the Workmen's Circle is especially visible in movements to expand education. The 1908 Workmen's Circle convention allocated $1,000 for an education bureau that developed into an education committee.[72] In 1910, the committee organized some public lectures and published the first issue of *Der Fraynd* (*The Friend*), which served as the official organ of the Workmen's Circle for the next fifteen years. Delegates at the 1912 convention passed a resolution stating, "education should be placed on equal footing with the other tasks of our order," and the greater New York branches organized a conference in August to discuss how the educational work of the Workmen's Circle should progress.[73] The participants agreed to publish a volume of academic articles in Yiddish, geared to a popular audience, on topics in the hard sciences, political and economic theory, and the social sciences. The Workmen's Circle published the book *The Universe of Man* and sold out the first edition of six thousand copies in 1913.[74]

The inclusion of articles in the hard sciences was likely a response to criticism, most notably from Chaim Zhitlowsky, that the Yiddish press did not engage seriously in discourse spanning the entirety of intellectual endeavors. Zhitlowsky prided himself on his command of a broad spectrum of academic subjects, and his translation of Einstein's theory of general relativity into Yiddish earned Zhitlowsky the admiration of the German Jewish physicist.[75] Zhitlowsky's vision of a Jewish civilization depended on both intellectuals and workers discussing in Yiddish those topics and ideas typically explored in liberal arts college curricula. Building on that vision, the Education Committee of the Workmen's Circle began to assist branches with programs that helped to transmit Yiddish culture through classroom instruction, theater, music, and art. The committee established Yiddish libraries and offered classes in Yiddish on a variety of subjects in 1913 and 1914. Workmen's Circle members also took Yiddish correspondence courses in the natural and social sciences through the People's University, which was established in 1913 by L. Rozentsvayg, Dr. Kaspe, and A. Sh. Zaks. In 1915, the Education Committee sponsored the production of plays in Yiddish, helping to elevate the fledgling Yiddish theater.[76]

The central debates in the Workmen's Circle involved conflicts between the old guard who had established the order as a fraternal organization and the new, more militant Bundists who sought a base for their vision of socialism and national Jewish autonomy in the Diaspora. Chaim Zhitlowsky led the Bundist members in pushing the Workmen's Circle leadership to establish Yiddish educational and cultural institutions that would support the Yiddishist movement.[77] Between 1911 and 1917, Bundists argued in convention debates that the Workmen's Circle should maintain local autonomy within branches acting in accord with the general tenets of the order but that there should be centralized support for educational and cultural activities.[78] The debate was framed as follows: should the Workmen's Circle be, as the old guard preferred, "primarily a fraternal order which also engaged in educational work" or, as the younger members advocated, "an idealistic, educational organization which also paid sick and death benefits"?[79]

The question of whether meetings of the Workmen's Circle should be held in Yiddish or English brought an ideological conflict to the fore and underscored one of the most fundamental questions faced by any group composed largely of recent immigrants. The debate involved two competing ideologies sitting on the spectrum of Jewish thought that included socialism, cosmopolitanism, and a new interpretation of internationalism. In the minds of most militant Bundists and other Jewish revolutionaries, cosmopolitanism was linked to right-wing social democrats in Russia, particularly among the elite, who favored the Russification of the Jewish people. In the United States, cosmopolitanism gained more acceptance because of Jews' relative freedom compared to what they had experienced in Russia. Jews who felt less coercive pressure to adopt the language, culture, and religion of the dominant group were more open to acculturating selectively, learning English and the American way of life while retaining their distinctive religious and kin-based identity. In addition, German Jews, who had established communities in New York and elsewhere from the 1840s on, had already acculturated to a great extent. American Jewish cosmopolitans, according to Maximillian Hurwitz, "looked forward to a time when all national distinctions would disappear and humanity become one worldwide brotherhood."[80] They thought that Jews should learn the dominant language as quickly as possible and abandon Yiddish as a cultural form as soon as a majority of Jews had mastered English. Cosmopolitans saw Yiddish as a temporary medium of communication among new immigrants.

Zionists and cosmopolitans agreed on this point. Indeed, many Zionists could be called cosmopolitans, although they espoused markedly different programs. But at the turn of the twentieth century, international social and political conditions nurtured a more revolutionary perspective, and many of those who had been Bundists or fellow travelers in Russia transported the concept of a radical national Jewish cultural autonomy into the Jewish Diaspora and constructed a new concept of internationalism. While in Russia, Bundists regarded both Zionists and many Russian Jewish social democrats as internationalists because both groups rejected the creation of a sovereign Jewish nation (with or without territory of its own) within Russia. In the Jewish Diaspora, Bundists reinterpreted internationalism as the preservation of distinct national cultures, including Yiddish.

Practical as well as theoretical factors entered the debate over the question of which language the Workmen's Circle would use to conduct meetings and offer classes. In 1906, the Harlem branch of the Workmen's Circle created the first of many branch-based socialist Sunday schools for members' children. The schools survived for a few years with an entirely English curriculum and no Jewish content.[81] According to one historian, students complained of being bored by the overly doctrinaire classes.[82] More important, Jewish parents were increasingly concerned with the growing gap between themselves and their English-speaking children. Yiddish-speaking immigrants from Russia watched their children develop the same disdain for their parents' foreign tongue that Jewish intellectuals and anti-Semites in the Russian Empire had cultivated in earlier decades. In addition, many parents felt a loss of power as they had to rely on their children's command of English to mediate the social and political problems of their new environment. To imbue their children with a sense of ethnic pride, and perhaps to regain a measure of parental authority, Workmen's Circle members began to enroll their children in religious and secular schools run by other Jewish organizations. The socialist Sunday schools declined and all but disappeared until the schools began to offer a Yiddish-based curriculum, and members came back to the Workmen's Circle. The Bundists' argument for Yiddish schooling persuaded Workmen's Circle members who may not have necessarily subscribed to the broad political principles of Yiddishism.

Bundists had not achieved a majority within the national organization until 1916. In New York, former Bundists and sympathizers came to dominate many branches. Once they did, those members asserted their rights to run the local branches under the principles of Yiddish socialism. The leadership of the Workmen's Circle shifted from the "assimilationist intelligentsia" to those who advocated Yiddishkite, a radical, predominantly socialist, secularly inclined form of Yiddish culture.[83] By a vote of fifty-five to forty-three, Workmen's Circle convention delegates resolved to establish a Yiddish program, principally for children, in which they "would be imbued with the radical spirit of their parents and become acquainted with the cultural possessions of their people."[84] The convention allocated $1,000 for a pilot Jewish national school in New York, though a significant number of delegates voiced their opposition to the programs and their funding.[85] By 1917, the educational work of the Workmen's Circle encompassed all the cultural activities of the order. Branches sponsored lectures; organized open forums on politics, economics, and social questions; and published books and journals on all forms of science and social science, including Chaim Zhitlowsky's *Socialism* and the newspaper *The Friend*. In addition, the Workmen's Circle conducted cultural activities such as concerts, theater groups, choirs, mandolin and symphony orchestras, and trips to art museums led by Jewish artists.[86]

Though Bundists demanded local branch autonomy when they were in the minority of the Workmen's Circle, they acted to centralize power in the order when they controlled the national organizational leadership. They hoped central authority might prevent a feared breakup of the order by branches pursuing their own political and social agendas.[87] Central authority also allowed the new leadership to impose an education tax on members in 1918 and to administer a greatly expanded education program.[88] As membership in the Workmen's Circle jumped again from sixty thousand in 1916 to eighty thousand in 1918, a substantial portion of Jewish workers embraced education as an intrinsic value. Formal higher education was still out of reach for most Jews; it was too expensive, and Jews were barred from such local institutions as Columbia University. Jewish secular education was valuable not because it was a necessary means to vocational or professional advancement or because it necessarily led to a rise in social class but because it transmitted language as the medium of cultural pride and a socialist vision.

At this time, the socialist program was not fully formed; many issues remained open to debate. Gender equality was a contested issue among Jewish radicals in educational and political organizations as well as in labor unions and workplaces. Women and men both engaged in radical ethnic culture through education in the Workmen's Circle, but women had to fight their way into full membership of the fraternal organization. Although the Workmen's Circle began nominally as a men's organization, women were present at the beginning in small numbers. Much of the order's early benefits were related to unemployment or sickness insurance and death benefits that covered the spouse as well, but few married women were able or willing to pay additional dues to the organization to become full-fledged members.

Some women argued passionately for equal access to the organization and advocated the formation of separate women's branches to serve working women who relied on their earnings to support themselves and to contribute to the support of their families. The first women's branch was established in 1901, and women were granted partial sickness and death benefits in exchange for dues that took their lower earnings into account. By 1908, women of the Workmen's Circle, many of whom were veterans of the Bund and the Russian Revolution of 1905, began to assert their citizenship rights within the organization. They demanded equal rights and status, and in 1908 the association accepted women as full members into all branches. Women in the Workmen's Circle employed a variety of strategies to exercise their citizenship. Some women continued to open designated women's branches, while other women began to join the newly created mixed-gender branches.[89] For all these women, Yiddish socialism was capacious enough to embrace gender equity. In order to achieve it, Jewish women struggled for inclusion throughout the institutions of the Jewish labor and socialist movements in New York.

Conclusion

Having lived as cultural foreigners in Russia, Jewish immigrants to America were generally better prepared for the difficulties of living in a foreign culture than were many other groups coming from countries in which they spoke the majority language and worshiped in the dominant religion's churches. The movement to elevate Yiddish as the medium of Jewish national culture emerged in Russia just in time for a generation of radical Jews to arm themselves in revolutionary thought before they immigrated and confronted the tenements and sweatshops of America. The 1905 generation of revolutionary Jews brought with them a clear sense of the interconnections among capitalist exploitation, national cultural repression, control over education, and the meaning of citizenship. In Russia, they answered the "national question" with a program of liberation among workers of all nationalities. The ability of workers to explore their distinct national cultures was central to their construction of a successful revolutionary movement, and revolutionary education was the key to national cultural autonomy and full citizenship. The expressions of Yiddish culture that included the founding of the Workmen's Circle schools in the United States owed their success to the Jewish experience of founding Yiddish-language schools in the Pale of Settlement. Women experienced an added dimension of liberation as the revolutionary movements in Russia and the militancy of the labor and socialist movements in the United States offered new opportunities for women to act as equal participants and full citizens. That experience helped women to emerge as leaders, even though they had to struggle for a voice within the institutions of the Jewish labor and socialist movements as well as in the dominant society.

Despite the grinding toil and poverty inflicted by the sweatshop system on the Lower East Side of New York, the United States was quite different from Imperial Russia. Russian Jews were much more culturally isolated in the urban ghettoes and shtetlakh of the Pale of Settlement than they were in America. Their cultural contacts were limited as a minority among dominant ethnic majorities within a larger cultural empire. In the United States, the cultural context shifted. By the turn of the twentieth century, Jews had become one of the largest ethnic groups in New York City, and radical Jews became more confident in their culture, with the creation of schools, theaters, labor unions, and cultural and political institutions. While this environment offered Jews an unprecedented freedom to explore revolutionary thought and organization, it also prompted the hope nurtured by progressive movements that democratic reforms were achievable. How, then, was the Russian Jewish revolutionary movement transformed in the American context? How did national cultural autonomy serve the activists and organizers of the Jewish labor and socialist movements in the multicultural city they came to inhabit?

2

The Revolutionary and Gendered Origins of Garment Workers' Education, 1909–1918

Many of the Jewish women who immigrated to New York during the volatile years surrounding the 1905 Russian Revolution immediately joined the fight for justice in their communities. Mass movements involving thousands of Jewish women on the Lower East Side included a kosher-meat boycott in 1902, a rent strike in 1904, and food riots in 1907. As they had done in Russia, Jewish women engaged as economic actors in what Paula Hyman calls "the public secular sphere."[1] They organized committees, made demands on powerful men, appointed leaders, spoke publicly, negotiated, went on strike, picketed, built alliances, provided mutual support, and harassed those who violated the strikes and boycotts. The Jewish institutions of the Lower East Side, especially the *Jewish Daily Forward* and the Jewish branch of the Socialist Party, supported these actions without reservation, in large part because women were acting militantly in the role of consumers. When women acted similarly as producers, it was another story. Jewish men were more reluctant to support women's activism in the unions, where men viewed leadership as political and, therefore, as a male preserve.

Jewish and Italian women organized as class-conscious workers en masse in the late fall of 1909 in the shirtwaist industry of the Lower East Side. In the strike and its aftermath, we can detect moments in which organizers were successful in reaching across ethnic and racial lines, extending Yiddish socialist traditions in a new environment. We see the early intersection of national cultural autonomy and mutual culturalism and the birth of the American union education movement. This process is not always visible because it came from the bottom up, in spite of the indifference and hostility some ILGWU leaders demonstrated toward other ethnic groups. From 1902 through 1912, successive iterations of the ILGWU constitution explicitly barred Chinese and Japanese workers from holding membership in the union.[2] Italian workers were often reluctant to join the ILGWU because of what they perceived as neglect or lack of interest, opting at times for locals affiliated with the rival Industrial Workers of the World (IWW).[3] But Jewish immigrants of the 1905 generation brought with them both a heightened militancy and a more sensitive strategy of multiculturalism in reaching out to other ethnic groups than did the conservative male leaders who came before.

Almost from the beginning of the ILGWU, male leaders of the International union constructed a dichotomy between young, radical immigrant women and older, seasoned, and what they termed "conservative" men. John A. Dyche, secretary-treasurer of the International union, reported to the 1906 ILGWU Convention on the children's cloak and reefer makers' local union in Philadelphia. He remarked that the industry was "naturally invaded by fresh arrivals from the old country" who spontaneously began to agitate. He acknowledged that these young women organized a union on their own and approached the ILGWU after having enlisted three-quarters of the industry's workforce. "No organizer took a hand in this work," he reported. "It was a sudden out-burst of revolt against intolerable conditions." He warned that this sudden growth brought with it "danger and weakness" because the new "recruits were untrained and undisciplined in the movement"; they "understand the power of the union, but cannot understand its limitation." He complained that they expected too much too soon and did not comprehend "the need for diplomacy and tact in dealing with employers." Finally, Dyche reassured the convention that the "joint executive board, together with the more conservative members of the union . . . have succeeded in keeping the members in check and avoiding unnecessary friction with the employers."[4]

Before the 1909 strike, women's membership and activism in the fledgling union was limited. Just as in the Workmen's Circle, a few local unions with relatively sizeable numbers of women held separate meetings for men and for women, and some established separate women's branches.[5] While this arrangement seemed to reinforce these women's marginal or second-class status, Nancy MacLean argues that women in these branches saw the meetings "as a necessary measure so that women could then fight their common battle with working-class men as their equals."[6] When the ILGWU had only a few thousand members centered around local unions representing the most skilled and stable job categories, the number of women remained relatively small. But by 1908, Bundists and other revolutionaries began to dedicate themselves to radical activity in the United States, and more women began to join the union.

Women entered the ILGWU through several portals of the Jewish labor and socialist movements. Like the UHT and the Workmen's Circle, *Forverts* (the *Jewish Daily Forward* or the *Forward*), a Yiddish-language daily paper founded by Abraham Cahan, was among several Jewish socialist institutions based in the Lower East Side that were instrumental in the founding and development of the ILGWU. From its beginnings in 1897, the paper, which went from a circulation of 20,000 in 1900 to more than 130,000 in 1918, predominantly in New York City, was an essential organ of Jewish socialist thought.[7] Cahan was a moderate socialist who deliberately included many viewpoints and promoted debates in the *Forward* and in public forums on questions that included the direction of the union movement in the Jewish community.[8] The *Forward* was more than a vehicle for news and opinion; it served as a beacon for would-be union activists, rallying Jewish workers and the Jewish community in support of strikes and in the formation of unions. Clara Lemlich organized a group of shirtwaist makers in the shop where she worked in 1906. Then she went to the offices of the *Forward* to find out "how to form a union."[9] The *Forward* attracted past and future ILGWU leadership to its staff. Benjamin Schlesinger became managing editor of the *Forward* after he was voted out of the ILGWU presidency in 1904 and held that position until he was recruited to run for the presidency again in 1914.

The Jewish section of the Socialist Party also proved conducive to the success of the ILGWU. Revolutionaries who had been radicalized in Russia were attracted to party politics soon after they arrived. Fannia Cohn immigrated to New York in 1904 at the age of nineteen after a brother was almost killed in a pogrom.[10] She joined the Socialist Party and, despite her middle-class background and wealthy relatives in the United States, chose to forgo a formal education. Instead, she went to work in the garment shops and set out to organize her co-workers. She helped to organize ILGWU Local 41 of the Brooklyn white-goods workers beginning in 1906 and, in 1909, at the age of twenty-four, became a member of the local's first executive board.[11] Workers turned to the Socialist Party first for aid in organizing co-workers in their shops and in their communities. For example, Pauline Newman, a leader of the 1909 shirtwaist strike and the ILGWU's first female organizer, who later became the director of its health center, organized a rent strike in 1907 and 1908 at the age of seventeen with legal support provided by the Socialist Party. The strike involved tens of thousands of tenants in the Lower East Side, many of whom needed immediate representation in court against landlords moving to evict them. The strike was only a limited success, and many families were evicted, but the struggle helped forge solidarity among women in the community and provided the opportunity for female leaders to gain experience and hone their organizing skills.[12]

In these and other struggles, Jewish women organizers applied the sensibilities and political worldviews that they had developed in Russia to the conditions in New York and the United States. Fannia Cohn was among the most outstanding young Jewish women of the 1905 generation. Her revolutionary experiences in Russia, steeped in Yiddish socialism, propelled her into fighting for unions, workers' education, women's equality, and multiculturalism in the United States. Cohn was born in Kletsk, Belarus, near Minsk, in 1885. Her father was a prosperous pharmaceutical merchant who sent her to private school. Her parents were literate and encouraged her exploration of books. Like many young middle-class women of her time, she discovered a public place for political expression in revolutionary movements.[13] In 1901, having been a committed socialist since the age of sixteen, Cohn joined the Socialist Revolutionary Party (SR), in which she was exposed to the ideology and strategies of the party's cofounder and principal theorist, Chaim Zhitlowsky. For the three years Cohn was active in the Minsk section of the SR, Zhitlowsky was at his most influential in the Bund, and Yiddish socialism was the expressed worldview of most revolutionary Jews in Russia and in the Russian Jewish Diaspora. Upon arrival in the United States, Cohn's revolutionary experiences and her espousal of Yiddish socialist ideology led her to the Jewish labor movement and the ILGWU.

Fannia Cohn met Rose Schneiderman in 1908 during a white-goods workers' strike, and the two bonded over their style of organizing. Faced with an increasingly female workforce that was predominantly Jewish but had a significant Italian element, and with little or no support from male union leaders, both women sought out rank-and-file women and groomed them as strike leaders, rather than relying on men to conduct the strikes for them. They were concerned with the strikers' morale as well as with the cultural and linguistic divides between the Jewish majority and the Italian minority. The concern that the union could become divided over cultural differences had occurred to ILGWU leaders from the earliest days of the union, when most workers were Jewish. At the 1903, 1904, and 1906 conventions, delegates put forth resolutions calling on the English-speaking Jewish leaders of the union to print convention proceedings and newspapers in Yiddish for the new arrivals. Then, as Yiddish became the principal language of union meetings, Italians complained that they could not fully participate in local deliberations. In a strategy that Cohn and others developed further with respect to other racial and ethnic groups, Schneiderman went to the heart of the Italian women's community and began to work with a priest in Brooklyn to identify potential leaders among the workers. She sought to create the same ethnic institutional supports in the Italian community that Jewish women workers enjoyed. At her suggestion, the New York Women's Trade Union League (NYWTUL) hired an Italian-speaking organizer to appeal to Italian professionals to back the white-goods workers' strike.[14]

Working-class Jewish organizations such as the ILGWU grew in response to rival organizations, such as the Industrial Workers of the World (IWW), which presented a militant alternative to the ILGWU and often attracted members of ethnic minorities. In 1907, the IWW created locals outside the ILGWU that divided the garment workers' movement for a time. The Wobblies appealed to several constituencies. The more militant garment workers, members of Daniel DeLeon's Socialist Labor Party and recent veterans of the Bund in Russia, supported the IWW's class-war rhetoric and mass mobilization tactics, which offered opportunities for grassroots activism. Local IWW leaders, including Morris Sigman, a future president of the ILGWU, led a series of strikes in 1907. The IWW was particularly adept in communicating with Jewish and Italian workers, distributing leaflets in Hebrew, Yiddish, and Italian.[15] The size and strength of the ILGWU increased dramatically in 1909 when the IWW locals in the garment industry elected to leave the IWW and rejoin the ILGWU, just before the Uprising of the Shirtwaist Makers. The right conditions were in place to nurture the most significant developments in the history of the ILGWU.[16]

Rising Up

In the fall of 1909, strikes among Russian Jewish women working in the shirtwaist and dress trades began to break out with increasing fervor. In November, thugs hired by garment manufacturers savagely beat a small group of young women who were picketing the factories they had walked out of several weeks before. The strikers, members of ILGWU Shirtwaist Makers' Local 25, called for a mass meeting and publicized it throughout Manhattan's Lower East Side. Thousands of garment workers responded, filling not only Cooper Union but three other halls for simultaneous meetings. These militants, many of whom were not union members, forced the ILGWU leadership to consider the demands of the strikers as well as those of unorganized workers and the Jewish community. The overflow crowd at Cooper Union heard speeches by union officials, AFL president Samuel Gompers,

Women's Trade Union League (WTUL) president Lenora O'Reilly, and Jewish community leaders. After two hours of speeches, Clara Lemlich, a young Local 25 executive board member, fresh out of the hospital after a beating on the picket line, seized the floor and called for a general strike. The audience voiced its approval, and according to some accounts, the chairman of the meeting, Benjamin Feigenbaum of the United Hebrew Trades and an editor at the *Jewish Daily Forward*, asked the audience to take "the old Jewish oath": "If I turn traitor to the cause that I now pledge, may this hand wither from the arm I now raise."[17] That electrifying moment, linking the voices of young women and older women and men in a sacred commitment to labor radicalism, has become legendary, for it precipitated a mass mobilization. At least fifteen thousand young women responded to the call for a general strike, followed by thousands more in the ensuing weeks. Estimates of the number of strikers range from twenty to forty thousand.[18]

Neither rank-and-file strikers nor union leaders anticipated the overwhelming response, and by all accounts confusion reigned during the first few days. Women walked out of shops uncertain as to where to go or what to do. Organizers from the UHT, the Socialist Party, and the WTUL jumped into action and began to run the strike on the streets. The *New York Call* and the *Jewish Daily Forward* appealed to the Jewish and socialist public to support the strike by donating money and joining the picket lines. Protestant middle-class reformers from the WTUL and Jewish and Irish working-class activists bore witness to police brutality, marched to protect striking women, hired lawyers, and raised bail for arrested strikers.[19] They organized pickets and turned monotonous picket lines into street meetings. They visited working women's clubs and sought public support by leafleting at religious services. Appealing to the desires of women in the working and middle classes for leisure activities with social significance, they held dances and sponsored benefits for the strikers.[20] The WTUL was particularly skilled at introducing tactics to keep the strike going among the young women and conducting a public-relations campaign to win the favor of the media and middle classes.[21] The uprising of 1909–1910 drew large numbers of women into the International union and solidified local unions that were organized and maintained on the shop level by women. Membership of the ILGWU catapulted from seventy-eight hundred members in 1908 to fifty-eight thousand members one year later.[22] Most important, Local 25 emerged as the key center for women's activism within the union.

Women were committed to recruiting the many Italians and even the small number of Blacks employed in the garment shops in the union. Mary

White Ovington, a white socialist who cofounded the National Association for the Advancement of Colored People (NAACP) in 1910, commented during the shirtwaist makers' strike on how friendly the young Jewish women were toward the young Black women. The strike provoked a debate within the Black community, largely because the AFL had a long history of racial exclusion and discrimination. The Cosmopolitan Club, an interracial group of socialists meeting in a Black church in Brooklyn, voted to endorse the strike.[23] Local 25 members reached out to Blacks in their churches in Brooklyn and Manhattan, urging Black teenagers and young women to join.[24] Though, as Maxine Schwartz Seller has noted, some union leaders failed to reach out to them, Black women participated in the strike as pickets, and at least one was an official in her shop union during the strike.[25]

Historians have discussed this moment as an important point of intersection between working-class and middle-class women reformers during the Progressive Era, as well as a complex nexus of radical thought, union building, and popular culture. The 1909–1910 uprising highlights a period of rapid social change for women and men when gender and power relations were being tested anew in work, popular culture, and politics. The public attention paid to the uprising and the variety of individuals and groups involved in the strike and strike support meant that these activities took on different meanings for each participant. The multiplicity of groups and perspectives involved in these events is reflected in the various ways historians have interpreted the meanings of the strike.[26]

Dubbed by one socialist publication "The Strike of the Singers of the Shirts," a reference to the poem by Thomas Hood published in England in 1843 that was popular among Russian revolutionaries, the uprising has served as a parable to inspire subsequent generations of young militant women in the ILGWU and throughout the American labor movement.[27] As Susan A. Glenn observes, these teenagers and young adults were mostly Russian émigrés who were involved in, or indirectly affected by, the radical movements accompanying the 1905 Russian Revolution.[28] Many women openly expressed frustration with the slower and more moderate approaches to building a union movement favored by the male leaders of the ILGWU.

The success of the more militant, broad-based strategy of striking, which included education through street-corner oratory and meetings, social events, publicity, and direct confrontation with employers and police, can be attributed to the experiences and perspectives of the Jewish female organizers of the WTUL and the ILGWU and of the strikers themselves. The radical practices and ideology of the young Russian women were evident at the moment that the ILGWU became a powerful economic and political force. Twenty-four-year-old Clara Lemlich had come to New York from Russia only five years earlier. As the *New York Call* pointed out, the majority of the strikers were "not all Socialists, but they come from a country where political and social questions are considered seriously and where the fight for radical measures claims thousands of human sacrifices."[29] Women who built and sustained the ILGWU, such as Rose Schneiderman, Fannia Cohn, and, later, Rose Pesotta, had all developed a militant and feminist consciousness in Russia. Another key organizer, Pauline Newman, was born in Russia and immigrated without her parents to the Lower East Side.[30] For the most part, it fell on them to educate and lead strikers who were in their teens and early twenties. They trained and encouraged rank-and-file activists to assume leadership quickly. They worked to create social cohesion and direct the militant energies of the strikers through hastily designed classes in union leadership that ended in celebratory dancing. And they were sophisticated in forming powerful support networks.

As historians Barbara Wertheimer and Nancy Schrom Dye have noted, the WTUL brought critical publicity and support to the garment workers' struggle.[31] An uneasy partnership of middle- and working-class women, the WTUL leadership tended to couch ideas in moderate reform terms. Mary Kenney O'Sullivan and William English Walling founded the WTUL in 1903 at a meeting of the American Federation of Labor. The organization welcomed all interested women and men, not just union members. O'Sullivan and Walling forged an alliance between wealthy patrons, settlement-house activists, and AFL officials to support the organization of working women, especially during the shirtwaist strike, in what Dye calls "the New York League's finest hour."[32] Socialist women who envisioned an end to the private ownership of productive property worked in the WTUL alongside women who embraced a worldview in which capitalism could thrive under humane conditions. Rose Schneiderman was the most important Jewish socialist organizer who carefully navigated those uncertain waters.

When Rose Schneiderman first won office as a member of the General Executive Board of the United Cloth Hat and Cap Makers in 1904 at the age of twenty-two, she became the first woman elected to that high office in any AFL union.[33] The New York chapter of the WTUL (NYWTUL) recruited Schneiderman into its leadership. In 1905, she won election to the executive board, and a year later she was chosen vice president.[34] In 1908, she became the NYWTUL's first full-time organizer in the ladies' garment industry. Schneiderman worked closely with the ILGWU until 1912, when she left the NYWTUL to work directly for the union.[35] Like ILGWU president Schlesinger, who went back and forth between the union and the *Forward*, Schneiderman went back and forth between her posts in the ILGWU and the NYWTUL until she became president of the NYWTUL in 1917.[36] For Schneiderman and Pauline Newman, who also took leaves from the ILGWU to serve as a WTUL organizer, the WTUL provided important personal as well as political support.

While women activists in the WTUL and the ILGWU worked closely with one another and each reached out to improve the circumstances of immigrant women, ideas about how to do that varied widely. Most starkly, ILGWU organizing efforts that supported ethnic and cultural expression contrasted with many Progressive efforts to Americanize immigrants. The difference between the strategies of immigrant Jews and middle-class reformers in addressing the difficulties of organizing a multiethnic immigrant workforce can be discerned by the way in which Jewish union activists viewed Italian workers during the shirtwaist strike. The *Call* reported that the initial response of young Italian women to the call for picketing was strong. But the bosses put enormous pressure on these strikers and, just as Schneiderman and other union organizers had done, sought support from authority figures within the Italian community. In one instance, Jewish manufacturers in Mount Vernon, just north of New York City, brought an Italian Catholic priest in to tell striking women that they would go to hell if they continued to strike. Organizers responded by holding Italian-language meetings with Italian music and dance programs.[37] The local union created space for these young Italian workers and their families to reinforce one another in the strike, not only casting labor demands in Italian terms but allowing workers and their kin to express their Italian culture within a union venue.

The WTUL's middle-class members, on the other hand, were fixated on what they saw as "cultural, social and language barriers" between them and the women they sought to organize and could not bring themselves to overcome them.[38] There is some evidence that the native-born white leaders of the WTUL turned a blind eye to a significant number of Italian women who did participate in the strike. Elizabeth Dutcher, a board member of the WTUL who was a militant suffragist and trade-union supporter, having been arrested several times for picketing and orating on the street corner on behalf of the waist makers, gave a lengthy interview to the *New York Call* on the first full day of the strike. The social worker and Vassar College graduate explained, "As the strikebreakers are all Italians, and the strikers Jewesses, there is a danger of racial feeling which we feel the masters are constantly inciting. The work of outside pickets in this strike, then, is to prevent police interference and race warfare."[39]

Evidence suggests that Dutcher was reacting more to stereotypes than to direct observations. The following day, Salvatore Ninfo, an Italian organizer for the Shirtwaist Makers' Union, responded without referring to Dutcher directly:

> There is a thousand of my people out, and they are standing solidly with their fellow workers, determined to win before they return to work. There is no race prejudice among us as some of the papers try to make out. We are all united for a common purpose. The Italian strikers are among the most active in doing picket duty and leafleting in the work of carrying on the strike. There is no chance of any of them breaking away form the union and returning to work.[40]

The Italian press was sympathetic to the shirtwaist makers as well. The *Call* reported on November 19 that the police arrested a Triangle factory striker named Bennie Press for distributing *Il Giornale Italiano* (the Italian newspaper), with "a true and detailed report" of the strike.[41] Indeed, Italian women would be expected to participate. As Jennifer Guglielmo explains, these Italian immigrant women, like Jewish immigrants, were familiar with a "culture of struggle" in their places of origin in Italy's rural south and its industrial north, as well as in the immigrant communities of the United States.[42] As Meredith Tax notes, the myth that Italian women were reluctant to strike was belied in the mass walkout of New England textile workers in 1912: "the Italian women of Lawrence proved that they could be as militant as any other strikers, provided they were organized by people who spoke their language and understood their culture and their special needs as women."[43] Still, the image of the passive Italian woman, first constructed by Italian elite trying to quell the militancy of peasant women in the 1890s, persisted.[44]

Jewish garment manufacturers believed the myth of Italian women's reluctance to unionize or strike and hired Italian workers in large numbers just as Jewish workers began to organize the industry.[45] Louis Levine estimated that in 1908 the "women's trade," composed largely of shirtwaist makers, was 55 percent Jewish, 35 percent Italian, and 7 percent native-born white women.[46] As Cohen and Schneiderman suspected, the garment bosses anticipated that Italians would make it more difficult for garment workers to build a union because of the wide gulf between Jews and Italians in language, culture, and experiences with unions.[47] Certainly, distinctions in language and family culture provided some of the most obvious difficulties in building interethnic solidarity in the ILGWU. Italians complained that they were frozen out of important strike meetings because they were conducted in Yiddish.[48] And parents and male family members gave single Italian women fewer liberties than their Jewish peers enjoyed. Italian women were expected home earlier and were often accompanied to strike meetings by family members. Nevertheless, Nancy MacLean argues, while the Italians' culture "perhaps restrained their willingness to be at the forefront, . . . it did not prevent them from sharing in the struggle."[49] Italian garment workers understood this situation clearly. After the shirtwaist and cloakmakers' strikes of 1910, Italians in the ILGWU began to demand their own branches and locals in which they could conduct union business and make decisions in their own language.

At the 1910 convention, much was made of the need to attract different nationalities. The union's journal, the *Ladies' Garment Worker*, had just begun to publish in Italian as well as in Yiddish and English that April.[50] The meeting heard calls not only for more material in Italian but also for leaflets and "two pages of the official journal given up to Polish."[51] While important, printed literature was not the critical issue. The convention passed a resolution noting, "we have found it impossible for the Jewish working people to organize the Italian working people in our trade," and proposing to create an "Italian bureau in New York" in order "to organize the Italian working people" in the trade.[52] Italians already active in the union sought to have voice in the highest union councils; a resolution proposed to designate an Italian member of the International union's General Executive Board. Finally, several Italian leaders in New York City locals, including Salvatore Ninfo, citing the "uneasiness" of Italian workers trying to fit into local unions conducting business in Yiddish, as well as Italian "pride in self government," called for the creation of a separate Italian local for Cloak and Skirt Makers by 1912.[53]

Some of the locals in the ILGWU in which radicals constituted a significant part of the membership took the first steps toward making room for Italians to exercise political power and cultural expression. The New York Cloak Makers' Local 9 began in 1910 to conduct separate meetings in Italian where Italian-speaking members could discuss the union's business and offer proposals for the consideration of the entire membership. In this way, Italian members could express their political interests as an ethnic group in a union context. Italian members of Local 9, Local 23, and Local 35 began to meet informally to discuss their common interest in the International union.[54] By 1913, Local 25 established an Italian Branch. But revolutionary leaders of the 1905 generation, especially women union members who, like Fannia Cohn, maintained a distinct outlook on multiculturalism and organizing, were not yet able to implement their ideas, particularly as these women continued to confront the gender-related anxieties and sometimes the wrath of their union brothers.

Union Structure and Gender Conflict

The 1909–1910 shirtwaist strike set the stage for gendered conflicts and contradictions within the ILGWU that mounted through the 1910s and 1920s. Women were limited by the division of labor in the industry that was, unfortunately, mirrored in the union organization. In the late nineteenth and early twentieth centuries, the ladies' garment industry was divided increasingly into more narrowly defined crafts and less skilled tasks. Men occupied the relatively few highly skilled crafts that commanded the highest pay. Cutting was at the apex of the shop's occupational pyramid: garments were cut in large stacks from a pattern using a specially designed power saw, and the accuracy and productivity of the workers who performed this task affected the profitability of the whole operation. Cutters protected their gender monopoly through an apprentice system that they created and controlled. No one could learn the skill except from a cutter, and male cutters only taught other men.

The workforce was further divided in the 1890s and the first decade of the 1900s because manufacturers allowed a system of subcontracting within the shops whereby veteran sewing-machine operators employed by the manufacturer could in turn employ "learners" at a fraction of the pay of a full-fledged operator. Men were more often continuously employed throughout their adulthood and maintained seniority in the shops, while the learners were almost always women employed by men. Indeed, better-paid men might accumulate some money and open up a manufacturing shop of their own. If the shop failed after a season or two, they simply went back to work for someone else. Women, however, had especially high turnover rates because they often left employment after marriage, at least temporarily.[55] As Meredith Tax argues, the privileged position of men as skilled, permanent workers and as employers of women had a direct effect on the structure and attitude of the early ILGWU leadership. The union officers excluded women from leadership, condescended to the women members, and ran "the union like a business."[56] As Daniel E. Bender argues, this gender divide in the workplace and union was reinforced by sexual harassment.[57] On the other hand, women as a group often emerged as a more creative and enthusiastic force for building the union than men were, and the union gained in strength when women became committed and engaged activists. This dynamic can be seen in the shirtwaist strike and its settlement.

The demand for a general strike of the entire shirtwaist industry in November 1909 came from women workers. Male leaders were reluctant to call a strike and had no confidence that these young women would respond if they did. Women not only responded in huge numbers; they picketed in greater numbers and often endured greater hardships than did the men. Women continued to strike in spite of hundreds of arrests, excessive fines, jail and workhouse sentences, and assaults on the picket line by hired thugs and police.[58] Their sacrifice may have been even more intense if, as Meredith Tax notes, many women gave up strike benefits in favor of men who were the principal supports of their families.[59] Because a majority of the workforce was female, fewer men were on the front lines during the struggle. Men were less likely to come away with the same understandings of militant action that women did during the shirtwaist strike. In the end, despite the fact that tens of thousands of women held out for several months through a harsh winter and swelled the membership of the union to a new high, union leaders compromised with manufacturers. Most settlements included substantially higher wages for the male-dominated crafts and included no provisions for a closed union shop, an agreement that required employers to hire only union members.[60]

Despite the mixed results in contract negotiations, the 1909–1910 uprising electrified the ILGWU. A few months later, the male-dominated ladies' cloakmaking industry conducted the largest strike in the history of American garment manufacturing to that date. As many as sixty thousand workers walked out. Louis Levine, in his 1924 history of the ILGWU, mirrored the opinion of many men, particularly the leaders of the International, as he reflected on the two strikes:

> The contrast between the two strikes was significant in several ways. In the women's strike, the "social consciousness" of the community was a potent factor. In the men's struggle, labor faced capital directly. One was sudden emotional outburst; the other was carefully planned. In the former, about 20,000 workers were involved. In the latter, the number of strikers was three times as large. As a result of these and other differences, the two strikes came to be thought of as prologue and principal act. The shirtwaist-makers' strike was an "uprising." The cloakmakers' strike was the "great revolt."[61]

Most remarkable in this passage is the gendered way in which Levine characterizes the two forms of struggle. For him, women's organizing linked an agenda of social consciousness to a strategy of community organizing but culminated in a "sudden emotional outburst." In spite of his regard for the women's strike, his description implies that the uprising was unreasoned. Because the men's strike did not (at least in Levine's reckoning) rely on broader community support but on male workers' power at the point of production, it seemed a more potent and assertive confrontation, and by comparison, the women's strike seemed a weaker defensive movement.[62] This analysis became the official history of the ILGWU and influenced how many scholars have thought about the early union. Historian Irving Howe carried on this narrative that the "girls" were responsible for jumpstarting the union movement and earned the reputation of being more militant than their male counterparts. Still, he noted, "what the girls began, the men completed" in the subsequent cloakmakers' strike.[63]

The 1909–1910 shirtwaist strike brought to the fore enduring tensions between the desires of local unions to maintain autonomy and the tendency for International leaders to centralize control. From the ILGWU's origins as an amalgam of small independent unions in 1900, its leaders labored to balance power within an increasingly complex organizational structure. As the union grew, new locals were established in various segments of the garment industry—cloaks, shirtwaists (blouses), dresses, skirts—grouping workers by skill or, in the smaller garment centers outside New York City, by geography. Initially these locals decided whom to organize, what their priority grievances were, when to strike, how to govern themselves, what dues to charge, and how to distribute funds and benefits. International officers began to assert their decision-making authority as they coordinated activities and distributed funds and other forms of support to locals. In 1905, for example, the International began to offer increased benefits, particularly during strikes, and hired and supervised auditors to check the books of local unions.[64] The tension between local militancy and International authority had clear gender implications. As women occupied no positions of authority within the International and remained in the ranks of the least-skilled jobs in the shops, efforts to concentrate power in the International were an inherent affront to women's power and influence. The Protocols of Peace, adopted in the 1910s, dramatically increased the power of the International union over its constituent locals, drawing resistance from local militants, especially women.

The Protocols of Peace and Union Militants

The ILGWU and several manufacturers' associations first signed the Protocols of Peace, a series of trade agreements, at the conclusion of the cloakmakers' strike in September 1910. Both parties enlisted Louis Brandeis, a Jewish progressive judge and legal scholar and later a U.S. Supreme Court justice, to help craft and administer the agreements. Brandeis envisioned the Protocols of Peace as an attempt at state-mediated industrial relations, a system that could mollify the most radical currents of union activism, ameliorate the worst conditions of industrial work, and bring order to the relations between capital and labor. He worried about the radicalism of labor as much as he worried about employers' abuse of workers. In reference to an expansion of the protocols to other industries, Brandeis wrote,

> On the one hand, the disclosures incident to the labor policies of the strong trusts and particularly the hours of labor, wages, and conditions in the steel industry are making many Americans recognize that unions and collective bargaining are essential to industrial liberty and justice. On the other hand, the abuses of trade unionism as we have known them during the last twenty years with their violence, restriction of output, and their lack of constructive policy, are in large part the result of the fact that they have been engaged in a bitter struggle for existence. When public opinion is brought actively to the support of labor unions these abuses will, I believe, tend rapidly to disappear.

Brandeis was adamant that the protocols embrace the elimination of any notion of a closed shop in which only union members could be offered employment. The American people, he charged, "will not consent to the exchange of the tyranny of the employer for the tyranny of the employee."[65]

As Richard Greenwald details, the settlement of the cloakmakers' strike involved negotiations between International union leaders, large manufacturers, and Brandeis as mediator, all under the heavy pressure of a court injunction that ruled the strike illegal. In settling the strike, the General Executive Board (GEB) of the ILGWU, led by President Rosenberg and Secretary-Treasurer Dyche, took over the strike committee and imposed a ratification process on contract negotiations that involved shop chairmen, not the full membership of the union.[66] The settlement, known as the first Protocols of Peace, established wages, hours, and holidays that were better than prevailing conditions and stipulated the creation of shop-based labor-management committees to establish piece rates (rates of pay per garment) for specific tasks. The terms of the protocols included provisions that the ILGWU give up the right to strike, while grievances such as wages, hours, and conditions of work were arbitrated by a Joint Board of Sanitary Control made up of representatives of the manufacturers, the union, and the government.[67] Union leaders then tried to replicate these protocols in a series of agreements throughout the ladies' garment industry.

The agreements lasted until 1916 but were fraught with weakness from the start. Union leaders who supported the protocols were divided on how to administer the agreements, and they precipitated a retreat from the confrontational dispositions that young Russian Jewish women brought with them into the union. More important, union leaders and members divided over support for the Protocols of Peace themselves. No longer allowed to strike, the largely female membership was required to submit to the decisions of a committee of employers and union representatives that they did not choose for the purpose.[68] As the protocols required restraint on the part of impatient and skeptical militant union members, administration of the agreements involved a further extension of control by moderate male leaders over the more militant female rank and file.

The struggle over control of the protocols came to a head in 1912. The New York Joint Board of Cloakmakers, whose directors included representatives from the various locals, International President Abraham Rosenberg, and General Secretary-Treasurer John A. Dyche, signed and administered the Protocols of Peace with the cloak employers' association. The ILGWU had created the New York Joint Board of Cloakmakers in 1903 to allow the four largely male locals in New York's cloakmaking industry to coordinate organizing efforts and to establish labor standards.[69] By 1912, the Joint Board represented fifty thousand union members. Dyche, who during his tenure between 1904 and 1914 became the most powerful International officer, insisted that he represent the union's position in negotiations. Resolved to organize workers in nonunion factories at all costs, Dyche went to an extreme to pressure employers who resisted the union. Dyche conspired with unionized manufacturers to lead the cloakmaking industry out on a three-day strike,[70] then settled and forced nonunion manufacturers to agree to an industrywide standard that union members had no hand in establishing.

The locals represented on the Joint Board, responding to what they saw as an infringement of their authority to speak for their members, voted to kick Rosenberg and Dyche off as directors of the Joint Board of Cloakmakers, ending the International's direct control over the protocols in the cloakmaking industry.[71] Dyche had taken a more conservative approach to the protocols and saw them as an opportunity to stabilize the union's membership. His goal was to limit the number of strikes in the garment industry in return for modest gains in wages and working conditions. But the more militant members of the Joint Board of Cloakmakers saw the limits on the right to strike as illegitimate constraints on their right to organize.[72] After Dyche's ouster, he criticized the Joint Board of Cloakmakers, accusing them of approaching negotiations "from the point of view of a Russian revolutionary."[73] The protocols were further weakened because a growing number of Italians allied themselves with Jewish radicals in the ILGWU, particularly in support of convention resolutions that proposed to create nationality-based subdivisions in the locals. An early resolution to restructure the International union along industrial lines, a move favored by left militants, won the support of many Italian delegates to the 1912 convention. Most important, the Italians supported the movement by Jewish radicals to end the Protocols of Peace.[74]

Women union members in the shirtwaist industry resisted the Protocols of Peace as well. The locals populated by women adopted the protocols in the spring of 1913, more than two years after locals in which men predominated first agreed to them. Having emerged from the militant uprising in 1909–1910 and maintained a vigilant movement that withstood violence and economic hardship, they were in no mood to submit to male control. As Meredith Tax points out, the protocols were "based on the union's ability to keep its members in line; it ruled out any displays of spontaneous militance such as the rejection of the arbitrated agreement in the shirtwaist strike."[75] Given the moderate union vision and collaboration with employers embodied by the protocols, the agreements ironically contributed to the education movement in the union that supported the most radical expressions of women militants. Though the protocols undermined militancy, they also provoked a call for education that even conservative elements in the International union were compelled to support. According to Susan Stone Wong, "If the Protocol was to work, the workers had to be taught that arbitration and conciliation, rather than class struggle, were the basis of American unionism."[76] The retention and training of members became increasingly important after the protocols were introduced. The process was legalistic and dependent on precedent in the industry and in individual shops. Its complexity demanded that a larger number of union members be knowledgeable about the agreements and mechanisms for enforcement if the protocols were to be useful.

Brandeis, along with Dyche and other International leaders, conceived of the protocols as a force to oppose the radicalism and militancy of the 1909–

1910 strike veterans. Education was the most important element of their conservative agenda. Louis Levine noted that "Justice Brandeis and other supporters of the protocol insisted on the necessity of an 'educational campaign' to wean the workers from the 'radical' ideas which they had acquired as a result of a 'generation of miseducation' and to teach them the value of the principles underlying the protocol."[77] Though this radicalized generation generally resisted the protocols, they responded to the idea of education, and women on the local level began to adapt education programs to fit their own needs and desires. The protocols opened the door to education intended to train and restrain union workers, but women and their male comrades, distrusting the protocols, appropriated educational opportunities to construct and refine their own worldview.

Education and Women's Militancy

The demise of the Protocols of Peace accompanied the rise of an educational movement among militant women and men through which they could forge strong bonds, grow intellectually, and develop political ideas and strategies. These militants influenced the conditions that supported education at the 1914 ILGWU convention, where the radical wing of the union held a majority of the delegate positions.[78] The assembly elected Benjamin Schlesinger as president and Morris Sigman as secretary-treasurer to rebuff the conservative administration of Rosenberg and Dyche. Schlesinger was supported by the militant elements of the union who wanted to end the protocols.[79] Those involved in the Socialist Labor Party (SLP) and the Industrial Workers of the World (IWW) held out hopes that Sigman, a former IWW leader, would also support a more confrontational stance.

The militants got a mixed bag in Schlesinger. In retrospect, it became clear that any president bent on increasing confrontation with employers would likely seek to concentrate power in the International at the expense of local autonomy. The radical members of Local 25 in particular organized to fight both the International union and the employers over the protocols, refusing to accede to limits on their right to strike. This local, predominantly populated by young Russian Jewish women, organized for Rosenberg's and Dyche's ouster and campaigned to broaden the union's social and political agenda. While presiding over the ending of the Protocols of Peace in 1916, Schlesinger also pushed to increase the dues for a unionwide strike fund that made locals increasingly dependent on the International. He also created a more effective system of local audits that asserted International control over the locals.[80] The one area in which Schlesinger tolerated an expansion of local autonomy was in education. Schlesinger also increased educational opportunities for union members through the International union offices, though within circumscribed limits.

The development of education programs in the ILGWU accompanied tensions between male leaders and women members and provided an important arena for the political struggles between conservatives and radicals. Women constructed education as a space to exercise their political voices in a way that was more accessible than the existing union structures controlled by men. The strategies that had been effective in building and maintaining the 1909–1910 strike evolved during the 1910s into formal programs, first in the educational department of Local 25 and then at the International level. This was a natural development. Union activists had always employed education in organizing workers in the needle trades. Some of the early cloakmakers' unions either grew out of educational clubs or were closely connected with societies for education and self-improvement.[81] ILGWU members also sought out education in the Jewish socialist movement.

Classroom-based institutions such as the Rand School for Social Science, established in 1906 as the first school in the United States dedicated primarily to workers and supported by the Socialist Party, offered formal educational forums to develop leaders among the mostly female membership of the ILGWU.[82] In the first decade of the twentieth century, many young garment workers found their way to public night schools and to programs at the Rand School before joining the ILGWU and creating its union educational programs. Clara Lemlich took classes in Marxist theory at the Rand School; Pauline Newman took classes at the Socialist Literary Society, where she met Jack London and Charlotte Perkins Gilman.[83] In 1914, Benjamin Schlesinger briefly established formal ties with the Rand School to provide trade-union courses for union members. About one hundred members attended classes in trade unionism, methods of labor organizing, and English. Though Schlesinger dissolved the relationship after one term, some locals continued to arrange courses with the school. In that same period, several locals organized union programs that ranged from a free circulating library to concerts and lectures.[84]

The Rand School attracted workers who were hungry for an education that appealed to their socialist sensibilities. Jewish women, who disproportionately attended the free evening public schools, compared to women of other racial and ethnic groups, were particularly enthusiastic about workers' education.[85] The leading Jewish women organizers who helped to build Local

25 all experienced their political awakening through education. Regarding Fannia Cohn, Pauline Newman, Clara Lemlich, and Rose Schneiderman, Annelise Orleck comments, "The link between education and liberation was reinforced for them when, as young girls, they heard Zionist, Yiddishist, and Socialist speakers attack Jewish religious education and gender roles as old-fashioned, narrow, and provincial."[86] These women sought out and built educational vehicles that were linked with their participation in struggles for social and industrial justice. American Jewish political movements that encouraged participation by women and equal access to education supported them.

Fannia Cohn, the leading visionary of ILGWU education, introduced educational programs in Local 41 as early as 1913. She judged that education was particularly crucial for young, inexperienced workers not only in order to teach them the basics about the labor movement but also to develop bonds among those who belonged to different ethnic communities, bonds that were strong enough to sustain solidarity and build a militant union. In addition to being concerned about the language barrier between these women workers, she worried that Italian as well as Czech, Polish, Slavic, and Arab women had very different cultural experiences with unions than did Russian Jewish women. Like many manufacturers and moderate union leaders, she assumed that workers from rural areas, principally the Italian and Slavic women, had no previous experience with trade unions.[87] For Cohn, the solution to these problems was an integrated program of education and social and cultural activities, including parties and monthly dances. The local created separate Jewish and Italian branches to accommodate workers' distinct language needs and cultural interests; both conducted musical entertainments and popular lectures. In appealing to the varied needs and desires of workers, apart from their most immediate concerns with wages, hours, and working conditions, Cohn created a way to help workers bond beyond what might occur on the shop floor when they were employed by a particular manufacture for a season that lasted just a few months.

As a result of the Local 41 education programs, unskilled workers remained members of the union during the slack season. This was a new development for the ILGWU. Garment manufacturing in the United States generally operated on two busy seasons each year, one in the fall and one in the spring. Without union controls, workers labored sixty, seventy, or more hours a week during these periods of three or four months each. A "slack" season in the winter usually meant that garment workers had no income for periods from several weeks up to two months; they were unemployed for even longer periods in the summer. Before the formation of the ILGWU, it was typical for workers to form a union in a shop for just one season, strike for what they could get, and start over the next season with different co-workers, in a different shop, or both. The workforce, particularly the less-skilled and lower-paid women who made up the vast majority of workers, was transitory; so were many small manufacturers. Because women commonly worked in the shops for a few years before they got married, male leaders expended almost no energy in retaining them as members, and the membership of the ILGWU turned over every few years.[88] But young women began to keep their membership in Local 41 to participate in the educational programs, allowing the union to build its strength and enabling women to act collectively and to aspire to leadership.[89]

ILGWU leaders recognized the effectiveness that education programs had in retaining members. In 1915, Local 25 of the shirtwaist makers created the most comprehensive and significant education program in the ILGWU. These activities, developed by Fannia Cohn, Rose Schneiderman, and Pauline Newman, were the forerunner of workers' education programs that the International later adopted, influencing programs in other unions around the country.[90] One of the most important innovations of Local 25 was the opening in the summer of 1915 of Unity House, a rented house in Pine Hill, New York. The weekend and summer retreat was operated by the women of Local 25 and accommodated up to fifty people at a time. It provided an important means for these young women to interact in a concentrated time and space, in an intimate environment that they controlled.[91]

Some male members of Local 25 were similarly inspired by the militancy of Local 25 women and the local's educational programs. Charles "Sasha" Zimmerman, a longtime leader of the dressmakers' union, attributed much of his early radicalization to his exposure to women leaders in the local. Zimmerman might have been more disposed toward accepting women's leadership than were many of his male peers because of the strong figures cut by his grandmother, mother, and sister. Zimmerman was born in the Ukraine in 1897, when pogroms were rampant. His father died of typhoid fever when Charles was six years old, and his mother supported the family with a small grocery store. During one attack, the family, consisting of his mother, older sister, younger brother, and grandmother, whom he credited with guiding his Jewish and secular studies, hid in the cellar: "And my grandmother—she was the one who actually had the biggest influence on me. She brought me up actually. She would read Tilim—you know who [sic] it is: in danger, they read Tilim. And she would sit and read Tilim in the house, in the cellar."[92]

In 1912, Zimmerman followed his sister to New York, where he worked in a series of trades, including carpentry. Around the end of 1915, Zimmerman's sister found him a job in the shirtwaist makers' shop where she worked and taught him to be a sewing-machine operator. In February 1916, Local 25 of the ILGWU organized the shop with a strike, and Zimmerman joined the union. Two weeks after the strike ended, the mostly female workers in the shop elected the nineteen-year-old Zimmerman shop chairman. As chairman, Zimmerman took responsibility for marshaling the women and men activists in his shop and organizing nonunion shops near his factory. "Every morning before going to work, we went to a nonunion shop, and we stopped them before they went in to work. Occasionally we were beaten up. I had a few girls there who were so good for the picket line. They carried an umbrella, rain or shine. It was always good for protection."[93] When Zimmerman went to Local 25 meetings, the intelligence and "spirit" of women socialists and anarchists such as Jenny Matyas and Rose Pesotta impressed him.

Local 25 was the largest and most important local union in the ILGWU in the 1910s, populated principally by unskilled and semiskilled young women workers. For the next few years, Local 25 education programs grew, and local women activists also pushed for an International education program. The International had greater resources that could expand the opportunities for women who were already active and could open doors for workers in other local unions who might not have access to local education programs. That effort bore fruit in 1916 when Fannia Cohn organized an ILGWU local of Chicago dressmakers. That year, the local sent Cohn to the ILGWU convention, where she was elected as the first, and only, woman vice president of the union.[94] At the convention, Cohn pushed hard for the creation of an International-level educational department. The convention created a Committee on Education whose members included Louis Hyman, the manager of Local 9; already a radical, he later became one of the union's Communist Party members.

In 1917, the GEB, controlled by male union leaders who were generally more moderate than the rank-and-file women leaders, formally established an International educational department and hired an outsider, Juliet Stuart Poyntz, as its director and assigned Cohn to assist her.[95] Poyntz was a Barnard College history instructor and a native-born white Protestant.[96] Her formal credentials in higher education and politically moderate American background stood in sharp contrast to Cohn, whose radical Russian Jewish background was much closer to the members she represented. Nevertheless, the educational programs were popular with the young militant women of

Local 25. The United States' entry into the Great War that had been raging in Europe since 1914 and the Russian Revolution of 1917 lent special urgency to the political discussions that took place in these programs and galvanized union members' participation.

Poyntz and Cohn established the International educational department with the opening of four Unity Centers housed in schools rented from the New York City Board of Education during the winter of 1917–1918. They located the centers in neighborhoods where members lived and often worked. Workers met to learn, sing, play music, and discuss politics. The programs were expanded in January 1918 when the International union opened a Workers' University at Washington Irving High School that offered a higher level of study, including courses that trained rank-and-file members to lead their locals. Poyntz and the other organizers intended to offer a counterbalance to the conservative philosophy underlying public education. "Courses were geared not to individual mobility as the public schools were, but to help female members understand their collective position in industry and society and giving them the skills to challenge it."[97] This contrast between collective and individual solutions to social problems marked the character of ILGWU education for decades. But struggles within the institutions of the radical Left also persisted. Poyntz became radicalized and left the employ of the ILGWU in 1918 after she was inspired to work for the Russian Revolution.[98] She moved increasingly leftward in her politics and joined the Communist Party in the early 1920s. Cohn, however, remained loyal to the Socialist Party and to the ILGWU. When Poyntz left, Cohn assumed the direction of the International's educational department.

Education served male leaders and women activists in different ways, and gender conflicts inherent in the formation of the International educational department intensified in 1918 when the ILGWU convention voted to impose an education tax on each member of the union. The GEB then formally assumed oversight of the work of the educational department at a time when the International union leadership was most suspicious of the political nature of the educational programs. These programs provided a place for young radical women to meet and agitate for an increasingly militant program for both the local and the International unions. Despite unwelcome pressure from below, International union leaders saw the important links between vibrant educational programs and the stabilizing of union membership. By 1919, over ten thousand students enrolled in a broad selection of classes that included literature, history, economics, and trade-union principles, and another seven thousand members attended concerts, plays, and lectures.[99] In 1920, the ILGWU convention voted $15,000 for educational and recreational work sponsored by the International union and various local unions that included dances, hikes, excursions, museum trips, three Unity Houses, and one Unity camp.

The educational programs generated positive public attention, providing cover for their advocates. Influential people, such as Charles Beard, the progressive Columbia University historian, helped promote the programs; he even taught evening classes in the ILGWU's Workers' University.[100] Other unions noticed as well. In the summer of 1919, a committee appointed by the Executive Council of the American Federation of Labor discussed the ILGWU educational programs and issued a report urging "all interested unions working through their Central labor Bodies" to "co-operate in organizing their educational work."[101] These outside boosters helped sustain Fannia Cohn in her constant struggle on the GEB to build and maintain the educational department.[102] As the only woman vice president on the GEB, Cohn felt isolated and vulnerable. But she learned early on that she could maintain a power base in the ILGWU within the educational department that was partly protected by the associations she forged with high-profile figures outside the union.

Education was also central to the creation of the Italian locals, particularly as Italian garment workers felt betrayed by the International union leadership under the protocols. Thousands of Italian women protested a 1913 strike settlement directed by Dyche but not approved by the membership. At least a thousand members left the ILGWU for the IWW and continued the strike.[103] The Rosenberg-Dyche and Schlesinger-Sigman administrations resisted earlier attempts by Italians to form their own locals, but by 1916, after the collapse of the protocols, the International granted a charter to Local 48 of the Italian Ladies' Cloakmakers, led by Salvatore Ninfo. This division was populated mostly by men and named for the abortive Italian revolution of 1848.[104] In 1919, the International chartered the Italian Dressmakers' Local 89, named for the French Revolution of 1789, headed by Luigi Antonini.[105] Antonini became the most prominent leader of the Italian dressmakers in 1917 when, in his second year as a paid general organizer for the ILGWU, he also became the editor of the Italian garment workers' newspaper *L'Operia*.[106] Antonini had opposed the creation of an Italian dressmakers' local until 1918, when he was granted significant authority within the ILGWU. From 1913 to 1918, he had argued that the Italians were not well versed in the operations of trade unions and were not ready to run their own local. By 1918, he credited the educational programs, particularly those in Local 25, with preparing the Italian members for political autonomy within the union.[107]

The more conservative members of the ILGWU leadership had cause to worry about the educational programs, particularly those of Local 25. A year after rank-and-file members' opposition in the local unions led to the defeat of the Protocols of Peace, left-wing members in Local 25 who had been active in its education programs created the Current Events Committee.[108] Initially inspired by the October 1917 revolution in Russia, members of the committee opposed the International union leadership on many fronts and led the anti-war movement among the rank and file during World War I. The ILGWU leadership supported the war and committed thousands of dollars to buying war bonds.[109] Soon, the Current Events Committee turned its focus to the issue of democracy within the ILGWU, explicitly criticizing local and International union leaders for manipulating the union's political mechanisms and collaborating with manufacturers.[110]

Conclusion

As the 1905 generation settled into the Lower East Side and inhabited the occupational and socialist institutional spaces of the Jewish working-class community, the Jewish labor and socialist movements were transformed. On the one hand, Russian revolutionary culture emboldened young women in particular to make demands on sweatshop and factory owners, on male co-workers and subcontractors of female "learners," and on leaders of the Jewish socialist institutions, including their unions. On the other hand, Progressive political actors responded to the elevated levels of militancy in the ILGWU in a very different fashion than did their counterparts in Russia. The Protocols of Peace experiment convinced some leaders in the union, particularly those at the top of the hierarchy, that the forces of the state and capital in America had an interest in stabilizing labor-management relations rather than crushing the labor movement. These differing views developed in the expanding union, causing new rifts between rank-and-file activists and International union leaders, often along gender and ethnic lines. As female activists designed their educational programs in the militant local unions they helped to build, they were at odds with most of the male leaders, who typically regarded women as second-class union members and a threat to their personal power. Even the more enlightened leaders of the union, who welcomed and encouraged women's participation and low-level leadership, were nonetheless suspicious of women's assertions of power at its upper levels. Women's success at the grassroots increasingly conflicted with an emerging bureaucracy of male leaders who believed that the gains made first on the picket line could and should be traded quickly for a structure of industrial democracy involving labor, capital, and the state. The gendered contest over power in the union strengthened some leaders' resolve against educational programs. But the need to attract non-Jewish workers into the union supported an environment in which radical women continued to experiment with educational programs. The advent of the Russian Revolution eventually ruptured the Jewish Left and, together with the postwar Red Scare, threw the ILGWU in turmoil just as it was achieving unprecedented strength.

3

Political Factionalism and
Multicultural Education, 1917–1927

In 1917, Jewish socialists in America cheered the news that the Russian people had overthrown the czar. At the ILGWU convention in 1918, President Benjamin Schlesinger sang the praises of the Revolution, hailing the victory by the proletariat not only over absolutist rule but also in taking control of the state from "representatives of the liberal middle classes." He declared, "Russia, heretofore a country of unmitigated political absolutism and economic oppression, the fort and stronghold of European reaction, suddenly blossomed out as the first truly democratic Socialist republic."[1] The union newspaper echoed this sentiment by publishing inspiring stories of heroism among Jewish women garment workers.

One such story that illustrated women's active participation, "A Pioneer of the Russian Revolution," centered on a woman named Hessie Helfman. Hessie grew up in a religious household in the Russian Pale of Settlement, and her parents took a dim view of secular political activities. In 1874, she moved to the city of Kiev, where she worked sewing garments and learned of the revolutionary movement from other women garment workers. Hessie was eventually sent to prison for hiding activists on the run from the police. There, she met other revolutionary women, who taught her more about the movement. On her release, she married another revolutionary, Nicholas Kolotkevitch. Hessie was arrested again and charged with aiding Kolotkevitch in producing bombs used in the 1879 attempt to assassinate the czar. After months of torture, the article explained, Hessie refused to give up her corevolutionaries. Finally, the military court sentenced her to death, and though she was nine months pregnant, Hessie was hanged. The article quotes Sergius Stepniak:

In the history of the revolutionary movement there were unknown brave girls who sacrificed everything on the altar of their ideal, and asking nothing in return. Theirs was the most thankless task. They risked their liberty and life by performing petty services, such as receiving letters for politi-cal refugees, giving them shelter overnight, delivering packages without enquiring as to their contents, and so forth. This was a most important work in the revolutionary movement.

The article underscored the dedication of many revolutionary Jewish women and concluded, "Such devoted Hessies helped prepare the ground for the Russian freedom which has recently become an established fact."[2] These revolutionary Russian women had counterparts in the women of the ILGWU, whom men and women alike regarded as more militant than the men. The story showed the transmission of socialist principles among women, whether in prison or at work. In the ILGWU, leaders transmitted tenets of Yiddish socialism through workplace activism, strikes and rallies, and educational activities.

ILGWU educational programs and departments were founded in the midst of dramatic global and national developments that affected how union leaders and radical activists thought about education. The Russian Revolu-tion and Russia's subsequent withdrawal from World War I occurred months after the United States entered the hostilities. Fearing support for the revolu-tion at home, particularly among recently arrived immigrants, and seeking to suppress antiwar sentiment, Congress passed Wilson's Espionage Act of 1917 and Sedition Act of 1918, making it illegal to support the enemy in any way. The Wilson administration interpreted these laws broadly to prohibit published articles or public speeches advocating peace, condemning war, or urging others to resist the draft. Eugene V. Debs, presidential candidate for the Socialist Party; "Big Bill" Haywood, leader of the Industrial Workers of the World (IWW); and Emma Goldman, a Russian Jewish anarchist and birth-control advocate, were among those arrested and imprisoned.

After the war, militant unionism and radical activity increased in the United States. In 1919, a strike wave spread across the country, including Seattle shipyard workers, Boston police officers, New York garment workers, and steelworkers from West Virginia to Colorado. That same year, radicals in the Socialist Party split off after the convention in Chicago barred left-wing delegates. Two major Communist parties formed: the Communist Party, led by Jay Lovestone, Charles Ruthenberg, Louis Fraina (later known as Louis Corey), Bertram Wolfe, and Juliet Stuart Poyntz; and the Communist Party of America, led by Benjamin Gitlow, James Cannon, and Ella Reeve "Mother" Bloor.[3] Activists in the IWW, such as Sasha Zimmerman, who had joined in 1917, were attracted to the burgeoning communist movement because of its efforts to reform the trade unions and to advance a militant agenda of strikes and workers' control. In 1920, William Z. Foster, a former IWW member and national organizer for the Great Steel Strike of 1919, formed the Trade Union Educational League (TUEL) among organizers, activists, and officers in the American Federation of Labor. They strove to push the conservative AFL to organize on a broader, industrial scale. The TUEL drew Communist activists such as Earl Browder and Mother Bloor and became informally affiliated with the communist movement after Foster visited Russia in 1921 for an international labor conference and became convinced of the Soviet model of social organization.[4]

The sweeping governmental repression of antiwar and militant labor leftists known as the Red Scare climaxed in the Palmer Raids on left-wing and immigrant organizations in early 1920. Attorney General Mitchell Palmer and his young assistant, J. Edgar Hoover, shut down union offices and left-wing journals, jailed thousands who continued to espouse pacifism and working-class militancy, and deported thousands more, including well-known Jewish radicals like Emma Goldman.[5] The Palmer Raids forced activists and leaders in the two Communist parties underground. At the behest of V. I. Lenin, these Communist parties, former left-wing members of the Socialist Party, and the TUEL merged in 1921 and formed the Workers' Party, which was legal and able to operate openly.[6]

Trade unions and immigrants, who constituted a substantial proportion of the industrial workforce, faced a political and social backlash that came to the fore in 1921. Congress passed the broadest immigration-restriction legislation in U.S. history, establishing strict quotas. The second Ku Klux Klan emerged as a nativist movement that used terror and intimidation to contain the threats they perceived to their Americanism and collective manhood from Jews, Catholics, immigrants, radicals, Blacks who were migrating north, and emancipated new women.[7] Organizations of manufacturers, contractors, and employers in a variety of industries and cities launched the "American Plan" to defeat unions, which they portrayed as un-American. This open-shop movement used intimidation, company spies, yellow-dog contracts (which required, as a condition of employment, that employees promise not to join a union), and blacklists against workers who tried to organize and employers who voluntarily recognized unions.[8]

Through this wave of repression, the underground Communist parties and the organizations associated with the wounded Socialist Party began to build new institutions. The split in the Socialist Party and factions within the communist movement, along with the anticommunist Left, contributed to the difficulties labor faced in the 1920s. But these conflicts created some opportunities as well, particularly as sophisticated educational programs became central to recruitment and institution building on the Left and a critical site of political contest.

Yiddishism and Union Education

The ILGWU education programs reflected the impact of the Russian Revolution on Jewish socialists in the United States. Union leaders generally applauded the ideals of the revolution and supported the transmission of revolutionary ideology through the newspaper and education programs. After Juliet Stuart Poyntz, director of the ILGWU educational department, left the union in late 1918, Fannia Cohn took over the direction of the International's education activities in her new post as executive secretary of education. She designed the heart of what came to be called social unionism in the ILGWU.[9]

In the fall of 1919, the ILGWU educational committee hired Louis Friedland, a professor of English at the College of the City of New York, as the new education director for the next year, under Cohn's supervision.[10] In his first article, Friedland outlined a vision of education that explained the goals of the architects of the union's education program, primarily Fannia Cohn. His exposition revealed the optimism generated by the Russian Revolution, often addressing students in union programs as "comrades in education." He argued that worker education should transform the "spirit" as well as the "aim" of all education and be integrated with all aspects of workers' lives, including their families and communities. He wrote about the "inspiring task" of preparing workers for social change. "For the time will come when the workers—all of them, hand and brain workers, will unite to control industry."[11]

Cohn and Friedland designed a two-tier system of education based on an idea Cohn first proposed to the General Executive Board of the International union three years earlier. They intended the program to be socially transformative, a new form of education that would raise the consciousness of workers toward a socialist vision and cultivate future union leadership from the ranks of students.[12] Cohn and Friedland devised one program, held at the Unity Centers for the "mass" of union members, which offered "intellectual, cultural and recreational instruction." The second program, called the Workers' University, trained "especially good material to act as officers, secretaries, leaders, shop committeemen, etc., in the trade-union."[13] The ILGWU also encouraged members to attend classes sponsored by other institutions such as the Workmen's Circle and the Rand School through class schedules published in *Justice*. When ILGWU members attended classes in 1920, Alexander Trachtenberg taught "History of the Working Class Movement" and "Russian Revolutionary History," and Scott Nearing taught "Dynamic Sociology," "Control of Public Opinion," and "Capitalism."[14] Beginning in 1921, students who showed promise as union organizers and leaders won scholarships to the Brookwood Labor College.

As a Socialist Party activist, Fannia Cohn joined key union leaders, academics, and workers' education advocates in founding Brookwood as a residential school in Katonah, New York, in Westchester County just north of New York City. Historian Jonathan Bloom calls Brookwood "the flagship of the workers' education movement." It drew students from the ILGWU, the Amalgamated Clothing Workers of America (ACWA), and the United Mine Workers, all of which later became instrumental in founding the Congress of Industrial Organizations (CIO). Though nonsectarian, many of its prime movers belonged to one or another socialist party. Brookwood's longtime director, A. J. Muste, was a seminary classmate of Socialist Party leader Norman Thomas. Muste, like most of the founders of Brookwood, had been a pacifist during World War I and was drawn to Quakerism and the labor movement as vehicles to bring about peaceful social change. The American historian Charles Beard, who had cofounded the Rusk Labor College in Oxford, England, two decades earlier, sat on Brookwood's board.[15] Fannia Cohn's influence was felt at Brookwood and extended through its students to the most reform-minded unions in the country. Brookwood courses were based on the pioneering educational design of the ILGWU, which included long, detailed course syllabi for the most advanced classes.[16]

On all levels of union education, Louis Friedland enthusiastically touted the advantages of bilingualism. In the view of Friedland and the Yiddishists, workers could best organize in a class-conscious movement when they were rooted in their ethnic cultures. And for them, language was the foundation of culture. Friedland wrote that the first priority of the education program was to teach English to the "large admixture of foreign born." But, in contrast to the English-only movements that prevailed in many states during the Progressive Era, he emphasized, "This does not imply surrender of such foreign language as our membership can handle."[17] "We are proud of the fact that we can command more than one language. We are glad that the literatures, the arts, the music, the culture, the riches of more than one country are open books to us."[18] Fannia Cohn pushed this multicultural agenda throughout the labor movement, successfully proposing that the American Federation of Labor Committee on Education recommend that union groups lobby public schools to offer "lectures and discussions in foreign languages." Quoting from the report, Cohn said, "good public policy demands 'that non-English speaking people must be given an opportunity to learn in the spirit of American institutions before they have mastered our language.'" She crowed that "this part of the report is a rebuke to all narrow-minded patriots who would follow the example of the worst reactionaries."[19]

Cohn's and Friedland's respect for cultural pluralism, informed by revolutionary Yiddishist ideals, was supported by a thriving Yiddish culture in New York. This moment after World War I marked what Irving Howe called "the beginning of the second and last upsurge of Yiddish theater in America," which lasted through the 1920s. New York City was the center of this movement, with twenty theaters producing Yiddish-language plays. Though the plays were extremely uneven, appealing occasionally to highbrow tastes and more often to broad, popular humor, a creative, intellectual, and experimental Yiddish theater emerged that addressed contemporary issues.[20] Chaim Zhitlowsky's boyhood friend S. Ansky produced one of the most enduring plays of the time, *The Dybbuk*. Written in 1914 and produced first in Europe in 1919 and then in New York in 1924 (after Ansky's death), *The Dybbuk* borrowed heavily from Chasidic folk tales that Ansky collected in his travels among the Jewish shtetlakh.[21] In it, a wealthy father of a bride-to-be is forced to confront his betrayal of a childhood friend. He breaks a pact with the friend that their children would marry, because the boy turns out to be poor. When the youth learns that he will lose his beloved, he dies heartbroken, and his spirit, or dybbuk, inhabits her body. In a court of rabbis convened to exorcise the dybbuk, the father is found guilty and forced to give half his earnings to the poor for the rest of his life.[22]

As Zhitlowsky explained in a 1926 English translation of *The Dybbuk*, his friend and fellow revolutionary drew from Chasidic culture because Chasidism was a democratic movement that subverted what he described as a "caste system" in the Jewish community led by a small group of intellectuals, religious leaders, and rich men who kept the masses of Jews illiterate and fearful. Chasidism was a movement that allowed any Jew, regardless of background, to participate in an ecstatic life filled with optimism. This development, Zhitlowsky believed, became the underpinning of Yiddishism: "The new philosophy inspired by Chassidism was in later years to find its expression, under the influence of science and rationalism, in Jewish revolutionary and nationalistic movements. It is not remarkable, therefore, that

I. L. Peretz, philosopher anarchist, D. Pinsky, revolutionary social-democrat, and S. Ansky Rappaport, socialist-revolutionist, and author of *The Dybbuk*, should have been the first to express the older Chassidism in modern Jewish literature."[23]

The Yiddish theater flourished at the same time that leaders in the Jewish labor and socialist movements were increasingly concerned over a growing gap between generations in language and ideology. Workmen's Circle leaders worried about the diminishing numbers of Jews who spoke Yiddish, especially after the Immigration Act of 1924 closed the door on those Jews coming from Russia.[24] As the second generation English-speaking youth began to come of age, Yiddishist Bundists of the first generation felt increasingly anxious. They equated the learning of Yiddish with the transmission of socialist ideals. For them, culture generally and language specifically were central to Yiddish socialism. Yet parents had to appeal to their own children in the second generation's native language, English. They hoped to hook the children through English-speaking clubs that would teach them the history of Jewish socialism and the importance of studying Yiddish. But they also understood that the circumstances in which Yiddishism emerged no longer existed in the same way in the United States. One officer of the Workmen's Circle wrote.

> We are a Jewish organization, and therefore we are adjusting ourselves to changing conditions among the Jews in America. The old waves of immigration, armies of refugees from Czarist persecution and from starvation in Central Europe, are no longer sweeping over the country. Whether we like it or not the doors have been barred and no more of our people are coming in. At the same time the sons and daughters of the first generations of members of the Workmen's Circle are growing up.
>
> Many of them don't speak or read Yiddish. Many of them are ignorant of the ideals that animated their fathers. How are we to get them to accept and embrace our great Socialist ideals? The clubs will get them, and then the English speaking branches. That is, if we know our business. We will organize our clubs in such a way that every boy and girl that hears about them will be eager to join, to participate in their activities, to become active, and ultimately to embrace our ideals.[25]

Efforts to revive the labor movement and to ensure the transmission of Yiddish socialist ideals overlapped in other educational venues such as camping, which combined informal education with healthful recreation.

Fannia Cohn championed the Pioneer Youth Camp, the sleep-away camp in Pawling, New York, that opened in the summer of 1924 for children of union members. Socialist and Jewish institutions, including the *Jewish Daily Forward*, the Rand School, Brookwood Labor College, and most of the needle-trades unions, gave money to buy the land, construct buildings, and hire staff. By 1926, the 142 children (77 boys and 65 girls) who attended from one to ten weeks came from twenty-nine different unions. The ILGWU, whose members sent twenty-five children that summer, used the camp, as well as the various Pioneer Youth day programs in New York City, more than any other union did.[26]

Pioneer Youth Camps were part of the strategy of social unionism that involved families in the labor and socialist movements. Pioneer Youth architects intended the day and overnight camps as a vehicle to build a non-Communist children's auxiliary to the unions. In 1926, the *Forward* helped to provide partial or full scholarships for students to attend camp; the funds included ten full scholarships dedicated to children of United Textile Workers union members who were involved in the protracted strike in Passaic, New Jersey that year. The presence of these children, most of whom the camp doctor reported to be underweight, stimulated discussion among all the young campers. "Questions about the strike, about the conditions of the workers and strikers' songs were current during their stay and when the other camp children found that these children lacked bathing suits and other suitable clothing, they raised of their own accord over $60.00 among themselves and their parents to buy these necessities and voted to send the $22.00 that remained to the strikers' funds."[27]

The importance of education in general and camping in particular to both the left and right wings of the Jewish labor and socialist movements is illustrated in the battles between Communists and Socialists within the Workmen's Circle. In January 1926, Communist-controlled branches formed the League of Progressive Branches, and Workmen's Circle officials charged that the League made decisions affecting its member branches independently of the Workmen's Circle's elected leaders. In response, the National Executive Committee dissolved sixty-four branches with seven thousand members whose leaders refused to leave the League. The Communist-affiliated members of the League assumed full control of twenty Workmen's Circle schools in New York and Camp Kinderland, the summer camp on Sylvan Lake in Hopewell Junction, New York.[28]

Kinderland was the jewel in the crown of Workmen's Circle educational programs. Planning began in 1922, when the order's executive board appointed a three-member committee to find a suitable site. The committee included Yankl Doroshkin, a left-wing member of Local 22, who approached Local 22 leaders to see if the Workmen's Circle camp could be built on the grounds of Unity House. Though the union agreed, the committee found an existing camp for sale, and Camp Kinderland was founded in 1923.[29] The camp was the primary retreat of the New York chapters, the order's largest concentration of members in the country. Workmen's Circle literature described the camp as a place where the ideals of education could be put into practice and socialist and Jewish cultural programs could be enjoyed. When Workmen's Circle leaders felt they lost Kinderland to Communist control, they organized a committee in the spring of 1926 to purchase a new camp on the same lake as Kinderland.[30] The chairman, R. Block, recalled with sarcasm and spite, "Our Left Winged friends assured us that the members of the Workmen's Circle were not interested in any cultural work. It is only they, the 'select' that are interested in educational work among the Jewish labor masses. After the[y] leave our organization, there will be no one to carry on the work." But, he said, Workmen's Circle members were resolved: "We will have a camp for children, where the future heirs of the W.C. will be educated to love and appreciate the socialistic and labor ideals for which their parents fought all their lives. A camp for adults, where our members could spend their vacation far from the stuffy and tumultuous city."[31]

While the struggle over Jewish political, social, and cultural institutions occupied time and energy on all sides of the Jewish Left, leaders of the Jewish labor and socialist movements engaged in another core aspect of Yiddish socialism, reaching out to leaders and workers from other racial-ethnic groups. Remarkably, they cultivated relationships with important Black leaders, often through educational vehicles. The association of A. Philip Randolph and Chandler Owen with the Jewish labor movement, particularly with important members of the ILGWU, dates to 1915–1916. Randolph and Owen met as students in 1915 and collaboratively developed ideas that led them into the Socialist Party. When they attended the Rand School for Social Science, they met a number of Jewish labor radicals, most importantly Morris Hillquit, a founder of the United Hebrew Trades who remained a close adviser to ILGWU officers. Owen and Randolph founded the Harlem branch of the Socialist Party and in 1917 became editors of the *Messenger*. That same year, Hillquit ran for mayor of New York City on the Socialist Party ticket and inspired Philip Randolph and his wife, Lucille Green Randolph, to run for statewide office as well.[32]

Randolph and Owen sought and received support from the Jewish needle-trades unions in their initial campaigns to organize Black workers. As early as 1920, the ILGWU journal *Justice* published appeals for funds to keep the *Messenger* alive.[33] The *Justice* editors' confidence that they could raise money among the garment workers was likely due in part to the hundreds of women garment workers who had been Randolph's and Owen's classmates at the Rand School and became their students in classes they taught there beginning in 1919. Among the Jewish and Italian garment workers at the Rand School were a handful of Black women, who began entering the needle trades in 1917. They were the most likely audience for *Justice*'s announcements in 1920 for lectures at the Rand School by Owen, on the "Political Situation and the Negro," and Randolph, on "Labor and the Negro."[34]

An editorial in *Justice* in June 1920 about the AFL convention that year noted the persistence of Black delegates who demanded formal inclusion in all local unions. The article remarked that while the AFL constitution provided for equal rights to Black members, "there is a wide chasm between theory and practice. . . . The Negro workers have not enjoyed the rights of workers, and it was their white brothers who stood in their way to securing their rights."[35] After the Black delegates had received what they perceived to be empty promises for inclusion the previous year, they demanded separate charters, particularly for the railway clerks, because of an explicit color bar in the Brotherhood of Railway Clerks constitution. *Justice* applauded the convention for protesting the union's policy and demanding a revocation of its constitutional provision against Negroes.

At the 1920 ILGWU convention, President Schlesinger submitted a report that observed the increase of young Black women who had "begun invading" the ladies' garment trades over the preceding few years in New York, Baltimore, Philadelphia, and Chicago. Black women were first "used by employers as a club against the organized workers in the shops." But, the report went on, the idea of unionization had spread among these workers, and Blacks were joining the union in increasing numbers. Union officers explained the Black workers' affinity for the ILGWU this way: "The friendly attitude of the members of our locals towards them, the fact that they have treated the colored women in a friendly and equitable spirit, has aided materially in revealing to the negro women workers where their true interests lie."[36] In addition, the General Executive Board expressed a desire to educate Black garment workers and considered hiring organizers dedicated to organizing Black women. Union leaders touted the donations they made to the *Messenger* as one way to support the organizing of Black workers in the ILGWU. This pattern follows the experience that many ILGWU members had when, as recent immigrants, they found their way to unions through reading the *Jewish Daily Forward.*

The ILGWU's interest in organizing Blacks seems disproportionate to their numbers in the industry. In 1922, the convention report suggested there were "scores" of African American women in the union who worked as iron-ers and pressers as well as operators, at a time when there were roughly one hundred thousand members in the ILGWU. Nevertheless, between 1920 and 1922, the Waist and Dress Joint Board of New York, made up of all local unions in those industries, including Waistmakers' Local 25, Dressmakers' Local 22, Cutters' Local 10, and Italian Dressmakers' Local 89, "held several meetings for Negro workers with considerable results."[37] Black women work-ers were praised for their participation in a recent strike, and the convention voted to donate $300 to Randolph and Owen's *Messenger.*[38] In 1923, Local 22 carried out an educational program addressed to Black women workers in West Harlem. They arranged for Black trade unionists and lecturers to address the women and their families on the merits of joining the ILGWU. During the summer of 1923, Blacks actively helped to organize ILGWU Local 132 for button workers. That winter, Local 22 reported that it conducted a general strike with the support of Black members.[39]

Throughout the 1920s, radical Jewish leaders reached out in sympathy to Black co-workers in spite of the fact that employers in many industries, including the needle trades, hired Blacks as strikebreakers or to weaken union organizing drives. The presence of Blacks in the ladies' garment industry did not seem to play any appreciable part in the cause of the bit-ter conflicts between Jewish Communists and Jewish Socialists. However, the effect of this rivalry may have been to boost interest in Black workers as both left factions worked to develop African American allies. A. Philip Randolph became increasingly important to the union's efforts to organize Black women in the garment industry after he helped to found and then led the Brotherhood of Sleeping Car Porters and Maids in 1925. That relation-ship helped the ILGWU succeed to some degree in these years in organizing Black women and elevating a few to local leadership positions.[40]

In spite of the ILGWU's organizing efforts, overall membership began to decline after 1920, helped along by the internal conflict between the Com-munists and Socialists. Women's membership dropped even faster than men's, and relatively few Black women remained members of the ILGWU. However, the keen interest that Jewish radicals of all sectarian persuasions had in organizing Black workers and developing ties to Black organizations and leaders survived. ILGWU leaders in power and in the opposition managed to build important relationships even in the organization's weakened state. By 1925, the numbers of Black women in the ladies' garment trades had risen to approximately five thousand workers in the principal localities of the ladies' garment industry: New York, where the majority of the trade was still based; Philadelphia; Chicago; and Baltimore. ILGWU leaders recognized that a majority of Black women workers were not members of the union, but they attributed the situation to the problems in organizing the industry overall. By the end of 1926, the union had lost almost 40 percent of the members it had just five or six years earlier. Even so, ILGWU leaders continued to appear sanguine at the prospects of organizing Blacks. They consistently remarked on the "fine fighting qualities" of Black members who struck in New York, Philadelphia, and Chicago.[41] That attitude served the union well in years to come.

Local 25 Militancy

Government repression, open-shop campaigns, membership declines, and intraleft squabbles have understandably distracted historians from seeing the initiatives that later revived the ILGWU, particularly those concerning ethnicity and race. Some of the most innovative strategies for organizing across racial-ethnic cultural lines emanated from rank-and-file members active in union locals. Often, these initiatives came from the most militant quarters. Local 25 militants in particular established new venues to nourish radical multicultural education. At Unity House, these young women transmitted their vision of socialism through an educational program that included social and recreational activities and the celebration of different ethnic cultural traditions. Unity House was an experiment in cooperative ownership by workers; it was a showcase for workers' ability to control their own business, their own education, and their own recreation. Jennie Matyas, an activist in Local 25 since joining in 1910 at the age of fifteen, helped to pioneer the educational programs in the ILGWU and sat on the committee that opened the first Unity House, or Unity Village, as it was originally called.[42] In 1920, she described the bucolic estate of over eight hundred acres in the Pennsylvania Blue Ridge Mountains (now known as the Poconos) as more than just a place for rest and relaxation: it was a "model for the labor movement of the world." Workers bought this retreat as a group; they devised the extensive program of swimming, boating, hiking, horseback riding, theater, lectures, and dining and operated it cooperatively. The operation of Unity House required a complex organization: a committee to hire staff, supervise, keep books, hire contractors, set prices, and organize bookings. Matyas declared that Unity House was "a test" of workers' collective ability to run their own affairs.[43]

Because these workers were women, Unity House was simultaneously a showcase for women's ability to articulate their vision for the future and to control their own destiny. A number of male observers in the ILGWU acknowledged over the years that Unity House was a particular creation of the young women of Local 25. One member, Nathan Shaviro, echoed Jennie Matyas's characterization of Unity House: "It is a testing and training for the future where they will control their entire lives. And those glorious girls at the Unity House have demonstrated their ability for such a life." Shaviro commented at length about the integration of play and politics and ethnic cultural forms in the programs at Unity House and about the spontaneity those programs engendered among the young women:

> They may be gravely discussing some of the present problems and a moment later gleefully clapping their hands and kicking the ground because someone had succeeded in making a good hit in bowling. . . . We learn how to make enjoyment creative and educative. We learn games, dances, songs, dramatic sketches. Intelligence and meaning permeates our fun, and the play warms up our intelligence.

In keeping with Fannia Cohn's call for multiculturalism, Unity House programing made the celebration of multiple cultures central to the political frame of worker education. Shaviro described a Labor Day pageant: "There was a symbolic Greek dance, and a Japanese sketch, and a labor sketch. . . . This followed by Jewish and Russian folk songs which melt the wall between performers and the audience."[44]

The Italian local unions similarly pursued broad educational programs rooted in Italian ethnic and radical culture. In 1920, Local 48 purchased a building, naming it the Italian Labor Center, in which they operated a grocery cooperative that served Italian workers from many trades throughout New York City. Also in 1920, Local 89 delegates to the ILGWU convention proposed that the International invest in the socialist Italian-language newspaper *Avanti* as a vehicle to support the Italian labor movement in the same way that the *Forward* supported the Jewish labor movement and the *Messenger* supported the unionization of Black workers.[45] And Local 48 helped to found the Italian Chamber of Labor, a fraternal organization that provided education and mutual insurance benefits to Italian workers and their families.

The founding of Villa Anita Garibaldi in 1920, Local 89's own retreat and vacation home, was one of the most important elements of local autonomy for the Italian union members. The convenient Staten Island retreat allowed the Italians their own space to enjoy their own culture, especially food. Women in particular were attracted to the Villa, in part because they found it difficult to bring family members to meetings and rallies but were able to bring children and other family members to the vacation home. The Villa was open to other Italian community members, including members of other unions. Local 89 manager Luigi Antonini used the Villa to build loyalty to himself and the union among his members and Italian workers throughout New York's labor movement by associating himself with the retreat. In 1925, the Villa had to be closed because of financial losses. It is a measure of how important the Villa was to the larger Italian community that Carlo Tresca, the former IWW leader and widely known intellectual in the American Italian Diaspora community, publicly criticized Antonini for mismanaging the retreat.[46] As anarchists, Antonini and Tresca were allies in domestic and international movements that ranged from the defense of Sacco and Vanzetti to the formation of an anti-Mussolini, antifascist front. Local 89's educational activities served those efforts.

In Local 25, educational programs overlapped with rank-and-file efforts to demand reform in the union, beginning with the Current Events Committee formed in 1917 to discuss the Russian Revolution, the war, and industrial developments. In 1919, Sasha Zimmerman joined with other members of Local 25, mostly women involved in educational work, to form the Workers' Council of the waist makers' union.[47] The name they chose for the group was a direct translation of the Russian word *Soviet*, though they confined their agenda to local issues.[48] Radicals in the union locals tried to democratize the ILGWU, starting with the shop-delegate movement beginning that year. Local 25 activists organized a Shop Delegate League that agitated for a restructuring of the local's system of governance. Union members traditionally elected local union executive board members from slates determined by existing leaders. It was possible to elect insurgent candidates, but only with great difficulty. The "Leaguers" argued that the only fair system of representation would be one in which two delegates from each shop were elected to a council that replaced the executive board. This democratizing movement threatened the officers of the International's General Executive Board (GEB), most of whom were managers of local unions. The shop-delegate movement attracted members of leading radical groups active in the needle trades from 1919 to 1922. Current and former Wobblies (IWW members), socialists who followed Daniel DeLeon, Italian syndicalists, and, most important, members of the nascent Workers' Party of America adopted the agenda of shop-floor democracy and the shop-delegate strategy.[49]

In 1920, President Schlesinger and Secretary-Treasurer Sigman moved to thwart the Shop Delegate League in Local 25 by breaking up the union into smaller industrial locals.[50] The ILGWU convention voted in 1920 to form Local 22 out of the dressmakers' shops represented in Local 25. GEB leaders hoped to weaken the radical tendencies percolating among the young women of Local 25.[51] Nevertheless, the members of the new dressmakers' local that organized formally in 1921, most of whom were former Local 25 members, had militant political leanings. The shop-delegate movement spread, and groups formed in Local 22 as well as in important locals such as the New York Suit Operators Union, Local 1, and the New York Cloak Finishers' Union, Local 9. In 1921, the GEB again tried to suppress the shop-delegate movement in Local 22 by expelling twelve members of the newly formed executive board, including Sasha Zimmerman, who was active in the TUEL.[52]

In 1921, William Z. Foster appointed Zimmerman as the New York regional director of the TUEL, elevating Zimmerman to one of the most visible posts in the communist movement.[53] As James R. Barrett notes, "The TUEL built its strongest and most durable movement in the needle trades."[54] Because the TUEL was ostensibly an educational group, not a formal trade union, it provided the ILGWU leadership with another reason to be wary of educational activities. Communists intended to take control of American trade unions through the TUEL by "boring from within," that is, joining existing unions rather than establishing competing organizations. In 1922, the TUEL established a needle-trades section, and the leadership of the ILGWU, most of whom were committed members of the Socialist Party or anarchists, linked the movement for union democracy with the insurgency of the Communist Party.[55]

The intensifying rivalry between Socialists and Communists was complicated because the fight against union bureaucratic control was also a fight to expand women's rights, attracting a broad spectrum of activists from various political positions. Zimmerman recalled that left-wing socialism and other radical ideologies were particularly pervasive among the young women in Locals 25 and 22. In the early 1920s, a number of Local 22's executive board members who supported the movement for democratic reform were women. Many women who were not Communists, particularly in Local 25 and, by 1924, Local 22 as well, lined up with Communists in the shop-delegate movement.[56] Zimmerman later explained:

Well, first of all, Local 22, coming from previous Local 25, always had a radical element. Even when it wasn't the fashion, they had a lot of the young girls there who were socialists, you know, and had a socialist background, like Saran Shapiro, Bessy Mirsky, Jennie Matyas. Before I was active, I remember Jennie Matyas, who already made speeches in 1918 in Webster Hall. I was still a newcomer, and she was already an old-timer making speeches. Mollie Friedman came later. Cayman. A number of these girls who were socialists. And it was always a general socialist ideology among the active members of Local 25. Juliet Stuart Poyntz, who was the educational director. So there was an element of that: the socialists and the anarchists and the Wobblies were combined and worked together. When the Communists came in, they cashed in on this sentiment that existed all the time. . . . Many went with the Communist Party after it was organized.[57]

Sectarian Conflicts

While the ILGWU international leadership stewed over the insurgency among radical young women, the threats from outside organizations loomed ever larger. For Socialist unions such as the ILGWU, competition from the Communists centered on educational, cultural, and recreational institutions. Throughout the 1920s, Communists sought to win democratic control of unions, fraternal organizations, and summer camps and founded newspapers and other rival institutions to those that they could not control. Though conservative leaders of the ILGWU may have wanted to abandon education programs which fostered dissent within the ranks, the programs were necessary to countervail the Communist education movement. ILGWU leaders had to tolerate some risk associated with keeping the programs alive.

The conflict between Communists and Socialists heightened on many fronts in the Jewish labor movement in 1922. Left-wing Jews founded the Yiddish language *Freiheit* (Freedom) that year in opposition to the Socialist *Forverts* (Forward). The TUEL, through its publications, attacked the United Hebrew Trades and the Workmen's Circle for their support of ILGWU secretary-treasurer Morris Sigman, whom they charged with "class collaboration."[58] Though Communists considered Schlesinger a foe of the Communist Party, he hesitated in confronting the Communists in the ranks of the union.[59] His indecisiveness angered fervent anticommunist socialists on the International's General Executive Board. In January 1923, intent on combating the communist movement in the union, the GEB seized on an apparently empty rhetorical threat by Schlesinger to resign, forcing him to make good on the promise.[60] Morris Sigman, next in line of succession, assumed office as president of the ILGWU. Soon after, TUEL members captured the majority of Local 22's executive board and made significant gains in Locals 1 and 9, among others. In response, Sigman took the most decisive and strident action that escalated the fight against the Communists: he demanded the resignation of members of local executive boards who belonged to the TUEL. When fourteen women of the nineteen-member Local 22 executive board objected, Sigman expelled the entire board, replacing them with eighteen men and one woman.[61] In a local union populated mainly by women, Sigman made a sweeping statement in appointing men: he implied that women were not to be trusted politically; as a group they were too radical. This was reflected in the union staff, as only three women organizers could be identified as being in the employ of the International in the period between 1922 and 1924, down from at least eleven in the years between 1920 and 1922.[62]

Morris Sigman's hostility toward the Communists was apparent in his report to the 1924 convention of the ILGWU. In a section entitled "Left Hysteria in Our Locals," Sigman outlined the grievances he had against the Communists who had managed to gain dominance or substantial influence over several local executive boards in Chicago and Philadelphia, in addition to those in New York. Sigman argued that, under the guise of the TUEL, the Communist International in Moscow directed the work of the Communist Party members of the ILGWU. "These 'idealists' did not hesitate to look for allies among that class of riff-raff and malcontents which may be found in every big labor union, persons who, for some shady reason in the past, have had a grudge against the Union and its officers. These became their chief supporters and 'comrades' and were naturally only too ready to do their bidding and nefarious work."[63] The GEB ordered, and the 1924 convention affirmed, that no delegates to the convention could be seated if they maintained membership in the TUEL.

A debate that accompanied the charges against one local union militant exemplified the gender tensions exacerbated by the anti-Communism of the Sigman administration. The 1924 convention denied Rose Wortis seating as a delegate, in spite of her resignation from the TUEL two months earlier. Wortis was a longtime activist of Locals 25 and 22, a member of their educational committees, and a founder of Unity House. Wortis's principal accusers were male leaders of the GEB, while most of her defenders were women.[64] Still, Wortis framed the fight around democracy, not gender. Wortis and her supporters posed objections that resonated with union members not connected to the Communist Party. Though she had in fact withdrawn her membership from the TUEL, members of the credentials committee argued Wortis did so for the wrong reasons. In her own defense, Wortis said,

> I believe this Convention should have all opinions represented. You have done me a great injustice. I have never besmirched the members of the Executive Board or the officers. I deny that the Trade Union Educational League is a dual organization. Your refusal to let me explain its purposes proves that you are afraid to hear the truth. Your refusal means that you are afraid of our arguments, and it means that your objection is not well founded.[65]

The sectarian conflict placed militant women from different factions, who had worked together in the same local union fights, in different camps. Members were torn between loyalties to the revolution and the union, on one hand, and injustices they felt their comrades suffered at the hands of revolutionaries and institutional leaders, on the other.

Rose Pesotta, like Wortis, represented an important constituency at the 1924 convention. One of the most prominent anarchists in the union, Pesotta rose through the ranks of Local 25 and Local 22 as an educational department activist, and around the time of the convention she began her studies at the Brookwood Labor College.[66] As a committed anarchist, Pesotta struggled with her political allegiances in the deepening crisis involving the socialists and communists in the American Jewish socialist and labor movements and in the Soviet Union. Her distaste for communism was at least as personal as it was political because four years earlier Bolshevik sympathizers killed Pesotta's father in Russia.[67] At the ILGWU convention, she rose to offer a resolution for the delegates to demand that Lenin and the Soviet government free political prisoners, particularly the socialist and anarchist critics of Bolshevism. In her speech, she reminded the delegates, especially the Communists in attendance, that rumors of Soviet repression of fellow anticzarists had been reaching America for years, though she and others had refrained from acting on them because, she said, "we in America, partly knowing the truth, could not come out in the open at a time when Russia was hounded by enemies."[68] Pesotta offered this condemnation at a critical point in the Sigman administration's own repression of her comrades, particularly in education. Like other revolutionaries, Pesotta was doubly conflicted, especially as the politics of the Russian Revolution intersected with the politics of the ILGWU. Even as these contradictions emerged, the general consensus among leftists was that both the revolution and the union should succeed.

The reaction to the communist movement in the ILGWU was heavy-handed, and it garnered sympathy for Communist activists among otherwise unaffiliated rank-and-file and notably younger members. In December 1924, the International oversaw new elections for Local 22. It insisted that all candidates for union office sign a sworn declaration that they were not members of "any 'leagues' directed by outside influences."[69] According to Sasha Zimmerman, who was then a member of the Communist Party (he won election to the Local 22 executive board again in 1925), Communist Party members of the Local 22 board at the time all lied willingly.[70] It was an open secret but hard to prove. So Morris Sigman used a flimsy pretext to suspend the executive boards of Locals 1, 9, and 22 again in June 1925, in a way that roused the ire of the majority of the rank and file—non-Communists included—in the cloak-makers' and dressmakers' locals. During a May Day event in 1925, attended by Communist members of the ILGWU, a speaker who was not a member of the ILGWU ended his talk with a pro-Soviet slogan. Sigman and the GEB suspended the local board members who had attended the event for violating the union's constitutional ban on belonging to a dual (rival) union. Within hours of the suspension, the Sigman administration moved to take physical control of the offices of the three locals. Local 22 members got wind of the takeover of Locals 1 and 9 and rallied supporters to occupy the offices of Local 22's West 21st Street building. Hundreds of volunteers, Communists, and non-Communist reformers who had opposed Sigman's strong-arm tactics held a round-the-clock vigil inside and outside the building. Groups of young workers organized themselves into squads headed by captains, generating a heady esprit de corps. One historian remarked, "To the youthful 'guards' these night sessions held the thrill of duty for cause combined with fun."[71]

With increasing support for the ousted Communists building among non-Communists, the Communist members of the suspended local executive boards formed the Joint Action Committee (JAC) in July 1925 to fight the suspensions. Dissenters elected Louis Hyman, manager of Local 9, as JAC chairman and Sasha Zimmerman as secretary. They called a rally in Yankee Stadium, and on July 10, forty thousand union members and Communist sympathizers showed up. Following speakers at the rally who demanded "free speech and no dues," Hyman and Zimmerman encouraged union members to stop paying dues to the ILGWU and instead pay directly to the JAC.[72] On August 10, the JAC called for a work stoppage to demonstrate its strength in the union, and thirty thousand ILGWU members responded, filling seventeen rented halls.[73] The JAC then began to collect dues and settle grievances in the shops in which the majority of members supported its cause. In retaliation, ILGWU leaders pressured employers to fire members who refused to pay dues to them. Zimmerman remembered well the commitment of non-Communists who sacrificed their livelihoods in the face of the injustice.

> When I reviewed in my mind afterwards the extent of this support that we had from the cloak industry, from among rank-and-file cloakmakers, I found religious Jews, and all kinds supported the Joint Action fight. And no matter what they did to get them to register, many people were thrown out of shops, because they refused to register. They wouldn't register in the ILGWU. They lost their jobs, and they gave up their jobs and were starving and went around, for months, without a job. Yet they stuck to it. It was the most amazing thing.[74]

The political conflict spun out of control. Violence erupted between ILGWU business agents and leadership loyalists, on one hand, and the Joint Action Committee and its supporters, on the other hand. Certainly to protect themselves and perhaps to provoke one another, each side in the conflict turned to gangsters for professional muscle. Employers, taking advantage of the chaos, stepped up the hiring of goons to beat up workers on strike.[75]

The hostilities in the ILGWU involved key leaders of the Jewish labor and socialist movements. As the crisis worsened, Morris Hillquit and Abraham Cahan, editor of the *Jewish Daily Forward*, approached Morris Sigman to broker a peace between the ILGWU International leadership and the Communists.[76] As a result of a negotiated settlement, the union held new local elections. Union members elected Louis Hyman as general manager of the New York Joint Board, including all cloakmaking and dressmaking locals, and Zimmerman as manager of the dress division.[77] Sigman agreed to call a special union convention in November 1925 in which he would allow for a referendum of the membership to consider reforming the formula for representation by locals to the union conventions.

At the convention, Zimmerman, speaking for the Communist group, and David Dubinsky, manager of the elite Cutters' Local 10, serving as Sigman's lieutenant, emerged as the most influential leaders for their respective sides. During a floor debate between Zimmerman and Dubinsky on the issue of representation, Dubinsky offered a more moderate reform than leaders of the two sides had agreed on in closed-door negotiations. Convinced that Dubinsky and the Sigman faction had reneged on the deal, Zimmerman and Louis Hyman led their delegates out of the convention. In a meeting that same afternoon outside the hotel that hosted the convention, a member of the Communist Party Central Committee, controlled by William Z. Foster, ordered Hyman and Zimmerman back into the convention, since they had no authority from the party to leave the union and form a dual union. Hyman and Zimmerman returned to the convention and ran as president and secretary-treasurer, respectively, against Sigman and the current secretary-treasurer, Abraham Baroff. Sigman and Baroff won reelection with a vote of 158–110 under the newly adopted moderate reforms that still favored smaller local unions.[78]

While tensions within the ILGWU continued to simmer in plain view, factions within the communist movement were chafing against one another under the surface. The two major factions, which Theodore Draper notes emanated from the early rivalry of separate Communist parties that merged, were led by William Z. Foster and James Canon, on one side, and Charles Ruthenberg and Jay Lovestone, on the other. A smaller faction led by Ludwig Lore included Sasha Zimmerman, Rose Wortis, and Ben Gold of the furriers' union.[79] In 1924, Zimmerman resigned his official post in the TUEL after James Canon accused him of being a "dangerous opportunist."[80] Zimmerman remained in the Communist Party as a loyal member but suffered a number of humiliations in addition to the order to go back into the 1925 convention.

Hyman and Zimmerman, now firmly in charge of the New York Joint Board, launched a general strike of cloakmakers in July 1926 that nearly destroyed the union.[81] Thirty thousand cloakmakers walked off the job, and after eight weeks, Hyman and Zimmerman reached what they felt was a reasonable settlement with employers. But at a strategy meeting of the New York Communist Party, William Z. Foster and the party leadership ignored Zimmerman's judgment and mandated that the strike continue. Zimmerman and Hyman reluctantly complied. The strike dragged on for six months and nearly bankrupted the union. Employers began to hire gangsters, including the Legs Diamond mob, to beat up picketers. Zimmerman responded by approaching Arnold Rothstein, one of the most notorious gangsters in New York, for protection. With the presence of gangsters, the union treasury depleted, and hundreds of thousands of dollars unaccounted for, Sigman finally had firm grounds for taking over the New York Joint Board and expelling the Communists from the union at the end of 1926.[82]

The Union's Decline and the Marginalization of Women

The belligerence of ILGWU leaders in this period involved not only the suppression of Communists but also the marginalization of women, women's culture, and Fannia Cohn, one of the most visible women leaders in the International. At the 1924 convention, Sigman encouraged Mollie Friedman, a protégée of Fannia Cohn, to run as a vice president in place of Cohn. Consistent with gender roles in the Jewish labor and socialist movements, the ILGWU had an unwritten but oft-spoken rule that only one woman at a time could be a vice president of the union. Friedman won the seat. But Cohn used her relative security as an activist in the wider labor and socialist movements to push back and open spaces for women to enter the union's polity. Even in the period of the most intense hostilities, the ILGWU leaders never disassociated themselves from the Jewish labor and socialist movements. The conflict between the socialist and anarchist leaders of the ILGWU and rank-and-file members linked to the Communist Party made the leadership's connections to the institutions dominated by Socialist Party activists all the more vital. Fannia Cohn's prominent position in Socialist Party–backed organizations of education and camping—pursuits that resonated with Yiddish socialist sensibilities about how to build unions—made her fairly invulnerable to expulsion, if not free from humiliation.

Fannia Cohn was embittered but persevered in propagating socialist notions that challenged prevailing assumptions of progressive education. The Workers' University continued to grow in the 1923–1924 school year. Cohn and Alexander Fichandler, a new associate, created an impressive program that brought university professors and labor- and socialist-movement intellectuals to the evening-and-weekend school for union activists. The faculty aimed to appropriate and contest concepts such as "civilization" and to prepare union activists to critique and rebuild major social institutions. The course bulletin announced, "A new civilization is in process of being built up. If the workers' movement is to be powerful in helping to shape that new civilization, workers must know the underlying principles and the dominant trends of our modern life."[83] The abstracts of the fourteen courses offered in 1923–1924 show a focus on developing critical thinking skills that included logic, polemical argument, and social criticism through courses in psychology and social psychology, sociology, literature, and history. Cohn and Fichandler believed that workers and their representatives needed to understand economics and history on as sophisticated a plane as university students did. Appropriating the cult of expertise that emerged during the Progressive Era, the Workers' University enabled workers themselves to become the experts. Though this would still create an elite within the ranks of labor, it widened opportunities for the rank and file.

The courses and the teachers represented different views of socialism and the labor movement. But taken as a whole, the curriculum suggests that these union leaders anticipated a radical change in European and American society that workers needed to understand and in which they must be involved. David J. Saposs, the labor economist and historian trained by John R. Commons who was on faculty at the Brookwood Labor College, offered "American Labor in Modern Civilization," which was organized around themes that the labor movement needed to debate, including "racial composition and distribution of union membership." Louis Levine remarked in his description of "Economic and Social Developments in Europe," "The Russian Revolution, the revolutions in Germany and elsewhere are the more spectacular and significant phases of a movement in which all of Europe is involved. It will take decades before the new economic and social forms are sufficiently crystallized to serve as the foundations of a new civilization."[84] In "Social and Political History of the U.S.," Columbia University professor H. J. Carman urged,

> We should endeavor to understand why we have industrial classes, why American capital is centered in the hands of a minority of the population, why we have a railroad problem, why the majority of the people of this country are concentrated in cities, and why many of these are without landed property, why we have great industrial organizations, combinations and protective tariffs, why in recent years there has been a growing tendency in the United States toward industrial democracy, and why America has embarked upon the policy of economic imperialism.[85]

These expressions of radical inquiry and socialist vision came under increasing pressure during the 1920s. The Palmer Raids, immigration restriction, and conflicts between Socialists and Communists all had a moderating influence on ILGWU leaders. Fannia Cohn also worried about the developing generational divisions in the first- and second-generation immigrant families. The children of immigrants grew up with a decreasing ability to speak their parents' first language, and popular amusements, which proliferated in the 1920s, forged a distance between workers and their ethnic cultures.[86] To address these concerns, Cohn began to produce dramatic plays and to argue for the importance of drama and pageantry for the labor movement. When workers and their families participated in theater, Cohn believed, it became "the most effective medium of dramatizing the labor movement and at the same time it offers young trade unionists an opportunity for self-expression. Naturally, it will stimulate in them a greater interest in the movement. Such performances will surely attract older people also, to whom it will be a reflection of their own past experiences."[87]

Fannia Cohn struggled to preserve a socialist ideal as her base of young radical women declined in the turmoil of the union's internal conflicts. She designed the ILGWU education programs in the Workers' University and the Unity Centers to be models of cooperative decision making, similar to Unity House. "To guard against an over-centralization of educational control, we have established a Permanent Joint Conference of the educational committees of our local unions."[88] The conference helped to ensure that the programs offered by the International educational department met the needs articulated by local unions and their members. Each class in the Unity Centers elected two representatives to a Student Council, which helped to decide curriculum along with faculty. But her efforts at democratic unionism were stifled as Sigman and the General Executive Board moved to take control of Unity House from Locals 25 and 22.

At the 1924 convention, the measure to wrest control of Unity House passed, and the International union began to run the resort in December. Ostensibly, the move was meant to allow the union to operate Unity House "for the benefit of all the local unions affiliated with the ILGWU and also to improve and enlarge it." But the union did little to hide the principal reason in the 1925 report. Though the 1924 summer season, operated by Local 22, made a profit, more than half the guests were not members of the ILGWU, and many did not belong to unions at all. In a veiled reference to the presence of Communists, the report complained that "frequent clashes and animosity between visitors representing various shades of opinion in the Union and the labor movement in general were very much in evidence."[89] International Secretary Abraham Baroff took over the chairmanship of the Unity House Committee.

The socialist vision embedded in the union's education programs moderated as partisan infighting intensified. The International's 1924–1925 course offerings were similar to those of the previous year, but there was a marked difference in how the program was framed. The introduction no longer spoke of a new civilization or an impending change in social relations. Instead, it spelled out what officials in the educational department were trying to accomplish. They wanted students to "learn some of the economic laws underlying the development of the present order" and to celebrate the victories of the labor movement. The program continued to emphasize collaboration among workers from multiple ethnic groups by showing how all workers, including those "speaking other languages and members of other races, struggled for many years."[90] But few course descriptions explicitly expressed a socialist vision. In addition, these courses attracted a greater proportion of male over female students. At a time when ILGWU officers were forcing women out of local and International leadership positions and taking over control of Unity House, the 1924 educational report to the GEB noted, "in fact, many of our classes are attended mainly by men."[91]

After union leaders dropped their support for Fannia Cohn's membership on the GEB, she continued, even stepped up, her assertion that women deserved to take leadership in their union. Cohn offered a new course in the Unity Centers for the 1924–1925 term titled "Woman's Place in the Labor Movement." Her course description read,

> The trade union movement is based on the principle of equal opportunity for men and women. Women have enjoyed the same right as men to hold office and to select women as officers in trade unions. Why have so few women taken advantage of these rights? Is it due to lack of ability or lack of confidence in their ability? Or is it due to women's individualism or her inexperience in group action? These and similar questions will be considered.[92]

Some of these rhetorical questions may point to a conclusion that women were, in part, responsible for electing an almost entirely male leadership of the ILGWU. But raising these questions was tantamount to fomenting rebellion against the GEB that had forced her out of power. Fannia Cohn continued to needle her male opponents, not simply by refusing to leave her position in the educational department but also by continuing to encourage women to take leadership roles in the union.

The educational program of the International, including Unity House, was in all probability saved from the axe because of the manner in which the Communists competed with the Socialists for the hearts and minds of union members. In Sigman's report to the 1925 convention, he summarized the transgressions of the Communist-associated members of Local 22's executive board that, in his mind, justified their expulsion. For one thing, Sigman was infuriated when the Local 22 board used its own bonds as security to guarantee a $2,000 loan to "a Communist group which was engaged in the forming of a summer camp." The secured loan violated union rules, but more important to Sigman, it "was also a hostile move against the summer camp owned and managed by the International Union, the Unity House in Forest Park, which has sufficient facilities for housing all members of the ILGWU who may desire to spend their vacation in a first-class workers' camp."[93]

This competition between Communists and Socialists in the Jewish labor and socialist movements through educational, social, cultural, and recreational programs made Fannia Cohn an asset to the ILGWU. Though her programs may been a haven for radical women, their absence would have left the ILGWU without a way to combat Communist efforts to reach out. However, the International educational department cut its list of courses in half for the 1925–1926 school year. Most of those dropped were from the extension division, which sponsored lectures and discussions to coincide with local union meetings. Through those meetings, Cohn and her staff had gained access to the largest number of union members on a regular basis, providing a critical means to recruit for the educational programs and connect the educational programs to local union work. Nevertheless, Cohn continued to teach her course on women and to find ways to advance her vision of social unionism.

Conclusion

Though the rivalry between left factions nearly destroyed the ILGWU and weakened it to the point where union density dropped precipitously through the 1920s, the "warfare" in the union may have actually sustained the drive for a multicultural movement against social forces that demanded "100% Americanism." Underlying the two main rival groups in the union, the Socialists with their anarchist allies on one side and the Communists on the other, was a common sensibility that considered multiculturalism an essential ingredient of a revolutionary worldview. That sensibility was reinforced as the two factions competed for the attention of garment workers from various backgrounds. In the period that saw the closing off of immigration to most of the world, government repression of radicals, the antiunion "open-shop movement," the rise of the new Ku Klux Klan, and dominant cultural pressures to assimilate, Jewish radicals maintained their ethnic identities and a demonstrated desire to appeal to African Americans.

The struggle between radical worldviews took on a gendered dimension that reflected the structure of the garment industry and union leadership. Marginalized women and sympathetic men sought a political voice at all levels of union authority, including education. The efforts to control the content of courses and the operation of institutions such as Unity House were contests over union citizenship: who belonged and who deserved a voice. Just as in czarist Russia, where Jews developed educational and cultural forms to resist Russian domination, Fannia Cohn and others clung to their faith that education would serve to build a more democratic, inclusive union.

4

Reconstructing a
Multicultural Union, 1927–1933

All the warring factions on the Left came to recognize the mutually destructive consequences of continuing belligerence. In 1927, a committee of fifty ILGWU cloak- and dressmakers, loyal to the Communist Party faction, formed for the purpose of bringing an end to the hostilities. They published an appeal to "workers and their organizations, to all communal institutions, to all literary and cultural associations, to all fraternal orders and particularly to all the influential communal workers of our city" that deplored the depths into which the union had plunged and urged the wider Jewish socialist movement to help resolve the conflict. The handbill complained of the return of sweatshop conditions: weekend and extended work hours, reduced wages, and arbitrary firings. "After reviewing the present situation, we came to the conclusion that during the internal strife our Union has not only failed to make any headway but has, on the contrary, been so completely demoralized and so weakened that to-day our Union is absolutely unable to protect the interests of the workers in the shop."[1] This effort at rapprochement failed. Ultimately, the committee claimed that President Morris Sigman threw them out of his office, refusing to entertain the notion of reconciliation.

Sigman's personality was well suited for war against the Communists and ill prepared for peace. A letter to *Forward* editor Abraham Cahan in October 1927 demonstrates Sigman's obsession with the personal animosities and political intrigue that characterized the conflict between the Communists and the non-Communist Left in the ILGWU. Sigman had filed a libel suit against the Yiddish daily *Freiheit*: "The Communists have subjected me in their press to an ugly personal attack all during last summer and have not spared even Mrs. Sigman, making the wildest and filthiest insinuations concerning her management of our little lake casino in Iowa."[2] He named those within the union who he thought were conspiring to oust him, and he accused his predecessor, Benjamin Schlesinger, of building support to return as president. He had confronted Morris Hillquit, a founder of and attorney for the ILGWU, about sponsoring Schlesinger's return. Sigman was still suspicious when Hillquit angrily denied the rumor.

Conservative and moderate union leaders believed that the struggle within the International during the mid-1920s required a stubborn and entrenched personality, and Morris Sigman had the right temperament.[3] However, pragmatic leaders on the General Executive Board (GEB), most importantly David Dubinsky, realized that after recalcitrant Communist leaders were expelled, a reconstruction of the ILGWU could only happen under a new administration of the International. Dubinsky, though the principal aide to Sigman in his war against the Communists, helped to engineer Sigman's exit from power. As Sigman suspected, Morris Hillquit did recruit Benjamin Schlesinger to return to the ILGWU. Even more devastating to Sigman, his confidant, Abraham Cahan, also supported a negotiated transfer of power. At the 1928 convention, GEB leaders proposed the creation of a new position, executive vice president for New York. The effective powers of the job would keep the day-to-day affairs of the union out of the president's hands and made the new official heir apparent to the International presidency should Sigman resign. The convention adopted the proposal, elected Benjamin Schlesinger to the new position, and reelected Sigman. A few months later, Sigman resigned, opening the way for Schlesinger's third ascendancy to the presidency of the ILGWU.[4]

Sigman's departure from the ILGWU did not signal an immediate turn in fortunes for the garment workers' union, but over the next five years it brought powerful political, economic, and ideological developments that influenced the progress and direction of union building. On the one hand, ILGWU activists faced new obstacles. Stalin's accession to power in the Soviet Union led to an open dual-union movement in the United States and to splits in the Communist Party. The Great Depression that began in the winter of 1929–1930 ushered in new depths of privation for garment workers. Manufacturers stepped up the hiring of non-Jewish and non-Italian workers, partly because the new restrictions on immigration dried up the usual source of cheap labor and partly in the hope of keeping workers divided along language, racial, and ethnic lines. On the other hand, the more moderate administration of Benjamin Schlesinger and David Dubinsky tolerated and at times encouraged Fannia Cohn and other activists to develop multicultural programs of education and to reach out to new constituencies, especially African American workers.

Radical Jewish Culture and the Communist Opposition

After the expulsion of the left-wing leaders from the ILGWU, Communist Party members continued to agitate among ladies' garment workers and their families. They did so throughout the needle-trades unions, in men's garments, and especially in furs, where Communists established the dominant union in the industry in the 1930s, led by Benjamin Gold. The nature of that agitation and organization, and Communists' entreaties toward Black and women workers especially, paralleled Fannia Cohn's educational, social, and cultural work in the ILGWU. This is not surprising in that through the 1920s and early 1930s, Russian and Polish immigrant Jews were heavily represented in the leadership of the Communist Party, especially in New York City and even more so in the garment trades. The Communist Party was headquartered in New York City, where a third of the national membership of the party and, according to Harvey Klehr, most Jewish Communists lived and worked.[5]

The influence of Russian Jews and Yiddish socialism on Communist activities is apparent in the CP's educational and social culture. As Paul C. Mishler and Randi Storch have demonstrated, local Communists in the United States resisted certain directives from the Soviet Union that did not conform to their realities, particularly concerning ethnic identity. After many immigrant Communists left the Socialist Party in the early 1920s, they reformed the foreign-language federations that had been their entrée into socialism. But the Communist International (Comintern), the decision-making authority of the Communist Party, subscribed to the theory that ethnic groups tended to be insular and divided the working class. From 1925 to 1928, the CP formally disbanded the foreign-language federations, emphasizing the Comintern directive to "Americanize" the movement. But, Mishler notes, "as the bonds of ethnic allegiance among radicals weakened, their radical politics weakened too."[6] Among such groups as Finns and Jews, ethnic cultures were the seedbeds in which radicalism was cultivated. Randi Storch has explored the practical problems with attempts to Americanize the communist movement in Chicago. Because many Communists were foreign born, they "did not mingle easily outside their ethnic enclaves." Efforts to create ethnically mixed groups among steelworkers "complicated the ability of activists to communicate and act together," while Finnish and Latvian groups resisted them altogether. Groups of ethnic Communists began to leave the party when their ethnic associations were discouraged. In fact, Chicago Communists were most successful when they organized within ethnic groups. As Storch points out, Chicago Communists organized social activities that included picnics, symphonies, choruses, and dances to "foster solidarity and emphasize party values" and served to raise money for the *Daily Worker* newspaper as well as ethnic presses.[7]

By 1930, the newly founded International Workers' Order (IWO) fraternal order, the Communist Party counterpart to the Workmen's Circle, attracted many ethnic Communists. The affiliated fraternal societies "maintained ethnic radical culture through sponsorship of singing groups, folkdance ensembles, and children's activities."[8] In 1931, nearly fifteen hundred Communists and fellow travelers (sympathetic to but not formal members of the party) belonged to thirty-one IWO branches, of which thirteen were explicitly Jewish.[9] Like Unity House in the ILGWU and the Brookwood Labor College, Communists created various institutions of adult education, leisure, and camping that "represented their aspirations." Like Yiddishists who remained in the Socialist Party orbit, Communist Jews created ethnic cultural programs for their children, who were being educated in American schools and influenced by bourgeois values. In the 1920s, Communist parents organized the Young Pioneers of America, which sponsored afternoon, weekend, and summer-camp programs. Branches were most popular with Jewish and Finnish Communists and were often explicitly organized in ethnic groupings.[10]

The importance of summer camping illustrates both sides' commitment to Yiddishist ideals. In rural and pastoral settings, the camps satisfied some of the Russian Jewish longing to own land, as well as reflecting the agrarian socialist tradition of some Yiddishists, such as Chaim Zhitlowsky. Czarist regimes denied Jews the right to own land. Land was a source of wealth and status in Russia. But for Jews crowded into the shtetlakh of Russia and the tenements of American cities, land also represented an ideal. Land meant open spaces and freedom to explore healthy and cooperative lifestyles, even if only for brief periods. For parents, it also represented a future for which to struggle.

The 1930 cover of a publication describing the history and function of the Workmen's Circle camp depicts two young children, perhaps brother and sister, at a study table looking longingly out a large picture window at an ideal camp scene (see figure 4.1). The children see campers diving and swimming in a lake near tents pitched on the shore. A counselor is teaching one camper to swim, and other campers are playing baseball and tennis. The sister stands with one hand on her schoolbook. Across the table, her brother sits with a hand poised at an inkwell. Their mother, wearing a kitchen apron, does not look out but down, with her eyes closed. She stands by gently but firmly, with her hand resting on her son's shoulder. The mother's face appears empathetic to the children's desires, even saddened that her children cannot be at camp. Icons of recreation, dance, music, study, nature, and farming border the entire scene. The illustration spoke to Jewish parents and children who longed to be out of the city and in the idyllic settings of camp but who had few options. The picture also shows the links between education and recreation. The mother is not scolding the children for being distracted from their book learning; after all, the camp is a more advanced educational experience. Seen another way, the mother's reverent countenance and the placement of the children's and mother's hands indicate something more solemn. The boy's hand and pen recall the pointer used in reading the Torah, and the hands of the young girl and mother are placed as if they were making a pledge. They reflect the sacred character of education and a commitment to pursue education, recreation, and culture as inextricably linked endeavors.

The Workmen's Circle founded camps as vehicles to transmit Yiddish socialist ideals. From the beginnings of the Russian Bund in 1897 and the founding of the Workmen's Circle a few years later in the United States, advocates for competing ideological tendencies argued about perpetuating Yiddish as the cultural medium for working-class Jews. For the first thirty years of the Workmen's Circle, those who championed Yiddish held sway, but not without being conscious of those who disagreed. Yiddishists in the United States faced demographic forces in the Diaspora and had to contend with the fact that their children were growing up with English, not Yiddish, as their first language. During the 1920s and 1930s, the Yiddishists in the Jewish labor and socialist movements, across the partisan spectrum, were extremely sensitive to the practice and teaching of ethnic culture. In "Why a Yiddish Camp," P. H. Geliebter explained the role of the Workmen's Circle camp in 1930:

> A camp must also be a place where children can be brought up in a social and cultural environment. Although children should not be taught during the summer months as they are taught in a classroom, nevertheless every camp activity must be run so as to bring the children into this social-cultural atmosphere. . . . Due to Socialistic spirit and Yiddish language, our camp has another color, another character. Just as we are proud of this difference in our camp, so are we also proud that it is different in respect to language. Those who oppose Yiddish may, if they want, argue with us, but those who send their children to camp realize that the Workmen's Circle Camp is striving toward a higher ideal.[11]

Figure 4.1. The Workmen's Circle established sleep-away and day camps for Jewish youth and families to transmit ideals of Yiddish socialism. This 1930 cover of the Workmen's Circle camp publication illustrates the integral relationship between formal study, recreation, and aspirations for an ideal society.

Similarly, one Kinderland veteran remembered the Yiddishist ideals that were central to the Communist-led camp over the years. Gedalia Sandler wrote, "An important part of the diverse daily program was the shule-hour. . . . The children signed up for special classes in speaking, reading, writing and singing Yiddish. Children took most delight in learning how to write a letter home in Yiddish." She recalled the writers, poets, and activists who visited the camp, including "Sholem Asch, Mme. Sholem Aleichem, Ben-Tsion Goldberg and his wife, Sholem Aleichem's daughter, Tom Mooney's mother, Michoels and Itzik Feffer."[12]

In addition to their attention to a revolutionary Yiddish identity, Jewish communists shared with Jewish socialists a concern for organizing Black workers and, to some extent, appealing to women. When ousted Communists formed the Needle Trades Workers' Industrial Union (NTWIU) in late December 1928 to organize furriers and workers in the ladies' and men's garments industries, they recognized the "special need" for organizing Black and women workers.[13] Communists were well aware of the gender dynamics in their struggles against the socialists, especially the fact that male leaders of the ILGWU blamed women for the Communist insurgency. One appeal directed at women, "whether working in the shop or in the home," illustrates Communist attempts to capitalize on the union leadership's perceived shortcomings.[14] The broadside, "A Call to All Women," addressed "Women dressmakers, cloakmakers, furriers and wives of union men!" and spoke of their sacrifices. It urged women to attend a mass meeting to "raise [their] mighty voice in protest" against Sigman and other union leaders for contributing to the conditions of their degradation. Still, in spite of high-profile women Communists such as Elizabeth Gurley Flynn, Helen Keller, Rose Pastor Stokes, and Meridel Le Sueur and the dedication of women Communist garment workers such as Rose Wortis and former garment workers such as Clara Lemlich Shavelson, the national leadership of the Communist Party was virtually all male, and the party had trouble attracting women.[15]

The CP's appeal to Black workers intensified throughout the 1920s. In 1925, the same year that A. Philip Randolph and Chandler Owens, committed members of the Socialist Party, founded the Brotherhood of Sleeping Car Porters (BSCP), the Communist Party founded the American Negro Labor Congress (ANLC).[16] Along with sympathetic groups such as the African Blood Brotherhood, the ANLC attracted a small number of influential Blacks.[17] In 1928, the Comintern advanced a formal policy that deemed southern Blacks a subjugated nation whose liberation should be encouraged.[18] From that time forward, race issues became central to Communist

Party strategies, and Communist institutions and movements intentionally strove to integrate Blacks and explore Black issues. Communist organs and literary journals such as the *New Masses* attracted Black writers and artists, including Richard Wright and Claude McKay.[19]

In 1931, Communists conducted one of their most successful campaigns by supporting the "Scottsboro Boys," nine young men accused of raping two white women in a boxcar in Alabama.[20] They were on trial for their life, facing execution. The National Association for the Advancement of Colored People (NAACP) was at first reluctant to represent the young men, worried that they might be guilty, but decided to support them after the Communist Party took on the case. The CP earned a positive reputation for taking bold action and mobilizing supporters nationwide. This strategy was brought home in New York, Chicago, and other cities as the Unemployed Councils of the Communist Party stepped up organizing in the early 1930s among unemployed workers, many of whom faced eviction from their homes.[21] The Unemployed Councils organized mass rallies and marches demanding jobs and pointedly encouraged the participation of Black workers, who suffered unemployment and eviction at far higher rates than either native-born white or white immigrant workers.[22] Interracial groups of Communists worked in immigrant and Black neighborhoods to put evicted and unemployed people back into their homes and to turn utilities back on. Confrontations with sheriff's deputies and police put pressure on local officials, and as a result, Chicago's Mayor Anton Cermak suspended evictions briefly in 1932.[23] For a growing number of Black workers, the Communist Party was viewed with respect.

Fannia Cohn's Vision

Though the Communist Party had fewer than ten thousand formal members nationwide in 1929, it had a significant presence in the garment industry. For the ILGWU and other institutions affiliated with the Socialist Party, educational mechanisms served to counter parallel Communist programs. Fannia Cohn, whose ideas about union, education, and ethnicity predated the formation of the CP, thought deeply about what methods of education were best suited to reaching across ethnic and racial cultural divisions to involve members in the union. In the educational department bulletin of the 1927–1928 school season, Cohn wrote, "since teaching methods are really influenced by the instructor's knowledge of the group to whom he is presenting his material, our Educational Department makes every effort to acquaint the instructors with the character—social and racial background—and the experience of the group he is teaching, to give him some idea of their social aims, aspirations and hopes for the future."[24] Like the Communists, Cohn sought to counter the values in the public schooling of workers' children through the Pioneer Youth Camps. "The school and the playground develop a standardized type of behavior and an outlook altogether unsympathetic to our own. Not only is questioning discouraged, but we are too often shocked to find that our children hold in contempt the ideals for which the labor movement stands."[25]

Fannia Cohn's advocacy for a system of multicultural union education was unmatched in the ILGWU during the 1920s. Though she never regained her previous level of authority after she was dropped from the GEB in 1924, the GEB allowed Cohn increasing visibility in the wider labor movement after the reconstruction of the union. The ILGWU, and Fannia Cohn in particular, successfully used educational programs to integrate white, Jewish, and Black union members as early as 1927. In the spring of that year, the educational department, under the direction of Cohn, began supervising the weekly entertainment and education programs at Unity House, the union's retreat. In September, she produced a musical pageant based on Walt Whitman's poem "The Mystic Trumpeter." Staged in twenty tableaux-vivants, the show included 150 actors, dancers, and chorus members and was meant to convey "a social message to suffering humanity."[26] The cast members were mainly ILGWU members but also members of the Workmen's Circle, Brookwood Labor College, and several unions including the Pullman porters. Twenty-five hundred spectators witnessed the involvement of Black porters in the ILGWU pageant. As with many union educational events, a social dance among all members and guests followed the program.

The choice of Whitman's poem allowed Cohn to express a militant and iconoclastic message of racial and gender inclusion. Walt Whitman's collection of poems *Leaves of Grass* challenged Victorian morality as well as poetic form from its first self-publication in 1855 to its last iteration in 1891. His brazen celebration of sexuality, including homosexuality, shocked critics and titillated his admirers, in such poems as "I Sing the Body Electric." In "I Hear America Singing," a poem the ILGWU used as the foundation of another pageant in 1940, Whitman extolled the "varied carols" of mechanics, carpenters, masons, and other male workers plying their trades, as well as those of "the mother, or of the young wife at work, or of the girl sewing or washing."[27] After seeing the ravages of chattel slavery firsthand as a reporter in New Orleans, Whitman returned to his native Brooklyn in 1848 to found the antislavery newspaper the *Brooklyn Freeman*.[28] His abolitionist sentiments were expressed brilliantly in "The Mystic Trumpeter," along with a general call to rise up for social justice. The participation of Black actors reinforced the vision that the trumpeter reveals, referring to American slavery and indirectly pointing to the degraded conditions of African Americans in the 1920s.

> O trumpeter! methinks I am myself the instrument thou playest!
> Thou melt'st my heart, my brain—thou movest, drawest, changest
>   them, at will:
> And now thy sullen notes send darkness through me;
> Thou takest away all cheering light—all hope:
> I see the enslaved, the overthrown, the hurt, the opprest of the whole
>   earth;
> I feel the measureless shame and humiliation of my race—it becomes
>   all mine;
> Mine too the revenges of humanity—the wrongs of ages—baffled feuds
>   and hatreds;
> Utter defeat upon me weighs—all lost! the foe victorious!
> (Yet 'mid the ruins Pride colossal stands, unshaken to the last;
> Endurance, resolution, to the last.)

Whitman begs the trumpeter, "Sing to my soul, . . . give me some vision of the future" that ultimately embraces both men and women:

> O glad, exulting, culminating song!
> A vigor more than earth's is in thy notes!
> Marches of victory—man disenthrall'd—the conqueror at last!
> Hymns to the universal God, from universal Man—all joy!
> A reborn race appears—a perfect World, all joy!
> Women and Men, in wisdom, innocence and health—all joy!
> Riotous, laughing bacchanals, fill'd with joy![29]

Through "The Mystic Trumpeter," Cohn connected with the more militant members of the union. Revolutionaries, including anarchists and Communist Party members, often interpreted Whitman's work, especially the line "I see the enslaved, the overthrown, the hurt, the opprest of the whole earth," as a call for revolution.[30]

The ILGWU leadership countered the Communist appeal to women with a renewed effort by the educational department to reach women members and the wives of male members. In the "1927–1928 Educational Department Bulletin," Fannia Cohn, now education director as well as executive secretary of the Education Committee, called women's attention to the classes and lectures discussing "the organizability of women and their place in the labor movement": "The wives of our members may be interested in studying the power of women as consumers, how to acquaint children with the labor movement, the contribution of trade unionism to the welfare of the family, the part the trade unionist's wife can play in the labor movement."[31] These themes were consistent with previous years' classes. But Cohn made a more pointed appeal to members' wives that spoke just as directly to the male members of the union and may have been equally aimed at the ILGWU leadership. She wrote,

> If the labor movement is to win the full-hearted support and cooperation of the wives of its members, they must be taken into the confidence of the organization and inspired to realize their own importance as a social force. In order that their husbands may frankly share their experiences with them, they must be fully informed about the affairs of the organization. So informed, they will be willing to place at the disposal of the labor movement their will-power and practical common sense and influence, to aid their husbands in their daily struggles.[32]

Cohn was instructing the men of the union how to win the loyalty of women who had fought as union members and union family members before. Many of these women might have responded well to the Communist Party's recognition of women's contributions to workers' struggles. Cohn offered a concrete example of how men could offer practical support to women's education and activism. She recalled previous lectures and discussions designed to attract women: "At that time a special appeal was made to the husbands that where there were young children to be taken care of, that they should stay at home and relieve their wives for that evening."[33]

Cohn secured her place in the ILGWU through her education activism and, in part, by targeting as wide an audience as possible when she was advocating for women in the ILGWU. She wrote and distributed a series of ten articles on the subject of women in unions in 1927. The articles appeared in *Justice* and *Labor Age* and "in 30 percent of the labor press" in the United States.[34] Cohn drew continued attention to the ILGWU from the non-Communist Left. In light of the CP's similar efforts to attract women, the leadership of the ILGWU could not afford to dismiss her. She pressed on through the 1920s, expanding her influence on the political culture of the labor movement.

Her articles in the *American Federationist*, among other places, brought wide attention to the ILGWU's educational activities and the rationale for establishing them during a period of decline and retreat for many unions. In "Educational and Social Activities," Cohn answered critics who questioned the importance of the whole range of educational programs, including theater, social, and recreational programs. "It is our aim to cultivate in our members an appreciation of beauty and art which tends so much to increase the enjoyment of life, and, at the same time, to awaken the will to despise the dirty tenements, oppose unsanitary conditions in their shops and abolish slums." Formal classes, she argued, taught workers not only methods of organizing in their industry but also economic principles, politics, and the impact of major social forces. She argued in the tradition of the Yiddishist ideal that these classes needed to address the history of struggles by workers from diverse backgrounds:

> They heard how other workers, members of other races, speaking other languages, also struggled for many years; how they attempted to get more joy and happiness out of their miserable existence; how their attempts to unite for common interest were met with persecution and oppression from the ruling classes; and how, in spite of it all, they too succeeded finally in winning the improved conditions which prevail today, and in raising society to a higher level.[35]

This article reveals an aspect of Fannia Cohn's vision of unionism that rankled Dubinsky and other International union leaders. She articulated a union culture that fostered rank-and-file democracy through education and would act as a counterbalance to hierarchical and centralized power in the International union. She declared,

> We encourage the worker to carry to his shop and to the business meeting of the union the reflection and added grasp of facts, because we know the trade-union policy is not to be formed only in the Executive Council of the International. The living policy is formed in the daily routine of the shops, in the meetings of locals and shop chairmen, and in the union study groups.[36]

By the winter of 1929–1930, however, questions of union governance became secondary to concerns over the decline in union strength. The union had briefly recovered only a portion of the membership it had lost during the previous decade, and the Communist Party's NTWIU competed with the ILGWU to attract garment workers. Cohn's efforts to reach out to Black workers, among other groups of workers, were far too valuable to the union for leaders to censor her.

ILGWU Efforts to Organize Black Workers

During the 1920s, the ILGWU leadership at the International and local union levels began to seek ways to draw Black workers in New York City into the union by building bridges to Black middle – and working-class communities. Though ILGWU organizers and officers were concerned with organizing members of all groups, Blacks were the largest ethnic minority in the Jewish-dominated ladies' garment labor force after the Italians, and it is likely that organizers did not perceive as strong an antiunion consciousness among these other groups as they did among Blacks. Organizers were explicit about the difficulties in organizing Black workers, who had historically been offered limited opportunities or denied membership in most AFL unions and been hired as strikebreakers by northern employers.[37] In addition, some Black leaders encouraged Blacks to take strikebreaking jobs as an entrée to otherwise restricted trades.[38]

In late 1927, International and local union leaders including Luigi Antonini, Fannia M. Cohn, and Julius Hochman helped form the Trade Union Committee to Aid the Pullman Porters Union. New York State Federation of Labor officer Tom Curtis, Abraham I. Shiplacoff of the International Pocketbook Workers Union, and Frank R. Crosswaith of the Brotherhood of Sleeping Car Porters (BSCP) led this committee. It sought to raise upward of $25,000 among progressive, almost exclusively white, unions for the BSCP to use in legal fights with the U.S. Mediation Board and the Interstate Commerce Commission.[39] The committee vowed to continue its work for the BSCP beyond the "present crisis, but also to aid them in securing their desired affiliation with the American Federation of Labor (AFL)."[40] One appeal, endorsed by other members of the Jewish labor movement, such as M. Feinstone of the United Hebrew Trades, addressed the common interests of the working class regardless of race: "Their struggle is our struggle. Race and color should not count. If they fail, we fail. . . . The success of their efforts will mean power to organized labor. Negro workers in every other industry will be encouraged into joining the union of their trade."[41]

ILGWU support for the BSCP went beyond providing much-needed funds. Like Communist Party members, union leaders demonstrated their willingness to socialize with Black union members through educational programs. Cohn used her new responsibilities for scheduling and programing at Unity House to invite members of other unions to visit the summer retreat, and members from twenty-two international and national unions attended Unity House in the 1928 season.[42] Cohn also became an important ambassador from the ILGWU to other unions and organizations trying to organize Black workers. She represented the ILGWU at conferences of the BSCP and joined the Urban League as a representative of the ILGWU in 1928.[43] Cohn's connections with these organizations made her a valuable asset to local unions' efforts to organize Black workers in the late 1920s and early 1930s. Other ILGWU officers were conscious of the opportunities to participate in interracial dances and other social activities as a means to build relationships among Jewish, Italian, Black, and other working-class communities. In October 1928, for example, A. Philip Randolph extended an invitation to the ILGWU and other unions to buy tickets to a Big Ball in December that would raise money for a strike fund. To the letter from Randolph, ILGWU Secretary-Treasurer Abraham Baroff added, "The Conventions of the ILGWU and the GEB have supported the struggles of our black brothers. Let us support the heroic fight of the Pullman porters by purchasing tickets to their dance. Too long have black workers been used by the bosses to break the strikes of the Unions."[44]

In return for the support the BSCP received from the Jewish labor and socialist movements, Randolph and other BSCP union dignitaries frequently spoke at ILGWU meetings and conventions. Randolph sat on the boards of a number of important socialist institutions, including WEVD, the radio station launched in October 1927 in honor of Eugene V. Debs.[45] WEVD was a powerful new vehicle to communicate with existing and potential union members. The station allowed unions to broadcast a wide range of programs, from organizing and strike appeals in a variety of languages to music and other cultural shows aimed at specific ethnic constituencies.[46]

In late 1929 and early 1930, the ILGWU dressmakers enlisted the support of the New York chapter of the Urban League and the BSCP in their organizing drive. These Black organizations assisted in a largely unsuccessful campaign to organize the estimated three to four thousand Black dressmakers working in the city's garment industry.[47] During this campaign, the ILGWU appointed Floria Pinkney, an African American woman, as an organizer specifically for Black women. A. Philip Randolph publicly endorsed Pinkney's appointment, helping to cement the relationship between the unions.[48] Pinkney, a dressmaker, was a protégée of Fannia Cohn. Before becoming active in the ILGWU, Pinkney had attended training sessions in group leadership at the YMCA, the earliest women's group to promote racial integration.[49] Then, in 1926 and 1927, Cohn nominated Pinkney for a scholarship to attend the Brookwood Labor College, where she trained to become a union organizer.[50] Pinkney remained active after the organizing drive. In 1931, the Industrial Assembly of the Brooklyn YMCA selected Pinkney to attend the YMCA's world assembly in Geneva, Switzerland.[51]

The dressmakers' union held a series of meetings in Harlem, beginning with a meeting on September 26, 1929 at St. Luke's Hall that featured a speech by Randolph. According to the convention report that year,

> The keynote sounded at the meeting was that the exploitation of the colored people in the sweat shops even exceeds that of the white workers, but the Unions ought now to eradicate this inequality together with other injustices prevailing in the dress shops. The International, as the Negro workers know, has never made any distinction as to race or color in accepting members and will insist that the scales of wages and hours and other work conditions are alike for every member of the Union.[52]

The organizing drive in the dress industry was momentarily successful. In 1930, Local 22 recorded a membership of almost 14,000, including a fair number of Black workers.[53] But the bank failures and business slump that began in late 1929 caught up quickly with the ladies' garment industry. Manufacturers laid off thousands of workers, and membership in Local 22 dropped to less than 8,000 by the following season. By November 1931, the ILGWU had only 45,452 members, less than half the total in 1920, and only 30,000 were paid up to date in dues. Local 22 retained just 3,386 dues-paying members.[54] The decline in dues-paying membership had a devastating effect on International educational efforts. The union only devoted $7,845 to education in a twenty-nine-month period from November 1, 1929, to March 31, 1932, barely covering Fannia Cohn's salary.[55] Programing was reduced mainly to activities Cohn could run herself. She likely dipped into her own savings or asked for money from family members to keep a few programs alive.[56]

In spite of the miserably low numbers of garment workers who joined the ILGWU in the early 1930s, and even though Blacks accounted for a relatively small proportion of dressmakers (perhaps 13 percent), officials in Local 22 persisted in appealing to African Americans. The union concentrated on Harlem, with the assistance of major Black institutions. Letters in 1931 from Local 22 officials expressed thanks to BSCP officials such as Ashley L. Totten, the general secretary, for speaking at a membership meeting in Harlem, though the meeting was poorly attended.[57] The dressmakers placed ads regularly in the *Amsterdam News* announcing meetings specifically for its Black union members, held at the Urban League headquarters on West 136th Street.[58] ILGWU leaders also weighed in on national politics, linking Jim Crow segregation, employers' attempts to pit Black and white workers against one another, and the lynching of southern Blacks, which was brought to national attention through the Scottsboro case.

At the May 1932 convention of the International union, a telegram from President Schlesinger and General Secretary Dubinsky to Alabama Governor Miller demanding "a pardon or retrial of the Scottsboro Boys" was read. "The Twenty-First Convention of the International Ladies' Garment Workers' Union . . . solemnly protest against the convictions of the seven young negro workers at Scottsboro, Alabama on evidence universally believed to be tainted with race and class prejudice and hatred."[59] The 1932 convention adopted resolutions supporting the young men that drove home specific Jewish sympathy for African Americans. One resolution introduced by the delegates of Local 1 read, "The progressive workers of the United States, especially those who come form Czarist Russia are only too well acquainted with the frame-up as a weapon of racial prejudice. The 'blood-frame-ups' of the Czarist forces against the Jews (the famous Mendel Bailes case) are parallel. Against these attacks of the ruling class upon the oppressed races and classes, labor must raise its voice."[60] Another resolution from the Local 9 delegates suggested that the Scottsboro case was tied to the overall suppression of Blacks and efforts to divide the working class. They called on Alabama and the federal government to end lynching and called "on all local organizations and the entire membership [of the ILGWU] to participate actively in the movement for the release of the seven Scottsboro boys and for the struggle for equal social, political and economic rights of all Negro workers."[61]

As significant numbers of workers from other ethnic groups began to appear in the industry, the union expanded its appeals. In late 1930 and 1931, activists and union officials in the dressmakers' union began to call attention to the growing numbers of workers from other backgrounds. In December 1930, the Dressmakers Trade Union Circle, a group formed by anarchists in the union, suggested appointing Spanish and Greek organizers "with the object of meeting those elements that are constantly coming into the industry."[62] In July 1931, the Organization Committee of Local 22's executive board recommended calling a meeting of Spanish-speaking members and inviting a "special Spanish speaker" to address them.[63]

Though the union's primary emphasis remained on organizing Black workers, cultural appeals were not always sensitive to the racist stereotypes that pervaded the dominant society. An article in the union's newspaper, *Justice*, at the end of 1930 described a concert by the Hall Johnson Negro Choir, which had performed at several ILGWU functions: "The songs sung by the . . . Choir breathe the spirit of Negro Life and Sentiment. Not all of their songs are serious. Many of them have the delightful, unconscious humor of the old-time slave."[64] This image of a slave—content, loyal to the master, and enjoying the simple pleasures of life despite his bondage—is an example of the "Tom" character, one of a handful of Black stereotypes that dominated Hollywood films from the 1910s to the 1940s.[65] While these stereotypes may have influenced the impressions of some leaders in the International, they were not typical of the overtures made to Black leaders and workers. The greatest gains in organizing African Americans, as well as members of dozens of other racial-ethnic groups, resulted from carefully developed educational programs, foremost in the Dressmakers' Local 22, beginning at the end of 1933. But that was only possible because the political upheaval in the Left had abated to a certain degree, and a key Communist faction was purged from the party and made its way into an alliance with the socialists. While the needle trades remained fractured, few permanent gains in organizing a multicultural union could be sustained.

The Lovestoneite Communist Faction

By 1928, the leaders of the Jewish labor and socialist movements were weary of warfare with the Communists and sought paths toward reconstruction of the ILGWU. On December 12, Benjamin Schlesinger, newly reinstated as ILGWU president, convened a meeting of the New York City Joint Board of Cloak and Dressmakers, the executive boards of all affiliated locals, and the members of those locals. Out of that meeting, the GEB issued a "Manifesto" laying out the conditions under which members of all political factions active among workers in the ladies' garment industry could maintain membership or rejoin the union.[66] In the short run, this overture did not immediately result in the repatriation of Communists and former Communists. But it established a new, although limited, tolerance for dissent in the union and created the possibility for Communist Party members and former Communists to reenter the ranks of the ILGWU. When the Communist faction led by Jay Lovestone, founded in 1929, reentered the ranks and the leadership of the dressmakers' and other locals, the stage was set for the rebuilding of the ILGWU.

This manifesto reflected the more pragmatic positions of moderates in the GEB, including David Dubinsky, who became the strong second-in-command to Benjamin Schlesinger, just as he (Dubinsky) had been to Sigman. As Schlesinger's health was failing, Dubinsky stepped in as acting president, sometimes for months at a time. Like the Communist appeal the previous year, the manifesto decried the divisions in the ranks generated by the ideological wars between the various left factions. "It is high time that you lay aside all personal, political and tactical differences and once more unite as a man in support of the common cause for which we were organized—the fight for economic justice and human rights of the workers in our industry and their families."[67] The GEB promised to reinstate former members of the union, regardless of political affiliation, if they promised to adhere to the union's constitution, specifically the bar against acting on orders from outside organizations. Although this position was largely a restatement of the leadership's stance during the conflict with the Communists in the mid-1920s, it reversed the expulsion orders under the Sigman regime. The union reinstated members as of February 1, 1929, and postponed local union elections until the first week of February. This opened the possibility that Communists and former Communists could vote and run for office. To ensure a fair election, the manifesto established a complex mechanism of oversight by which representatives from all levels of the union and outside observers supervised the local elections.[68]

The manifesto coincided with the ascendancy of Joseph Stalin in Russia. After V. I. Lenin's death in 1924, Stalin, Leon Trotsky, and Nicolai Bukharin struggled for power, each advocating a different strategy and ideological path to continue the Communist revolution. Most revolutionaries considered Trotsky to be on the left, arguing for a "permanent revolution" in which workers would replicate the Russian Revolution by overthrowing capitalist governments around the world. Bukharin, on the right, counseled a slower approach, both in Russia and around the world. He argued that conditions in each country differed dramatically and that a single revolutionary strategy could not apply universally. Indeed, the question of American exceptionalism was key in the debate. Bukharin, head of the Comintern, argued that the advanced nature of capitalism and democratic institutions made revolution in the United States less likely than in other countries. Stalin favored a universal strategy, but he was conscious of the nuances of foreign relations and international affairs and was willing to build relationships with capitalist countries if he felt the Soviet

Union would benefit.[69] Each theorist had supporters in the worldwide communist movement, including the Jewish labor movement. Stalin defeated Trotsky in the summer of 1928, forcing the international revolutionary to flee and live in exile, often one step ahead of assassins, until he was finally murdered in Mexico City in 1940. Trotsky's expulsion led a small number of key American Communists, such as James P. Canon, Martin Abern, and Max Shachtman, to split from the American Communist Party. Stalin's defeat of Bukharin that same year and the initiation of the Soviet "Third Period" had an even greater impact on the fortunes of the ILGWU.[70]

The official Comintern pronouncement of the Third Period followed the revolutionary theory that capitalism was on the brink of collapse.[71] Under this theory, the first period of global revolutionary uprising from 1917 to 1923 was followed by the second period of capitalist stabilization from 1923 to 1928, and the Third Period of sustained revolutionary movement would see the overthrow of capitalist regimes.[72] The Comintern decided toward the end of 1928 that those unions controlled by non-Communists in the United States and elsewhere were corrupt and could not be reformed from within.[73] The Profintern (International Federation of Trade Unions, a constituent body of the Comintern) ordered William Z. Foster to form an alternative, or dual, union structure in the United States. In doing so, the Profintern tacitly admitted failure in its efforts to radicalize the AFL. So Foster ended the Trade Union Education League (TUEL) and formed the Trade Union Unity League (TUUL) to set up unions independent of the AFL in various industries. Up until that point, Sasha Zimmerman and others had formed an opposition group within the ladies' garment industry, operating independently of the ILGWU leadership, but they always expressed their desire to cooperate as one union. In January 1929, Foster, with the reluctant acquiescence of Zimmerman and other Communists exiled from the ILGWU, announced that the Needle Trades Workers' Industrial Union (NTWIU) was formally independent. Zimmerman objected in principle to the formation of a dual union; he had been convinced of Foster's "boring from within" strategy in setting up the TUEL in 1921. The fiat issued by the Comintern, without considering what Zimmerman and others believed was a majority opinion, did not sit well. According to Zimmerman, the Communist Party had always tolerated a degree of opposition, even in the pages of the *Daily Worker*, up to at least 1927.[74] This policy began to change, and by 1929 Stalin and Foster, Jay Lovestone's rival in the factional conflicts within the party, demanded obedience from Party members to the decisions made in Moscow. Bukharin and Trotsky supporters pushed back. Lovestone, the secretary of the Communist

Party in the United States since the death of Charles Ruthenberg in 1927, was the highest-ranking Communist Party official in the United States to express opposition to Stalin's reforms and to side with Bukharin.[75]

Sasha Zimmerman grew increasingly uncomfortable with Foster's demand for obedience, especially in light of inexplicably poor judgment from Moscow. He remembered that the NTWIU, in its earlier manifestation as an autonomous union intending to rejoin the ILGWU, was stronger than the ILGWU, controlling more shops in 1929.[76] That year, the NTWIU called for a general strike in the dress industry and led a number of shops out. In the 1920s, the growing power of jobbers—middlemen who controlled what shops produced garment lines under any given manufacturer's label—reached critical levels. But William Z. Foster, who was used to the power relations in the steel industry, with only a handful of major employers, refused to allow Zimmerman to settle with individual jobbers who agreed to the union's terms. Foster believed that the entire garment industry had to succumb to the union's demands to win the strike. Zimmerman argued that Foster did not understand the dynamics of the industry. In time, a jobber would be able to line up any number of manufacturers among thousands not facing strikes, and many more shops outside Manhattan, to continue to produce the garment lines. Zimmerman ignored Foster's directive and settled with jobbers and shops that would do so.[77]

In June 1929, the Communist Party expelled Jay Lovestone, Sasha Zimmerman, and other notable Communists such as Benjamin Gitlow, Bertram Wolfe, and Will Herberg—all first-generation-immigrant or U.S.-born Jews of Russian parentage—as a result of their persistent and publicly aired doubts. The group, known as the Lovestoneites, organized a new party. They confidently called it the Communist Party Majority Group, because the faction led by Foster had been a minority within the American party but was favored by the Comintern. Other Lovestoneites active in the ILGWU and instrumental in the rebirth of the union in the 1930s included Louis Nelson, Jennie Silverman, and Minnie Lurye, a former secretary to Jay Lovestone.[78] Silverman, who was Jewish, came to the United States from the Ukraine in 1919 after a pogrom in which all of the males in her village were killed, perhaps in an attack against Bolsheviks during the civil war that followed the Russian Revolution.[79] Lurye, born in 1909, was the daughter of Communist activists in Chicago and later married Bill Matheson, a Chicago labor activist. In 1930, Lurye moved to Paterson, New Jersey, to support a textile strike, then moved to New York City, where she and Silverman shared an apartment.[80] Juliet Stuart Poyntz, the first director of the ILGWU educational department, was also part of the Lovestone faction. Though she was no longer working for the ILGWU, she remained in contact with Zimmerman through their shared political activities.[81] For the next two years, from 1929 to 1931, representatives of the Lovestoneites and socialists, united to some degree in their opposition to the Communist Party, carried on discussions aimed at repatriating the former Communists into the institutions of the Jewish labor and socialist movements, principally the ILGWU.

From the time Sasha Zimmerman went back to work as an operator in a dress shop in 1930, he strategized along with other Lovestoneites about how best to rejoin the ranks of Local 22, to work his way back into the leadership of Local 22, and to rebuild the union.[82] Though the International's GEB had expelled Zimmerman from the ILGWU in 1926, Zimmerman sought reentry to the union through the local. The International was weak and fractured, and the GEB left decisions for reentry up to the locals. As head of the Lovestone delegation in the ILGWU, Zimmerman approached Local 22 manager Max Bluestein in the spring of 1931 to negotiate the reentry of the former Communists into the dressmakers' union. At the depths of unemployment in the industry, representing only a small proportion of dressmakers, and facing opposition from the Communist Party, Bluestein had good reasons to form an alliance with expelled Communists. After a number of conferences, Lovestoneites such as Louis Nelson, Pearl Halpern, Louis Rosenthal, and Isadore Stenzor rejoined Local 22 and other ILGWU locals.[83] Bluestein agreed to a joint administration led by the Progressive Group that included the Lovestoneites.[84] The new administration sought "to have an honest and progressive and militant organization" that would weed out corruption and build an organizing movement among the dressmakers.[85] Zimmerman joined Local 22 on May 15, 1931, and immediately headed up the newly formed "committee of twenty-five," activists who organized new union members, "pulled" shops, and recruited more volunteers for organizing campaigns.[86] The following year, he won election to the Local 22 executive board.

At the beginning of 1933, the ILGWU was weaker than it had been since before the Shirtwaist Makers' Uprising in 1909. Union leaders suspended publication of *Justice*. Sweatshop conditions that had prevailed in the garment industry twenty-five years earlier returned with the Great Depression. Garment manufacturers took advantage of the political strife that divided the ILGWU, as well as the enormous surplus of workers competing for paid work. In an effort to avoid dealing with the union, manufacturers established thousands of small subcontracting shops in New York, Philadelphia, Boston, and Chicago, as well as "runaway" shops in rural areas up to a hundred miles outside the urban centers. Subcontractors competed with one another to make garments for larger manufacturers by bidding down the cost of producing clothes. Sewing-machine operators, pressers, and cutters labored in urban and rural districts throughout the country under conditions of long hours and low pay. The standard pay for the fastest dressmaker in New York was thirty cents an hour.[87] They worked in overcrowded factories with bad lighting, poor ventilation, and excessive heat and cold. More than two decades of struggle that had raised garment workers' standard of living were wiped out in a few years.

Zimmerman led Local 22 to reestablish an educational department and tied its work directly into the movement to reorganize the dress industry. In February 1933, Local 22 created a separate branch for the lowest-skilled and lowest-paid jobs in the industry: finishers, drapers, examiners, and cleaners. The educational department appealed to them to engage in programs that would train them to lead in the union-organizing efforts. At the inauguration ceremonies for the new branch, union leaders, echoing the words and sentiments of visionaries such as Fannia Cohn, reminded the members of the union's earlier accomplishments. They emphasized the centrality of social unionism as a strategy and as a vision:

> You dressmakers, with the ILGWU, have the distinction of being pioneers in many activities. You were, for instance, the first to establish five days' work and the forty hour week. You started the workers' education movement, and conducted recreational and social activities. We still believe that workers who play and sing together will also work and fight together, not for immediate demands alone, but also for ultimate goals, for a new world, founded on the happiness of all who work, in whatever useful capacity.[88]

The concert program that followed the ceremonies, intended to appeal to the increasing ethnic and racial diversity among the dressmakers, included performances by leading artists. The Romanian violinist Sandu Albu played the "Spanish Dance" from *La Vida Breve*, Russian baritone Stefan Kozakevich sang Russian folk songs, and William Bowers sang Negro spirituals.[89]

Like Cohn, Zimmerman located power in the union among the rank and file. Cohn's vision of shop-based power fit nicely with the shop-delegate system that Zimmerman championed as a Communist in the early and mid-1920s and again as a Lovestoneite in the early and mid-1930s. This vision of local power was helpful to Zimmerman as he worked to reestablish himself politically, creating a power base in an International union controlled by his former rival David Dubinsky.

After the death of President Schlesinger, Dubinsky won the presidency of the ILGWU in 1932. Zimmerman was elected in early 1933 as the secretary-manager of Local 22. Though a shell of a formerly strong organization, Local 22 remained one of the largest locals in the ILGWU. The experiences of Dubinsky and Zimmerman in the union during the 1920s likely motivated their actions in their respective offices in the 1930s. Dubinsky was anxious to dramatically increase the membership of the International, yet he was wary of losing power in a weak organizational structure. Zimmerman, who reassumed office with a local membership that numbered about three thousand, representing only 10 percent of the non-Italian dressmakers working in New York City, was anxious to create a stable power base that would protect him from being ousted from the union once again. Although Dubinsky, seeking to build an anti-Communist bloc, supported the reentry of Zimmerman and other former Communists into the Local 22 leadership, their relationship remained tense. Both men desired to increase the size of the union while maintaining a stable political hierarchy, and each had reason to distrust the other.[90]

Conclusion

At the weakest point in the union's history, a core of committed and seasoned organizers remained. They were well prepared, with a strategy shaped by a particular socialist worldview, to rebuild the union with an increasingly diverse membership. Fannia Cohn at the International level and Sasha Zimmerman on the local level never stopped trying to appeal to Blacks, Hispanics, and others in the workforce, even as the union faced near collapse. From the mid-1920s until the nadir of union strength in early 1933, Fannia Cohn kept ILGWU education programs going almost single-handedly. During this difficult period, she sustained a steady drumbeat in the union, in the Jewish labor and socialist movements, and throughout the AFL, emphasizing the vital function of union education and the critical need to organize workers of all groups into a movement defined by a transformative social vision. She continued to organize education and social programs at Unity House, which she consistently held up as a model for the ideals of the labor movement. Zimmerman, who had cut his teeth as a union leader in Local 25 and had been influenced early on by strong radical women, intuitively adopted Fannia Cohn's methods. When the New York ladies' garment workforce unexpectedly erupted in a near-perfect show of solidarity in August 1933, union leaders, especially those in Local 22, were ready to welcome and involve the new international membership.

PART II

5

All Together Different

*Social Unionism and the Multicultural
Front, 1933–1937*

On August 16, 1933, the dressmakers in New York's garment industry went out on strike despite, or perhaps because of, the dire condition of
the ILGWU. Beyond the most optimistic expectations of union leaders, sixty
thousand mostly female dressmakers walked off their jobs and flooded union
halls throughout the city. Two months earlier, the U.S. Congress passed the
National Industrial Recovery Act (NIRA), a foundation of President Roosevelt's first New Deal, promising for the first time "that employees shall have
the right to organize and bargain collectively through representatives of their
own choosing and shall be free from the interference, restraint, or coercion
of employers of labor, or their agents."[1] David Dubinsky was among those
labor leaders who saw that provision as a watershed moment for unions. But
the promise carried no teeth. Without a government mechanism to implement unions' right to exist and to enforce labor-management contracts, little
changed in how unions organized.[2] Indeed, the NIRA offered management
within each industry the opportunity to create "codes" that established uniform wages and maximum hours based on prevailing rates and conditions.
For many small garment manufacturers who were competing in a cutthroat
industry, fearful of going out of business because of competitors underbid-
ding them or unions demanding higher wages, the codes held out the hope
of a rationalized system and a stable, low-wage structure. For many union
activists, especially in the garment industry, the threats inherent in the NIRA
provided more motivation to organize than did its promises.

The ILGWU began to sign up new members at a rate that stunned the
industry. More workers walked out, and as many as twenty thousand dressmakers struck in out-of-town centers such as New Haven, Connecticut,
and Camden, New Jersey.[3] Neither Sasha Zimmerman nor David Dubinsky expected the rush of workers who responded to the dressmakers' call to

strike. Zimmerman remembered, "The response was so overwhelming that we were astonished ourselves. We had estimated that 30,000 workers might go out, or at most 35,000. The actual outpouring was in the neighborhood of 70,000, shops we had never been near, shops that did not have a single union member. We did not have halls enough to hold them, so we had to take an armory. It was enormous, just enormous."[4] The energy and confusion that reigned among the tens of thousands of new recruits recalled the shirtwaist strike twenty-four years earlier. Like that organizational surge, the 1933 strike required immediate conscription of a new class of leaders. People had to hire halls to accommodate the strikers and to register and instruct new union members. Strike leaders needed to rally troops, to run picket lines, and to hold those lines against strikebreakers. At the same time, local union leaders were negotiating with hundreds of garment manufacturers. For union leaders on all levels, maintaining order on the streets, at the union offices, in strike halls, and in the shops required a level of coordination that proved difficult, but not impossible, to achieve.

Zimmerman and other veteran union leaders called on years of experience running strikes, leading mass meetings, and identifying leadership among new recruits. In addition, just as in the 1909–1910 strike of shirtwaist makers, the dressmakers relied on Socialist Party activists to train strike leaders quickly. Union organizers pressed rank-and-file members such as Maida Springer-Kemp into service for the union. Springer-Kemp, who joined the union only a few months prior to the strike, remembered the heady atmosphere and disarray that accompanied it.

> I was working in a shop when the call for the general strike went out. They poured out by the thousands. The Local 22 couldn't keep up. I was asked to learn something about parliamentary procedure. The young socialists would come to teach parliamentary procedure. My husband must have thought I took leave of my senses. . . .
>
> The strike committee is almost a euphemism. They were so overwhelmed that they took anyone, and you started work; it was that informal. . . . I just came out with my shop and went to one of the halls assigned and was overwhelmed by what was going on. You joined committees and had sandwiches, pumpernickel and corned beef. . . . You were a part of an activity that was going to change the economics of your life.[5]

Only four days into the strike, individual manufacturers began to seek settlement with the dressmakers' joint board, which comprised the four local

Figure 5.1. This is a bon-voyage party for Maida Springer-Kemp, second from right, the night before she departed as an AFL delegate to England in 1945, shortly before the end of World War II. Springer-Kemp began her union activism on the August 1933 dressmakers' strike committee and rose through the ranks to become one of the most prominent African American women unionists in the country. Charles S. Zimmerman, right, Springer-Kemp's mother, far left, and Springer-Kemp's sixteen-year-old son, Eric, second from left, pose with her. (Cornell University, Martin P. Catherwood Library, Kheel Center for Labor-Management Documentation and Archives, ILGWU Records, collection 5780p, box 20, file 1)

unions in the industry. The union established settlement headquarters inside Stuyvesant High School on East 15th Street near 1st Avenue. With shops ready to negotiate, Charles Zimmerman recalled, "people stood in line to settle."[6] By the eighth day, most of New York City's dressmaking industry was operating under a new union contract that provided for a thirty-five-hour work week with no overtime hours allowed and a guaranteed minimum wage of ninety cents an hour.[7] Within a few more weeks, ILGWU locals representing workers in underwear and children's dresses won similar victories, and the union signed up almost all of the one hundred thousand workers in the industry. By September, the ILGWU had grown fivefold to over two hundred thousand members—nearly twice the number of workers who had joined the union at the height of its power in the early 1920s. The union membership, roughly 75 percent women, encompassed a greater diversity of cultures than ever before. In addition to the Jewish and Italian workers who made up the majority of the membership, the Jewish-led union organized over four thousand Black and over three thousand Spanish-speaking workers, many of whom had never before been union members.[8]

The extraordinary victory in New York was fragile, and union officials at all levels recognized the immediate concerns presented by the abrupt expansion of the ILGWU. Leaders confronted the challenges of rebuilding the union's infrastructure and inculcating union principles before the newcomers drifted away from the organization. They had to learn how unions organized and then formulate and articulate their demands. They had to learn how to exercise the power of an organized workforce to win everything from pay raises and shorter hours to safer work conditions and a more reasonable work pace and to establish systems to enforce concessions won from employers. Hundreds of union members had to be trained as shop-floor leaders who could represent co-workers in grievances, monitor contracts, and lead workers out on strike when necessary. Some had to learn English, and many needed to become public speakers. As leaders, they would have to rally co-workers to action, even though some of them had never taken such actions before. Most important, workers from many different racial-ethnic cultures had to learn to trust one another.

The young female membership challenged the ILGWU to build a militant union movement among workers whom many union leaders in ladies' garments and other industries regarded as unorganizable.[9] Days after the August strike ended, the editors of *Justice* wondered in print about how to proceed:

> The great problem confronting the dress workers' unions in New York—and that goes also for the International in New York and elsewhere—however, is how to consolidate the gains of the great strike, how to muster sufficient man material to administer the machinery of the huge dressmakers' organization and to keep at the same [time] alive the interest of the rank and file in the activity of their union.

They advised local and International union officers to "concentrate at once upon building up the spiritual and moral resources within their midst, on concentrating a bond of genuine fraternity between all members, regardless of views and convictions outside their trade union affiliation."[10] Implicitly, these union officials were reminding local and International leaders of the folly of the partisan warfare that had torn the union apart in the mid-1920s. Still, the emphasis that *Justice* editors placed on "man material to administer" the union suggests that they accepted gendered divisions and continued to assume that leadership of the overwhelmingly female union would remain almost entirely male.

Union leaders realized that many employers looked to exploit any division among workers—including race, gender, skill, and religion—to impede organizing and to weaken other collective action. Manufacturers sometimes either included or excluded various ethnic groups to maintain ethnic tensions among workers. For example, workers and union activists knew that some employers, including Jewish employers, looked specifically to hire non-Jewish workers. Young Jewish women had a reputation for militancy, and the desperate need for a job drove some Jews to conceal their identity. In Amelia Bucchieri's first job interview in 1931, she was asked by the boss, who was Jewish, if she was Catholic. She was, and she believed that was why she was hired. Her suspicions were confirmed when she got to know her co-workers. One Jewish co-worker who wore a crucifix told her, "If I don't wear a cross, I'll never have a job."[11] The suppression of Jewish ethnic culture was one of many tools employers used to keep workers scared and suspicious. The task for union organizers, then, was as much about reinforcing ethnic pride as it was about inculcating respect for ethnic difference.

New Education Programs

Within weeks of the dressmakers' unprecedented victory, Fannia Cohn urged union leaders to meet the union's challenges by embracing an expanded program of educational activities that she had pioneered and nurtured over the previous twenty years. Cohn defined education expansively to envelop the many complex facets of workers' lives. She predicated the design of union education on the assumption that workers and their families required structures to explore and develop new ideas about class, race, and society. Cohn and the union leaders and activists who embraced this assumption discussed education in what I categorize as three general areas: political education, social education, and multicultural education. These categories overlapped with one another and were conceptually and practically linked as Cohn and others consciously sought to define the meanings of different program activities in multiple educational contexts.

Cohn explained in *Justice* her integrated concept of union education to prepare young members for political participation. She emphasized that her program, which included formal evening classes in workers' schools and classes in residential summer colleges, was based on "the needs of the worker." Similarly to how Latin American radical Paulo Freire framed the ideal link between education and action forty years later, Cohn argued that workers would assume various political functions within the organization through firsthand experiences in shop and membership meetings and in conventions, calling the union the workers' "real school."[12] She explained the great importance of social and recreational activities such as music programs, dancing, pageants, and dramatizations as well as physical training, swimming instruction, and sports: "They draw the group together and create amiability and solidarity, and are of educational and artistic value. We believe that workers who dance, play, and sing together will also fight together for their rights." Cohn argued that the programs should provide a "vision of a future society based on cooperative effort supported by new spiritual and intellectual values. The underlying principle of workers' education is based on a conviction that the aims and aspirations of the organized labor movement can be realized only through the workers' own efforts in the economic, political, social and educational fields."[13] Cohn outlined a vision of a labor movement whose members would be trained and encouraged to make the most critical decisions in the operation and direction of the union. It was a vision that she and others referred to as *social unionism*, a form of union organization that touched members not only in the shops but also in their homes, in their communities, and with their families.[14] This view trusted that workers, if given enough opportunities, would naturally create lasting bonds among themselves, treating race and ethnic diversity as a strength rather than a divisive barrier.

With a limited budget to implement these ideas on the International level of the union, Fannia Cohn appealed to the local unions that were suddenly filled with new members and flush with resources. She outlined the design of activities in a 1934 guide written for local unions developing education committees. She reminded union activists that all social activities, such as dancing and sports, were organized in political and ideological contexts and that dancing and sports had been central ILGWU educational department programs since 1917. She urged that when members gather to enjoy social and folk dancing, group singing, calisthenics, basketball, and swimming groups, they should first discuss "social, economic, labor and health problems." "While our activities do aim to develop character and personality, we expect at the same time that our members will use their newly-gained knowledge in the service of our union, the labor movement generally, and the higher social aspirations of humanity."[15] While several local unions created educational programs in late 1933 and early 1934, Fannia Cohn's greatest influence was felt in Dressmakers' Local 22, which multiplied nearly tenfold to thirty thousand members during the August strike, as Sasha Zimmerman adopted her plan with zeal.[16]

Zimmerman announced the formation of Local 22's educational department in late November 1933 under the direction of his friend and close political ally Will Herberg. Like Zimmerman, Herberg was a key leader among the small Lovestone faction that was expelled from the Communist Party in 1929. Prior to his Local 22 appointment, Herberg directed the New Workers School, the Lovestoneite institution that paralleled the Communist Party's New York Workers School; the Rand School, which was affiliated with the Socialist Party; and other left-wing schools, which taught evening and weekend classes in a range of subjects. "The strength of a union lies fundamentally in the solidarity, consciousness and militancy of its members," he wrote. But, he warned, experience in strikes and workplace struggles were not enough to ensure a stable and loyal membership. Without an ongoing program of education, workers who rose to the occasion during extreme economic crises might "relapse into passivity as soon as circumstances change." Most of the young women in Local 22, he noted, had never been members of a union before and had no historical context in which to understand their strike activity. "Especially this is true of the large number of colored and Spanish-speaking dressmakers in our ranks today."[17] Of the four thousand Black members who joined the ILGWU in 1933, over twenty-seven hundred belonged to Dressmakers' Local 22. Local 22 also counted about two thousand Spanish-speaking members in 1934. Dressmakers' Local 22 and Children's Dressmakers' Local 91, whose ethnic and racial composition was nearly identical to Local 22's, were the prime locus of interracial concerns and of multicultural experimentation.

In the most ambitious local education program in the ILGWU, Herberg established eight education centers in neighborhoods around the city and gave special attention to programs aimed at the thousands of Black and Spanish-speaking workers who had recently joined the ILGWU. Zimmerman wrote about the new members: "The Dressmakers' Union is not satisfied with receiving them passively; it is bending all efforts to assimilate them into the Union body, to draw them into active participation in union work and leadership on an equal plane with everybody else. In this direction the educational program is expected to help."[18] Unlike Italian members a generation earlier, Black workers never demanded their own union locals, nor did

Figure 5.2. The Dressmakers' Local 22 was the first ILGWU local union to establish neighborhood centers around New York City to hold union meetings, classes, and other activities for members and their families, such as this 1936 class in the Harlem section of Local 22. (Filmstrip series—"The Union of the Women's Garment Workers, ILGWU," filmstrip no. 3, "Part IV: Educational and Cultural Activities," Cornell University, Martin P. Catherwood Library, Kheel Center for Labor-Management Documentation and Archives, ILGWU Records, collection 5780p, box 57a)

the ILGWU offer them this option. There were many fewer Blacks than Italians employed in the industry, and they were almost always a small minority in shops dominated by Jews and members of other ethnic groups. Equally important, they might well have viewed separate local unions as an extension of the Jim Crow practices that still existed in other AFL unions.[19] At the same time, Blacks familiar with racially segregated union locals may have known that there were some advantages to meeting apart from the majority group and electing their own representatives.[20] In 1933, Local 22 settled on a hybrid structure in which Blacks in Harlem could gather in a local union branch to make political decisions and to explore their identity as African American trade unionists. It established an East Harlem branch for Spanish speakers as well. Courses such as "The Negro in American History" offered in the West Harlem branch reinforced that exploration, although it included material presented over the years to the entire membership in various venues.[21] These branches sponsored classes, choirs, orchestras, and lectures. Local union leaders encouraged each ethnic and racial group to sponsor elaborate balls and festivals that provided opportunities to demonstrate group identity and leadership. At the same time, Black and Spanish-speaking members participated in most of the programs offered by the locals and the International in their main centers in the midtown-Manhattan garment district.

Spanish speakers presented unique problems to the union. Puerto Ricans, who constituted a majority of the Spanish-speaking membership, were relative newcomers to New York, with a far smaller population in the city or

Figure 5.3. "Dramatization of 'Casey Jones' being 'sent to Hell a-flying' at the Harlem (N.Y.) Educational Center." Here Harlem children and some adults perform a classic union ballad. Most of these union members and their families are African American. But Jews and Italians still lived in Harlem in considerable numbers in the 1930s. It was not unusual to see some white children and adults participating in activities sponsored by the Harlem section of the ILGWU. (Filmstrip series—"The Union of the Women's Garment Workers, ILGWU," filmstrip no. 3, "Part III: The Union at Play," August 1938, Cornell University, Martin P. Catherwood Library, Kheel Center for Labor-Management Documentation and Archives, ILGWU Records, collection 5780p, box 57a. These filmstrips depicted activities from 1900 to mid-1938. This play took place between early 1934 and mid-1938.)

across the country than the other main ethnic groups in the union—Jews, Italians, and African Americans. Comparatively, they did not have the resources and mature ethnic institutions that the ILGWU could call on to support the unionization of Spanish workers. The New York State census of 1930 estimated that forty-five thousand Puerto Ricans lived in New York City.[22] Most of them came after the 1924 Immigration Act restricted the flow of cheap foreign labor into the United States and labor agents began to encourage and facilitate the migration of Puerto Ricans to New York. But the Spanish-speaking population of dressmakers was not homogeneous. It included workers from other countries, including Spain, Cuba, Panama, and Argentina. The task of Local 22 was to carve out space in which Hispanics could feel comfortable as a group, without neglecting the distinctions between them, and still be a part of the local union as a whole. In April 1934, the Local 22 executive board appointed Saby Nehama, a Spanish-born Jew, to organize the activities of the Spanish section and to "be in the office for the purpose of assisting to attend to the needs of the Spanish speaking members of [the] union."[23]

Zimmerman and Herberg sought to encourage a Hispanic rather than a specifically Puerto Rican section of the union. Local union leaders recognized that for many immigrant groups in the United States, Jews and Italians included, language was a more significant determinant of cultural identity than was place of birth. Some Puerto Rican migrants in New York City shared this view. In 1923, representatives of several Latino communities in New York formed La Liga Puertorriquena y Hispana, the Puerto Rican and Spanish League. La Liga served a diverse Hispanic population as a general benevolent and welfare society throughout the 1920s and 1930s. While not denying the predominance of Puerto Ricans, the group's first stated goal was "to unite all Hispanics without national distinctions."[24] The group opened an education center, taught English, held social and cultural functions, and lobbied government officials on issues that concerned the Spanish-speaking community.

For Spanish-speaking immigrants to New York in the 1920s and 1930s, the difficulties in confronting other ethnic and national groups helped to cement their Hispanic identity. Louise Delgado immigrated with her family from Puerto Rico in 1923, arriving in the primarily Jewish and Italian neighborhood of East Harlem when she was eight years old. She remembered that conflicts, including youth-gang fights over access to community swimming pools, raged between Italians and Hispanics, Jews and Hispanics, and Italians and Jews.[25] To non-Spanish-speaking people, Hispanics appeared a monolithic group. For Spanish speakers, their small numbers and common language meant that they had an interest in cultivating a common culture. The challenge for the union, then, was to figure out how an ethnic group identity, forged in part through interethnic conflict, could also serve to build intercultural solidarity. Cohn, Zimmerman, Herberg, and others knew that education was the answer and that union activism had the potential to build intercultural trust. Delgado recalled how she worked in a shop where the bosses were Jewish and Italian and the workers were all Italian except for herself and her sister. Initially, the Italian workers refused to work with Louise and her sister, until the local union's business agent interceded. Some time later, Louise witnessed the Italian boss abusing one of the workers, who might have been a family relation. She said, "I think one of the girls did something wrong and he took a dress and threw it in her face. So I got up and stopped the whole shop."[26] Louise led the women to the union headquarters and brought a complaint. A few weeks later, her Italian co-workers elected her chairlady of the shop. A program of education that built on this dynamic could solve the seeming paradox of interethnic working-class solidarity.

International officers were initially reluctant to devote substantial resources to Fannia Cohn and the International educational program, but organizers and union officers on the local level followed Local 22's example by replicating the practices of social unionism.[27] For some local leaders who were political comrades, establishing educational departments modeled after Local 22's program was quite natural. Louis Nelson, who won election as manager of Local 155 of the knit-goods workers in 1934, for example, was also a Lovestoneite and a former member of Local 22. He was one of the first officers in the 1930s, after Charles Zimmerman, to build an educational program. Still, local officers who did not necessarily share Zimmerman's ideological assumptions but ran unions with large numbers of Black and Hispanic members, such as in the Pressers' Local 60 and the Children's Dressmakers' Local 91, looked to Local 22's success in retaining and involving them.

The leaders of Local 91 were particularly enthusiastic. The children's dressmakers did the same work as the ladies' dressmakers, but on a smaller scale. Children's styles were often smaller-sized patterns of adult dress. It was not unusual for workers in one industry to find work in the other from one season to the next, so to some extent the memberships of Locals 22 and 91 overlapped. With about eleven thousand members in the mid-1930s, Local 91 was slightly more than one-third the size of Local 22. In the summer and fall of 1933, nine hundred Black and about seven hundred Spanish-speaking garment work-

Figure 5.4. Other local unions in the ILGWU that organized large numbers of Black workers followed the lead of Local 22. This meeting of the New York City Dress Pressers' Local 60 in April 1934 attracted scores of Black women and some Black men, many of whom joined the union in August 1933. Educational programs were key in the local union's strategy to keep these workers as members and to develop a cohesive, militant, loyal fighting force. Garment manufacturers often hired African Americans as pressers in the hope of dividing the workforce along racial lines and keeping wages depressed. (Cornell University, Martin P. Catherwood Library, Kheel Center for Labor-Management Documentation and Archives, ILGWU Records, collection 5780p, box 47, file 4)

ers joined the Children's Dressmakers' Local 91. Unlike Zimmerman, Local 91 manager Harry Greenberg was never a controversial figure in the ILGWU. Greenberg came into Local 91 and led a successful strike at the age of thirteen, and he rose quickly to become manager in the 1920s.[28] He remained loyal to Morris Sigman, Benjamin Schlesinger, and David Dubinsky throughout the 1920s and 1930s but never took a prominent role in the union's civil war and was not aligned with any political party. Gus Tyler described him this way: "I would have called him an anarchist if it were possible to describe him by any ideology, but Harry Greenberg was incapable of ideology. He was a pragmatist."[29] He had few ambitions beyond his role as manager. Though not an ideologue like Zimmerman, Greenberg embraced social unionism as an earnest trade unionist intent on building a loyal and militant local union. In early 1935, Local 91 began to publish *Our Aim* chronicling their activities. The uninterrupted run of this newsletter is one of the richest extant sources of information on social unionism in the ILGWU locals from this period.

Greenberg encouraged social unionism by hiring ideologically motivated staff to run the programs. When Bessie Weiss, Greenberg's first educational director, announced she was leaving her position, she suggested that Greenberg see Gus Tyler, who was working at the International union office. Greenberg attended a debate in which Gus Tyler participated, representing the Young People's Socialist League. The next day, he offered Tyler the job of educational director of Local 91, promising him a free rein in doing whatever he wanted in the program. Even though union careerists considered a job in a local a step down from a job in the International, which offered daily access to David Dubinsky, Tyler was excited by the prospect. In particular, Tyler was eager to work with the new mix of racial-ethnic cultures in Local 91. When Dubinsky asked him why he wanted to leave a coveted position, Tyler replied,

Figure 5.5. In this January 1935 photo of a class in trade unionism at Local 144 ILGWU in Newark, New Jersey, at least five Black women, seated in the second and third rows, are taking part. The union's retreat, Unity House, is advertised on the bulletin board. Unity House was an integral part of the IGLWU vision of social unionism. (Cornell University, Martin P. Catherwood Library, Kheel Center for Labor-Management Documentation and Archives, ILGWU Records, collection 5780p, box 9, file 22)

I grew up in a working-class family. But I want to know what the Italian workers feel, what the other workers feel, the Spanish workers—there weren't that many around—what the Black workers feel, even what the Jewish workers feel nowadays. And at 3 West 16th Street—which was where the headquarters was—I don't meet any workers. I never see a worker. I don't know what's going on. I'm living in an unreal world.[30]

What Tyler found when he went to Local 91 was a thriving culture of activists who were hell-bent on building a militant union with a mission to help transform society.

At the same time, union programs satisfied ordinary workers' desire for educational, social, recreational, and cultural experiences that were unavailable elsewhere, helping to enrich their lives or to transform them as individuals. Many of these young women did not have the opportunity to finish high school or to pursue college. The union opened many avenues for study and collegial activities. Maida Springer-Kemp described the richness of activities and how rank-and-file members felt as they participated in the programs

You worked from eight to four, from nine to five. [It] puts you in a different world. . . . You don't know how to dance? Teach you something [about] how to dance, . . . put[s] you in a different world. You are in an orchestra— [a] different world. You are in a chorus. . . . A variety of things put you in a different world. Your family comes with you. They come to hear you play. They come to an art exhibit all structured and set up to see your paintings, to see what workers are doing.[31]

In addition to workers who aspired to college, more highly educated Blacks and whites entered the ranks of the garment workforce during the Great Depression. Anita Burke Maurice, who was born in Barbados, began working as a garment worker in Manhattan at the age of fourteen in 1925. She worked mostly during the summer, mainly to earn money for clothes, and remembers making fourteen dollars a week, of which her mother only took two dollars. After she graduated high school in 1928, Maurice entered the New York Training School for Teachers as one of only a handful of Black students. She finished her course work, including Latin and French, at an accelerated pace and graduated in June 1930. But as it was the first full year of the Great Depression, she could only find substitute teaching assignments in schools that primarily served Black students. The city froze teacher hiring, and white teachers began to squeeze Blacks out of substitute jobs, even in the

Black schools. "The white teachers that graduated, they could work as salesladies in Macy's and Gimbels. But then, when the Depression got real bad, they didn't work there any more, so then we had competition. They worked in our schools, but we didn't go to white schools." Unable to teach, Maurice worked in garment shops as the best-paying option available to her.[32]

For immigrants such as Maurice, ILGWU music and choral programs that provided instruments and instruction free to members and their families offered material as well as cultural benefits. Music-education programs and the formation of choruses and orchestras appealed to the musical ambitions of workers from various ethnic backgrounds. Maurice found that the ILGWU programs in which she participated as a young woman reinforced the values of musical education with which she was raised. During her childhood, Maurice's father, who was the son of an Irish schoolmaster and had trained as a civil engineer, earned a modest salary as a factory handyman in New York. Though her family enjoyed few luxuries, Burke bought a $500 piano from Bloomingdale's in the 1920s for his children to learn piano and voice.[33] Many immigrant families saw a musical education as an important advantage, and some made large sacrifices to give their children the opportunity to develop their musical talents. This value was particularly prevalent among many immigrants who dropped into the working class in America from their positions as professionals, teachers, intellectuals, or shopkeepers in their countries of origin.

By the end of 1934, Local 22 enrolled fifteen hundred students in forty-five weekly classes held in the union headquarters in the garment center and in the Bronx, Harlem, Spanish Harlem, Williamsburg, Brownsville, East New York, Boro Park, and Coney Island. These programs included twenty-two classes in English, twelve in the principles of unionism, two in history, two in the structure and function of the union, three in public speaking, and one each in the history of American literature, social science, and economics.[34] In addition, Local 22 conducted twenty cultural groups with more than one thousand participants enrolled in four mandolin classes and orchestras, a general chorus, a Spanish chorus, a Harlem or Negro chorus, a brass band, five gym squads, and seven swimming classes.[35]

The local employed twenty-eight classroom teachers, two mandolin directors, three chorus leaders, a bandleader, and four gym and swimming teachers. By the end of 1935, its educational committee recorded twenty-four hundred participants in fifty-five classes and twenty-five cultural and recreational groups. In the 1935–1936 school year, the number of classes more than doubled.[36] Local 22 members and their families also frequented the local union library, one of several established in the ILGWU. They attended

Figure 5.6. Black and white union members engaged in a range of intimate social and athletic activities. Racial mixing in these venues helped build a trusting bond among union members. ("Souvenir Hallowe'en Ball Supplement," International Ladies' Garment Workers' Union, Boston, 1940, YIVO Institute for Jewish Research, Bund archives, ILGWU collection, file 15)

theater, lectures, and museums. For example, the educational committee organized trips for children to visit an art exhibit at Rockefeller Center and the Metropolitan Museum of Art. Many thousands more attended dances, picnics, pageants, and parades. These programs peaked in 1937, when the ILGWU reported over twenty-two thousand participants enrolled in educational programs nationwide.[37]

In rebuilding the ILGWU from the shop floor up, local officials and activists blended the functions of economic, political, social, and recreational activities. They considered the creation of and participation in the locals' educational programs as union "work," underscoring what the historian Michael Denning calls the "laboring of American culture."[38] Nora Lopez, a shop-level activist and member of the Local 22 Journalism Club, articulated this expanded concept of union work in an article titled "All in a Day":

> At five o'clock all those who are interested in the larger work of the Union are going—going their way to the various educational and cultural centers. There is gym work, basketball and swimming for the athletes; dancing, drama, chorus and mandolin orchestra practice for those musically inclined; and the study classes dealing with vital subjects concerning the well-being of the workers and their Union.[39]

Lopez's article illustrates the various categories of education in which union leaders and members engaged, constituting social unionism in the ILGWU. In treating each category in relief, we can see how union leaders thought problems and solutions could be addressed by various educational activities. Education activists intended these activities to educate union members on multiple planes. By examining the record closely, we can catch several glimpses into how ordinary members experienced those activities.

Political Education

As a practical matter, all levels of union leadership saw union education as the essential vehicle through which members, particularly brand-new members, would learn to act as dedicated citizens of the union. The ILGWU was organized in a complex political structure before the explosive jump in membership during the summer and fall of 1933. To maintain the integrity of the union, leaders were anxious that new members learn that structure quickly, including the various functions of union departments. They were equally anxious to identify and train shop-floor leaders to serve as chairpersons, local union executive board members, and activists in education and other committees. Union members needed to learn the practical day-to-day workings of the union in the workplace. How do union members lodge complaints about work conditions? How do members choose leaders and spokespeople? What services can members expect from various union departments, and what are members' obligations to the union? Most important, union leaders were concerned about maintaining the level of militancy expressed by dressmakers in the August strike. A remarkable number of rank-and-file union members had to learn sophisticated skills and practices of organization in each of the small shops in the industry.

Union leaders used educational activities as a means of exploring a wide range of political ideas, particularly as matters of ideology and strategy were in flux. In the period from 1933 to 1937, the principal players in ILGWU education were affiliated with several different political movements, and their ideas were played out in educational activities. There were differences among elected leaders and union educators in ideological perspectives and organizing strategies. On both the local and International union levels, Socialist and other anti-Communist leaders maintained alliances with anarchists who insisted on expressing different ideas. World and national events urgently demanded interpretation and response. Despite this ideological diversity, there was a broad agreement against fascism and the need to build militant unions which appealed to garment workers. While some workers responded to sectarian ideological overtures, other rank-and-file leaders were attracted to union militancy, participating in actions and programs sponsored by different groups. Zimmerman understood and seemed to tolerate differences among union members, sponsoring debates that included Socialists, Communists, and independent political thinkers. Dubinsky, a moderate member of the Socialist Party, still distrusted Zimmerman because he was an active leader in the Lovestone Communist faction. Fannia Cohn remained loyal to the Socialist Party but continued to irritate Dubinsky because of her lack of interest in criticizing the Communists. However, all agreed that broad educational programs were central to the rebuilding of the union. In this milieu, programs that introduced members to a broad liberal arts curriculum thrived.

For Fannia Cohn, Sasha Zimmerman, Will Herberg, and local union leaders who embraced social unionism, education meant more than teaching ordinary union members to function within the complex organization of the union, to assume leadership in union affairs, and to develop a trade-union consciousness that encouraged loyalty to the ILGWU and the labor movement. To them, education also meant developing a class consciousness that imagined a socialist society eclipsing the misery and exploitation inherent in the capitalist system. They believed that workers needed both practical and theoretical education in militant unionism, particularly regarding shop-floor struggle. Beginning in 1934, Will Herberg attracted some of the leading radical theorists of the socialist and labor movements to teach in the program. Educators from the Rand School of Social Science, the New School, and Columbia University taught economics, trade-union theory, Marxist analysis, and history to thousands of ILGWU members.[40] One semester, for example, Lovestoneites Bertram Wolfe and Irving Brown taught Marxist theory; Leo Huberman, who later founded *Monthly Review*, taught American social history; and the radical pulp mystery writer Bruno Fischer taught "The Machine Age and Literature." Themes that ran through many of the course outlines included such shop-floor issues as the piece rate, explained in the context of capitalist exploitation.[41] From the standpoint of various academic disciplines, instructors encouraged workers to be vigilant in holding the line against even the smallest incursion by employers on workers' control and power.

To bring new union members into "active and equal participation in union work," Local 22 established a central Dressmakers Educational Center at Washington Irving High School, modeled after and located at the same site as the International union's Workers' University.[42] The local offered advanced classes on economic, social, and trade-union subjects to those students considering whether to run for shop- and local-level offices. For the rank and file, Local 22 offered more elementary classes in the seven residential sections of the local around the city. Because the classes had open enrollment, candidates for leadership in the local were largely self-selected, though union officials urged those members whom they hoped to groom for leadership to attend classes.

Zimmerman and other Local 22 activists used the courses to recruit minority members into the union's leadership. Several Black women who enrolled in them soon assumed higher-profile roles in Local 22. Lillian Gaskin, Violet Williams, Gussie Stanford, and Edith Ransom were elected to the Local 22 executive board in 1934.[43] Eldica Riley and Ransom, who was elected to the paid position of business agent in 1935, both chaired important committees in the union and helped form the Negro Labor Committee, a coalition drawn from AFL unions, in 1935.[44] Other classes attracted young women interested in expanding their political roles by offering them practical skills for shop-floor leadership and local union activism. The public-speaking class, for example, was designed specifically to create an Active Speakers Group that traveled from shop to shop to spread news, to recruit for activities, or to mobilize for mass action.[45] Students in Local 22 classes, most of whom were women, joined the Union Defenders Committees that were organized to patrol shops to enforce contract provisions, especially maximum hours and restricted workdays, and to report violations by employers and complicit members.[46]

Figure 5.7. "Negro Officer of Dressmakers' Union Local 22, ILGWU." *Front row, sitting, from left to right*: Rosina Presscott, convention delegate; Juanetta Smith, executive board member; Edith Ransom, business agent; Lucille Lane, convention delegate; Oretta Gaskins, Election Committee. *Back row standing, from left to right*: Clarissa Bostic, executive board member; Eldica Riley, executive board member. Black and Hispanic women won election to key local union positions after the August 1933 strike, almost always by a majority-white union electorate and at a time when union power resided on the shop floor and local union levels. (Cornell University, Martin P. Catherwood Library, Kheel Center for Labor-Management Documentation and Archives, ILGWU Records, collection 5780/14, box 39, file 10)

After 1933, Black and Hispanic women were elevated to shop chairperson, committee, and local executive board positions, becoming better represented in the places where critical decisions were made. Shop chairpersons monitored the terms of the contracts, settled disputes that arose, and recommended to the local union whether to strike a noncompliant employer.[47] Their role as the eyes, ears, and voice of the union in the shops was critical to the health of the union. Sasha Zimmerman noted that in the two and a half months from mid-September to the end of November 1933, shop chairpersons reported over 11,700 complaints to the union. During this short period, they held 1,482 shop meetings, and the local union held 173 jobbers' group meetings. In one month alone, the union found eight hundred shops violating the maximum-hour provision of their contracts with the ILGWU.[48] Both the local union's careful count and the high number of reported violations reflect shop leaders' serious attention to contract enforcement.

In the 1930s, the ILGWU continued the practice, begun in the early 1920s, of appealing to Black strikebreakers rather than vilifying them. The union promoted feelings of interracial camaraderie in the shops that opened opportunities for Black and Hispanic women to be elected to office from shops in which they were minorities. In a union newspaper article, Freddie Mae Haynes, a Black woman born in North Carolina, admitted to crossing the picket line in the early days of the dressmakers' strike. "Where I was born, there were no unions for colored people," she explained. Haynes soon joined the strike and later won election as her shop's chairlady and as executive board member of Local 91. "I was colored; but that didn't make any difference. There were about two hundred workers in Reinsdorf [dress shop] and it made me feel all of a sudden that every one of them was my sister." She remembered that prior to the union, she and the other Black women pressers were cut off from the rest of the shop and did not even know the names of the white sewing-machine operators. She declared, "Now we know them all."[49] The unusually large size of Reinsdorf's workforce gave even more significance to Haynes's election as a Black worker in a predominantly white shop.

Women benefited from opportunities to prove their organizational and political skills to male members in recreational and social functions of the educational departments of the ILGWU, just as women commanded the grudging respect of men for their leadership acumen in the founding and operation of Unity House in the 1910s and 1920s. For example, women took charge of the Local 22 Spanish section's Grand Solidarity Balls in January and November 1934 and the Dressmakers' International Ball organized by the English-speaking Harlem, or Negro, section in January 1935.[50] The November Grand Solidarity Ball, which featured an orchestra directed by Señor Del Pozo, attracted fifteen hundred people.[51] Women chaired the committees that ran these extravagant events, which required considerable resources and administrative talent. Female activists created elaborate programs, disseminated publicity, sold tickets, and rented facilities; auditioned and hired professional orchestras; arranged for and supervised decorations, catering, and the taking of photographs; and directed the evenings' events. In the program for the Dressmakers' International Ball, held at the Rockland Palace in Harlem, a photograph shows that Black women composed the majority of

Figure 5.8. Arrangement Committee for the International Dressmakers Ball, January 19, 1935. Black women and some men developed organizational and leadership skills through high-profile educational activities that garnered the attention of the entire union. The Arrangement Committee for this celebration included Edith Ransom, front row, fourth from the left, a salaried business agent for Local 22, and other women soon to be elected to the Local 22 executive board.

the Arrangement Committee. The mutual culturalism of Local 22 meant that representatives of other cultural groups were willing to lend their support while allowing the appropriate individuals to lead. The committee's chair, Isabelle Harding, and secretary, Edith Ransom, were Black women who organized a group that included Jewish and Spanish women and a handful of men.[52]

Social Education

In the period between 1933 and 1937, local and International union officers expressly promoted the political enfranchisement of all their members, particularly their African American members, through the social and cultural programs of social unionism. In November 1934, Local 22 formed a theatergoers group and took about one hundred members of mixed racial and ethnic backgrounds to see the controversial play *Stevedore*. Written by Paul Peters and George Sklar, *Stevedore* was produced by the Theater Union, an early Popular Front group whose executive board included an ecumenical mix of "Socialists, Communists, and some liberals with no official adherence to any party."[53] *Stevedore* tells the story of a group of African American dockworkers attempting to organize in the face of opposition from an exclusively white dockworkers' union.[54] Black actors, some of whom were members of the well-known Hall Johnson Choir, played leading roles, and the play featured a score replete with African American hymns. Because the play advocated militant unionism and interracial cooperation, it was banned in several cities in the United States in the mid-1930s.[55] Before the play, the Local 22 group heard a lecture by David M. Rossi titled "The Negro in Life and Drama." After the performance, they accepted an invitation to meet the cast. A Local 22 officer described the event:

> The scene of fraternization of the colored and white workers of the stage with the colored and white workers of the shops was really touching. Short speeches by actors, stories of discrimination, hope for a united front of black and white, and the relating of an experience of a colored member of Local 22, who was at the Chicago convention where a case of color discrimination was dealt with in a spirit of solidarity by the whole convention, had a great effect on all present.[56]

The "colored member of Local 22" recounted a dramatic action that David Dubinsky and the General Executive Board of the ILGWU (GEB) had taken in May 1934 at the start of the union's national convention. When the delegates arrived, they found that the hotel they originally reserved refused entry to the Black members of the delegation. The entire body of convention delegates, several thousand strong, marched out of the hotel into the Chicago streets and into a hastily reserved hotel that would accommodate them.[57] Local 22 and the International union had taken some steps to improve the political representation of Black and Spanish-speaking membership. Dubinsky and the GEB agreed to a proposal made by Charles Zimmerman to add two delegates each from the Harlem section and the East Harlem Spanish section to the Local 22 delegation to the 1934 International convention.[58] In all, there were only a handful of Black delegates present in Chicago. But union leaders intended the move to show the thousands of Black members back home that the union would go to great lengths and expense to insist on their equal status. These gestures were important symbols of interracial commitment that shored up the foundation of regular classes and group activities in which Black, Spanish-speaking, Jewish, and Italian workers participated.

Social unionism taught workers to connect with one another by building intimate bonds among garment workers from various cultural backgrounds. The tens of thousands of rank-and-file members and their families who participated in local and International union educational activities in the 1930s did so for a variety of reasons, but the planners ensured that their horizons would be broadened and union commitments strengthened by their participation. Some may have come simply to learn English or to play baseball, while others were attracted to the political and ideological movement that underlay social unionism. Women and men chose to spend their leisure time with the ILGWU because the classes, groups, teams, and trips satisfied deepseated needs and desires. Will Herberg and his staff were conscious of both the desires of members and the potential for building organization. They ran classes in conjunction with programs that were intended "to meet the many sided cultural interests" of the members: "Every section, too, is to run periodical social affairs at which the ties of friendship and solidarity among the members of our union can be strengthened and cemented."[59]

Herberg encouraged the active participation of members in designing the programs and activities, heightening members' enthusiasm and sense of ownership in the union. Maida Springer-Kemp emphasized that approach. "The purpose of the education committee was to have a cross-fertilization of ideas. And I think many of the activities, even the early ones, came out of discussions—things that members said."[60] Committees worked to encompass the broad interests of their members, who spanned cultures and generations. The educational departments organized classes in the latest dance steps and basketball leagues to interest teenagers and arranged trips to museums for more mature members. The union thrived because social unionism tapped into workers' natural impulses to establish personal relationships, to identify with their ethnic cultures, and to share elements of their culture with friends from around the world. Above all, the union thrived because women responded to the manner of union building implicit in social unionism.

Local 22's education programing reflected a particularly feminine approach to organizing and a vision of a union movement that took workers' family and community life into consideration. Female activists and men such as Zimmerman who were influenced by strong women organizers understood that family involvement in union activities likely increased workers' affinity for

Figure 5.9. This young Black couple is dancing in what may be a dance contest in late 1930s. Other dancers, Black and white, are cheering them. The singers may have been cast members from *Pins and Needles*. It is an unusual picture in this period to see white singers entertaining while Blacks are dancing. (Cornell University, Martin P. Catherwood Library, Kheel Center for Labor-Management Documentation and Archives, ILGWU Records, collection 5780pn 45, box 24.)

the union. At the same time, the union's education programs provided some opportunities for young women to push back against the demands their families made on the new leisure time that workers enjoyed courtesy of the union contract. Although the hours that working women spent in classes were previously spent at work rather than at home, women's choice to join education programs helped them to preserve that time as their own.

The leadership of Local 22 took full advantage of the regular participation of thousands of members and their families in social and recreational programs. Just as corporate welfare programs of the 1920s in other industries appropriated emerging popular cultural forms such as baseball and basketball to create and reinforce an employer-affiliated identity among workers, locals formed athletic teams and the International organized leagues that included teams from various socialist institutions, such as the Workmen's Circle, to cultivate identification with the union and the labor movement.

Figure 5.10. This 1937 basketball game between the Dressmakers' Local 22 (dark tops) and the Children's Dressmakers' Local 91 (gray tops) on November 6, 1937, was one of hundreds played in the ILGWU women's basketball league in the mid-1930s. The photo shows that both teams had Black and white participants. The league played games in public venues around New York City in front of family and friends, who sometimes numbered in the hundreds. This game was played at the old Stuyvesant High School in Manhattan. (Cornell University, Martin P. Catherwood Library, Kheel Center for Labor-Management Documentation and Archives, ILGWU Records, collection 5780p, box 9, file 12)

During periods of mobilization, Local 22 used sites of recreational activities to educate and recruit members for organizing and strike-related responsibilities.[61] The participation of workers' families in the union's cultural activities facilitated activism and strengthened the union's bonds with members' relatives who were not employed in the garment shops.

Through direct participation in activities and the union's reportage of those activities, workers from all racial-ethnic groups learned to interact socially. Scores of photographs illustrate classroom, social, and recreational activities in the dressmakers' and other locals in which a proportionate number of Black women participated. In a conscious but genuine gesture, Black women, even if they were alone in a sea of white members, were often positioned in the front and center of the photographs. One 1937 photo-graph taken during a women's basketball game between Local 22 and Local 91 clearly shows that both teams were racially integrated (figure 5.10). Participation in sporting events, as athletes and as spectators, helped workers and families from all racial-ethnic backgrounds identify with one another as union members. The interracial character of athletics and their coverage in local and international newspapers helped to build interracial bonds in the workplace and on the picket line.

Activities such as the Dressmakers' International Ball of Local 22's English-speaking Harlem section were well attended by members of many different racial-ethnic groups, opening up spaces for interracial socializing that did not normally exist in most workers' neighborhoods. A photograph of one of the many subsequent balls shows well over one hundred people dancing or circled around a few couples strutting their stuff (figure 5.11). Most participants are white, but a number of Blacks are dancing together (see, for example, couples close dancing at nine o'clock and at two o'clock), and some Blacks are mixed in with white spectators. Hispanics, Italians, Jews, and African Americans all attended ILGWU dances. The most prominent dancers in the photograph are two couples in the center, one of which appears to be a Black man and a white woman.

The opportunity that dancing provided for interracial socializing illustrates the remarkable level of intimacy reached through ILGWU social events. Since the turn of the twentieth century, young men and women frequented commercial dance halls, which replaced ethnic and religious sites and festivals as their preferred locations for socializing and dating. The exclusion of Blacks from dance halls and other places of recreation frequented by white patrons functioned as a principal factor in breaking down ethnic identities among European immigrants and in defining whiteness in the North.[62] The close connection between courtship and social dancing made interracial participation a particularly bold step, even if no courting occurred. In 1930s New York City, many dance halls, restaurants, and hotels still refused admission to Black patrons. But under the auspices of the union, workers of all ethnic and racial groups mixed in union dances. Maida Springer-Kemp recalled, "You would go with your friends and your family and maybe be close to a few shop friends. You all knew that you all belonged to that same union and you were dancing with your friend or your husband or somebody . . . that you knew. . . . You were with the union and you were doing this as a part of that social activity."[63]

It was equally important to many Spanish-speaking activists that the union promoted interethnic and interracial participation in a safe and famil-

Figure 5.11. "Local 22 Dance." Undated, circa 1938. Social dancing was a central element to social unionism. Workers and their families bonded in celebration and a show of unity, while affirming the inclusion of all racial-ethnic groups. (Cornell University, Martin P. Catherwood Library, Kheel Center for Labor-Management Documentation and Archives, ILGWU Records, collection 5780pn 45, box 24)

ial environment and that the union allowed groups to meet separately. Celia Flores, a union activist born in Puerto Rico in 1916, remembered social activities outside the union, such as the dances in her East Harlem neighborhood social club and sleeping out in the park with friends on a hot summer's night. These neighborhood interactions were safe and familiar, with no fear of unwanted sexual advances from male friends. She said, "We were all like a family." If the union wanted to attract members through social and cultural activities, it had to provide a similarly safe and comfortable atmosphere. Referring to the union, Flores said, "They had dancing. I used to go to school to learn something about political things. They used to send us to tell the people to join the union; and in the union, they'd teach them how to write and read, how to vote. And that way, the union was like a family—that you'd go there, and they were so nice also, friendly, that people joined the union to live together."[64]

For some union members, the dances sponsored by the union were the only place they would go to dance with people from other racial and ethnic groups, even though they were aware of other interracial dance venues. Workers were eager to dance with their friends from work. Celia Flores went with her husband to ILGWU dances in the 1930s. "We danced, and they gave food, and they stayed until one o'clock in the morning." She remembered that Italian, Jewish, Puerto Rican, and Black people all attended. She explained why she went: "because all my friends go there, and we could meet there a lot of people that we knew. But otherwise I didn't go to no other place."[65]

The physical activity and social bonding associated with athletics and dancing helped to build a militant union. Members developed confidence in their own bodies through the physicality of these programs. They became strong in the company of one another and learned to cooperate. Within the political context of building a union movement, sports helped prepare workers to join a picket and to defend the line against strikebreakers or to risk

Figure 5.12. The ILGWU made direct appeals to Black workers by contrasting the democratic processes of the union with the Jim Crow South. Blacks remembered years later how the union taught them to vote and to participate in the political process. (Max D. Danish, ed., *International Ladies' Garment Workers' Union Illustrated: 23rd Convention, Atlantic City, N.J.* [Abco Press, 1937])

Figure 5.13. The ILGWU celebrated the militancy of Black women along with their social participation, underscoring their contributions to the union. Here, Boston police officers are arresting a striking ILGWU member. (Max D. Danish, ed., *International Ladies' Garment Workers' Union Illustrated: 23rd Convention, Atlantic City, N.J.* [Abco Press, 1937])

arrest. Photographic essays in educational literature consistently included physical-educational activities with images of picketing and arrests, reinforcing the integrated purposes of social, physical, and political education and underscoring Fannia Cohn's linking education with militant action. But the key to the remarkable success of social unionism was more than political education, militant consciousness, and the enthusiastic inclusion of members from various racial-ethnic groups in these programs; it was a conscious, sophisticated program of multicultural education.

Multicultural Education

Social unionism, at its core, provided a venue through which union members and officers encouraged the construction of working-class racial-ethnic identities and demonstrated their admiration for the many racial-ethnic cultures to which workers belonged. Social unionists sought to build on the cultural impulses they recognized among workers. The cross-racial solidarity cultivated by local union programing germinated in the shops as workers sang, told stories, gossiped, argued, and came to regard one another as fellow workers and individuals. In 1934, Rose Pesotta, the only woman vice president of the ILGWU at the time and a general organizer for the International union, described workers in the garment shops singing to pass the time more enjoyably. "Such concerts are not uncommon. . . . Good music, folk songs of all nationalities in all languages, arias from favorite operas, difficult music from well-known symphonies, and jazz are in the repertoire." Revolutionary songs from various political factions mixed in with Spanish and Swedish folk songs and Negro spirituals. "This, sung by an international, interracial group of workers sounds really pleasant."[66]

Social unionists understood that urban density could create opportunities for interethnic and interracial trust as well as conflict. Attitudes sometimes improved just with living and working in close proximity, and the union looked for and used those organic bonds. Anita Burke Maurice explained how her life in New York offered opportunities to dispel ethnic bigotry. She grew up in an anti-Semitic environment. "And in Barbados, you learned the Bible. You had Bible scriptures, you know, and we heard, 'And the Jews killed Jesus.' And we heard all of that. And I was afraid of the Jews."[67] This fear was reinforced by her father, who worked as a "fix-it man" for a Jewish-owned lamp company in New York; Burke complained that the Jews cheated him out of his wages. But he moved his family to a predominantly Jewish section of Harlem when Maurice was a girl. After she befriended a Jewish girl across the hall in her apartment house, her ideas about Jews changed. Amelia Bucchieri also remembered close relationships in the shops between workers of different racial and ethnic backgrounds. Bucchieri was born in Mount Vernon, New York, in 1917. Because of the Depression, she had to leave full-time school at the age of fourteen; she went to work in Manhattan's garment center in 1931. She remembered Jewish, Italian, Puerto Rican, and Haitian co-workers. "I had friends all over down there. We shared lunches together: whatever they'd have left over from supper they'd bring for lunch, and I was eating all kinds of ethnic food."[68]

The bonds formed between workers of distinct racial and ethnic backgrounds by learning and sharing aspects of one another's ethnic cultures was the most powerful effect of social unionism. The programs organized by local unions appealed to rank-and-file workers in part because the climate engendered through these activities permeated the daily lives of workers in the shops. When the union ameliorated the causes of ethnic and racial con-flict, workers expressed a heightened interest in sharing their ethnic cultures. Maida Springer-Kemp remembered that she and friends from her shop would go to a theater performance once a month. Her closest friend was a Jewish woman who liked to bring her to the Yiddish theater. Springer-Kemp said, "She liked me, and I liked her. She wanted me to have a sense of enjoy-ment of the Yiddish theater. We would go to the opera. I would invite them to Harlem. We would have this exchange of things." When workers went out together, Springer-Kemp recalled, they went out as union members. Without the union, "there would not have been the camaraderie. There never would have been the sense of purpose. The union was the instrument helping to create" these bonds.[69]

Union-sponsored social events served to develop ethnic identity within the union context, as well as creating venues for intercultural mixing. The Italian Dressmakers' Local 89, for example, frequently held dances featuring Italian music. In February 1934, *Justice* reported that five thousand Italian dressmakers attended a dance arranged by the Williamsburg and Browns-ville branches of Local 89 at Arcadia Hall. Luigi Antonini, manager of Local 89 and a vice president of the International, was the only speaker for the eve-ning. Members of Commendatore Clemente Giglio's Company, well known among Italians as stage and radio performers, entertained the crowd, and dancing lasted until the early hours of the morning. John Gelo, assistant manager of the local, arranged the entertainment and musical program. It started with the "March of Local 89," composed by Maestro P. Lupo, leader of the orchestra engaged for the evening.[70]

The Spanish section of Local 22 held its Grand Solidarity Ball on Satur-day evening, January 6, 1934, setting a vivid example of how education archi-tects sought to incorporate the families and communities of members into the union. The Spanish-speaking activists organized the fete to consolidate gains from the August 1933 strike by creating bonds among Spanish work-ers. The dance was meant to "launch [an] extensive program of educational and social work of the union" among the two-thousand-plus Spanish-speak-ing dressmakers who had recently joined the local.[71] The dance at the New Harlem Casino on West 116th Street attracted 450 union members and their families.[72] A Spanish orchestra played a mix of Spanish love ballads, popular Latin tunes, and folk songs from various Spanish-speaking countries.[73] Other union members were invited and attended, but the strategy was to allow Spanish workers a space to celebrate their ethnic identity while proudly dis-playing their dance, food, music, and language for the non-Spanish-speaking guests. In subsequent dances—some sponsored by the union as a whole, others by ethnic sections—Puerto Rican, Cuban, Panamanian, and Spanish workers attended alongside their Jewish, Italian, African American, and Afro-Caribbean friends. Workers and their families consistently received the message that they were invited to identify as ethnic union members.

In addition to the more than sixty-five hundred Black and Spanish-speaking members, Local 22 organized workers from an impressive variety of ethnic and racial groups. The local often boasted the results of a membership census taken in October 1934, showing that more than thirty-two nationalities were represented among its nearly thirty thousand members. It counted 19,842, or 70.5 percent, "Jewish"; 2,569, or 9.5 percent, "Colored"; 1,850, or 6.5 percent, "Spanish"; 1,053, or 3.7 percent, "American"; and 2,924, or 9.8 percent, "other." The others were then broken down into twenty-eight nationalities, ranging from German (655) and Polish (522) to twelve ethnic groups with less than five members; Japanese, Chinese, Malayan, Hindu, and Bulgarian were listed, although only one union member came from each group (see table I.1).[74] Local 22's efforts to count each and every distinct racial-ethnic group represented among its membership demonstrated the leadership's celebration of diversity.

Union leaders looked for opportunities in every popular cultural form in which they were engaged to build a union identity by educating members about their co-workers' distinct racial-ethnic cultures. Morris S. Novik, who managed WEVD, the ILGWU's New York City radio station, wrote to Charles S. Zimmerman in the spring following the 1933 organizational surge regarding the programing for the coming months: "I am personally so sold on the idea of converting radio, and our station in particular, into a lively medium of union education and propaganda that I would be only too glad to help you in every way possible." Novik could barely contain his excitement at the prospect of broadcasting programs that would appeal to all of the union's racial and ethnic groups. While emphasizing that the programs should be "entertaining and of high caliber," he was adamant about taking into consideration the distinct tastes of African American workers, Spanish- and Yiddish-speaking workers, and "American" workers (native-born whites of northern and western European ancestry). To address this diversity, Novik suggested presenting a number of singers, each of whom was known to the Jewish community and could perform numbers in various languages. He suggested finding a prominent Black singer who could sing spirituals, which are "always acceptable to most groups and will be especially appreciated by the Jewish and Negro groups."[75]

Unity House continued to be an important site for intercultural mixing. In the 1930s, the International and local unions promoted Unity House as a reasonably priced resort in the Pocono Mountains, a luxury that otherwise only the wealthy could afford. Unity House also expanded the vacation options for Black and Hispanic workers who might be excluded from accommodations they *could* afford. The eight-hundred-acre park included a large dining hall where guests ate communally, an open-air theater, a library, bungalow-style rooms, tennis courts, horse stables, and a large swimming and boating lake. Workers stayed for the weekend or for a week or two. Unity House programing included music, plays, and lectures that spanned the breadth of popular, classical, political, and ethnocultural themes. A Sunday-morning "International Hour" presented music from different cultures and by artists of different ethnic and racial backgrounds. One Sunday in August 1935, Anna Appel, a popular actor in the Yiddish theater, read from Sholem Aleichem on the same program as Yohichi Hiroaka, who performed on the xylophone. The following day, an academic lecturer, Professor Fagin, spoke after supper on the topic of "Conflicts in Negro Literature."[76] During the 1935 season, the Unity House committee brought the Hall Johnson Choir and the Eva Jessye Negro Choir to the resort.[77] This opportunity had its limits. Though relatively inexpensive, a vacation at Unity House was beyond the means of many garment workers with little or no disposable income, and Black and Hispanic workers were still disproportionately represented in the lower-wage jobs in the industry. But activists of all racial-ethnic backgrounds attended union-funded planning meetings and training institutes at Unity House.

The Spanish-speaking membership presented Local 22 with a unique opportunity to explore mutual culturalism by involving families in the programs of social unionism. Like all union divisions, the Spanish section facilitated family members' participation in all educational and cultural activities. The Puerto Rican community was close-knit, and families looked out for one another, particularly their unmarried daughters. In this respect, the Puerto Ricans seemed similar to how Jewish unionists described the Italians in the 1910s. For them, the decision to join a union and to become involved in rallies, strikes, and other union activities often involved consulting the entire family. Louise Delgado remembered organizing dressmakers in the 1930s and 1940s. "We used to have a Puerto Rican organizer . . . [who] was dynamite. In the nighttime, she would pick me up, and we'd go there and speak to the mothers and the fathers and the children, the

Visit Unity's Official Opening

FRONT ROW (left to right): Josephine Lloyd, Mamie Santora, Judith Raines, Sophie Weissman, Lillie Feinberg.

BACK ROW (left to right): Raymond Orsini, Sam Rogers, Harry Greenberg, Gus Tyler, Arthur Samuels.

Figure 5.14. Union activists from all ethnic and racial backgrounds had regular opportunities to stay at Unity House, even if some could not afford a stay there. Local 91 sent a delegation of officers and activists for the season's opening weekend in June 1935. (*Our Aim*, July 1935, 6)

husbands, . . . [everybody,] just to sign the cards in order, you know, to organize the shop."[78] Though organizing Puerto Rican workers may have been labor intensive, convincing the whole family to embrace the union meant that when a strike was joined, the union could count on the support of members' relatives.

In the Spanish section of Local 22, leaders conducted meetings in Spanish; members listened to reports and voted on strikes, contract settlements, and political issues. At the section headquarters in East Harlem, union leaders sponsored lectures and organized classes in the Spanish language on trade-union principles as well as on dance and music.[79] Louise Delgado's leadership in calling a walkout and pressing a grievance, described earlier, exemplifies how these skills facilitated collective action.

Figure 5.15. Local 22 Hispanic members explored their ethnic identity in the Spanish section through cultural events such as this Flamenco dance performance in the 1930s. (Cornell University, Martin P. Catherwood Library, Kheel Center for Labor-Management Documentation and Archives, ILGWU Records, collection 5780pn 45, box 24, file 9)

English classes helped Spanish speakers, just as they had Yiddish and Italian speakers, to take a lead in shops and to break down the barriers that many employers constructed to keep workers divided. English classes alone may have encouraged a common sense of Americanness as they helped foreign-born workers speak with other union members, confront bosses, and navigate the exigencies of daily life in New York City. At the same time, the union also sponsored language classes in Yiddish, Spanish, and Italian for members to communicate in one another's language and to help the American-born children of immigrants understand their parents. In offering both options at the same time to all workers, the union reinforced the understanding that workers did not have to give up their ethnic cultural affiliations to coalesce into a solid union.

Carmen Rosa, though exceptional in her level of activism, embodied the possibilities created by the Spanish section's programs. An article in *Our Aim* described Carmen's ethnic origins and her path to union activism. Rosa was born in Puerto Rico in 1906. Her paternal grandfather went to Puerto Rico from Cadiz, Spain, and died resisting the Spanish during the anticolonial war at the end of the nineteenth century. Her mother was of indigenous descent and native to Puerto Rico. Rosa married as a teenager and reluctantly moved to New York with her husband and two young children in the 1920s. After her husband left her, she went to work in the garment industry to support her family. In the 1930s, she took every class offered by the union, including an English-language class. Rosa was elected chairlady of her shop, attended weekend union leadership courses at the Brookwood Labor College, joined the education committee of the local union, and was elected to the local union's executive board.[80]

Figure 5.16. The Local 22 Spanish section's mandolin orchestra was one of many groups formed to promote ethnic pride in the mid-1930s. The Spanish section met in East Harlem, where many of the Puerto Rican members lived. ILGWU educational programs were open to members' families. This picture shows two children who are members of the orchestra: one is sitting in the front row, third from the left; another is sitting in the third row, far right. (Filmstrip series—"The Union of the Women's Garment Workers, ILGWU," filmstrip no. 3, "Part III: The Union at Play," Cornell University, Martin P. Catherwood Library, Kheel Center for Labor-Management Documentation and Archives, ILGWU Records, collection 5780p, box 57a)

AT BROOKWOOD INSTITUTE

Figure 5.17. Fannia M. Cohn, seated, cofounded the ILGWU educational department and Brookwood Labor College in Katonah, New York. Cohn built bridges between these and other institutions she helped to found or in which she was active. Union leaders used Brookwood as another vehicle to promote Black and Hispanic leadership. Here, members of Local 91 are attending a summer institute at Brookwood. *Standing from left to right*: executive board member May Daindridge, executive board member Marie Simmons, executive board member Carmen Rosa, local educational director Gus Tyler, Pearl Bailes, and Ruth Sussman. (*Our Aim*, August 1936, 8)

Social unionism resonated deeply among the multicultural membership of Local 22 because of the ways in which the union embraced cultural diversity within its ranks at important public events, integrating social, cultural, and political performance, such as in the 1934 May Day parade in New York City. Two photographs of that event contain a number of clues as to how the members of Local 22 saw the role of ethnic identity in building their union (figures 5.18 and 5.19). In one, the members posed around Sasha Zimmerman, who is standing in the center dressed in a three-piece suit. Most women and some men are dressed in traditional peasant and village costumes from eastern, northern, and central Europe, the Middle East, Spain, Mexico, South America, and perhaps the West Indies or Africa.[81]

Pride in the ethnic and cultural diversity of the local is unmistakable, as is the political context in which that pride was expressed. Many of the members are sitting in or standing near the horse-drawn float that Local 22 constructed for the parade, shown in figure 5.19. In place of a Maypole, a single upright fist is clenching ribbons held at the other end by members in costume, showing the united power of an ethnically and racially diverse membership. On the right flank of the float, those sentiments are expressed rhetorically. Crowned by a rendering of the Western Hemisphere, the medallion reads, "The Power of Labor Lives in Organization and Militancy." The central slogans read, "Workers of 32 Nationalities United: Dressmakers Union Local 22, ILGWU" and "One Army under One Flag Fighting for One Cause—The Cause of Labor." The horse drawing the float is draped with a banner reading, "Down with Nazism."

Figure 5.18. Local 22 members pose around manager Sasha Zimmerman (standing in three-piece suit) dressed in peasant costumes from several of the members' thirty-two national cultures. (Photo by H. Rubinstein, Cornell University, Martin P. Catherwood Library, Kheel Center for Labor-Management Documentation and Archives, ILGWU Records, collection 5780/14p, box 1, file 15)

Figure 5.19. Local 22 members constructed this May Day float in 1934 to illustrate the links between multiculturalism, union militancy, and anti-Nazism. (Cornell University, Martin P. Catherwood Library, Kheel Center for Labor-Management Documentation and Archives, ILGWU Records, collection 5780/14p, box 1, file 15)

Taken together, the image unifies a number of key themes. Leaders and members of Local 22, like the rest of the Jewish labor and socialist movements, opposed Nazism both in Europe and in the United States. The Nazis crushed the free-labor movement that operated freely in the Weimar Republic and developed a sophisticated ideology of racial supremacy that denigrated all cultures that were not "Aryan." Nazism linked anti-Semitism, anti-Communism, and the suppression of an independent labor movement with the singular supremacy of a German national culture. In constructing this float, Local 22 leaders and activists suggested that a militant labor movement was needed to defeat Nazism in the United States as well as abroad by organizing aggressively, going out on strike, and conducting boycotts. The strength of the movement they envisioned was predicated on the inclusion of workers from all racial-ethnic backgrounds. In advocating a mutually supportive and culturally diverse movement, Local 22 activists did not mean multiculturalism to be a blending or absorption of cultures into a single monoculture but rather a celebration of the workers' many distinct cultures. Although this ideal was modified at times, for example, by the union's efforts at forging a unified Hispanic movement, union activists clearly rejected a singular dominant ethnic culture. In elevating workers' various ethnic cultural identities in the context of building the union, Local 22 stood in direct opposition to the master-race ideology of the Nazis.

Conclusion

The mutual culturalism that underlay social unionism prevailed in the ILGWU for four years. In that time, the members of the New York dressmakers' union, more than any other unit, demonstrated a successful alternative model of union building and leadership. Local 22 presented opportunities for women, as well as for men, to help determine their destiny. Social unionism in the ILGWU during the mid-1930s reflected the sensitivity of Yiddish socialists to the linkages between Jewish identity, revolutionary political organizing, and mutual ethnic cultural celebration among union members and comrades. As in Russia at the turn of the century, for Jewish garment workers, the face of capitalist exploitation in the American sweatshop was most often Jewish. When the union was nearly mortally wounded at the onset of the Great Depression, young Jewish women had to suppress their ideas and even their Jewish identities to get jobs with Jewish bosses. But the revival of the ILGWU and the surge of radical movements ushered in a shining moment of Jewish cultural pride predicated on mutual culturalism. With the ladies' garment industry almost completely unionized, expressions of ethnic Jewish cultures mingled prominently with expressions of African American, Hispanic, and Italian cultures in the ILGWU. A membership composed mostly of young women asserted their racial-ethnic identities as they developed their political consciousnesses and engaged in building a militant union.

Women took charge of their own education, participating in the economic and political decisions that affected their lives. They assumed positions of responsibility through educational, social, recreational, and especially cultural activities. In doing so, women took the opportunity to link their roles in their family, community, and union. As we will see in the following chapters, the forces supporting this movement were far broader than the ILGWU or the Jewish needle trades. Many dynamic factors had to intersect at specific times and places for social unionism to succeed. By the same token, as international events developed, the nature of the welfare state evolved, and the political affiliations of key leaders shifted, social unionism was altered considerably.

6

Politics and the Precarious Place of Multiculturalism

The extraordinary revival of the dressmakers' local unions and the ILGWU resulted in two-year contracts signed in late 1933 and early 1934 that established minimum wages and a limit of thirty-five hours per week with no overtime.[1] Employers in New York City and the union's "Eastern Out-of-Town" district, which included Staten Island, New Jersey, Long Island, and Westchester County, organized themselves into five employer associations to negotiate and administer the contracts. To institute uniform standards across the shops, ILGWU leaders welcomed this level of employer consolidation. However, the structure of the dressmaking industry in the region remained chaotic, with more than three thousand establishments employing an average of thirty-one workers each in 1934. Manufacturers that sold directly to retail stores operated some of those establishments. But, more often, the manufacturers hired "jobbers," who acted as middlemen. They took the fabric, which may have been cut at the manufacturing plants, and contracted with small sewing shops to do the bulk of the work; some jobbers cut the fabric or did some of the finishing work themselves. While some ILGWU members were employed in "inside" shops run by a manufacturer or jobber, most worked for the "outside" shops of the contractors.

Manufacturers created this decentralized system during the 1920s to promote competition between contractors who lowered their prices—and, therefore, the wages they paid—to get work from the jobbers. The union referred to this as the "auction block" system, in which contracts were awarded to the lowest bidders. Even if manufacturers and jobbers signed contracts with the union establishing a minimum wage in their shops, they denied any responsibility for contractors.[2] To avoid the union, a number of contractors, on their own volition or at the behest of jobbers, regularly "ran away," closing up shop in one location and opening in another, often with a new name, and hiring a new nonunion workforce. During the 1920s and early 1930s, the ILGWU was ill equipped to combat this situation. After the 1933 strike, however, the ILGWU fought back more effectively than ever. The massive participation of union members in the educational programs supported an impressive mechanism of contract enforcement that relied on representatives from each of the thousands of shops to monitor the terms of the contracts and to pursue runaway shops. The programs served to cement interracial relations and to mobilize members by the tens of thousands to support contract negotiations in late 1935 and early 1936.

Though social unionism prevailed for several years in the mid-1930s, neither members nor leaders in the ILGWU universally or unconditionally accepted the social unionism formulated by Fannia Cohn and others. Social unionism continued to be nurtured and sustained by the institutions of the Jewish labor and socialist movements, particularly as the ladies' garment industry remained chaotic and the institutions of state-sponsored labor-management oversight remained ineffective. But international and domestic developments provoked a reorientation in the worldview of union leaders. Over time, social and political forces that operated below the surface of the multicultural experiment weakened the union's commitment to the mutual embrace of ethnic cultures, especially when leaders no longer deemed it critical to the health of the union.

The Politics of the Jewish Labor and Socialist Movements

The rising tide of the Jewish Left in the 1930s, including Communists, Socialists, anarchists, Trotskyites, and the small Lovestoneite group, lifted the ship of Yiddish socialism and provided the most important ideological and political support for social unionism in the ILGWU. In the early days of the union's rebirth, the transmission of socialist ideals through cultural forms permeated the Jewish labor movement. The ILGWU, the *Jewish Daily Forward*, the Workmen's Circle, the Rand School for Social Science, and the United Hebrew Trades drew staff from one another, and their members participated in the other groups' activities. At the International's 1934 convention, delegates approved a motion that "the General Executive Board issue an appeal to all [ILGWU] members in the United States and Canada to affiliate themselves with the Workmen's Circle in their own interest and in the interests of the labor movement."[3] Following that convention, ILGWU locals, including Dressmakers' Local 22, Cutters' Local 10, and Knit Goods Workers' Local 155, organized Workmen's Circle branches among their membership, and the Workmen's Circle sponsored a men's basketball team that played in the ILGWU league. The ILGWU also recruited for the Young Circle League, the young adult section of the Workmen's Circle.

Socialist theories of culture were discussed in the classrooms and theaters of the Rand School for Social Science, an important institution supported by the Socialist Party, the Workmen's Circle, and socialist-led unions such as the ILGWU, the Amalgamated Clothing Workers of America (ACWA), and the Brotherhood of Sleeping Car Porters (BSCP). ILGWU officers such as Fannia Cohn and General Organizer Frank Crosswaith taught at the Rand School, ILGWU local unions sent officers to training classes there, and many ILGWU events were held at the school. In 1934, a group of students from the Rand School formed the Rebel Arts Group to produce plays, music, and murals exploring the intersection of art and revolutionary ideology. Many ILGWU locals used Rebel Arts materials in their own literature. And several ILGWU dramatic groups participated in a two-day labor drama festival held at the New School for Social Research in April 1935, along with the theater groups from the Rebel Arts, the Young Circle League, and the Brookwood Labor College.[4]

In the founding issue of the Rebel Arts Group's cultural magazine *Arise*, it averred that the new magazine

> *will* take sides in the class struggle—the side of the working class. It will be a cultural forum for artists in all fields who are eager to contribute to the great movement of workers of hand and brain which fights for the con-quest of society for the benefit of the masses. Realizing that art is a weapon, and should be used by workers for the working class, *Arise* will wield that weapon for the toiling masses along the whole cultural front—graphic arts, photography, literature, the drama, the dance, music, criticism.

Arise argued that the socialist artist is a "class conscious fighter" who "is with the victims of capitalist brutality and fascist savagery. He is with all of the oppressed proletarians whose dreams are shattered on the rocks of a cruel system and whose children are starving in the midst of the superabundance that made inevitable the want of many."[5] The Rebel Arts Group explained the relationship of arts and politics for the movement of which Local 22 was a part. The plays and outings organized by Local 22 activists, such as the union's attendance at a performance of *Stevedore*, emphasized the plight of exploited workers under capitalism. Through these experiences, Local 22 officers and activists, as constituents of a militant socialist movement, sought to expose the culpability of capitalism in fanning the flames of racial discord among workers.

Figure 6.1. Local 91 used this Rebel Arts–produced drawing for a cover of their publication *Our Aim* in February 1935. It contains elements employed by American social-realist artists of the 1930s who felt free to appropriate religious iconography for secular radical propaganda. A working mother and her crying child are being evicted from their apartment in the middle of the night. The action is enforced by the police, who are representatives of the state acting as agents of capital. A specter, evocative of Mother Mary, is pointing with the three-finger sign of the Holy Trinity toward the slogan "Local 91 Gives Relief to Members in Need." These artists and unionists were not yet convinced that the New Deal welfare state would provide for and protect workers and the poor.

The Jewish wing of the Communist Party (CP) continued to express Yiddish socialist ideals as strongly as their Socialist Party and Lovestoneite counterparts did. The CP, whose New York leadership was dominated by first- and second-generation Russian Jews,[6] focused heavily on interracial organizing and engaged in a broad spectrum of popular cultural activities. It sponsored athletic leagues and dances and operated a number of camps, including Camp Unity, a retreat on the Hudson River in which Blacks and whites mixed easily. They sent activists to the Workers' School in New York and children to the Young Pioneer camps.[7] The ILGWU competed with the Communist Party both politically and socially for the loyalty of its members.[8]

That competition was most acute during the Comintern's Third Period but remained even when international events softened the antagonism between Communists and Socialists in the needle trades. When Hitler became chancellor of Germany in 1933, he intensified the rearmament of the German military and stepped up anti-Soviet rhetoric, and the Nazi regime brutally crushed the German Communist Party. Stalin and Comintern leaders became alarmed and sought alliances with liberal capitalist states, socialist parties, and liberals to confront fascism, which they considered the preeminent global threat to the Communist revolution and the Soviet state. By the end of 1934, the Comintern began to disband the Trade Union Unity League (TUUL), and the constituent Needle Trades Workers' International Union appealed to the ILGWU on behalf of its members for admission to the ILGWU.[9] By 1935, Moscow's Third Period fully transitioned into the Popular Front Against Fascism. In the United States, as elsewhere, the Popular Front took hold for almost five years as an unprecedented period of left-wing cooperation and creativity. While rivalries persisted, the level of enmity reached during the 1920s all but disappeared by the mid-1930s.

During the Popular Front, workers who developed a political consciousness through activities sponsored by radical political groups were often open to exploring various, even competing political affiliations. For immigrants who were constrained in their countries of origin by custom, law, or limited resources from joining available educational and cultural institutions, the choices available to them throughout the Left were especially tempting. This was true for Mary Boyer, who immigrated from Minsk, Russia, in 1930 at the age of seventeen and began working in a garment shop two weeks after she arrived. The sole supporter of her family and, according to her self-description, a shy person, she socialized largely with a few friends from her neighborhood on Eastern Parkway in Brooklyn. Boyer attended public night school, but the Local 22 education

Figure 6.2. This photograph of Mary Boyer (front, second from right, wearing dark shirt and light shorts) and friends during a stay at Camp Unity, from her personal effects, demonstrates interracial friendship and affection that developed in the left-wing camps. (Courtesy of Mary Boyer)

programs exposed her to more expansive ideas such as those in a course she took on political economy. The powerful confluence of political and social cultures that thrived during the Popular Front inspired workers to action. In the mid- to late 1930s, Boyer frequently attended demonstrations and pickets. Around 1937 she joined the Popular Front organization the League for Peace and Democracy. She did not dedicate herself to one political group or party but went along with whichever group was organizing effectively.[10] Through participation in events organized by the ILGWU and by rival organizations led by Communist Party members, Boyer and others reinforced their commitment to shared Yiddishist ideals including interracial worker solidarity.

Boyer realized a new passion when she began attending athletics and calisthenics classes. She joined every sport she could: "Everything, even the teams. Really, I learned how to swim there. I learned how to play tennis there. I learned softball. I mean, they did everything." Boyer made lifelong friends through her participation in athletics and continued to swim three times a week in her mideighties.[11] Boyer participated in the 1937 May Day parade down Broadway, ending in Union Square, in which a twenty-foot-high float of a working man reading the *Daily Worker* led the CP contin-

Figure 6.3. The 1937 May Day parade, during the Popular Front period, was a rare moment of political unity among left sectarian groups, including Socialist, Lovestoneite, and other non-Communist participants. The CP contingent is led by this twenty-foot-high float of a working man in overalls reading the *Daily Worker*, seen here turning the northeast corner of Union Square. (Photo by Harry Rubenstein, Cornell University, Martin P. Catherwood Library, Kheel Center for Labor-Management Documentation and Archives, ILGWU Records, collection 5780p, box 27, file 3)

gent (figure 6.3). Communists, Lovestoneites, Socialists, Trotskyites, and members of other political groups marched under Local 22's banner. In film footage of the parade, a large, racially integrated contingent of proud, fashionably dressed Local 22 members appears prominently among the marchers.[12] This public event was an ideal venue to show off the products of their labor. Then a group of Local 22 workers in soccer uniforms fills the frame. In a photograph of the parade, Mary Boyer is among members of her gym class dressed in their athletic outfits (figure 6.4). Through the union, she was able to merge her two passions, sports and politics.

The union linked sports and politics in myriad ways. In opposition to the Nazi regime, ILGWU locals sent resolutions to the American Federation of Labor's Committee on Fair Play in Sports urging a boycott of the 1936 Olympics in Berlin. Local 91's resolution argued that American participation in these games "would represent a virtual endorsement of the Nazi reign of terror, directed not only against all religious, national and racial minorities, but also against the entire free trade union movement of Germany."[13] The ILGWU helped to organize the World Labor Athletic Carnival, a counter-Olympics held August 15, 1936, on Randall's Island.[14] An article in Local 91's *Our Aim* proclaimed, "The carnival was not only a protest against the Hitler-ized Olympiade, however, it was also an expression of labor's rising interest and participation in the development of its own culture, its own athletic institutions."[15] The carnival drew ten thousand spectators and was a showcase of interracial cooperation for the ILGWU, as Black athletes participated side by side with white teammates. Local 91's four-person relay team, drawn from their basketball players, included Ginger Bailes, a Black garment worker. Members of Local 91 won several events, including the La Guardia Cup relay, and Governor Herbert Lehman presented the trophy to the four women alongside union officers and representatives of the city.

A small delegation of union athletes went to the aborted Olympiad in Barcelona, Spain, the international counter-Olympics organized to protest the games hosted by Nazi Germany. One African American member, Dorothy Tucker, stepped up her political activity as a result of her trip. She recalled, "While we were there we got caught right in the middle of the Spanish Revo-

Figure 6.4. Local 22 teams, and other union athletic groups, often participated in political events. Mary Boyer, kneeling in front on the right, marched in the 1937 May Day parade wearing her Local 22 gym outfit. For these union activists, athletic participation in the union was a conscious political activity. (Courtesy of Mary Boyer)

lution. When I got back to New York, I was asked to go around to the various locals and tell them about the labor olympics."[16]

The union's support for Spanish loyalists resonated with other union members, including Spanish-speaking members from Puerto Rico who came to New York specifically with a socialist background or more generally as young veterans of political activities. Celia Flores was born in Guayama, Puerto Rico, in 1916 and raised by her paternal grandfather and her father, a carpenter who made enough money to hire help for the household. She remembered being involved in politics as a young teen. "Over there in Puerto Rico, they all have a political leaning. . . . We had fun. Every time they have an election, I was in the crowd doing something, because I was very active always."[17] Chencha Valdez, who was born in Carolina, Puerto Rico, in 1911, remembered that her father, though illiterate, was such a devotee of the Socialist Party that he refused to go underneath a banner bearing the logo of another political party.[18]

In the 1930s, the Spanish members of Local 22 became increasingly involved in the ILGWU's efforts to raise awareness of and support for the antifascist forces in the Spanish Civil War. Saby Nehama hosted a delegation of Spanish workers traveling across North America. He introduced the delegation to the Local 22 executive board, which listened to the worker-soldiers' reports and voted to increase its donations for food and medical supplies. Gestures such as these helped Spanish-speaking members to identify with Local 22 as Hispanic union members engaged in a movement for global justice and human rights. At the same time, the Spanish section of Local 22 could point to its commitment to Spain's loyalists as earnestly as its rivals the Communists did.

Zimmerman and Dubinsky: A Fledgling Alliance

Political differences and fledgling alliances characterized the relationship between key leaders inside the ILGWU. In the mid-1930s, local unions still exercised substantial autonomy from the International, and men who did not belong to the Socialist Party led the two largest locals. Luigi Antonini, an anarchist, led the forty-thousand-members Italian Dressmakers' Local 89, representing almost one-fifth of the entire ILGWU membership. Italians interacted with other union members in various activities, but Antonini, who served as the first vice president under David Dubinsky, was more concerned with maintaining Italian autonomy than in exercising political domination within the ILGWU. Former Communist Sasha Zimmerman, with a core of

Lovestoneites, led the second-largest and most politically active union, the Dressmakers' Local 22, with almost thirty thousand members. Some smaller local unions were also headed by managers who were not Socialist Party members: fellow Lovestoneite Louis Nelson helped to rebuild Local 22 after the 1933 strike and then won election as manager of Local 155 of the knit-goods workers.

Still an ideological Communist, Zimmerman hoped to agitate for revolution when he came to head the dressmakers' local. He viewed the position as an ideal office from which to pursue what he called his "extracurricular activities."[19] This high-profile position gave him broad exposure to the union's membership, and he was elected to the International's General Executive Board as vice president in 1934. For Zimmerman, local union autonomy meant that he could operate politically as a Lovestoneite, with comrades such as Jennie Silverman and Minnie Lurye, who were rank-and-file activists and deeply involved in the educational department. Zimmerman viewed Local 22's educational department in part as a power base to protect himself against another ouster in the future, as educational activities fostered loyalty to Local 22 and to Zimmerman as well as to the ILGWU.

As manager of the dressmakers' local, Zimmerman challenged Dubinsky by seeking to reorganize the structure that sustained Dubinsky's authority. Just as he had done in the early and mid-1920s, at the 1934 convention Zimmerman introduced a resolution that would have realigned the balance of power. As head of Local 22's delegation, Zimmerman again charged that the formula for assembling joint boards and conventions, in which each local was given equal weight, was "a gross violation of union democracy and of the equal rights of the members."[20] The Local 22 delegation proposed that representation "be allotted strictly on the basis of the number of members enrolled in the particular Local" and that locals, particularly those with smaller treasuries that were less able to pay for delegates to attend faraway conventions, be fully represented at conventions even if their entire delegation were not present.[21] Dubinsky, the former manager of the cutters' union, Local 10, rose to power as a leader of the small local with the most highly skilled and best-paid garment workers. The resolution failed, but if adopted it would have undermined the cutters' power in the International, along with Dubinsky's base of support.

Though Zimmerman was an irritant to Dubinsky, he was just as concerned as Dubinsky with the threat posed by the Communist Party. The vast number of shops in which employees were organized as union members included large numbers of Communist workers. Even before the NTWIU disbanded, thousands of Communists had joined the ILGWU as a matter of simple pragmatism. And Communist Party members held the leadership of locals in ladies' cloaks and on joint boards in other cities.[22] In Local 22, they formed a significant minority and won election to some of the leadership positions that Zimmerman created for the newly expanded organization. Each of the neighborhood sections that Zimmerman established after the August strike elected a chairman who ran meetings. Two of eight chairmen elected in the fall of 1933 were Communists.[23] In 1934, Zimmerman ran for reelection as Local 22 manager and won by more than a two-to-one margin against his Communist rival, with six thousand votes in a local of thirty thousand members. Nevertheless, the Communists had a significant power base, and Zimmerman knew better than anyone how political fortunes could turn on a dime.

Zimmerman relied on his political acumen but earned the respect and admiration of his political supporters and political antagonists alike, in part because of a warm and open personality. Nettie Harari Shrog, an activist with the left opposition group in Local 22 that was dominated by members of the Communist Party in the early and mid-1930s, recalled working against Zimmerman in a local election. The opposition group put her and her friend Millie Weitz in a hotel the night before the election. They worked as poll watchers because they did not trust Zimmerman to run a fair election. Nevertheless, Harari Shrog maintains that Zimmerman was approachable. A few years later, after the opening of the ILGWU Broadway production of *Pins and Needles*, in which she had a prominent role, Harari Shrog remembered that Zimmerman talked to her after the show. "He came over to me. He told me how much he liked me. He was really a nice man. As a matter of fact, he was very easy to talk to. I used to drop in on him and tell him if I had a complaint. I would tell him directly."[24]

Zimmerman and Dubinsky at times worked together to contain the Communists, often expanding opportunities for ethnic groups. But, the political sectarian rivalry that played out in the ILGWU did not always guarantee greater *autonomy* for ethnic groups. For example, a Communist minority among the dressmakers agitated for a separate Spanish-language local, similar to the Italian Dressmakers' Local 89. The group of eighty-four members presented a petition to David Dubinsky asking him to bring the proposal to the General Executive Board. Dubinsky initially supported the measure but withdrew his support, perhaps after realizing the group was composed largely of Communists.[25] Though the effort was unsuccessful, Sasha Zimmerman took steps to ensure that the Spanish members of the union were represented on the local's executive board and at the International's convention.[26]

Dubinsky remained a loyal member of the Socialist Party until 1936, but he was never an ideologue. As president and secretary-treasurer of the International, Dubinsky had broad authority to initiate and execute policy for the ILGWU.[27] He established departments and hired staff who researched industry trends, conducted organizing campaigns across the country, ran general strikes in the garment industry, and promoted educational activities. Dubinsky represented the entire ILGWU in relations with other unions in the United States and abroad, with large employers and employer associations, and with local, state, and national political leaders. He supported the concentration of power in the union hierarchy, held firm on maintaining male dominance in the union leadership, and was more interested in stabilizing the garment industry than in realizing an ideal socialist vision.

Dubinsky aimed to consolidate the authority of the union in the office of president. Almost immediately after he became president upon the death of Benjamin Schlesinger in 1932, Dubinsky moved to contain the autonomy of several locals. At the 1932 convention, he publicly accused Locals 1, 9, and 22 of mutiny. The locals had refused to pay a three-dollar tax per member to cover a $140,000 bond taken as a loan to finance the 1929 cloakmakers' general strike.[28] Communists won an influential number of seats on those locals' executive boards, giving Dubinsky an added motive to move against them. In early 1934, the International union's General Executive Board sustained charges against the officers and executive board of Local 9 for "illegitimate and consistent support of the dual union and by their incitement to and practice of sabotage and destructive tactics designed to undermine our organization."[29] The GEB barred local officers and board members from holding office and conducted a new election.

Dubinsky's pragmatism allowed him to be flexible. He tolerated dissent in the union within limits, but not division in the needle-trades' labor movement. His distaste for Communism was not ideological as much as it was political. He considered the Communists dual unionists whose intention was to destroy the garment workers' organization. So Dubinsky saw Zimmerman, a charming and talented organizer, as someone who would effectively diminish the threat of the dual union. Both Dubinsky and Zimmerman had an interest in building a vital and stable union, as well as in maintaining their own personal authority. Education was central to both of their efforts, so Local 22 and International education programs complemented one another for several years.

The Politics of Generation, Gender, and Race

The success of social unionism did not quell the doubts that older men tended to have about the seriousness of educational and cultural activities and about the leadership of women from all racial-ethnic groups. Just as in the late 1910s and 1920s, when young semiskilled women made up the core of the union's revolutionary wing and operated through educational activities, young women dressmakers embraced the education programs in the mid-1930s. Gus Tyler believes that the presence of radical militants and female members in Local 22 was the mixture that produced the extraordinary educational activities in Local 22.

> They were hot with the idea that you educate the working class. . . .
> They also understood that education doesn't mean just classes. Education means you get people involved. So Local 22 was on fire to get people involved. . . . Over the years, I've come to a conclusion that, between the two sexes, assuming that all human beings have a social instinct, women have a sharper social instinct than men. . . . Women have a feeling about socializing. I think it's almost a learned reaction on the part of men. . . .
> Men also socialize, but this was female organization in Local 22, and it was emotional. And people just wanted to be with one another. In addition to which they had leaders who wanted to educate the working class and make a revolution tomorrow morning.[30]

Tyler admired female militancy. But in his 1999 interview, he also reflected male leaders' long-held view that women's activism was emotional rather than rational, much as Louis Levine had characterized it in his 1924 history of the ILGWU.

Gender and age dynamics within the Jewish membership limited the reach of social unionism. In general, older men and younger women in the ILGWU assigned different meaning to their educational activities. Maida Springer-Kemp remembered that some older men resisted the social forms of organizing promoted by locals. They would ask rhetorically, "We organized the union by dancing?" She said, "You have to accept the mentality of those early pioneers" who saw social dancing and art classes as a "luxury." "They were so grounded in adversity and their earnings. . . . They were so marginalized, and they were so outside the general pale of the social system." Springer-Kemp acknowledged that women more than men saw the social aspect of union work as intricately tied to the political and economic work of the organization.[31]

An article titled "Impressions of Unity House Institute" that appeared in Local 91's newspaper *Our Aim* is a particularly stark example of the different meanings the same programs held for men and for women. Two members of Local 91's executive board, Max Heller and Olive Pearman, attended a five-day workshop sponsored by the International at Unity House in May 1935. Local 91 published articles written by each: Heller wrote "As a Male Sees It," and Pearman wrote "The Feminine Angle." Heller's account of the five days focused entirely on the classes he attended, which were impressive indeed. Joel Seidman from the Brookwood Labor College taught an economics class on labor under the National Recovery Administration (NRA). There were classes in English, parliamentary law, the economics of the ladies' garment industry, and public speaking. Heller was enthusiastic about his experience and urged that other members be given the opportunity to attend. In contrast, Pearman began her account by describing the bus trip from New York City. The members sang labor songs, popular songs, and various ethnic songs. She described the ethnic, gender, and skill makeup of the contingent. "There was a pretty little Italian girl asleep on the shoulder of a charming Polish miss. . . . Here a Cuban, Jewish, German, Negro quartette. . . . Cutters, truck drivers, pressers, and cloak makers, of whom most of our male section was composed were busy discussing . . . whatever truck drivers, cutters, etc. discuss."[32] Pearman, who was Black, wrote at length about the camaraderie across racial and ethnic lines. Like Heller, she expressed enthusiasm about the courses. In her account, however, we learn that the classes were "evening lectures which were a welcome interlude between a strenuous afternoon of rowing, hiking, handball, tennis . . . and an evening of dance and song."[33] Olive Pearman's account reveals that the union structured classes in the context of social, recreational, and cultural activities. Pearman came away from her stay at Unity House with the sense that the interracial and interethnic community of men and women workers created through intimate social activity was the foundation that supported the union's political and economic work. From Heller's account, we have no sense that he experienced Unity House in the same way.

Male leaders of the union remained ambivalent about women's rising authority, even while they encouraged women to take on leadership responsibilities. The experiences of Lillian Gaskin offer evidence that the culture of male leadership in the ILGWU made it as difficult for Black women as it was for Jewish women to advance in the union structure. Gaskin was an activist in Local 22 before the August 1933 strike and was among the first Black women to win election to the local's executive board. In early 1935, on Sasha Zimmerman's recommendation, David Dubinsky asked Gaskin to take an assignment in Chicago to organize Black women employed in several plants owned by Ben Sopkins.[34] The union's principal model for organizing outside New York City involved sending a veteran activist from New York on the road for months at a time. With few resources beyond their salaries, organizers found contacts and allies among local unions, churches, and other sympathetic organizations. Sometimes they would work in a targeted factory and build relationships with co-workers. They went door to door in unfamiliar neighborhoods, often without a local escort. It was up to the organizer to build a union movement. The work was often frustratingly slow and quite lonely. Gaskin left behind her friends and comrades during a critical local election, about which she regularly inquired. In one letter to her fellow executive board members after a month in Chicago, she wrote, "Accept my heartiest congratulations in the results of the recent elections. While I am not with you in the flesh, I assure you I am spiritually always with you. Many of you realize what it cost me to leave you in the midst of the campaign. But it was the call of duty to my fellow workers, and I answered it."[35]

Lillian Gaskin's progress reports show that she formed a social club for workers at Sopkins's plant, utilizing methods employed by other women organizers such as Rose Pesotta. Gaskin wrote, "Thru the club I was able to contact the girls and later started visit[ing] them in their homes, in this way I was able to get 8 girls to work for me on the inside."[36] As Rose Schneiderman had done as early as 1908, Gaskin worked through local clergy to reinforce sympathy for the union among Black workers on the South Side of Chicago. She spoke to various groups, including the Illinois Federation of Colored Women's Clubs, and built coalitions to support the organizing drive. After months of work building a union movement in the Sopkins factories, Gaskin wrote to Zimmerman in early September complaining that Dubinsky had replaced her with Abe Plotkin, a Jewish male organizer.

> Now that I have things running smoothly, the work is to be taken from me and turned over to Plotkin. I had a letter from the President today telling me to return to New York next week. Of course orders are orders, but just the same I don't feel that I am being treated fairly, I was taken from my job and sent here, and if you can remember I didn't want to come, and now that I've succeeded in getting a hold on Sopkins, it's give[n] over to Plotkin to undo all I've done.[37]

Gaskin's complaint was not unusual for women organizers in the ILGWU. Fannia Cohn saw her authority undercut time and again. Nevertheless, Gaskin resigned herself to returning and asked Zimmerman to see about getting back her old job in a New York garment shop. More than a month later, Gaskin wrote Zimmerman another letter in which she expressed a great deal of anger and resentment. She had spent four weeks with her parents in Brockton, Massachusetts, waiting for word on her status with the International. She was broke and had not received a paycheck for three weeks. She was confused as to whether she should keep up correspondence with Sopkins workers or to whom she should report. She remarked, "Please understand that I do not mind waiting, but I feel that I am being used as a cat's paw, and I am asking you to let me know just what is expected of me." She continued with a thinly veiled threat:

> There are several ugly rumors in New York about my having been sent to Chicago last March, I am trying to not believe that the International would stoop to such practices. I have been asked to ask the President just what the status of 6,000 Negroes in New York is in the International. I think it would be well for you to consider that point. You probably don't know that Negroes are fast refusing to support organizations or firms that refuse them proper representation or consideration. And I for one would dislike very much to see any disturbance in the union at this time. I am afraid that if you, as Mgr of Local #22 don't concede to some of the demands of the negro-membership, you will have a dual situation to deal with.[38]

Subsequent correspondence from Gaskin makes it unclear whether she was prepared to provoke a dual union among Black workers or to criticize the union among Black activists and organizations. She wrote another letter to Zimmerman almost two weeks later in a desperate but much softer tone: "Each week passes and I find myself in the same predicament. Winter is just around the corner and I am unprepared, I am sorry to bother you with my affairs but I know you understand me better than the others do, and I can say what I feel to you. I am sick and tired of borrowing from my people, I must continue to be self supporting."[39]

Zimmerman's response was measured. He had been away and received both letters on his return. He wrote that he was "rather surprised at the tone" of her letter but let her know that he had spoken to Dubinsky.[40] According to Zimmerman, Dubinsky said he had told Gaskin that the assignment in Chicago was temporary and that she had been recalled. Zimmerman asked Gaskin to refer further inquiries to the International. Gaskin replied simply that her questions were answered and that she did "not need to bother the President."[41] Instead, she inquired again about work in a garment shop.

Though Gaskin was in the employ of the International, not Local 22, Zimmerman's unsympathetic response and distant posture suggests a weakness in his leadership. Zimmerman cultivated Gaskin's activism in Local 22, but when he recommended Gaskin for the International organizing job, he apparently relinquished his mentor role. Union work demanded long hours, often disconnected from family and neighborhood community. Though the camaraderie of the movement and the social aspect of ILGWU organizing offered some compensation, it was lonely work. Women had a more difficult time than men did, with fewer options for companionship, and male officers and organizers had wives who played supportive roles at home. Women on the road rarely enjoyed the same benefits. Black women, with fewer support networks, were even more isolated than were their white sisters. Without acknowledging these conditions, Zimmerman provided little emotional or material support.

Lillian Gaskin's concern about whether she should continue correspondence with Chicago workers suggests an additional limit to the ILGWU's model of organizing. Gaskin was a rank-and-file activist, attracted to the union largely because it engendered a community of fellow workers. Union leaders encouraged organizers to build personal relationships and to form group bonds. They asked Gaskin to go to an unfamiliar city, to form social bonds with workers of her own racial group, and to convert them to the ideal of the union. The union then abruptly severed her ties to the community she helped form. Gaskin left Chicago worried that the workers with whom she formed relationships would suffer. Even if the union had made it clear to Gaskin that her work would only be temporary, the reality was jarring. In early 1936, Gaskin found herself living outside New York City, disconnected from the local to which she had devoted more than two years and cut off from the relationships she had developed as part of her job.

Frank Crosswaith's experiences differed substantially from those of Lillian Gaskin. In November 1934, Dubinsky turned to Crosswaith, a well-known Black organizer in the socialist labor movement, to lead the International's efforts to organize Black workers.[42] A powerful speaker and a prolific writer, Crosswaith had helped to organize the Brotherhood of Sleeping Car Porters. He was an ideal hire for Dubinsky. Crosswaith had been a member of the Socialist Party since 1915 and a confirmed anti-Communist. His long association with the Socialist Party was primarily through its Jewish wing. In October 1918, as the age of twenty-six, Crosswaith won a scholarship from the *Jewish Daily Forward* to attend the Rand School of Social Science. Like his friend A. Philip Randolph, Crosswaith admired the United Hebrew Trades

Figure 6.5. The ILGWU hired Frank Crosswaith as a general organizer in 1934 to work with the thousands of Black workers who joined the union the year before. The union supported Crosswaith, a gifted speaker and writer, as he founded and led the Negro Labor Committee in 1935. (Cornell University, Martin P. Catherwood Library, Kheel Center for Labor-Management Documentation and Archives, ILGWU Records, collection 5780pn45b3f116a)

and proposed as early as 1923 creating a United Negro Trades organization to unionize the masses of Black workers in New York and elsewhere. The organization he helped found in 1925, the Trade Union Committee for Organizing Colored Workers (TUC), depended on support from the AFL and individual unions that was not forthcoming. The TUC folded after little more than a year in existence. From mid-1929 to late 1934, Crosswaith worked full-time for the Socialist Party and was the only speaker the party put on national tour.[43]

Crosswaith was also a high-profile proponent of an important dissenting ideology within the Socialist Party, which resonated among Jewish socialists. He rejected the dominant position in the Socialist Party articulated by Eugene V. Debs, the party's standard bearer for twenty-five years, that Blacks should be organized into unions and into the Socialist Party strictly as workers. Debs argued that Black workers should not be treated as having any cultural distinction.[44] Despite the policies of some local branches, the national party did not officially embrace a platform of racial social equality even as it struggled for economic and political equality for Blacks.[45] Crosswaith supported the development of a race consciousness in the Socialist Party and urged leaders to become acquainted with Black newspaper editors and to sponsor forums on issues important to Black people. He urged Socialist Party leaders to develop structures that addressed needs peculiar to Blacks, similar to those programs in the Communist Party, such as a Negro news service.[46]

Crosswaith was the principal ILGWU spokesperson for Blacks and addressed numerous union meetings, conventions, and mass rallies. His articles in *Justice* drew attention to the progressive attitude of the Jewish unions in particular. "Those of us who are in the labor movement know that in the needle trades unions the Negro worker receives a square deal."[47] He taught classes in the ILGWU educational program, including "The Negro in American History," which followed Black accomplishments and contributions. In the strike mobilization during contract negotiations in the winter of 1935–1936, Crosswaith played a critical role in marshaling Black loyalty to the union. At a rally at the Manhattan Opera House drawing five thousand members in 1936, Crosswaith assured the gathering of the "solidarity of the Negro and White workers" and amplified the point in a *Justice* article, "Negro Dress Workers Ready for Battle," the following week. He stated that "the bosses in the industry used to count upon the unorganized Negro workers as their 'ace in the hole' to maintain low, debasing wages and long hour regulations." But now, he insisted, most Negro garment workers were in the ILGWU and were "ready for any eventuality."[48]

Crosswaith's sentiments were reinforced in several issues of *Justice* that highlighted Black dressmakers. In early January, the dressmakers' section featured "Sadie," who "was born in North Carolina and blessed with all the solemn guarantees of the august Constitution of the United States of America" yet "is made a stranger in her own country by race prejudice." She was a "step-citizen of the land of her birth, but she is a full citizen of the ILGWU and our Dressmakers' Union."[49] Two weeks later, "Fay," a Black woman from South Carolina, was also called a "step-citizen" of the United States but a full citizen of the union, because, Crosswaith wrote, "we despise the prejudices of race, color and creed that split the working class into warring factions and permit the Hitlers of the earth to lord it over millions."[50]

In 1935, with the backing of the ILGWU, Crosswaith founded the Negro Labor Committee (NLC), which he patterned on the United Hebrew Trades.[51] As the NLC suited Crosswaith's talents for thinking aloud on a broad scale, the ILGWU continued to pay his salary while he organized Black workers in Harlem. It is not clear how successful the NLC was during its four years of functional existence. Its sixteen-member board included at least seven from the ILGWU, one from the United Hebrew Trades, and at least two from the Brotherhood of Sleeping Car Porters.[52] Crosswaith was the primary spokesperson and organizer for the group. He spoke at numerous meetings in which Black workers were organizing themselves or being organized by various AFL and CIO unions. Although the Harlem Labor Center, where the NLC had its office, hosted a number of union-organizing meetings, Crosswaith seems to have exaggerated his accomplishments. He claimed at one point to have organized fifty thousand Black workers in Harlem, including four thousand who joined the ILGWU. But those workers had entered the ranks of the ILGWU a year before the union hired Crosswaith.[53]

Fundamentally, the UHT was an inappropriate model for the Negro Labor Committee. Originally, the UHT was created as a network of small unions populated by Jewish workers who had been ignored by or denied membership in the American Federation of Labor. These unions banded together to organize and promote the creation of similar unions within various trades. But the UHT operated within the larger context of the Jewish socialist and labor movements. The organization drew strength and support from the local newspapers and fraternal societies, then from the *Jewish Daily For-*

ward and the Workmen's Circle. Once some of those UHT unions bonded to form unions such as the ILGWU, the UHT continued to support the new amalgamation.

To have operated like the UHT, the NLC would have sought and received support from the *Amsterdam News*, the principal African American orogan in Harlem, and perhaps the National Urban League, which served functions similar to the Workmen's Circle and the settlement houses of the Jewish Lower East Side. But the *Amsterdam News* was ambivalent toward organized labor, having provoked a strike by its own employees in the mid-1930s.[54] Although several officials of the Brotherhood of Sleeping Car Porters sat on the Negro Labor Committee, including A. Philip Randolph, the BSCP did not appear to have solicited assistance from the NLC or from Crosswaith personally. Crosswaith concentrated on organizing Blacks into unions that represented white workers in their trade. But with the advent of the CIO, Blacks found themselves increasingly included in the new industrial organizations. The interracial unions that formed in mining, garments, textiles, rubber, steel, packinghouse, electrical, and auto manufacturing made the Negro Labor Committee seem obsolete.

The Politics of International Union Education

Within the ILGWU, education remained the principal force for organizing and maintaining a militant, cohesive, multicultural union membership. As David Dubinsky sought to consolidate power at the International level, he also put his imprint on education. After the summer 1933 strike, Dubinsky and the General Executive Board turned down Fannia Cohn's repeated requests for increased funding for the educational department.[55] However, wary of the new members organized into the union in the dressmakers' August 1933 strike, Dubinsky and other male leaders of the ILGWU remained dubious about union consciousness among the young women whom they dubbed "NRA babies." By the end of 1934, David Dubinsky recognized the need to build the International's educational program. Leaving Cohn with only marginal responsibilities, he poured substantial amounts of money into the educational department and hired new staff to coordinate programs burgeoning throughout the locals.

Dubinsky initially turned to men who shared the Yiddish socialist understanding of culture and politics. When he began to consider rebuilding the

International's educational department in 1934, he first approached Louis Schaffer, labor editor of the *Jewish Daily Forward* and a Socialist Party activist, and put him in charge of recreational and cultural activities.[56] Like Dubinsky, Schaffer was not an ideologue; he was more of a militant trade unionist. Gus Tyler called him a *coch leffen*, Yiddish for "mixing spoon," meaning someone who likes to stir up excitement. Schaffer was particularly fond of staging big events, such as demonstrations and pageants. He brought Tyler, his assistant labor editor at the *Forward*, to work with him at the ILGWU. When Schaffer hired Tyler at the *Forward* in 1933, Tyler had the feeling that Schaffer was already angling to move to the ILGWU. Tyler admitted to Schaffer in his job interview that he did not know how to write Yiddish and that his "grammar and spelling are very inventive," but Schaffer seemed to care more that Tyler was young, smart, and a socialist—the sort of person who would appeal to young garment workers.[57]

Nominally a subordinate to Fannia Cohn, Schaffer worked directly for Dubinsky. He began to direct the cultural activities of the International educational department and was responsible for building up the union's orchestras, choruses, and theater. Schaffer hired Lazar Wiener to conduct the ILGWU orchestra and chorus. Wiener had been conducting the Workmen's Circle orchestra and chorus and continued to hold posts there and in the ILGWU throughout the 1930s. He introduced a broad program of music to both organizations that included standard Yiddish music, Italian opera, Negro spirituals, and popular music, to foster an appreciation of musical cultures among the multicultural groups of union-member musicians and singers and their audiences. To the Local 91 chorus he directed, Wiener wrote,

> You have already learned that your only salvation lies in the unity you obtained by organizing with your fellow workers. Any further gains you can hope for must depend upon the continuance and strengthening of that unity. . . . The members of Local 91 who have joined the chorus in ever-increasing numbers have learned that great lesson taught by all workers' educational activities. They have learned to sing together just as they have fought together.[58]

The orchestras played at union-sponsored pageants, labor rallies, and in public performances at Carnegie Hall and Town Hall, helping to generate and publicize a multicultural union identity.

At the same time, Dubinsky worried about the changing ethnic demographics of the ILGWU membership, especially outside New York City and other urban centers. In the 1920s, the open-shop campaign among garment manufacturers accelerated, and many shops moved out of the city, first into New Jersey, Connecticut, and Pennsylvania and then further west and south. The ILGWU followed the shops into rural America and organized a new group of white, native-born, Christian workers. Gus Tyler remembered, "The membership now no longer was Jewish New York, Chicago, and Boston. They now had a thing called 'the shiksas from Shamokin' [a small town north of Harrisburg, Pennsylvania]. They were a symbol. . . . That was the new membership."[59] The majority of members remained in urban centers where Jews resided and included Chinese in San Francisco, Mexicans in Los Angeles, and Spanish-speaking workers in Puerto Rico. But Dubinsky believed, or at least traded on the perception, that white, non-Jewish workers represented a sea change that must

Figure 6.6. Lazar Wiener (top row, center), choral director for the ILGWU International chorus and the Workmen's Circle chorus, poses with the Local 91 choral group, which he also directed. (*Our Aim*, February 1935, 6)

Figure 6.7. Lazar Wiener periodically combined smaller ensembles to form the combined ILGWU orchestra and chorus, which performed at Town Hall on January 25, 1936, as a show of force during industrywide negotiations. (*ILGWU Illustrated*, published by the ILGWU educational department for the May 1937 Twenty-Third Convention in Atlantic City, New Jersey)

be attended to. The "out-of-town" locals in rural areas were crucial to Dubinsky's lock on power in the ILGWU. They all had small memberships, especially in comparison to Locals 89 and 22, and were isolated geographically from one another. Their links to the ILGWU were directly through the International offices. Each local had as many delegates to the International convention as did the large locals in New York and other cities. Contrary to Dubinsky's expectations, however, some new members were militant unionists. In Pennsylvania, for example, many white women came from coal-mining families with a long history of labor activism.[60]

To meet the needs of these new workers and to advance his own objectives, Dubinsky wanted a new education program directed by someone more "vital" than Fannia Cohn.[61] Dubinsky was embarrassed by Cohn's thick Yiddish accent, although he too had an accent. His main concern was ensuring that political moderates led the educational department. Apparently, Dubinsky asked Schaffer and Tyler to seek out an education director who had "general appeal."[62] Tyler suggested Mark Starr, a Welsh-born trade-union educator from a coal-mining family, who was teaching at the Brookwood Labor College. In 1935, Dubinsky hired Starr as director of the International's educational department in a deliberate move to undermine Fannia Cohn. Though Starr nominally became Schaffer's boss, Dubinsky wanted Starr to concentrate on classes and lectures, while Schaffer developed the theater and athletics. Fannia Cohn was "endlessly and bitterly resentful" that Dubinsky had passed her over in favor of Mark Starr as educational director.[63]

Soon after Starr took office, he froze Cohn out of the work he felt was most critical and recommended that Cohn be restricted to supervising museum trips, lectures for foreign-language groups, and the preparation of courses in union history and labor problems. In one memo, he added parenthetically, "Her continued overwork and nervous strain make it imperative to lessen her load."[64] Cohn was outraged and wrote to Dubinsky about the humiliation and mental torture she was forced to endure. While limiting her formal responsibilities, Dubinsky and Starr never overtly forbade Cohn from pursuing her activities, though they allotted her only a small budget. Gus Tyler had the impression that Fannia Cohn may have again used her own money to pay his and other people's expenses to take cross-country trips to do educational work.[65]

Deeply humiliated, Fannia Cohn nevertheless continued to push her vision for social unionism. Indeed, she began openly and unapologetically to advocate for women's leadership in the ILGWU and the labor movement through *Justice* articles and educational department literature. Her collected writings are a testament to her tenacious commitment to members, especially women, the ideal of the union, and education as the principal vehicle to realize that ideal. They also demonstrate her relentless challenge to male leaders' portrayal of women as weak and ill suited for leadership. The same year Dubinsky hired Starr, Cohn published a pamphlet in which she asked, "Can women have strong unions?" She argued that women had shown themselves to be "courageous fighters," having "struggled side by side with men" to build the union since 1909. Women, she suggested, may even be better suited for struggle: "Their endurance is greater than men's." Cohn declared that the union depended on men's support of women's activism. "The strength of unions therefore depends upon women's understanding and active participation. This can best be achieved if men, with their longer experience, will encourage women to take their place in their unions and in the labor movement."[66]

In a pointed article titled "Can Women Lead?" published in *Justice* in early 1936 and reprinted as a pamphlet, Cohn directly confronted the most offensive gender stereotypes held by men at the top of the International. She lambasted men for defining leadership according to "male qualities." She blamed male leaders for limiting women's leadership opportunities and promoting competition among women vying for what few places existed. She admonished men to create spaces for women leaders and exhorted women to demand those spaces. Cohn suggested that educational activities in the union gave women "new social and cultural values," which would lead women to make those demands and induce men to accept them.[67]

Despite the shortcomings Cohn pointed out, social unionism flourished during this period. Throughout 1934 and 1935, the union celebrated multiculturalism at social events such as dances. *Justice* reported that six thousand dressmakers and friends attended the Dressmakers' International Ball sponsored by the Harlem section of Local 22 on January 19, 1935. "Over the stage hung a huge banner showing dressmakers of various races, colors and nationalities parading through the garment district with arms upraised and fists clenched, marching on to victory under the flag of the union."[68] The parallel between the vigorous, coordinated movements of dancing and of strikers' pickets and marches was made clear visually. The power of social unionism to mobilize the multicultural membership of the dressmakers' locals came into sharp relief during the contract negotiations in the winter of 1935–1936.

The contracts negotiated during the great upsurge in membership two years earlier were set to expire on January 1, 1936. *Justice* reported that the United Dress Manufacturers Association presented demands such as mandatory overtime, elimination of a minimum wage, and the freedom to discharge employees that would have undermined the gains won in the 1933 strike. Members involved in every aspect of union activity were mobilized. In December 1935, the Local 22 Educational Committee established a council representing twenty-seven sports, social, and cultural groups with thirty-three delegates "to meet periodically to coordinate the work and exchange experiences," bringing the classes, athletic teams, and social clubs into the political structure of the local.[69] Among the delegates was Dorothy Tucker, who starred on the Local 22 basketball team and later went on to the Barcelona counter-Olympics. Underscoring the connections between sports and union militancy at the height of strike mobilization, a photograph of Tucker and her Local 22 teammates posing next to the Italian Dressmakers' Local 89 women's basketball team ran under the headline "Ball Tossers Talk General Strike" (figure 6.8). The caption noted that though the game had been hard fought, the "General Strike was the sole discussion subject after the last whistle."[70]

Figure 6.8. "Ball Tossers Talk General Strike." Athletic competition, militant unionism, and interracial solidarity come together in sharp relief during preparations for a general strike in 1936. In the mid-1930s the ILGWU women's basketball league included teams of mixed race and ethnicity, such as Local 22, and teams made up of one ethnic or racial group, such as the Italian Dressmakers' Local 89. ILGWU members had many options to socialize within their ethnic and racial groups as well as with members across groups. Dorothy Tucker is in the top row, sixth from left. (Cornell University, Martin P. Catherwood Library, Kheel Center for Labor-Management Documentation and Archives, ILGWU Records, collection 5780p, box 9, file 18)

Throughout January and into the middle of February 1936, *Justice* reported on the mass mobilization of the 110,000 union members employed in the New York City–area dress industry, demonstrating the integrated strategy of social and cultural programing, mutual culturalism, and militant unionism. Julius Hochman, as chairman of the Joint Dress Board, called a mass meeting at the Manhattan Opera House of building chairmen and Union Defender Committee (UDC) members in early January to coordinate the work of all local unions in preparation for a general strike. Local 89 had already mobilized six hundred members of the "Italian Union Defender's Committee." Manager Luigi Antonini stated, "We need vanguard groups for various union activities in peace time as well as in time of strikes. We also need defense groups against various enemies, above all the Fascists, who are trying to disrupt our unity." Local 22's UDC numbered one thousand members, formed at eleven neighborhood section meetings in December.[71] Five thousand members "stormed the doors" of the Opera House, eclipsing Hochman's prediction by two thousand members. Hochman, Antonini, Zimmerman, and Crosswaith, along with other union leaders, addressed the activists.[72]

Three successive meetings at Madison Square Garden with tens of thousands in attendance led to the settlement of contracts in February 1936, avoiding a strike. The contracts were signed in the office of Mayor Fiorello La Guardia, who sponsored talks between the union and the employers.[73] Even more impressive than the 1934 agreements, the three-year contracts held jobbers responsible for wages paid by contractors and limited the number of contractors that did business with the jobbers, undermining the auction-block system. Contractors were forbidden from moving their shops out of the nickel-fare transit zone, preventing shops from running away with the intention of making it more difficult for union members to get to work. Card-holding union members had to be hired first into available jobs. Dressmakers won recognition for union-management committees that under the new contract had the authority to demand admission to all shops to settle with manufacturers and jobbers on piece rates. But with the NRA finally put to rest in the spring of 1935 and the immediate challenges to the National Labor Relations Act (Wagner Act), which President Roosevelt signed in July 1935, the ILGWU required a citizen army of union members to enforce the complicated terms of the new agreements. In this respect, social unionism was critical.

In the immediate aftermath of the 1936 dress-industry negotiations, Starr and Dubinsky worked together to create a more professional standard for the burgeoning corpus of organizers, business agents, and local union executive board members. On March 2, 1936, Dubinsky gave a talk that was later incorporated into a mandatory "Training for Trade Union Service" course for new officers, conducted by the International's educational department. While Dubinsky gave a nod to the importance of officers' experience in strikes, most of the advice he laid out was about working in moderation with employers and friendly politicians, even when it is explicitly at odds with what the members think they want. He reasoned that while the successful leader "must study what the masses are saying, he must not be the blind expression of the mass wish. No leader can evade the responsibility of giving advice and of using his influence to guide the membership. He must give this advice and assume his responsibility even if it is in opposition to the popular view at the moment."[74]

Though the militancy of the rank and file won the unprecedented industrywide agreement, the International emerged stronger, more centralized, but more cautious and more predisposed to take a moderate path than ever. In negotiating contracts, Dubinsky warned, demands must be "rational and realizable, not Utopian, or else the employers will ridicule the whole program of the Union." Because of the "justice" of the union's demands, public officials such as Governor Herbert H. Lehman and Mayor Fiorello La Guardia "were anxious to conciliate the existing differences" between labor and employers during deadlocked contract negotiations. Successful negotiations depended on the good word of the union in upholding previous contracts, "even if the agreement . . . sometimes works to the disadvantage" of union members. Yet Dubinsky advised union leaders to be flexible in enforcing agreements "when the Union is weak or during periods of economic depression," even if it meant working longer hours than the contract called for. He acknowledged that in this approach the "rank and file might lose its morale. They may argue that you do not need a union to take cuts. However, the point is to keep the army together and to spread the organization over the whole field in preparation for labor advance."[75]

Politics of State Reform

Zimmerman and Dubinsky clashed over a number of important political issues, reflecting the contrast between militant local rank-and-file activism and the politically cautious centralized hierarchy. The settlement of these controversies came to define the union's identity as a workers' organization and its relationship to the state. The clearest marker of Zimmerman's and Dubinsky's divergent political views is their position toward the National Industrial Recovery Act (NIRA) and the federal agency it created, the National Recovery Administration (NRA). Dubinsky and others later credited the NIRA as the reason why nearly the entire dressmaking workforce answered the August 1933 call to strike.[76] Section 7a of the NIRA was the first federal acknowledgment that workers had the right to organize unions. Industrial-union leaders explained that their ability to claim that "the President wants you to join a union" was the single most important factor in labor's upsurge. But union activists and leaders, particularly on the local level, experienced many other factors that fueled the movement's rebirth, and many leaders responded to the NRA with a great deal of ambivalence.

Far from seeing the NIRA as the "Magna Carta of labor," as William Green famously called it, some local and International leaders voiced fears that the NIRA would strengthen the power of manufacturers.[77] The strike movement had been brewing in the locals since the spring of 1933, before the NIRA was announced, and a strike by five thousand dressmakers in Philadelphia in May 1933 anticipated the mass outpouring in New York in late summer. Militants in the ILGWU, especially in New York, pointed to the success in Philadelphia as a justification for devoting the union's limited resources to aggressive organizing. By the time NRA officials announced plans for a garment-industry code, the Joint Board of Dress and Waist Makers and the Communist Party's Needle Trades Workers' International Union (NTWIU) had been working for months, independently of each other, toward a general strike by New York's dressmakers in the fall.

Union officials treated the NIRA as a crisis as well as a blessing. Indeed, the front-page article in the revived publication *Justice* initially credited the seemingly spontaneous desire of garment workers throughout the country to join the ILGWU to the excitement inspired by the NIRA. But the International's official organ acknowledged the fear that employers were forming their own associations "for the purpose of railroading through a code" to ensure the continuation of sweatshop conditions. The paper called on workers to organize and to join the ILGWU "to save the dress industry from the unspeakable chaos into which it has been dragged."[78] David Dubinsky accelerated a date for a strike because the NRA was due to establish a code of hours and wages for garment workers in late August. Union leaders believed that if they could establish higher standards through direct negotiations with employers, they could demand higher minimum standards for the entire workforce in NRA hearings. With the triumph of the 1933 strike, Dubinsky turned toward the NRA with optimism.

Union leaders with closer links to rank-and-file organizing worried that Dubinsky and other International leaders were prone to dismiss the importance of militant local movements as they extolled the virtues of new state structures. Rose Pesotta argued that the young militants acting earlier in Philadelphia inspired the August strike in New York that year: "In the spring of 1933 the garment workers of notorious open-shop Philadelphia, driven by sheer intuition that the time is ripe for reorganization, quit work marching out in a spontaneous strike. This was a signal. That 'wash-out' as we called the Philadelphia general strike was ample proof that the courage and militancy of the girls is still strong." "Incidentally," she added, "this strike preceded with several months the NRA."[79]

During the August 1933 strike, the New York Joint Board of Dressmakers, which included Dressmakers' Local 22, Italian Dressmakers' Local 89, Cutters' Local 10, and Pressers' Local 60, issued a newsletter that was openly ambivalent about the NIRA. In the first issue of the *Organizer*, the joint board reprinted section 7a of the NIRA, advised workers to "read clause 7 carefully," and encouraged workers to use the provision that gave them the right to organize. They warned that the act gave employers the opportunity to set minimum codes of wages and hours without consulting labor. "No sooner had the bill been passed than employers of various industries began a feverish campaign to organize for the purpose of working out codes called for by this Act." In industries such as textiles and dry goods, employers submitted codes that the *Organizer* said "actually amounts to a maximum." Because workers in these industries had weak unions, or none at all, employers were the only voices heard in hearings to set standard wages for the workforce. The *Organizer* concluded, "In the final analysis the workers will receive only as much as they have the power to command."[80]

Rose Pesotta emphasized that the codes only established meaningful terms and conditions of employment if manufacturers were pressured by militant dressmakers. The codes would drag down conditions in the industry if left to the whim of manufacturers. She implored workers not to be distracted from organizing by the NRA and argued that those codes "supplemented but by no means supplant the collective agreements." She warned that section 7a "became an effective tool in the hands of the open shop company-union bosses, who used it and have planted more company unions than the labor movement ever knew before."[81] Indeed, the mechanism of the NRA often proved to be a useless framework for garment workers.

A few months after the August 1933 strike, David Dubinsky dispatched Rose Pesotta to Los Angeles to organize Mexican and white dressmakers. She formed an organizing committee among a small group of committed activists, began publishing a newspaper in English and Spanish, and broadcast a union radio show on stations in Tijuana, Mexico, and in Los Angeles. A mass meeting drew more than a thousand workers who agreed to a general strike, spurring the local NRA administrator to call for a meeting between the union and representatives of manufacturers. According to Pesotta, "After three sessions with them, nevertheless, it became clear to us that our manufacturers meant no business; in fact, they even balked at the suggestion that the words 'union' or 'ILGWU' should be inserted into the proposed agreement."[82] The negotiations continued even as workers struck and employers locked out other workers, and at the end of the season many workers lost their jobs.

Pesotta settled in for a long strike with only a few hundred workers. She created a commissary for strikers and their families, and later she added a relief store to provide weekly groceries. Pesotta found innovative ways to publicize the strike in the media through dramatic activities, including a Halloween party that ended with costumed children walking the picket line. After a core of about sixty firms signed agreements with the ILGWU, Pesotta established a multicultural program of educational activities.

Figure 6.9. David Dubinsky, ILGWU president, steps off the train in Los Angeles to greet vice president and general organizer Rose Pesotta during an organizing campaign in early 1934. (Photo by Arrow Studio, LA; Cornell University, Martin P. Catherwood Library, Kheel Center for Labor-Management Documentation and Archives, ILGWU Records)

We hope to win the members through educational work which has already begun. We hold classes in public speaking and parliamentary law, and later we shall hold regular classes in labor problems, labor literature, etc., in both languages, English and Spanish. We are also planning to hold social gatherings giving our members a chance to learn that a trade union is not all discussion but play and merriment as well. The girls will add color to these affairs—they all own evening gowns and dancing shoes.[83]

Like Pesotta, Charles Zimmerman distrusted the newly formed state apparatus to referee labor-management conflicts. At the union's 1934 convention, Zimmerman opposed Dubinsky's resolution to support the National Recovery Administration and presented a minority report denouncing it. Dubinsky later admitted resenting Zimmerman for taking this stand.[84] The incident fed Dubinsky's lingering suspicions of the former Communist. Just as the ILGWU's International leaders had embraced the Protocols of Peace a generation earlier, Dubinsky saw in the NRA the potential that union-management relations could be rationalized and that recent union gains could become permanent. He was prepared to cement alliances with liberal politicians and manufacturers who made it easier for him to stabilize the union. Increasingly, Dubinsky toned down his already mild socialist rhetoric in return for state guarantees protecting the rights of unions.

Zimmerman warned about accepting a partnership with the state. In the wake of massive grassroots agitation in 1934, epitomized by the San Francisco general strike, President Roosevelt proposed a "truce" between labor and capital, encouraging workers to allow the mechanism of the NRA to replace the disruptive act of striking.[85] Zimmerman inveighed against those who supported the NRA, implicitly criticizing Dubinsky, who took a public stance in favor of the act. Zimmerman warned against what he believed to be the same impulse that embraced the NRA and support for FDR's call for a voluntary pledge to refrain from going out on strike.

> The reckless and uncritical enthusiasm with which this proposal has been hailed in some quarters is certainly not the attitude likely to bring any good to the trade unions. . . . The strike is a weapon that labor must always have at its command and be ready to use it if its voice is to be listened to with respect in the councils of the employers. . . . Even when it comes to enforcing decisions of the NRA boards or government bodies, where such decisions are unfavorable to the employers, the threat of a strike has been found to bring better and quicker results than official prosecution which the employers usually and with good reason regard as an empty threat. The workers cannot, therefore, afford to surrender, even through [sic] voluntarily, temporarily or indirectly, the only weapon that has proved of any value to them.[86]

Zimmerman held his position against the NRA for several years. In a report on the status of Local 22 written in 1937, Zimmerman gloated about the union's success in spite of the NRA. He reminded readers that the local's leadership had warned about becoming complacent and relying on the mechanisms of the NRA to enforce conditions in the dress industry. "We emphasized that the only way to preserve our gains and make further advances was to unite our ranks, strengthen our Union and place our entire dependence upon our own organized might."[87] This stance enabled the union to remain intact and to continue to grow even after the NIRA was struck down by the Supreme Court in 1935. In the end, though these conflicting views over the NRA illustrated potentially divisive ide-ological differences, ILGWU leaders chose to cooperate with one another.

The U.S. presidential election of 1936 was the watershed moment in the transition from socialism to liberalism for Dubinsky and many other Jew-ish labor leaders. Dubinsky had been concerned with the direction of the Socialist Party since the advent of the Popular Front. Norman Thomas, an ordained Presbyterian minister and former conscientious objector, led the Socialist Party after the death of Eugene Debs in 1926. Thomas had entered the party first to work on Morris Hillquit's campaign for mayor of New York City in 1917 and first ran for office himself in the 1920s. By 1935, after two suc-cessive presidential bids, he had welcomed Communist Party members into the Socialist Party, which worried Dubinsky and other "old guard" socialists. In the New York City municipal elections that year, over two hundred thou-sand votes were cast for socialists. Franklin Roosevelt was concerned that Thomas could be a spoiler in New York State for the 1936 election and asked David Dubinsky, Sidney Hillman, and Max Zaritsky, among others, to form the American Labor Party (ALP), a "nonpartisan" party that would allow socialists to vote for Democrat Roosevelt for president, Democrat Lehman for governor, and Republican La Guardia for mayor. Citing the Communist influence in the Socialist Party and the fear that a Roosevelt defeat would see the collapse of the New Deal and be a blow to labor, Dubinsky asked the General Executive Board of the union to endorse Roosevelt. Zimmer-man and others balked, objecting to the violation of the principle that the union would not support any party representing capitalism, which had been central to the founding of the ILGWU. The GEB then passed a milder state-ment expressing sympathy with what was soon to become the ALP. Zimmer-man and others in the Jewish needle trades as well as A. Philip Randolph did support Thomas in the election. Soon after, however, particularly after the Supreme Court affirmed the Wagner Act, the coalition between Jewish needle-trades leaders and Roosevelt's New Dealers was cemented.[88]

Conclusion

The struggle for citizenship is at the center of the narrative of the ILGWU in the mid-1930s, but its rank-and-file members and its International lead-ers espoused different visions of citizenship in the workplace and the polity. The August 1933 dressmakers' strike followed the passage of the NIRA with language that promised to protect workers' right to organize. Whether gar-ment workers and organizers regarded the law as a wolf in sheep's clothing or as rhetorical ammunition, the dressmakers asserted their rights through the strike. While some leaders of the International union worried aloud about the supposedly unorganizable "NRA babies," including thousands of young Black and Hispanic women, the dressmakers' local seized on a campaign of promoting the full union citizenship enjoyed by these new members. Their embrace of members' racial-ethnic cultures was as critical to their idea of citizenship as was members' participation in union elections, organizing, contract enforcement, and strikes. Still, women were limited in the leadership positions they could assume, particularly at the higher levels. At the same time, with the advent of the NRA, union leaders sought an equal place at the table with government and industry leaders. Through the American Labor Party, Dubinsky and other leaders in the Jewish labor and socialist movements sought to influence the political direction of the city, state, and country. But union leaders' access to the political process came at the price of abandoning the multicultural foundations of the militant union that brought them to power.

PART III

7

From Yiddish Socialism
to Jewish Liberalism

The Politics and Social Vision of
Pins and Needles, *1937–1941*

Two months after the ILGWU opened its Broadway review in the refurbished Princess Theater on 39th Street, Brooks Atkinson raved, "*Pins and Needles*, performed by workers in the garment trades is witty, fresh, and box office." Noting the "sparkling" music and lyrics of the score, the *New York Times* theater critic called chief songwriter Harold Rome the "discovery" of the show. For many people in theater and labor, *Pins and Needles* accomplished what its creators hoped: a triumphant and exuberant expression of workers' and unions' place in American politics and culture. Atkinson concluded, "Most of the wit, humor, and sentiment that the review makers have assembled spring logically from the culture of the union garment workers who play it."[1]

What the show said about workers' culture embodied a swiftly changing set of ideas about race, gender, politics, and the labor movement. As a cultural product, *Pins and Needles* involved a complex combination of losses and gains for union members, especially for those who had embraced mutual culturalism. Atkinson hinted at that change when he praised several numbers written by Harold Rome: "'Doing the Reactionary' and 'Sing Me a Song of Social Significance' have done more than anything else to remove the Fannie Brice curse of 'rewolt' from the stagecraft of the labor movement."[2] Brice, the comic star of the Ziegfeld follies, was known for her exaggerated Lower East Side Jewish accent. One of her signature skits in the mid-1930s was a satire of the leftist choreographer Martha Graham in which Brice's character cries out in a Yiddish accent, "Rewolt!" *Pins and Needles* had no such ethnic signature.[3]

Producing Pins and Needles

Less than a year after David Dubinsky hired Louis Schaffer to take over the recreational and cultural activities of the International union's educational department in 1934, Schaffer focused his energies on an ambitious project to create a theater production company for the New York City labor movement. With Dubinsky's support, Schaffer brought the plan to the American Federation of Labor convention in 1935. Though a number of unions expressed interest, neither the AFL nor any individual union was willing to commit funds to finance the enterprise.[4] Anxious to proceed anyway, the General Executive Board of the ILGWU approved the full financing of Labor Stage Incorporated under the nominal direction of Julius Hochman, manager of the New York City Joint Dress Board and vice president of the ILGWU. Schaffer became the executive director.[5]

In the fall of 1935, Schaffer rented the Princess Theater on 39th Street and 6th Avenue, a location near Broadway and within the northern edge of Manhattan's garment district. The playhouse originally seated 499 spectators but was renovated in the summer of 1936 to fit 600 seats, and Schaffer had the upper floors of the theater converted to rehearsal and office space. The Broadway venue was central to Schaffer's vision: to create a show that would appeal to mass audiences, beyond union members and the working class.[6] Schaffer tapped the talents of Harold Rome, a Yale University graduate who had attended law school and studied architecture. Rome had written songs for Gypsy Rose Lee and worked at the Green Mountains resort in the Adirondack Mountains during the summer of 1935.[7] His lyrics touched lightly on social issues, and his music evoked the idiom of Tin Pan Alley: melodic, upbeat, and devoid of any specific ethnic or racial markers. Within a year, Rome had created *Pins and Needles*.

The Labor Stage production of *Pins and Needles* that drew Atkinson's plaudits opened on Broadway on November 27, 1937. In the original cast, with one or two exceptions, the forty-four actors were all union members who auditioned for the parts. The show, a musical comedy revue that poked fun at conservative politics, was unusually successful, becoming the longest-running musical in Broadway history until *Hellzapoppin* eclipsed its record.[8] *Pins and Needles* ran for more than two and a half years on Broadway with three companies, two of which also toured throughout the United States and Canada, and was performed at the White House. In the combined three-and-a-half-year run of the Broadway and national tours, *Pins and Needles* comprised close to fifty skits, most of which had musical numbers. Each show included between nineteen and twenty-two of these skits.[9]

Developments in international and domestic affairs and transformations in the Jewish labor and socialist movements influenced those changes in the program as skits were dropped and added. *Pins and Needles* was produced during the 1936 presidential campaign, when Dubinsky and other leaders of the Jewish needle trades formed the American Labor Party to back Roosevelt. Six months after Roosevelt's victory, the Supreme Court upheld the National Labor Relations Act (NLRA), or the Wagner Act, establishing for the first time a federal mechanism to enforce contracts signed in the garment industry. Though the ILGWU continued to engage in aggressive organizing and contract negotiations with employers around the country, the Wagner Act helped to balance labor-management relations. The NLRA guaranteed unions a legal process within which they could organize workers, negotiate multiyear contracts and mandatory union membership, and enforce the provisions of those contracts. For Dubinsky and Zimmerman, the war with garment manufacturers was over, and the U.S. government became the guarantor of the peace. For the manufacturers, peace with the union offered a greater degree of stability within the industry. Union officials and garment manufacturers developed a common interest in reducing the destabilizing influence of shop-level militancy. The show criticized the state only mildly, and numerous skits revealed declining commitments to shop-floor militancy, ethnic and racial diversity, and gender equity. Behind the scenes, the production of *Pins and Needles* reinforced an expanding cultural bureaucracy within the ILGWU that favored men, ignored racial injustice, assaulted ethnic and racial identity, and undermined the notions of equity fostered in the local unions' educational programs.

Conceived at the height of the Popular Front, the initial production of *Pins and Needles* revealed the ambivalence Dubinsky and Schaffer shared about Communists and the relationships they built among liberals and radicals alike. To direct the revue, Schaffer turned to Charles Friedman, who was best known for his leadership in the Workers Laboratory Theater (WLT) and its successor, the Theater of Action (TOA).[10] WLT/TOA produced some of the best-known agit-prop (agitation-propaganda) plays of the 1930s. Friedman was an unlikely choice for Schaffer, who made no secret of his rabid disdain for Communists and later vowed to rid *Pins and Needles* of any Communists he discovered.[11] The WLT/TOA was from its founding in 1929 closely associated with the Communist Party.[12] But Schaffer, who admired Friedman's skills and success, probably weighed the benefits of having a talented director working with politically moderate material against the likelihood that Friedman was a Communist or a fellow traveler. The Popular Front had taken hold, and Schaffer may have been willing to chance the participation of talented Communists as long as they behaved. Schaffer, who intended to earn a profit for Labor Stage and the ILGWU, must have been aware that Clifford Odets, an active member of the Communist Party, had produced three critical and financial successes on Broadway that year: *Till the Day I Die*, *Awake and Sing*, and *Paradise Lost*.[13] Charles Friedman quit on the opening night of *Pins and Needles*, and Schaffer replaced him with Robert Gordon, a well-known Broadway actor and playwright.[14]

Whatever the reservations of some union leaders, other leaders and many members enjoyed and supported plays written and performed by Communists. Communists and sympathetic allies such as Clifford Odets were leading lights in the agit-prop and workers' theater movements. During the summers, the union regularly sponsored Popular Front theater groups that included prominent Communist Party members, such as the Theater Union, producer of the play *Stevedore*. Albert Maltz, a founder of the Theater Union, wrote *Black Pit*, a dramatization of union organizing in the Pennsylvania coalfields.[15] During the summer of 1935, Unity House presented the Theater Union's production of *Black Pit* with the original cast, as well as Clifford Odets's *Awake and Sing*, while at least one local union produced *Paradise Lost* in its own dramatic group.[16]

Schaffer recruited other left-wing talent to help create *Pins and Needles*. He hired Marc Blitzstein to write a skit called "FTP Plowed Under." Blitzstein authored *The Cradle Will Rock*, an agit-prop musical about a strike in the fictional Steeltown, USA, produced by the Federal Theater Project (FTP) of the Works Projects Administration (WPA). He had watched as the WPA closed down the show on the day of its premiere in 1936.[17] Still angry about the treatment of his play, Blitzstein took the opportunity in *Pins and Needles* to criticize the WPA for engaging in censorship under pressure from the right wing. He joined the Communist Party sometime between 1936 and 1938, allying himself with other party members.[18] Arthur Arent, who headed the writing team for the *Living Newspaper*, another left-wing project sponsored and then abandoned by the Federal Theater Project, contributed a skit to *Pins and Needles*.[19] Lee Strasberg of the Theater Guild and Group Theater taught acting at Labor Stage to *Pins and Needles* actors and ILGWU members. In addition, Elia Kazan, Martha Graham, and Katherine Dunham all taught at Labor Stage.[20]

In the spring of 1936, Louis Schaffer recruited ILGWU members who were active in the union's recreational and cultural programs to audition for *Pins and Needles*. As director of the International's dramatic, athletic, choral, dance, and orchestral programs, Schaffer had a large pool of recruits to choose from. After Dorothy Tucker returned from the aborted Spanish Olympiad, she remembered, "I joined the choral group the union had and we gave a concert at Carnegie Hall. Schaffer naturally attended and he was surprised to see me there. He came up to me after the show and said, 'I didn't know that you could sing, I just thought you were an athlete.'"[21]

Union members and their families, some of whom had trepidation about the enterprise, acknowledged the new opportunities that *Pins and Needles* provided. Immigrant parents were wary of programs that kept their daughters in the city after work hours, but the benefits of education and the promise of higher wages sometimes overcame their concerns. Ida Mandel, a member of the original cast, recalled,

> My parents were European and looked down on performers. As a matter of fact, I was supposed to be a school teacher. Naturally my parents tried to discourage me. I explained to them that it was part of the cultural activity for the union. The fact that it was a Broadway play helped. Since my girlfriend's father was a Rabbi and she was able to go with his permission, my parents gave in. When they learned I would earn [Actors'] Equity wages, which were considered good at the time, they were sold. Another way I convinced my parents to let me get into the show was by explaining to them that while I couldn't afford to attend college out of state, I would be able to travel across the country and be continuously learning at the same time through real life experiences.[22]

The fact that the cast was composed of union activists gave the show a great deal of credibility, as well as trouble for its producer. Nearly half the original *Pins and Needles* cast came from Local 22, where members were used to voicing their opinions about labor culture.[23] Sasha Zimmerman and others encouraged the union members to make decisions for themselves on the form and content of their activities, and Schaffer had to confront a cast of union members who assumed they had a say in what would be produced at Labor Stage and how it would be done. After an early performance of *Pins and Needles* in the summer of 1936, a number of cast members complained that the play was too light on political and labor themes and demanded that the play express class consciousness more overtly. To save *Pins and Needles*, Schaffer agreed to produce John Wexley's *Steel*, which dramatized the struggles of the Steel Workers Organizing Committee. It opened in December 1936, while production and rehearsals continued for *Pins and Needles*.

A class-conscious morality tale, *Steel* depicted virtuous strikers pitted against scurrilous employers, their police lackeys, and immoral scabs. Wexley was well known to ILGWU audiences. His popular play about the Scottsboro case, *They Shall Not Die*, was produced in early 1934 by the Theater Guild and performed at Unity House in 1935.[24] *Steel* ran for fifty performances at Labor Stage, two shows each weekend.[25] It toured New York, Chicago, Pittsburgh, and the Midwest in March and April 1937 and played at the ILGWU convention in Atlantic City in May 1937.[26] The cast of *Steel* was drawn mostly from the Cutters' Local 10 dramatic group.[27] Like the steel workers they portrayed, the cast was almost entirely male. It is not clear how happy many members of the *Pins and Needles* cast were about *Steel*, since most were left out of the production. Nor is it clear if Schaffer invested in this production as a way of defusing a mutinous group of players. In any case, Schaffer was dissatisfied with what he said was the overly serious nature of *Steel* and continued to push for funds to produce *Pins and Needles*, a play he said was decidedly "amusement and not class conscious."[28]

On the basis of *Steel*'s success and performance at the convention, the ILGWU allocated money for the more lighthearted *Pins and Needles*.[29] Bent on producing as professional a show as possible, Schaffer held back the official opening of *Pins and Needles* for nearly a year and a half until he felt the cast, most of whom were still working full-time in the shops while rehearsing at night, was ready. He increased rehearsal time and, after a year, took the cast to Unity House for a free two-week stay, during which the cast rehearsed daily and performed for vacationing members and union leaders on July 4, 1937.[30]

Within weeks of the play's opening on Broadway, its success extended far beyond the New York labor movement. Theatergoers reserved tickets months in advance. At first, the shows played only on weekends, since most of the actors were still employed as garment workers. After Schaffer arranged to hire the actors full-time with pay, the production played a full week's schedule. Schaffer formed a second company to perform five-o'clock matinees for union members at reduced cost. The show's success on Broadway created a demand across the country, and the first company began a national tour in April 1938.[31] That tour ended January 30, 1939, after at least 319 performances in thirty-four cities, grossing $333,000 and netting over $80,000 for Labor Stage.[32] The company played for three weeks each in Philadelphia, Boston, and Los Angeles, six weeks in Chicago, and five weeks in San Francisco, with shorter stints in small cities throughout the country and in Ottawa and Vancouver, Canada.[33] After the first company took leave of New York City, the second company took over the evening performances, and Schaffer formed a third company to play the matinees. The final tour of *Pins and Needles* began when the show closed in New York on June 22, 1940, after 1,108 performances. The second road show ended nearly a year later in Los Angeles on May 31, 1941.[34]

David Dubinsky and Louis Schaffer were thrilled with the popular success of *Pins and Needles*. The show struck the right balance of memorable tunes and a social message that did not offend the liberals with whom Dubinsky sought a political alliance. A two-page spread in *Life* magazine in December 27, 1937, confirmed the popularity of *Pins and Needles*, particularly among the middle classes. The article noted that critics applauded the show's "gay disarming propaganda, its racy wit, its novel capacity to laugh at Labor as well as Capital."[35] A whole page was devoted to a skit called "Vassar Girl Finds a Job," with a song called "Chain-Store Daisy," about downward class mobility. The Vassar girl, played by Ruth Rubinstein, enters the job market with high hopes of a professional career but laments that the only job she can find is in Macy's corset department. She sings, "I had a yearning for all higher learning and studied to make the grade. For subjects pedantic I shunned the romantic, and look at the kind of grade I made." Ironically, Rubinstein and the ILGWU players were proof positive of the expanded opportunities opened up through workers' education. In 1936, the CIO established the Department Store Organizing Committee (DSOC), chaired by Amalgamated Clothing Workers president Sidney Hillman, and launched an organizing drive among Macy's employees. DSOC signed its first contract covering several departments in Macy's in 1939 and continued to organize department-store workers through the run of *Pins and Needles*, raising the standard of living for the workers represented in "Chain-Store Daisy."[36]

The show poked gentle fun at the wealthy "carriage trade" in one of the few skits showing workers on strike, called "Lesson in Etiquette." A wealthy society matron advises union members in a song called "It's Not Cricket to Picket." But it was precisely to this class that Labor Stage meant to appeal. While by all accounts thousands of union members and their families saw multiple productions of *Pins and Needles*, the show could only be sustained by middle-class theatergoers. *Pins and Needles* appealed to entertainment and political celebrities and other major public figures. The ILGWU proudly published photos of Edward G. Robinson, Paul Muni, Frank Morgan, Mayor Fiorello La Guardia, Governor Herbert Lehman, Eleanor Roosevelt, and Albert Einstein attending performances.[37] While the broad popularity of the show underscored the excellence of the comedy, score, and acting, the professionalization of *Pins and Needles* changed the culture of education in the ILGWU.

Figure 7.1. *Pins and Needles* poked gentle fun at the middle-class audiences that came to see the show. Undated, circa 1937–1940. (Lucas and Pritchard Studio, Cornell University, Martin P. Catherwood Library, Kheel Center for Labor-Management Documentation and Archives, ILGWU Records, collection 5780p, box 27, file 22)

The Decline of Local Union Education

At the end of 1937, Local 22 began to reduce and narrow the purpose of its education programs. The local's education director, Will Herberg, left for a position in the International union research department and was replaced in October 1937 by Lewis Corey, another member of the Lovestone Communist faction. Corey, also known as Louis Fraina, expressed his intention to limit social and recreational programming.[38] Corey dramatically reduced the number of classes offered after the 1936–1937 school year. Local 22 offered 120 classes for 1935–1936, 102 classes for 1936–1937, and only 29 classes in 1937–1938, abandoning many of the classroom-based courses that promulgated the ideology of socialism. The local ended its athletic, music, and drama groups in the 1939–1940 school year. Corey argued that there was a difference between adult education and workers' education, or that which is of "value to the individual alone and what is of value to the individual and the union."[39] He maintained that the union must concentrate only on those activities that aim "to provide workers with the knowledge and culture what will directly aid in the organization and struggles of labor."[40] He illustrated the point in reference to dancing: "Stage, modern and tap dancing may be used for exhibition purposes at union meetings and entertainments, hence it is of value to the union. But social or ballroom dancing is purely individual, hence it should have no place in a union education program."[41] Contrary to

Julius Hochman, I.L.G.W.U. Vice-President, backstage at Labor Stage with Albert Einstein

Figure 7.2. Publicity photo of Albert Einstein meeting with Julius Hochman (front left, in jacket and tie), head of the New York Dress Joint Board and international vice president, with *Pins and Needles* cast members looking on. In a departure from previous union activity photos, no Black cast member is pictured in the group. (Photographs by Harry Rubinstein, Vandamm and Katherine Joseph, "Pins and Needles Presented by Labor Stage with the ILGWU Players," Cornell University, Martin P. Catherwood Library, Kheel Center for Labor-Management Documentation and Archives, ILGWU Records, collection 5780pubs, box 23, publication 437)

the ideas Fannia Cohn and others cultivated in the union over the preceding two decades, Corey did not conceive of workers' participation in social and recreational activities as important in and of themselves. In Corey's view, these activities were only ornamental.

While Corey restricted Local 22's educational programs, the International increased its offerings with more moderate aims than the Local 22 activities had before 1937. The General Executive Board authorized an expansive educational department under Mark Starr, and by the end of 1937 its programs outnumbered those offered by Local 22. The International's curriculum tended toward caution, underemphasizing concepts of class struggle. For example, International classes to train officers replaced local classes designed to mobilize masses of workers for organizing and striking. Union members who enjoyed arts and ethnic culture with a supportive community of co-workers increasingly competed in International union educational programs for a chance to perform professionally in popular entertainments staged by the union.

Labor Stage created opportunities at the expense of local union political culture. The production of *Pins and Needles* redirected the paths of rising union militants away from more radical political roles they might have otherwise assumed. Dorothy Tucker, the second African American union member to join the cast of *Pins and Needles*, came to the attention of Louis Schaffer in part because of her Local 22 political activity. Local education programs began to close as Labor Stage opened its doors. Ruth Rubinstein came to Labor Stage reluctantly, only after Local 32 canceled a modern-dance class she had taken for a year.

> We would come faithfully once a week—I think it was on a Tuesday right after work—and we'd have this class, and we'd go home. And suddenly, without any warning, we came, and they told us this was the last class, . . . no more. There were only about five or six of us, and it wasn't worth their while. They didn't say that exactly. And they weren't paying her [the teacher] that big a wage too. . . . [A union official told the students,] "If you're interested in [dancing], go to Labor Stage." The first we ever heard of it. It hadn't been publicized in the Union. He says, "Go to Labor Stage; they have all kinds of activities there." So we did![42]

While *Pins and Needles* occupied the limelight, Local 22 continued to produce other plays in the late 1930s written and performed by union members. The local union performed these plays largely in union or community environs, involving members at every level of production, including script and lyric writing. The plays had a greater capacity for militant interpretation by performers and audience members. Ethel Kushner, a cast member of *Pins and Needles*, nevertheless joined other union members who lamented the effect *Pins and Needles* had on local union culture. Kushner articulated a strong argument against the commercialization of labor theater. In an article titled "Build a Labor Theater," Kushner touted *Sew What*, a musical that she wrote and that the Local 22 theater company produced, as a collective venture created almost entirely by union members.[43] Echoing Fannia Cohn and the Rebel Arts Players, Kushner argued that labor theater must be created collectively by workers and derived from their own experiences:

> That our people have the desire, the will and the ability to do so has already been proven in a way. I speak of our labor revue, *Pins and Needles*. But the true labor theater I speak of carries the experiment a good deal further. We need no professional writers, professional directors, professional scenic designers and costumers, and we look for no great monetary returns. We are not competing with Broadway.[44]

Cast Struggle

Increasingly, International programs in dramatics, chorus, modern dance, orchestras, and even athletics became a proving ground for members who aspired to the professional ranks of the *Pins and Needles* cast. Instead of acting for their own edification or to build a union movement, members in union education programs began to compete for recognition. One program for *Pins and Needles* explained that in dramatic classes "beginners are taught how to act, receiving instruction in all the necessary fundamentals—diction, body movement and dramatic expression. When they have mastered these basic principles, demonstrating that they have done so in one-act plays which they hope to put on, they are moved up to the central acting company, the ILGWU players."[45] In chorus, the program says, union members are taught how to read music. "Whenever a promising singer is spotted, he is given a scholarship with a well-known vocal teacher."[46]

Union members found themselves in competition with one another and with outsiders who used deception to gain access to the singing, dancing, and acting classes. Education programs that had been constructed on a foundation of cooperation and class cohesion began instead to advance an unhealthy adversarial and cliquish spirit. Lee Morrison, who was not a garment worker, was attracted to Labor Stage because Katherine Dunham was staging dances in the later productions of *Pins and Needles*. Morrison took dance classes that were supposed to be for union members, but he got in through a union connection.[47] Irwin Corey used the union card of his friend's father and pretended to be him. He then created a "stage name" for himself, using his real name.[48] The competition led to ill will between casts and among various groups. Ethel Kushner noted, "The first company was not only upset about the ringers, but they were even intimidated by the new members of the cast who were legitimate ILGWU members. I felt a great deal of resentment from them."[49] Kushner, who had at one point replaced several first-company cast members and had the most solos, blamed Schaffer for the bad feelings among members. "There was always this resentment between the first and second companies—mostly on the first company's part because Schaffer fostered it. He told them that he had replacements for each and every one of them and if they did not do what he asked them to—they would be replaced."[50]

Despite the public image created by *Pins and Needles*, behind the scenes labor relations between the cast and the executive director who produced *Pins and Needles* involved a struggle between a union-conscious membership and a boss who fought for control. The show purported to demonstrate issues sensitive to garment workers, while the cast was losing its voice. When *Pins and Needles* resumed production after the close of *Steel*, cast members continued to assert their right to a partnership in decision-making. Ruth Rubinstein Graeber remembered that when Harold Rome and Louis Schaffer chose her to do "Chain-Store Daisy," some cast members objected that she already had two solos while other cast members had none or only one. Rubinstein Graeber said she volunteered to refuse the piece. "I was a good union member. I didn't want to do anything antiunion."[51] But Harold Rome and Louis Schaffer held firm. Rome threatened to pull the number from the show if Rubinstein did not do it, and Schaffer threatened to fire anyone who continued to object.[52] The tensions between the production team and the actors were well known. The 1937 *Life* article noted with amusement, "twice the actors, displeased with their material, staged sit-down strikes during rehearsal."[53] Louis Schaffer increasingly asserted his role as the boss, demanding control over production and the perks that accompanied his status. When the show later moved to a larger venue, Schaffer oversaw renovations of the Windsor Theater that included an apartment for him, his wife, and his daughter.[54]

From the beginning, Schaffer encouraged the auditions of "ringers," actors with professional experience or training with aspirations toward professional careers in the theater. In the original *Pins and Needles* cast, only Al Eben and Paul Seymour were not garment workers. The two obtained union membership cards for the purpose of joining the cast of *Steel*. Eben's father was ILGWU Local 117 Manager Louis Levy, a vice president of the International, and a member of the Unity House committee that had sponsored many theater programs for the union during the summer.[55] With the close of *Steel*, Schaffer hired Eben and Seymour for *Pins and Needles*.[56] Soon after *Pins and Needles* opened on Broadway, Schaffer began to add ringers, eventually replacing most of the cast of original garment workers. Some of the professionally minded actors did go on to pursue stage or screen careers. Gene Barry, who went on to star on Broadway, in movies, and as television's Bat Masterson, was probably the most famous actor to start in *Pins and Needles*. Irwin Corey, who made a career as a character actor in the persona of "Professor" Irwin Corey, also began his career in the second company of *Pins and Needles*.[57] Nettie Harari Shrog had a successful cabaret-singing career in New York City until the mid-1950s.[58]

Schaffer's motivation for replacing the garment workers with professionally minded actors was likely as political as it was artistic. ILGWU officials called the road cast "The Ambassadors to Labor." In many of the cities in which the show toured, local ILGWU and other union groups threw dinners, banquets, and parties for the cast. The show served to illustrate for unions around the country a new image of organized labor less concerned with workplace confrontation and more with achieving security through cooperation with the state. In spite of the shift toward a more moderate political agenda, the message in *Pins and Needles* was still centered on the lives of workers. But a banquet in San Francisco during the show's stay in that city during 1938 called into question the purpose of the *Pins and Needles* tour.

The *Pins and Needles* cast complained when ILGWU Local 341 officers arranged a formal dinner for them at a prominent Chinese restaurant in the heart of San Francisco's Chinatown. Ruth Rubinstein Graeber remembered, "The local gave us this wonderful dinner in a Chinese restaurant, the best I ever had in my life. . . . We found out afterwards, and I was furious, the members were taxed a dollar each toward the dinner for us. Isn't that horrible? And who was invited? The bosses, the Chinese bosses."[59] Most of the workers in the San Francisco local union made the minimum wage in the union contract of fourteen dollars a week. If the dollar levy for the dinner was true, it was a harsh burden. It was particularly insulting that union officials had invited few Chinese workers to the dinner. Like the performances in Manhattan that catered to the middle class, the dinner demonstrated that

Pins and Needles was at times as much an ambassador *of* labor as it was an ambassador *to* labor. In this case, it was a union showcase aimed more at the garment manufacturers than the workers.

Suppressing Race and Ethnicity

The climactic moment for *Pins and Needles* as an emblem of the ILGWU's political and cultural liberalism came on March 8, 1938, when a truncated cast played a command performance for Franklin and Eleanor Roosevelt at the White House. Dubinsky did not tell the cast about the White House event until the day of the performance and, on behalf of the cast, refused the president's invitation to dinner after the show. According to one cast member, Dubinsky was afraid the cast "wouldn't know how to act, or know which fork to use."[60] The White House production pointed up one of the dearest concessions ILGWU leaders made in building a relationship with the state and its more conservative constituents. Dubinsky, violating the spirit of racial equity that permeated many of the local unions and his own earlier actions, chose to omit Olive Pearman, the only African American in the cast at the time, from the White House performance. Pearman concluded quite simply, "I was eliminated from the show because I was black."[61] Ironically, Eleanor Roosevelt would not have minded Pearman, having invited African American opera star Marian Anderson to the White House three years earlier.[62]

Through *Pins and Needles*, Louis Schaffer worked to re-create the image that Dubinsky desired. In contrast to dramatic programing in the Dressmakers' Local 22, Schaffer made no real attempts to ensure that Blacks and Hispanics were well represented in the cast. Initially, Olive Pearman was the only Black person in the show, though she had only a supporting dancing role and worked as the company seamstress on the road.[63] Schaffer added more African Americans to the show only after the cast pressured him to do so. There were no Hispanics in any of the three companies, in spite of a ready pool of Puerto Rican and other Spanish-speaking union members who were engaged in union dance and choral programs. In contrast to plays such as *Stevedore*, *Pins and Needles* ignored all references to race issues.

Schaffer was particularly concerned that *Pins and Needles* not be seen as upsetting local sensibilities as the show toured Chicago, San Francisco, and Los Angeles. When local customs dictated segregated accommodations, Schaffer capitulated. Schaffer and his Labor Stage staff repeatedly warned the cast that they would not tolerate public dissent regarding the show's management policy in these matters. He threatened cast members with dismissal for

Figure 7.3. Cast members pose for a photo at the White House with Franklin Delano Roosevelt and David Dubinsky (seated, left). The truncated cast and performance excluded Olive Pearman, the only African American actor in the cast at the time. ("Command Performance of *Pins and Needles* in White House, March 3, 1938," ILGWU Justice photo by Katherine Joseph, Cornell University, Martin P. Catherwood Library, Kheel Center for Labor-Management Documentation and Archives, ILGWU Records, collection 5780/102, box 3, file 15)

walking out of a restaurant in Denver that refused Pearman service. In 1938, Schaffer and the road manager, Sam Schwartz, insisted that Olive Pearman and Dorothy Tucker, the only other African American in the cast, observe the Jim Crow culture in Los Angeles hotels. Pearman and Tucker stayed in a hotel miles away from the rest of the cast when the show played in Los Angeles—just four years after Dubinsky had led the union's entire convention delegation out of a segregated hotel in Chicago. Nettie Harari Shrog remembered the reaction when some cast members found out that Pearman and Tucker could not stay with the rest of the cast in the hotel: "We were going to picket the place and make a big to-do about it." But Schwartz heard about the plans and called Schaffer, who "thundered back at him and said, 'Anybody who does that is going right back to New York, and a replacement will come in.'"[64]

Olive Pearman withstood the humiliation of Jim Crow segregation longer than any other cast member did. Pearman was the only African American to open *Pins and Needles* and the only one to begin the road show. In the ten-month run of the first road show, Pearman frequently had to find her own accommodations in neighborhoods far away from the theater and from where the rest of the cast stayed. Occasionally, Pearman was lucky to room with friends or relatives; in Philadelphia, she stayed with a cousin.[65] Still, Pearman recalled her role in *Pins and Needles* as one of the most extraordinary and wonderful periods in her life.[66] Two letters she wrote home reveal the depth of her experiences. In Ottawa, Canada, Olive Pearman and the cast met the mayor and visited the Canadian Parliament. She wrote about meeting her "mother-in-law," actually the mother of her fiancé, Bob Avant, and her future sister-in-law while playing in Chicago. Avant, who was also African American, was active in the Chicago teachers' union; he and Pearman had met at the Brookwood Labor College.[67] She wrote about all the dresses she made on the road, for herself, family, and cast members,[68] and about the parties and banquets that she attended in Chicago and Los Angeles.

Pearman was able to enjoy herself and to help out her family with the money she made from the show. The *Philadelphia Independent* reported her income and expense money at thirty-five dollars plus seven dollars per week.[69] In one letter, she sent fifteen dollars for her younger brother's graduation. In addition, she told her mother, "Take a picture of Reg for about $2.50. . . . I'll pay for it. And buy him an autograph book. I think they cost .89 or a dollar. And if he needs a class pin and picture, get it."[70] Nevertheless, life on the road for Olive Pearman was often a profoundly lonely existence. When personal tragedy struck, Pearman found herself miles away from any friend and thousands of miles away from family. Within a few days after writing that letter to her mother, Olive Pearman received word that Bob Avant had died.[71]

White cast members in both road companies found ways to show support for Pearman, Tucker, and Dorothy Harrison, another African American who toured in the second road company. Cast members, sometimes in groups of up to thirty, continued to walk out of restaurants that refused service to Blacks. In at least one instance, Herman Rosten, a member of the second road tour, remembered how he used dancing to confront the Jim Crow policy of one dinner club. When the cast arrived with Dorothy Harrison, the maitre d' claimed to have lost their reservations. Rosten persisted, and the maitre d' took him aside and said, "You're a nice Jewish boy. You should realize we can't let you in with the shvartza."[72] Rosten deliberately raised his voice and threatened a lawsuit. The management then let them in with the understanding that the group would sit in the back and agree not to dance. "So we went in and the first thing I did was to dance with Dorothy Harrison. Nobody left the dance floor, nobody left the club and nobody gave a shit. We all had a wonderful time."[73]

When local customs and Labor Stage management permitted, Olive Pearman and Dorothy Tucker roomed with white cast members. During a five-week run in San Francisco, Pearman and Tucker roomed with Nettie Harari and Ruth Rubinstein. Harari, a second-generation Syrian Jew, and Rubinstein, a Polish Jew, developed deep relationships with Pearman and Tucker that lasted their entire lives. Their apartment in San Francisco was the venue of numerous social and political gatherings. Harari Shrog remembered that they would cook dinners for people they met on the road. Rubinstein Graeber recalled that Harry Bridges, the left-wing organizer of the longshoremen's union, used their apartment at night for meetings when the women were doing the show.[74]

Union members in the cast continued to find ways to resist Schaffer's authoritarian leadership, particularly in regard to race matters. Dorothy Tucker said that union members, backed by director Robert Gordon, pressured Schaffer to have a Black actor sing a number. Schaffer finally relented by creating a humiliating character for Tucker.

> Finally they decided to have me do a new number called "Mene, Mene, Tekel." But they had me dress up as a mammy, and I really wasn't the mammy type so they hired a ringer, Dorothy Harrison, and she did it. But we really got on Schaffer's back and made him change the concept. (I really yelled about that; I was a militant then.) Eventually we won and Harrison didn't have to do it as a mammy.[75]

Chafing against the careerist attitude Schaffer seemed to foster, Tucker was more concerned about the representation of Blacks in the union production than she was with her own success. She gave up the opportunity for a coveted role to ensure that African Americans would not be shut out of the production, then worked to keep Blacks from being denigrated.

Some white cast members were insensitive to the extraordinary difficulties faced by the few Black cast members on the road. Ruth Rubinstein Graeber remembered one day when other cast members were impatient at having to wait for Pearman and Tucker before the cast left for a party in their honor hosted by Gypsy Rose Lee at her Malibu house.

> Some of the men were getting very irritated, and they said, "Oh, let's leave! Why should we wait? That's terrible! Let them find a way to get there by themselves." So some of us were real angry. [We] said, "Look! They're way out in Watts. The buses don't run very often. They have to take a bus to come into town." So we waited, and they finally came. And we could have taken some of those men and hit them.[76]

Figure 7.4. Louis Schaffer wanted a "mammy" role in the show. He hired Dorothy Harrison in part because of her body type. The cast objected to the stereotype. Schaffer relented but managed to include stereotyped images in the number, "Mene, Mene, Tekel." Harrison plays a Christian preacher warning about totalitarianism. The Aramaic song, taken from the Book of Daniel, was a metaphor for the Soviet invasion of Finland. Nazi swastikas adorn the bottom of the backdrop to blend the images of Russian and German aggression. The images on the backdrop appear to be in blackface. (Photographs by Harry Rubinstein, Vandamm and Katherine Joseph, "Pins and Needles Presented by Labor Stage with the ILGWU Players," Cornell University, Martin P. Catherwood Library, Kheel Center for Labor-Management Documentation and Archives, ILGWU Records, collection 5780pubs, box 23, publication 437)

By the time *Pins and Needles* went on the road, the cast included several actors who had never worked in the garment shops and were never schooled in local union attitudes in confronting racial injustice. Though some actors did have a sense of race equity through associations with radical groups outside the ILGWU, others did not. In Harry Merton Goldman's rich oral history of *Pins and Needles*, the only two cast members who remembered being uncomfortable with Blacks were ringers who did not come out of the ILGWU culture.[77]

Pins and Needles did open some opportunities for African American artists. Archie Savage, a Black dancer with Katherine Dunham who later performed in *Pins and Needles*, noted that "Dunham's first professional New York show was due to Schaffer. He produced her dance group's Sunday night concerts at the Windsor Theatre when *Pins and Needles* was dark."[78] Dunham later choreographed new dance numbers for *Pins and Needles*, which brought more Blacks into the show. These aspects of the show did celebrate Black culture, though Dunham and her troupe, including Savage, Randolph Sawyer, and Alice Sands, were professionals, and their entrée came at the expense of Black and Hispanic union members who had little or no access to the stage.

Pins and Needles reflected a declining interest on the part of International officers in appealing to the multiple cultures of union members. They played down the presence of African Americans, ignored Hispanics altogether, and undermined Jewish ethnicity. Louis Schaffer was intent on demonstrating to the public that the ILGWU was not an ethnically Jewish union. Schaffer and his staff persuaded actors to change their Jewish-sounding names, pressured women to surgically alter their appearance, and replaced "Jewish-looking" actors. At least two actors changed their names. One remembered, "The press agent, Lee Mason, decided I should change my name from Hyman Goldstein to Hy Gardner. Eventually I made it legal. Sylvia Cohen became Sylvia Cahn."[79] Many cast members were aware of Schaffer's intentions from the beginning. Al Levy, an original cast member, said, "We managed to get it across with our accents. But eventually Schaffer weeded out those people with thick Jewish accents. People who looked Jewish were also weeded out."[80] Both Nettie Harari Shrog and Ruth Rubinstein Graeber said that Schaffer asked them to get nose jobs, and Ethel Kushner remembered that Lynne Jaffee had a nose job during the run of the show.[81] Schaffer insisted that one cast member wear her crucifix prominently in performances. Rubinstein Graeber remembered that Schaffer "wanted to show that not everybody's Jewish" in the cast.[82] It is not clear how even an oversized emblem might be detected by theater audiences, but Schaffer was concerned with the public appearances and publicity photographs. The gesture could not have been lost on garment workers with fresh memories of having to suppress their Jewish identities to get factory jobs.

Jewish cast members in *Pins and Needles* had little choice but to forgo religious observance, even on the High Holy Days. Labor Stage produced shows on Friday nights, Saturdays, and Jewish holidays. Ruth Rubinstein Graeber remembered that the first road show began the tour on the first night of Passover. This schedule provoked tensions for cast members from observant families. Rubinstein Graeber recalled that her father stopped speaking to her for a month or two after she played on Yom Kippur.[83] Since the production company made no provisions for kosher food, observant cast members such as Eugene Goldstein had to make do with provisions sent through family and by eating only vegetables in restaurants.[84] One cast member remembered with some derision when families bid farewell at the train station with all kinds of Jewish food.

> When we left New York and started the road tour the parents of the cast members came with bundles and bundles of food for them. Most had never been west of the Hudson. They were fairly ignorant and they came from old world families. They asked themselves how do you eat on a train? Our poor children will starve. After all, they thought, there were no dining cars on subways! So they brought food. They brought chicken, chicken soup, chali bread, bottles of pickles, bagels, matzos, kishka, knishes, bottles of borscht and a hell of a lot more. Boy did that train smell like a delicatessen![85]

While he might have been ridiculing the scene, it nevertheless demonstrates the anxieties some families felt about the show's competition with their ethnic culture.

Amelia Bucchieri's memories indicate that shop workers involved with *Pins and Needles* blended the show's music and the multicultural tradition of the local unions and continued to have an effect even on members who were not enrolled in classes or participating directly in union programs. Bucchieri is the American-born daughter of a French-immigrant father and an Albanian-immigrant mother. Though she began working in the garment shops in 1932 and participated in the dressmakers' strike of 1933, she did not participate in the union's educational or social activities until after World War II. She remembered that during the 1930s there was always a great deal of excitement in the shops generated by members who were involved in the union's chorus and various plays, including the ILGWU's Broadway production *Pins and Needles*: "They would practice in the shop, those that were in the chorus. It let us know what they were going to sing. And they always made sure that we had to come and see them. . . . But their voices were beautiful, and people were happy in the shops, and they sang all day long, . . . whether it was an Italian song or it was a spiritual or it was a Jewish rhyme."[86] Bucchieri learned the songs and idiomatic expressions from various cultures, including Yiddish. "I got to know all the Jewish sayings, and I still know them."[87]

From Yiddish Socialism to Jewish Liberalism

The changing libretto for *Pins and Needles* reveals the shifting ideology of the ILGWU leadership and the larger Jewish labor and socialist movements as world events moved closer to world war. If the initial production had an anthem, it was

"Men, Awake!" written by Harold Rome. The song evoked the show's all-male production team: Louis Schaffer, the executive director who reported to ILGWU vice president and Labor Stage president Julius Hochman; Harold Rome, who wrote most of the lyrics and all of the music; Sointu Syrjala, who designed the sets; the first director, Charles Friedman; and the second director, Robert Gordon. Despite the history of women's militancy in building the ILGWU, the song called to men. It was a martial ballad with rhetoric that closely resembled "The Internationale," the anthem adopted by the Communist Party but also played throughout the Left, including in ILGWU locals. Local 22, for example, opened its mass meeting to install new officers of the union in April 1934 with "The Internationale" and "Solidarity Forever."[88] Less militant than "The Internationale," "Men, Awake!" nonetheless alluded to common revolutionary themes. Suggestive of *The Communist Manifesto* and replete with references to class oppression, the first verse implores workers to act in their class interest:

> Workers, all! Heed my call!
> You who toil and sweat and slave,
> From the cradle to the grave!
> You who strive with hand and brain!
> You who live in fear and pain!
> You who slumber! Countless number!
> You in mines and fact'ry stalls,
> You within the sweat shop walls,
> You in life's forgotten heap,
> You who sell your souls for keep! men, awake!
> Heed the warning! men, awake!
> The day is dawning!
> Break the chains that keep you bound
> and trample to the ground the barricades that hem you 'round![89]

Though "Men, Awake!" calls for workers to "Break the chains that keep you bound," there is no direct reference to a violent confrontation. "The Internationale" refers to a war against tyranny and threatens that if need be, "We'll shoot the general on our own side." The most common refrain vows,

> 'Tis the final conflict,
> Let us stand our place
> The International working class
> Shall be the human race!

"Men, Awake!" articulated the socialist agenda at the moment it was written in 1936, when Dubinsky and others began to leave the Socialist Party. Socialists were still committed to the idea of abolishing the ills of sweated labor and poverty, but they were less certain about the methods to achieve those goals. Dubinsky and other leaders in the Jewish labor and socialist movements had been pushing the socialist agenda further away from its revolutionary goals throughout the 1930s. By May 1939, union officials, who had by then fully embraced New Deal liberalism, felt that world events made "Men, Awake!" too incendiary, and Schaffer pulled the number.

In 1937, *Pins and Needles* began to articulate the changing emphasis from class-conscious socialism to cross-class liberalism within the Jewish labor movement, a shift from Yiddish socialism to Jewish liberalism. In this period of the show's run, from 1937 to 1941, leaders in the Jewish labor movement were casting about for language to define their changing relationship to capital and the state. Louis Yagoda, organizing director for the increasingly prominent English-speaking branches of the Workmen's Circle, argued, "The ideology of the early Workmen's Circle was brought into it by idealists and radicals who had received their training in the arduous camps of political parties and revolutionary movements."[90] But by 1940, the socialist parties were weak and fractured: The American Communist Party suffered from defections and the sudden demise of the Popular Front after the Nazi-Soviet Non-Aggression Pact was made public in August 1939, just before Germany invaded Poland, precipitating the Second World War. Some members of the Socialist Party, such as Dubinsky, left with the formation of the American Labor Party. Important to the ILGWU, the Lovestone Communist Party Majority Group made the unprecedented move in American radical history to formally disband itself in 1940. In order to "sell" what Yagoda termed "Circle-ism" and socialism to younger Jews who were a generation removed from czarist Russia, he said, "the E-S [English-speaking section] organizer, aware of deep-dyed prejudices against stereotyped words and phrases has devised a phraseology which puts across our social usefulness without frightening shibboleths, yet without diluting our meaning."[91]

Yagoda was signaling Jewish labor elites' increasing abandonment of militant and revolutionary socialism. The opening number of the play for the first two years, and one of its enduring hits, was "Sing Me a Song with Social Significance," a love song in which a young woman warns her suitor that she will not love him unless his songs have social content. The song itself was devoid of any social analysis; the most striking element of the song was the title. "Social Significance" was a euphemism for something other than socialism. Rome and Schaffer's "social significance" did more than distract from the language of socialism generally and Yiddish socialism specifically; it signaled the orientation of a newly emerging liberal agenda that would replace the socialist agenda.

From the early days of the ILGWU, garment production, militant union building, and consumer actions, such as the rent strikes and food boycotts and riots in the first decade of the twentieth century, were inextricably linked. Capitalism was condemned for creating "wage slavery." As ILGWU leaders moved toward liberalism, they began to deemphasize union members' identity as producers. Throughout the run of *Pins and Needles*, skits and numbers gave shape to the ILGWU leadership's notion of social organization. Civilization became increasingly equated with a form of benign capitalism in which bosses and government treated workers with fairness and workers enjoyed a middle-class lifestyle. However, *Pins and Needles* did not present a vision of society in which workers made economic decisions. Musical numbers more often appealed to workers as individual passive consumers, not as organizers of boycotts and not as militant producers. As Harry Merton Goldman notes, in the number "Economics I," the scene "uses a Rube Goldberg chain reaction to satirize America's capitalistic system. What starts out as a bank policy filters down through manufacturer, wholesaler, and retailer until, finally, it's the consumer who gets it in the end."[92] The worker is conspicuously absent from the equation. In the number called "The Pluto Boys," a skit that Schaffer added for the second road company after the Broadway show closed in June 1940, commercial advertisements dressed as devils sing, "We're the ads, and we scare the daylights out of you. We make you buy our products."[93]

These references were balanced by warnings against the seductions of wealth and privilege, lest workers aspire *too* high. In "It's Better with a Union Man," Bertha, a sewing-machine operator, is lured away from her shop-floor lover by a polygamist who offers her champagne and caviar.[94] In this number and others, the show portrayed women as naive, vulnerable, and as objects of sexual desire. In "One Plus One Equals One," produced for the second national tour, the dismissal of Bertrand Russell from the City College of New York for allegedly sleeping with his students is satirized. In the clever number "Dear Beatrice Fairfax," a woman laments that despite buying all the products that are, according to their advertisements, supposed to make her attractive to men, "nobody makes a pass at me." While these skits satirized the advertising industry and the workplace, the songs expressed women's longings to attract men, rather than expressing aspirations for economic and social justice. Few numbers placed members in the shop or complained about industrial conditions. Numbers that did show women at work depicted the workplace as a venue for romance rather than a crucible of class consciousness.

Boss gives secretary dictation, in "1+1=1," the Bertrand Russell sketch

Figure 7.5. The workplace was generally depicted in *Pins and Needles* as a place to frolic rather than a locus of class struggle. 1940. (Photographs by Harry Rubinstein, Vandamm and Katherine Joseph, "Pins and Needles Presented by Labor Stage with the ILGWU Players," Cornell University, Martin P. Catherwood Library, Kheel Center for Labor-Management Documentation and Archives, ILGWU Records, collection 5780pubs, box 23, publication 437)

Pins and Needles expressed the newly dominant ideals in the ILGWU, the union's place in the New Deal coalition, and a view of foreign affairs similar to that of President Roosevelt. In "Four Little Angels of Peace," Hitler, Mussolini, an unnamed Japanese general, and Britain's Chamberlain are lampooned and criticized for their propensities toward militarism and imperialism. Each is treated to harsh satire. The Chamberlain character sings,

> Though we butchered the Boers on their own native shores and slaughtered the Irish no end
> Though in India we're sore slaying horde upon horde we were playing the part of a friend
> Yes our arms we increase, but we're really for peace, except in the case of a crook
> We conquered both spheres, now we're up to our ears, just trying to keep what we took.

The hostility that *Pins and Needles* expressed toward Britain for almost two years in "Four Little Angels of Peace" was also found in the skit "Britannia Waives the Rules": "Chamberlain and his colleagues in the British Cabinet" sing, "We're afraid of going red, so we spend our time instead playing potsy on the Nazi-Roman axis."[95] After the Stalin-Hitler pact in 1939, Stalin became the fourth angel of peace, replacing Chamberlain.

Months after Hitler invaded Poland on September 1, 1939, Roosevelt expressed a desire to stay out of the European conflict militarily. By September 1939, in addition to dropping the Chamberlain character from the "Angels of Peace," Schaffer dropped the "Britannia Waives the Rules" sketch that criticized Britain's part in appeasing Hitler.[96] In November 1939, Schaffer added the sketch "Stay Out Sammy" to *Pins and Needles* on Broadway. In the number, Dorothy Harrison warns her son Sammy not to go fight in a gang war that has erupted in the neighborhood.[97] The song echoed the sentiments of many Jewish American socialists. Most were disgusted by British and French appeasement of Germany but also favored staying out of Europe's war, just as most of them had done during World War I.

Many socialists still saw the war as a competition between imperial powers. Though the United States was not formally committed to the Allies, socialists were still anxiously expecting that Roosevelt would engage, as evidenced by the cartoonist Bernard Seaman, a journalist whose work was ubiquitous in the 1930s and 1940s in ILGWU's *Justice*, the *Forward*, and other Jewish labor publications. A January 1940 Seaman cartoon appeared in the *Call* depicting the

United States at the crossroads of war and peace.[98] Uncle Sam scowls at a waif-like personification of civilization who has lost hope for the prospect of peace and survival. The United States, Seaman argues through the cartoon, was abandoning civilization on the road to war. *Pins and Needles* closed in New York and began the second road show on June 22, 1940, the day Vichy France signed an armistice with Nazi Germany. During that summer, the Roosevelt administration began to sell Britain military equipment through third-party private companies, and in September he issued the executive order authorizing an early form of lend-lease that included the transfer of outdated destroyers to Britain in return for leasing long-term naval bases in Newfoundland and Bermuda. Reflecting these new developments, the second road tour dropped "Stay Out Sammy" and added the number "History Eight to the Bar," which called for intervention in the war.[99]

Many prominent Jewish socialists sided with the Roosevelt administration in its growing support for war. During the 1940 presidential election campaign, the Jewish Labor Committee (JLC) and the Workmen's Circle published their endorsements for Franklin D. Roosevelt. The JLC, which David Dubinsky helped to found and served then as treasurer, cited the Nazi threat

Figure 7.6. In early 1940, the Jewish labor and socialist movements were still split on the question of American entry in World War II, demonstrated by this cartoon of Bernard Seaman's, whose work was ubiquitous in the ILGWU, the Workmen's Circle, and other Jewish socialist publications. (Bernard Seaman, *Call*, January 1940, 3)

in Europe as the primary reason why the Jewish people must support FDR and entry into World War II. They declared, "The wealth of America must be put at the disposal of the defense of America."[100] They warned of a "fifth column," presumably referring, among others, to Communists who were supporting the Nazi-Soviet pact, whom they condemned as "the defenders of dictatorship, of tyranny, the inciters to racial hatred, the preachers of human inequality." Any mention of capitalist exploitation was conspicuously absent from their invective. This was an appeal for a cross-class united front against fascism, and the JLC was reluctant to alienate manufacturers and politicians who might otherwise be willing to finance the JLC's objectives.[101]

In making the case for a formal alliance with the liberal-democratic state and supporting Roosevelt in the 1940 election, the National Committee of the Workmen's Circle spoke directly to the majority of members who identified themselves as socialists.

> We have always urged our membership to support those political parties that stand for the abolition of the private ownership in the means of production, and for the establishment of a social order based upon freedom, equality and justice. . . . But the forthcoming Presidential election must be viewed in the light of the seriousness of our times. We must do everything within our power to render secure the well-being, the freedom, and the progressive ideals of the people of America, of the Jewish masses, and of the peoples of Europe in their struggle for safety, for life itself and for political democracy. It behooves us, therefore, to support the candidacy of Franklin D. Roosevelt, . . . who has manifested . . . his belief in democratic institutions, his devotion to the ideals of freedom, his hatred of reaction and totalitarianism.[102]

These statements laid out the framework for the Jewish liberal agenda for the next forty years. More than the 1936 election in which the ILGWU leadership first supported FDR, the 1940 election demonstrated the hope of the Jewish labor movement for a partnership with capital and the state in international as well as domestic affairs. Through that partnership, Jewish labor hoped to gain some access to American wealth to combat "totalitarianism," not to redistribute wealth. Words such as *totalitarianism* supplanted class-based language and created a hierarchy of oppression inside and outside of capitalism. Workplace exploitation became a less immediate concern for some Jewish socialist leaders in the face of fascism and, later, Communism.

Like others in the Jewish labor movement, leaders in the ILGWU sought ways to redefine their identity to reflect a moderating politi-

Figure 7.7. By mid-1940, David Dubinsky and other Jewish socialist leaders were resolved to support American entry in the war, constructing a historical narrative of American wars for freedom and democracy, through pageants such as *I Hear America Singing*, performed in Madison Square Garden at the 1940 ILGWU convention in New York City. (Cornell University, Martin P. Catherwood Library, Kheel Center for Labor-Management Documentation and Archives, ILGWU Records)

cal and social agenda derived from American liberalism rather than Russian-Jewish socialism. In 1940, Schaffer produced a pageant for the International convention called *I Hear America Singing*, which Labor Stage performed in Madison Square Garden for thousands of union members and others. Hundreds of union members acted, sang, and played in the union's orchestra as they performed the poetry of Walt Whitman put to music. A markedly different interpretation of Whitman than Cohn's staging of "The Mystic Trumpeter" thirteen years earlier, the pageant illustrated a steady march of American democracy from the Civil War to the present. On stage, a company of soldiers carrying a sign that read "The Great War" stood among the icons of freedom and democracy in the pageant. A union claim to American citizenship on behalf of its members, this pageant belied a more complex history of Jewish socialism and American foreign policy during World War I, when Socialist Party members of the ILGWU leadership and a significant number of rank-and-file activists in the union opposed U.S. participation in World War I.

Debate on the merits of isolationism reached a feverish pitch among factions within the Jewish socialist and labor movements. In a January 1941 letter published in the Workmen's Circle's *Call*, one member argued, "On the single meaningful issue of our generation, the defense of freedom, [Socialists] are on the side of the dictators. An isolationist policy has placed them there. It has placed them there as unmistakably as the Hitler-Stalin pact has done the same thing for American Communists."[103] So on the eve of the U.S. entry into World War II, ILGWU leaders worked to reinvent their ideological heritage in a way that positioned them as loyal citizens to support intervention in the current widening conflict.

For May Day 1941, only a few months before Pearl Harbor, August Claessens wrote a column in the *Call* that marks the rhetorical abandonment of a Jewish socialist vision.[104] Claessens was a standard-bearer for the Socialist Party for decades who resolutely protested World War I, arguing that the war was being waged against the interests of the world's working class. In 1919, Claessens was one of five Socialist New York State assemblymen banned by the assembly for "disloyalty during the war." On the eve of World War II, however, he called for a "truce in the class struggle."

> We may as well temporarily accept our capitalism as the best of all possible worlds in the face of what our comrades are suffering in the totalitarian lands. . . . Our capitalism always was and always will be our enemy and the obstacle to the fulfillment of our dreams of an orderly economic and social system but it is acceptable and endurable in contrast to the hell of Nazism, Bolshevism and Fascism. The wage system, the exploitation of the worker, slums, waste, degradation, economic disorder and misery become but minor ills in the sight of the plague now devastating the world. An American slum dweller is an aristocrat in modern comfort compared to the British family in the subway or bomb shelter.[105]

He goes on to make several more comparisons between the plight of the most marginal in American society and the greater sufferings of Europeans. He argues that the fight of American Jewish unionists is "for the moment, not for Socialism but for civilization, not for Social Democracy but just plain democracy."[106]

Conclusion

As the ILGWU became more powerful, Dubinsky saw the opportunity for the union to become an architectural partner in the construction of a liberal welfare state, rather than a vehicle to assume state power. As Dubinsky consolidated his authority in the ILGWU between 1937 and 1940, he looked at the political possibilities in the greatly expanded ILGWU and the cultural expressions of the union's educational department activities in a very different light than had social union visionaries such as Fannia Cohn, organizers such as Rose Pesotta, or local union leaders such as Sasha Zimmerman. On the eve of U.S. entry into World War II, the ILGWU was in the strongest position in its forty-year history. Union officials enjoyed close personal ties to Mayor La Guardia, Governor Lehman, and President Roosevelt, whom they were twice instrumental in reelecting. The Wagner Act helped the union rationalize labor-management relations in the ladies' garment industry, and the union continued to grow steadily. Communists ceased to be a serious rival in the ladies' garment trades. *Pins and Needles* was a sensation, becoming part of the popular American cultural lexicon.

The 1905 generation of young Jewish revolutionaries asserted their citizenship rights in the union and the community from the bottom up. From the 1910s through the 1930s, women's voices were amplified, and union activists explored mutual culturalism in programs directed by Fannia Cohn, at Unity House, and in local unions. While Yiddishism was transmitted through folk culture and workers' theater, the expression of American union citizenship in the New Deal state was facilitated through professionally produced popular theater. As union leaders centralized resources in the International education programs, the question of citizenship was expressed through the top-down production of *Pins and Needles*, but the cultural participation of ethnic-group members was ignored. The voices of Jewish immigrants, Blacks, Hispanics, and women were muted. The New Deal delivered more rights for union members, but with less direct say. The ILGWU professionalized its representatives, insisting on formal leadership-training classes, and increasingly turned to lawyers as stand-ins for organizers. When *Pins and Needles* opened in 1937, already non-Jews occupied the two most important union education positions in the International and in Local 22. In the end, in *Pins and Needles*, professional actors stood in for most garment workers.

Along with a growing rejection of socialism, leaders in the ILGWU increasingly abandoned the strategy of promoting the membership's diverse cultural heritages. The International union continued to support ideas of racial integration through educational, social, recreational, and cultural activities, but within a cosmopolitan cultural context. The union continued to showcase individual Blacks, for example, and to support important movements for civil rights. But the International educational program began to emphasize unanimity of culture and to promote an image that was decidedly American: English speaking, Anglocentric, and an expression of contemporary popular culture.

Epilogue

Cosmopolitan Unionism and Mutual
Culturalism in the World War II Era

Ideas of mutual culturalism that were derived from Yiddish socialism and integral to the practice of social unionism appealed to people on the margins of society: sweatshop workers, unskilled and semiskilled factory workers, immigrant Jews and Italians, Hispanics, African Americans, and women. But leaders of the ILGWU felt themselves moving from the margins of society to its center after their success in rebuilding the union and participating in Roosevelt's New Deal coalition, most importantly with the 1937 Supreme Court decision upholding the National Labor Relations Act. The context within which social unionism had meaning for leaders such as Sasha Zimmerman changed. The Communist Party diminished as a serious competitor to socialists and non-Stalinist Communists in the ILGWU during the Popular Front period. As ILGWU leaders gained access to political power, they began to accept the dominant American culture, which was English speaking; celebrated class mobility and middle-class consumption; encouraged leisure as a personal or family endeavor; and promoted individual solutions to social problems. Jewish leaders began to subordinate distinct ethnic cultures to a national American culture, abandoning one of the principal tenets of Yiddish socialism.

Mutual culturalism remained the dominant tendency in the Jewish labor and socialist movements, including the ILGWU, until passage of the Wagner Act stabilized labor relations and reduced the need for shop-floor militancy. Once the union leadership believed they no longer required the same level of rank-and-file activism, they did not feel the same urgency to appeal to workers as members of distinct racial-ethnic cultures. The relief of political tensions within the ILGWU eased competition between left factions, making International officers less intent on encouraging local educational programs, particularly those that promoted the celebration of dis-

Figure E.1. These young women are socializing under a banner that expressed the ILGWU's economic and social agenda during World War II. Union goals narrowed from a broad social agenda and celebrating a "union of many cultures" to pure and simple unionism of jobs, wages, and a dominant "American" culture. Undated. (Photo by Harry Rubenstein for *Justice*, Cornell University, Martin P. Catherwood Library, Kheel Center for Labor-Management Documentation and Archives, ILGWU Records, collection 5780p, box 9, file 8)

tinct racial-ethnic cultures. With the fate of millions of European Jews at stake and an impending world war, union leaders began to identify themselves and their political aims very differently. Moderate political ideas gained traction among Russian Jewish leaders, including a preference for cosmopolitan multiculturalism.

The radical political and social agenda of the Jewish labor movement was transformed into a more liberal agenda beginning around 1937 and accelerating through World War II. The ILGWU began to promote a singular American working-class identity at the expense of multiple cultural identities, and the CIO strategy that Lizabeth Cohen calls the "culture of unity" dominated the ILGWU's cultural agenda after 1937.[1] Led by President David Dubinsky and the General Executive Board, the power center in the ILGWU shifted from semiautonomous locals to the International. With only a few exceptions, male leaders kept women, who were critical activists in the locals, frozen out of power on the International level. The ILGWU often discouraged women from taking leadership roles. By the late 1930s, union leaders increasingly sought to build a union affinity rather than a class consciousness among their members and tended to appeal to members more as passive consumers than as militant producers. David Dubinsky and Mark Starr depoliticized education by promoting the International union's retreat, Unity House, as a place of recreation, rather than as a model for cooperative organization. The ILGWU, like the rest of the Jewish labor movement, maintained a strong commitment to civil rights and racial justice but abandoned many of the cultural mechanisms that built racial-ethnic understanding between workers and celebrated national and cultural distinctions.

With the advent of World War II, Local 22 and the International drastically changed the focus of their educational programs. The departments geared programs toward inculcating patriotism and reinforcing more restrictive gender roles. On May 20, 1942, the Education Committee of Local 22 reported, "Since war was declared, the policy of the Education Department has been to organize as many classes as possible to enable our members to be prepared in the National Emergency."[2] Local 22 offered classes in first aid, home nursing, and nutrition and formed the Women's Health Brigade. The International turned Labor Stage into a canteen where servicemen could dance with female ILGWU members. In the 1930s, the Union Defenders Committee (UDC) included many women whose vigilance maintained gains won through strikes and contract agreements. When union leaders reorganized the UDC for civil defense, they recruited men almost exclusively. In these ways, union leaders emphasized women's role as valuable supports to

Officers' Qualification Course in session. 1948

Glamour with the Union Label.

Strikes, new model.

Figure E.2. In this photograph from 1948 educational department literature, only men are seen taking an officer's qualifying course. Women are taking a class in design or fashion. The class is likely part of a curriculum training workers for professional work in the industry. The message is that men are suited for union leadership, while women can hope for better-paying jobs outside the ranks of the union. The woman on the right is bowling, with a caption reading, "Strikes, new model." In this context, bowling is not an activity of social cohesion to build a militant union but a diversion, both for women playing and for men watching. (Report of Educational Department, ILGWU: June 1, 1946–May 31, 1948, YIVO Institute for Jewish Research, Bund Archives, ILGWU collection)

the work of men in battle, rather than as empowered union members working to shape their own destiny.

For Jewish leaders, ideological changes came in degrees. Roosevelt's Four Freedoms—freedom of speech and expression, freedom of religion, freedom from want, and freedom from fear—were vague enough to be subject to radical social-justice interpretations.[3] In 1942, one activist, still struggling to rationalize support for FDR and the war, wrote in the *Call* that Roosevelt was a "humanitarian capitalist" who was in fact helping the cause of socialism with the New Deal and in his opposition to Hitler.[4] Jewish socialists thus supported the war enthusiastically. On Saturday, June 13, 1942, two and half million people lined 5th Avenue for more than eleven hours to view half a million participants march up 5th Avenue in the "New York at War" parade. ILGWU members, as they had done for so many May Day parades and strike rallies, showed up en masse. Several hundred members of the Wom-

Figure E.3. In this 1942 "New York at War" parade float, union members demonstrate their multiple ethnic cultures, as they did in 1934. But here, American military action and world war, not international workers' militancy, is the dominant theme. (*Justice*, July 1, 1942, 6)

en's Health Brigade marched in patriotic formation wearing white nursing uniforms with red and blue capes. As they had done in the 1934 May Day parade, dramatic floats expressed the political and racial-ethnic views of union visionaries. One float depicted a cannon constructed out of a giant needle and spool and covered with lists of war materials and garments manufactured by union members. Another float was a large replica of Abraham Lincoln seated at the Lincoln Memorial and guarded by one Black and one white soldier. The third float, titled "Americans All," was a globe surrounded by "flags of the United Nations" and flags representing the Four Freedoms.[5] The American flag was prominently displayed in front of the globe. Union members held ribbons attached to the globe, just as they had done with the 1934 May Day float. According to *Justice*, "Each marcher was in full national costume representing her nation of origin."[6]

In constructing and presenting these floats, the union was making an unmistakable assertion that the goal of racial equality was achievable through a fight against Nazi Germany. The union was defining the American fight as a movement that supported and was supported by multiculturalism. In these respects, the 1934 May Day and "New York at War" floats expressed similar themes. But in 1942, military mobilization became a surrogate for militant union building. A global struggle between democratic and humane capitalist states on one hand and fascism on the other became a surrogate for international class struggle. No longer did a socialist vision or a struggle to improve conditions of life and labor convey the blueprint for workers' liberation. The union defined World War II, like the Civil War, as the vehicle to achieve full citizenship for all racial-ethnic groups. In this context, the national costumes of union members were worn to demonstrate loyalty and subordination to the American nation, not as a defiant expression of national cultural autonomy.

Opportunities to resist social and racial injustices through local and International educational activities were increasingly limited in the late 1930s and early 1940s, but some militants clung to their principles. In 1942, Maida Springer-Kemp reluctantly accepted the position of Local 132 education director on the advice of her friend A. Philip Randolph, who encouraged her to see the post as an opportunity for what he called "creative dissent," using every means available to struggle for racial and economic justice. Springer-Kemp balked when International officers asked her to organize a blood drive to support the war effort. She was outraged that the U.S. military continued to segregate blood. Dubinsky insisted, so she complied with the request by arranging for Local 132 members to give blood in Chinatown, where blood was being collected for Chinese troops fighting the Japanese. She said, "We organized a blood bank with Black and white workers laying table by table, giving blood, because the Chinese didn't ask what color blood it was."[7]

Other Black women in the ILGWU found avenues to creative dissent through joining with A. Philip Randolph in the March on Washington Movement (MOWM), which pressured Roosevelt into signing Executive Order 8802, prohibiting government contractors from discrimination in hiring. Edith Ransom and Eldica Riley, Local 22 executive board members, held offices in the movement organization. Ransom served as secretary of the MOWM, and Riley represented Local 22 on the MOWM labor committee.[8] Notably, Randolph defended the MOWM's all-Black membership in terms that anticipated criticism of political and cultural organizing by Black and other racial-ethnic groups later in the twentieth century. Acknowledging the support by white and liberal groups, he argued that economic, religious, and racial groups had to form within their own communities to take the lead to fight "specialized" problems.

> For instance the problem of anti-Semitism is a specialized one and must be attacked by the Jews through a Jewish organization which considers this question its major interest. . . . The problem of lynching is a specialized one and Negroes must take the responsibility and initiative to solve it, because Negroes are the chief victims of it. . . . No one would claim that a society of Filipinos is undemocratic because it does not take in Japanese members, or that Catholics are anti-Jewish because the Jesuits won't accept Jews as members or that trade unions are not liberal because they deny membership to employers. Neither is the March on Washington Movement undemocratic because it confines its members to Negroes.[9]

He argued that other groups had an obligation to support those groups' taking the lead on specific issues and that other issues of concern to everyone demand leadership by intergroup coalitions. These distinctions and their rationale are reminiscent of how Yiddish socialists considered racial-ethnic groups as autonomous and mutually supportive.

After the war, individual ILGWU locals continued to employ elements of social unionism as a strategy to organize workers in factories owned by recalcitrant employers, particularly when organizing workers across racial and ethnic lines. The example of Local 424, in Johnstown, Pennsylvania, representing six hundred dressmakers at the Goldstein and Levin garment factory, illustrates how some employers and union organizers recognized the power of these activities and the ambivalence some International officers felt toward them. In 1946, Mark Starr circulated a memo that included an article written by Michael Johnson, manager of Local 424. Starr wrote, "I am always urging our education directors and organizers to write down human interest stories about particular experiences in slapping down Old Man Jim Crow. Such incidents by themselves seem small but they add up to something. Indeed, sometimes I feel that many of these minor incidents are more important than letting loose all the gobble-de-gook of the intercultural specialists."[10] Goldstein and Levin was a runaway shop that moved from Philadelphia to Johnstown in 1936 to avoid the union, which they were successful in doing for some time. An unusually large factory employing several hundred workers, the company sponsored social and recreational activities as part of a welfare capitalist program to deter unionization. After five attempts, the ILGWU successfully organized the employees into a union in 1945. When the union struck for recognition in the spring of 1945, Johnson reported that Black workers refused to participate in the strike, believing racist white workers led the union drive. Goldstein and Levin employed sixty to seventy Black women as pressers and initially included them in all social functions that were sponsored for its employees. But according to Johnson, the employer began to segregate workers and, by "using the devise of a social club," excluded Blacks from social activities. Management insisted it was responding to the will of white workers.

Johnson believed that the African American women continued to be skeptical about the union despite its victory and subsequent attempts to welcome Blacks into the organization as full members. However, Johnson successfully recruited some of the Black women onto the membership committee, where they worked to organize a victory dance to celebrate the strike's success and the installation of local officers. The union leadership encouraged Black women to attend the dance and to bring escorts. Johnson reported that a majority of members attended the dance, in spite of rumors warning of trouble if Blacks showed up. In addition, almost all the Black women showed up with their male escorts. Johnson wrote, "During the course of the dance, most of the Negro workers approached the officials of the Union and introduced their escorts. As we shook hands, I could sense acknowledgment on their part that the Union really did not believe in discrimination nor segregation in any form and that this dance was the demonstration of that."[11] Johnson recounted several subsequent examples of cross-racial solidarity, including an incident in which the local union sponsored a bowling tournament to include Black members. When a bowling-alley owner refused to rent shoes to the Black workers, the white workers refused to bowl and left the alley, just as the ILGWU convention had done in Chicago in 1934 and *Pins and Needles* cast members had done in the late 1930s. In another story, Johnson wrote about a white worker who came before the local executive board to plead for financial assistance for a Black worker who lost her home in a fire. Johnson noted that this was extraordinary since this white woman had spoken against the union and against Black workers before the union formed in Johnstown.

The ritual in which the women introduced their escorts to the union officials at the dance suggests the meaning Black women might have found in the dance. Even if these women were convinced of the sincerity of union leaders, their male escorts were less likely to have had similarly positive experiences. Black veterans returning from World War II faced Jim Crow discrimination in the South and the North. Despite CIO gains, unions in many industries still refused to accept Blacks as equal members in 1945. For those men who joined egalitarian unions, fears—including the vulnerability of their female kin to violence and sexual harassment in the workplace—must have remained high. At the dance, the introductions and handshaking provided an opportunity for white union leaders and Black men associated with Black women members to express mutual respect and to establish familiarity. These were essential ingredients in creating a bond strong enough to establish trust and build solidarity during periods of high-risk confrontation with employers. But Starr's characterization of the Local 424 events as a "human interest" story and as seemingly "small" and "minor" incidents indicates ambivalence, or a lack of understanding, on the part of many union officials.

After labor leaders turned away from socialism, the possibility of mutual culturalism still existed in places where interracial, cross-ethnic solidarity was imperative, though it was dampened by the liberalism of union leaders and by the national political culture. As ILGWU leaders moved closer to the center of political power in the United States, they alternately encouraged and dismissed the critical importance of social and recreational activities emanating from the lower ranks of the union. Mutual culturalism persisted at the grassroots, not only as an alternative to liberal cosmopolitanism but also as a militant, democratic challenge to cautious, top-down leadership.

Notes

NOTES TO THE INTRODUCTION

1. See Yevette Richards, *Maida Springer: Pan-Africanist and International Labor Leader* (Pittsburgh: University of Pittsburgh Press, 2000).

2. Interview with Maida Springer-Kemp, April 7, 1999.

3. See James R. Barrett, "Americanization from the Bottom Up: Immigration and the Remaking of the Working Class in the United States, 1880–1930," *Journal of American History* 79, no. 3 (1992): 996–1020. Other groups of workers infused labor-union movements with an ethnically specific radicalism well into the 1930s. For example, militant Irish Republic Army members who immigrated to the United States in the 1920s infused the leadership and activist core of the movement to organize transport workers in New York City during the 1930s. See Joshua Benjamin Freeman, *In Transit: The Transport Workers Union in New York City, 1933–1966* (Philadelphia: Temple University Press, 2001). For French and Belgian radicals in New England, see Gary Gerstle, *Working-Class Americanism: The Politics of Labor in a Textile City, 1914–1960* (New York: Cambridge University Press, 1989). For examples of Socialist Party language federations and socialist labor culture, see Elizabeth Faue, *Community of Suffering and Struggle: Women, Men, and the Labor Movement in Minneapolis, 1915–1945* (Chapel Hill: University of North Carolina Press, 1991), 50.

4. For a discussion of the ILGWU education programs and race relations, see Hasia Diner, *In the Almost Promised Land: American Jews and Blacks, 1915–1935* (Baltimore: Johns Hopkins University Press, 1995), 199–230. Whereas I argue the centrality of Yiddish socialism, Diner rejects the significance of socialism to explain union leaders' motivations in reaching out to Blacks and other union members.

5. For a brief discussion and a more narrow definition of social unionism, see Susan Stone Wong, "From Soul to Strawberries: The International Ladies' Garment Workers' Union and Workers' Education, 1914–1950," in *Sisterhood and Solidarity: Workers' Education for Women, 1914–1984*, ed. Joyce L. Kornbluh and Mary Frederickson (Philadelphia: Temple University Press, 1984), 43.

6. Steve Fraser and Gary Gerstle call this the "dominant order of ideas, public policies, and political alliances" of the New Deal. Steven Fraser and Gary Gerstle, introduction to *The Rise and Fall of the New Deal Order, 1930–1980*, ed. Steven Fraser and Gary Gerstle (Princeton: Princeton University Press, 1989), ix.

7. Walter Galenson, *The CIO Challenge to the AFL: A History of the American Labor Movement* (Cambridge: Harvard University Press, 1960), 3–4, 32. The three key AFL unions that founded the CIO in 1935, the ILGWU, the Amalgamated Clothing Workers of America (ACWA), and the United Mine Workers of America (UMWA), shared

common concerns about building a multiethnic, interracial industrial union movement. Ideas about how to build that movement flowed between these unions. The ACWA, which represented men's garment workers, was a sister union to the ILGWU. New York City–based Russian Jewish immigrants populated and led the ACWA as well. Sidney Hillman was an officer in the ILGWU before taking the reins as president of the ACWA. See Steven Fraser, *Labor Will Rule: Sidney Hillman and the Rise of American Labor* (New York: Free Press, 1991), 78–90. The UMWA, like the ILGWU, had been searching for ways to organize and retain the membership of Black workers. See Herbert George Gutman, "The Negro and the United Mine Workers of America: The Career and Letters of Richard L. Davis and Something of Their Meaning," in *Work, Culture, and Society in Industrializing America: Essays in American Working-Class and Social History*, 121–208 (New York: Vintage Books, 1976); Joe William Trotter, Jr., *Coal, Class, and Color: Blacks in Southern West Virginia, 1915–1932* (Urbana: University of Illinois Press, 1990), 111–15; Daniel Letwin, *The Challenge of Interracial Unionism: Alabama Coal Miners, 1878–1921* (Chapel Hill: University of North Carolina Press, 1998); Brian Kelly, *Race, Class, and Power in the Alabama Coalfields, 1908–1921* (Urbana: University of Illinois Press, 2001). In the 1920s, UMWA leaders availed themselves of educational programs created by Fannia Cohn, director of education for the ILGWU. One prominent UMWA district used materials and credited personnel from the Workers Education Bureau, cofounded by Cohn, with successful educational work throughout central Pennsylvania beginning in 1924. Paul W. Fuller, "Miners' Educational Work," *American Federationist*, March 1926, 324–26.

8. As Tony Michels has shown, much of the inspiration and literature for the Yiddishist movement in Russia came from Russian Jews living in the diaspora, particularly in New York in the 1880s and 1890s. In turn, Yiddishists who shaped the revolutionary movements in Russia in the late 1890s and early 1900s formed successive waves of immigrants who transformed the Jewish socialist and labor movements in New York and elsewhere. Tony Michels, *A Fire in Their Hearts: Yiddish Socialists in New York* (Cambridge: Harvard University Press, 2005), 67.

9. Randolph Bourne, "Trans-national America," *Atlantic Monthly*, July 1916; David A. Hollinger, *Postethnic America: Beyond Multiculturalism* (New York: Basic Books, 1995), 94–97.

10. Horace Kallen coined the term "cultural pluralism" in *Culture and Democracy in the United States: Studies in the Group Psychology of the American People* (New York: Boni and Liveright, 1924), but he had begun to develop his ideas in "Democracy versus the Melting Pot," *Nation* 100 (February 19 and 25, 1915).

11. James R. Barrett, "Americanization from the Bottom Up: Immigration and the Remaking of the Working Class in the United States, 1880–1930," *Journal of American History* 79, no. 3 (December 1992): 996–1020.

12. Benedict Anderson's work is helpful in understanding how Jews came to see themselves and at times to behave as a nation, not only in Russia but also as Russian Jews in the United States. Anderson proposes that "nationalism has to be understood by aligning it, not with self-consciously held political ideologies, but with the large cultural systems that preceded it, out of which—as well as against which—it came to being." Benedict Anderson, *Imagined Communities: Reflections on the Origin and Spread of Nationalism* (New York: Verso, 1991), 12.

13. Gerstle, *Working-Class Americanism*; Lizabeth Cohen, *Making a New Deal: Industrial Workers in Chicago, 1919–1939* (New York: Cambridge University Press, 1990).

14. The notion of "militancy" was and is fluid. For union members in the ILGWU from the first decade of the twentieth century through the 1930s, militancy meant a desire and willingness to engage in a range of activities that put them in danger of losing their jobs, incurring bodily harm, or going to jail. Women also risked public humiliation and censure and strained family or social relations. Militant activities included organizing drives, strikes, boycotts, leafleting, street-corner oratory, mass meetings, and pickets. Union activists also engaged in militant social activities, including some instances of interracial dancing. Militants often knowingly violated the law if they felt an action was just or strategically beneficial. While adherence to a revolutionary philosophy helped to indicate a member's level of militancy, there were always militant union members who were simply engaged in the struggle of the moment.

15. For a discussion of the role of labor culture in a militant union movement and the political tensions between the International and local unions within the ILGWU, see Elizabeth Faue, *Community of Suffering and Struggle: Women, Men, and the Labor Movement in Minneapolis, 1915–1945* (Chapel Hill: University of North Carolina Press, 1991), 126–31, 137–39. Faue demonstrates a clear connection between women's union activism in Minneapolis, local union autonomy, and the vibrant working-class culture emanating from the communities in which workers lived.

16. Yiddishists did not use the term *ethnicity*, which only came into scholarly vogue in the 1940s and 1950s. David R. Roediger, *Working towards Whiteness: How America's Immigrants Became White; The Strange Journey from Ellis Island to the Suburbs* (New York: Basic Books, 2005), 21–27; Werner Sollors, *The Invention of Ethnicity* (New York: Oxford University Press, 1988), xiii.

17. As Mae Ngai notes, the 1924 Johnson-Reed Immigration Act served to change the dominant notion of race from largely physiognomic (outward appearances that people attribute to race) to physiognomic and nationality based. The law defined racial categories and set immigration quotas or restrictions for nonwhite groups and created an additional category of white European ethnicities ranked by nationality. Through that act, the state interpreted ethnicity as a category in which less desirable white Europeans could be transformed through assimilation, certainly in a generation or two, while nonwhite people would remain in a subordinate social status generation after generation. Mae Ngai, *Impossible Subjects: Illegal Aliens and the Making of Modern America* (Princeton: Princeton University Press, 2004), 7–9, 21–55.

18. ILGWU Local 22, "Census of the Membership of the Dressmakers Union Local #22, I.L.G.W.U. as of October 1, [1934]," Cornell University, Martin P. Catherwood Library, Kheel Center for Labor-Management Documentation and Archives, ILGWU Records, collection 5780/36, box 1.

19. Roediger, *Working towards Whiteness*, 128.

20. Kathleen Neils Conzen, David A. Gerber, Ewa Morawska, George E. Pozzetta, and Rudolph J. Vecoli, "The Invention of Ethnicity: A Perspective from the USA," *Journal of American Ethnic History* 12 (Fall 1992): 4–5.

21. Hollinger, *Postethnic America*.

22. Roediger, *Working towards Whiteness*, 35–37. David Hollinger names five racial-ethnic categories in the United States: African American, Asian American, Euro American, Indigenous, and Latino.

23. On the portrayal of Blacks through minstrelsy, see David R. Roediger, *The Wages of Whiteness: Race and the Making of the American Working Class* (New York: Verso, 1999), 122–127. On post–World War II cultural elements of race, see Karen Brodkin, *How Jews Became White Folks and What That Says about Race in America* (New Brunswick: Rutgers University Press, 1994), 153–55.

24. James R. Barrett and David Roediger, "Inbetween Peoples: Race, Nationality, and the 'New Immigrant' Working Class," *Journal of American Ethnic History* 16 (1997): 3–34.

25. See, for example, Nancy Schrom Dye, *As Equals and as Sisters: Feminism, the Labor Movement, and the Women's Trade Union League of New York* (Columbia: University of Missouri Press, 1980); Elizabeth Ewen, *Immigrant Women in the Land of Dollars: Life and Culture on the Lower East Side, 1890–1925* (New York: Monthly Review Press, 1985); Meredith Tax, *The Rising of the Women: Feminist Solidarity and Class Conflict, 1880–1917* (New York: Monthly Review Press, 1980); Nancy MacLean, "The Culture of Resistance: Female Institutional Building in the International Ladies' Garment Workers' Union, 1905–1925" (Michigan Occasional Papers in Women's Studies 21, Winter 1982).

26. Dorothy Sue Cobble, *The Other Women's Movement: Workplace Justice and Social Rights in Modern America* (Princeton: Princeton University Press, 2003); Nancy F. Gabin, *Feminism in the Labor Movement: Women and the United Auto Workers, 1935–1975* (Ithaca: Cornell University Press, 1990).

27. Annelise Orleck, *Common Sense and a Little Fire: Women and Working-Class Politics in the United States, 1900–1965* (Chapel Hill: University of North Carolina Press, 1995); Faue, *Community of Suffering and Struggle*. See also Karen Pastorello, *A Power among Them: Bessie Abramowitz Hillman and the Making of the Amalgamated Clothing Workers of America* (Urbana: University of Illinois Press, 2007); Jennifer Guglielmo, "Negotiating Gender, Race, and Coalition: Italian Women and Working-Class Politics in New York City, 1880–1945" (Ph.D. diss., University of Minnesota, 2003).

28. On the ideology and iconography of gender and labor struggle in the 1930s, see Faue, *Community of Suffering and Struggle*, 69–99.

29. Alice Kessler-Harris, *Out to Work: A History of Wage-Earning Women in the United States* (New York: Oxford University Press, 1982), 254.

30. See Alice Kessler-Harris, "Problems of Coalition-Building: Women and Trade Unions in the 1920s," in *Women, Work, and Protest: A Century of U.S. Women's Labor History*, ed. Ruth Milkman, 110–38 (New York: Routledge, 1985); Alice Kessler-Harris, "Organizing the Unorganizable: Three Jewish Women and Their Union," *Labor History* 17, no. 1 (1976): 5–23.

31. ILGWU, "Report of the General Executive Board to the Twenty-First Convention of the International Ladies' Garment Workers' Union, May 2, 1932, Philadelphia," 19; ILGWU, "Report of the General Executive Board to the Twenty-Fourth Convention of the International Ladies' Garment Workers' Union, May 27, 1940, New York," 25, addendum D.

1. Vladimir Medem, *The Life and Soul of a Legendary Jewish Socialist: The Memoirs of Vladimir Medem*, ed. Samuel A. Portnoy (New York: Ktav, 1979), 296. The negotiations with Russia, conducted through Plehve, likely involved Turkey and its foreign debt. A few years earlier, Herzl had met with the sultan of Turkey to secure an agreement in which the Ottomans would allow Jewish settlement of Palestine. The negotiations, which broke down, centered on Turkey's considerable foreign debt, which Herzl offered to address in an intricate scheme (of what may now be called insider trading) that involved wealthy European Jews buying up Turkish bonds on various foreign exchanges. Only these Jews would have foreknowledge of the issuance of the bonds. See Theodor Herzl, *The Diaries of Theodor Herzl*, ed. Marvin Lowenthal (New York: Grosset and Dunlap, 1962), 335–58.

2. Medem, *Life and Soul*, 297.

3. Tony Michels argues that Yiddishism was incubated among the Russian Jewish Diaspora in New York first in the 1880s and exported through published books and newspapers to the Pale of Settlement. See Tony Michels, *A Fire in Their Hearts: Yiddish Socialists in New York* (Cambridge: Harvard University Press), 66–67.

4. David H. Weinberg, *Between Tradition and Modernity: Haim Zhitlowski, Simon Dubnow, Ahad Ha-Am, and the Shaping of Modern Jewish Identity* (New York: Holmes and Meier, 1996), 94.

5. Ibid., 96.

6. Melech Epstein, *Profiles of Eleven: Profiles of Eleven Men Who Guided the Destiny of an Immigrant Jewish Society and Stimulated Social Consciousness among the American People* (Detroit: Wayne State University Press, 1965), 300. His father was described as both a Chasid and an adherent of the Maskilim, modern thinkers inspired by science and the humanities.

7. Ibid., 301–2.

8. Michels, *Fire in Their Hearts*, 129; Weinberg, *Between Tradition and Modernity*, 89.

9. *Pogrom* is a Russian word meaning "interethnic violence"; it was not limited to attacks on Jews. But in the Jewish lexicon, it came to mean the violence visited on Jews by their gentile peasant neighbors. *Encyclopedia Judaica*, vol. 4 (New York: Macmillan, 1971). The Pale of Settlement was first determined under Catherine the Great in the 1790s. Only in this zone on the western edge of the Russian Empire, roughly nine hundred miles long and one hundred miles wide, was Jewish settlement permitted. Most Jews lived in villages, or shtetlakh. Over the course of the nineteenth century, various Czarist regimes relaxed the laws maintaining the Pale, only to return to violent enforcement of the restrictions during periods of economic or political upheaval. At times, Jews would be allowed to relocate to cities throughout the empire, and then they were forced to leave jobs, homes, and sometimes families to relocate in the Pale. Within the Pale, Jews were typically outnumbered by Russians and other ethnic groups. They were limited in what they could own—most important, they were forbidden to own land—and in how they could make a living. See Irving Howe, *World of Our Fathers: The Journey of the East European Jews to America and the Life They Found and Made* (New York: Harcourt Brace Jovanovich, 1976), 5.

10. Henry J. Tobias, *The Jewish Bund in Russia: From Its Origins to 1905* (Stanford: Stanford University Press, 1972), 229.

11. Herzl, *Diaries of Theodor Herzl*, 390.

12. Medem, *Memoirs of Vladimir Medem*, 298.

13. A. L. Patkin, *The Origins of the Russian-Jewish Labour Movement* (Melbourne: F. W. Cheshire, 1947), 20–21.

14. Ibid, 50. Under Alexander II's father, children as young as eight or nine were put into the military for up to twenty-five years. In the late 1850s, Alexander II reduced the military term to five years. At that time, most European empires used children in military service.

15. Ibid., 51.

16. Weinberg, *Between Tradition and Modernity*, 37; Tobias, *Jewish Bund in Russia*, 7–10.

17. Weinberg, *Between Tradition and Modernity*, 51.

18. Emmanuel S. Goldsmith, *Architects of Yiddishism at the Beginning of the Twentieth Century: A Study in Jewish Cultural History* (Madison, NJ: Fairleigh Dickinson University Press, 1976), 168–71.

19. Michels, *Fire in Their Hearts*, 131.

20. As quoted in ibid., 30.

21. Ibid., 130; Emmanuel S. Goldsmith, *The Story of the Yiddish Language Movement* (New York: Shapolsky, 1987), 170–72.

22. Karl Renner, "State and Nation," in *National Cultural Autonomy and Its Contemporary Critics*, ed. Ephraim Nimni, 13–41 (New York: Routledge, 2005).

23. As quoted in Joseph V. Stalin, "Marxism and the National Question," *Prosveshxhentye* 3–5 (March–May 1913), transcribed and translated by Carl Cavanagh, Marxist.org, www.marxist.org/reference/archive/stalin/works/1913/03.htm.

24. Otto Bauer, *The Question of Nationalities and Social Democracy*, trans. Joseph O'Donnell (Minneapolis: University of Minnesota Press, 2000), 258. Originally published as *Die Nationalitatenfrage und die Sozialdemokratie* (Vienna: Verlag der Wiener Volksbuchhandlung, 1924).

25. Frederick Jackson Turner, "The Significance of the Frontier in American History," in *Rereading Frederick Jackson Turner: "The Significance of the Frontier in American History" and Other Essays*, ed. John Mack Faragher, 31–60 (New York: Holt, 1994), 47.

26. As quoted in Edna Nahshon, "*The Melting Pot*: Introductory Essay," in Israel Zangwill, *From the Ghetto to the Melting Pot: Israel Zangwill's Jewish Plays*, ed. Edna Nahshon, 211–63 (Detroit: Wayne State University Press, 2006), 213.

27. David. A. Hollinger, *Postethnic America: Beyond Multiculturalism* (New York: Basic Books, 1995), 92.

28. Ibid., 94–97; Randolph Bourne, "Trans-national America," *Atlantic Monthly*, July 1916.

29. Patkin, *Origins of the Russian-Jewish Labour Movement*, 42–43.

30. Weinberg, *Between Tradition and Modernity*, 81.

31. Ibid., 36.

32. Ibid., 83–84.

33. Jonathan Frankel, *Prophecy and Politics: Socialism, Nationalism, and the Russian Jews, 1862–1917* (Cambridge: Cambridge University Press, 1981), 215–17.

34. From Chaim Zhitlowsky's 1917 essay "Tsienizm oder sotsyalism," as quoted in Michels, *Fire in Their Hearts*, 133.

35. Weinberg, *Between Tradition and Modernity*, 96.

36. As quoted in Michels, *Fire in Their Hearts*, 133.

37. Tobias, *Jewish Bund in Russia*, 11–21.

38. Thanks to Roni Gechtman for this distinction, which he employs in his work on the Bund. See Roni Gechtman, "Socialist Mass Politics through Sport: The Bund's Morgnshtern in Poland, 1926–1939," *Journal of Sport History* 26, no. 2 (1999): 326–52; Roni Gechtman, "Yidisher Sotsializm: The Bund's National Program in the Context of the Second Polish Republic" (Professor Bernard Choseed Memorial Lecture, YIVO Institute for Jewish Research, 2000).

39. Tobias, *Jewish Bund in Russia*, 62–67.

40. Susan A. Glenn, *Daughters of the Shtetl: Life and Labor in the Immigrant Generation* (Ithaca: Cornell University Press, 1990), 38.

41. Tobias, *Jewish Bund in Russia*, 160–76.

42. Weinberg, *Between Tradition and Modernity*, 98.

43. Goldsmith, *Architects of Yiddishism*, 171–72.

44. Weinberg, *Between Tradition and Modernity*, 100.

45. Tobias, *Jewish Bund in Russia*, 335–43.

46. See David Levering Lewis, *Prisoners of Honor: The Dreyfus Affair* (New York: Holt, 1974), 47–62.

47. Marvin Lowenthal, introduction to *Diaries of Theodor Herzl*, by Theodor Herzl, xix. Lowenthal points out that Herzl never noted in his diaries or dispatches at the time that he felt Dreyfus was anything but guilty. Deep suspicions that Dreyfus was framed in part because he was a Jew came to light a few years later, after Herzl published *The Jewish State*. Herzl credits the Dreyfus Affair with his nationalistic awakening only in 1899. Nevertheless, Dreyfus became a symbol for anti-Semitic injustice soon after the World Zionist Organization was formed in 1897.

48. Theodor Herzl, *The Jewish State* (1896; repr., New York: Dover, 1988), 75.

49. Ibid., 137.

50. The first meeting of the Zionist Congress in 1897 in Basel, Switzerland, drew 197 self-appointed delegates, most of whom came from western Europe, while most of the world's Jews lived in Russia and eastern Europe. Herzl, *Diaries of Theodor Herzl*, 214.

51. Herzl, *Jewish State*, 144

52. Ibid., 96.

53. Ibid., 146.

54. Ibid.

55. Ibid., 99.

56. Ibid., 117.

57. Ibid., 116.

58. Ibid., 132.

59. Walter Laidlaw, "Makes an Analysis of Census Figures: Federation of Churches Predicts That in Future Brooklyn Will Gain More than Manhattan" *New York Times*, September 4, 1910, 8; Joseph Jacobs, ed., *The American Jewish Year Book, 5676* (Philadelphia: Jewish Publication Society of America, 1915), 347.

60. Jacobs, ed., *American Jewish Year Book*, 348–49; Howe, *World of Our Fathers*, 61.

61. Annette P. Bus, "Lower East Side, New York: Turn of the Century," in *Encyclopedia of the American Left*, ed. Mari Jo Buhle, Paul Buhle, and Dan Georgakas (Urbana: University of Illinois Press, 1992), 439.

62. Benjamin Stolberg, *Tailor's Progress: The Story of a Famous Union and the Men Who Made It* (Garden City, NY: Doubleday, Doran, 1944), 37. Tony Michels, who calls the German socialist movement "the midwives of the Jewish labor movement" in New York, discusses the ways in which the German socialists tolerated multiple ethnic groups. In the 1880s, Russian Jewish immigrants with no mature socialist culture of their own learned socialism from the Germans among whom they lived on the Lower East Side of Manhattan. Michels, *Fire in Their Hearts*, 43.

63. Joseph Brandeis, "From Sweatshop to Stability: Jewish Labor between Two World Wars," *YIVO Annual* 16 (1976): 12–13; Louis Levine, *The Women's Garment Workers: A History of the International Ladies' Garment Workers' Union* (New York: Huebsch, 1924), 69.

64. Howe, *World of Our Fathers*, 297.

65. Levine, *Women's Garment Workers*, 103.

66. Workmen's Circle, *Forty Years Workmen's Circle: A History in Pictures, 1900–1940* (New York: National Executive Committee of the Workmen's Circle, 1940), American Jewish Historical Society Archives.

67. "Twentieth Anniversary Souvenir Journal, Grodner Branch 74, 1906–1926," New York, 5, American Jewish Historical Society Archives.

68. Workmen's Circle, *Forty Years Workmen's Circle*, 15.

69. There were at least fifty branches in the United States in 1904. Nora Levin, "The Influence of the Bund on the Jewish Socialist Movement in America," *Gratz College Journal*, 1971, 57.

70. Howe, *World of Our Fathers*, 294; Maximillian Hurwitz, *The Workmen's Circle: Its History, Ideals, Organization and Institutions* (New York: Workmen's Circle, 1936), 34, 38.

71. American Jewish History Society Archives, Workmen's Circle collection, 1903–1993, Box 1, Folder: Workmen's Circle Collection, Administration–Anniversary, Year Books.

72. Hurwitz, *Workmen's Circle*, 155.

73. As quoted in Isaiah Trunk, "The Cultural Dimension of the American Jewish Labor Movement," in "Essays on the American Jewish Labor Movement," ed. Ezra Mendelsohn, *YIVO Annual of Jewish Social Science* 16 (1976): 359.

74. Hurwitz, *Workmen's Circle*, 159.

75. Epstein, *Profiles of Eleven*, 316.

76. Judah Joseph Shapiro, *The Friendly Society: A History of the Workmen's Circle* (New York: Media Judaica, 1970), 124.

77. Epstein, *Profiles of Eleven*, 314; Hurwitz, *Workmen's Circle*, 38; Trunk, "Cultural Dimension of the American Jewish Labor Movement," 364.

78. Hurwitz, *Workmen's Circle*, 35–36.

79. Ibid., 36.

80. Ibid., 37.

81. Trunk, "Cultural Dimension of the American Jewish Labor Movement," 360. A 1940 Workmen's Circle publication reported that an English-language Sunday school opened in 1900, but there is no information on where it was or how long it lasted. See Workmen's Circle, *Forty Years Workmen's Circle*, 19.

82. Trunk, "Cultural Dimension of the American Jewish Labor Movement," 360.

83. Ibid.

84. Hurwitz, *Workmen's Circle*, 39; Trunk, "Cultural Dimension of the American Jewish Labor Movement," 361.

85. Trunk, "Cultural Dimension of the American Jewish Labor Movement," 361.

86. Hurwitz, *Workmen's Circle*, 158–62.

87. Ibid., 28.

88. Ibid., 55.

89. Ibid., 207–12.

NOTES TO CHAPTER 2

1. Paula Hyman, "Culture and Gender: Women in the Immigrant Jewish Community," in *The Legacy of Jewish Migration: 1881 and Its Impact*, ed. David Berger (New York: Brooklyn College Press, 1983), 158–59; Paula Hyman, "Immigrant Women and Consumer Protest: The New York Kosher Meat Boycott of 1902," *American Jewish History* 70 (1980): 91–105. For the citywide and national scope of the protest, see Rosalyn Baxandall, Linda Gordon, and Susan Reverby, eds., *America's Working Women: A Documentary History, 1600 to the Present* (New York: Vintage Books, 1976), 185–86.

2. See the Constitution of the ILGWU, 1902, 32.

3. Jennifer Guglielmo, "Negotiating Gender, Race, and Coalition: Italian Women and Working-Class Politics in New York City, 1880–1945" (Ph.D. diss., University of Minnesota, 2003), 119–22.

4. John A. Dyche, "Report of the Secretary-Treasurer: Report and Proceedings of the Seventh Annual Convention of the International Ladies' Garment Workers' Union, New York, N.Y., June 18–21, 1906," 15–16.

5. Nancy MacLean, "The Culture of Resistance: Female Institutional Building in the International Ladies' Garment Workers' Union, 1905–1925" (Michigan Occasional Papers in Women's Studies 21, Winter 1982), 59–60, 63; Roger Waldinger, "Another Look at the International Ladies' Garment Workers' Union: Women, Industry Structure and Collective Action," in *Women, Work, and Protest: A Century of U.S. Women's Labor History*, ed. Ruth Milkman (Boston: Routledge and Kegan Paul, 1985), 98.

6. MacLean, "Culture of Resistance," 59.

7. Irving Howe, *World of Our Fathers: The Journey of the East European Jews to America and the Life They Found and Made* (New York: Harcourt Brace Jovanovich, 1976).

8. Ibid., 518–43.

9. Meredith Tax, *The Rising of the Women: Feminist Solidarity and Class Conflict, 1880–1917* (New York: Monthly Review Press, 1980), 208.

10. Annelise Orleck, *Common Sense and a Little Fire: Women and Working-Class Politics in the United States, 1900–1965* (Chapel Hill: University of North Carolina Press, 1995), 23.

11. Ibid., 48. In a 1953 letter to Local 62 manager Louis Stulberg, Fannia Cohn expresses some doubts about this chronology: "I want to . . . call your attention to the fact that I did not participate in organizing Local 62, as in 1911 I was not as yet a member of the ILGWU. I was then preparing for my college examinations. . . . I joined the International in 1912. I was inspired to do so by the overwhelming shock of the Triangle Fire. Against the opposition of my family, I insisted that I wanted to make my contribution to the labor movement and ignored their advice that I first complete my education and then join the movement. I felt that to speak for the workers and be able to voice their grievances and aspirations, I should live the same life as they do. I was amply remunerated for my choice. As soon as I joined the Union in 1912, I was elected to the Special Emergency Convention

of the ILGWU in Yonkers." This letter was written forty years after these events, when Cohn was in her sixties, and she may not have recalled the chronology correctly, or she may have been distinguishing between her activities as a member of the local and those with the International union. Fannia M. Cohn to Louis Stulberg, January 2, 1953, Cornell University, Martin P. Catherwood Library, Kheel Center for Labor-Management Documentation and Archives [hereafter Kheel Center], ILGWU Records, collection 5780/22, box 2, folder 2.

12. Orleck, *Common Sense and a Little Fire*, 29–30.

13. Ibid., 4, 9, 22.

14. Ibid., 47.

15. John H. M. Laslett, *Labor and the Left: A Study of Socialist and Radical Influences in the American Labor Movement, 1881–1924* (New York: Basic Books, 1970), 106.

16. Louis Levine, *The Women's Garment Workers: A History of the International Garment Workers' Union* (New York: Huebsch, 1924), 120–25, 42.

17. *Souvenir History of the Shirtwaist Makers Strike*, as quoted in Levine, *Women's Garment Workers*, 154, reprinted from the *New York Call*, November 23, 1909. The original articles in the *New York Call* did not report this detail. The *Souvenir History* paraphrases a slightly longer pledge recounted in a November 23, 1909, article from the *Forverts*.

18. Tax, *Rising of the Women*, 206. One left-wing journal claimed in an article printed during the strike that forty thousand women walked out: see Rose Strunsky, "The Strike of the Singers of the Shirt," *International Socialist Review* 10 (1909). So did the *New York Evening Journal*. See Nan Enstad, *Ladies of Labor, Girls of Adventure: Working Women, Popular Culture, and Labor Politics at the Turn of the Twentieth Century* (New York: Columbia University Press, 1999), 132. The *New York Times* quoted B. Wataskin, an organizer for the Ladies' Waist Makers' Union, as saying that he expected forty thousand workers would go out on strike; *New York Times*, November 23, 1909, 16. The rolling nature of the strike made all estimates inexact. Some manufacturers settled with the union immediately, and thousands of workers went back after the first day. As more and more manufacturers settled, thousands more workers went out on strike for the first time. This process continued throughout the winter.

19. Nancy Schrom Dye, *As Equals and as Sisters: Feminism, the Labor Movement, and the Women's Trade Union League* (Columbia: University of Missouri Press, 1980), 91–92.

20. MacLean, "Culture of Resistance," 27, 37.

21. Tax, *Rising of the Women*, 215–16, 28.

22. Nancy L. Green, *Ready-to-Wear and Ready-to-Work: A Century of Industry and Immigrants in Paris and New York* (Durham: Duke University Press, 1997), 53.

23. Tax, *Rising of the Women*, 215–16.

24. Ibid., 216. Philip S. Foner and Ronald L. Lewis, eds., *The Black Worker: A Documentary History from Colonial Times to the Present*, vol. 5, *The Black Worker from 1900 to 1919* (Philadelphia: Temple University Press, 1980), 108.

25. Maxine Schwartz Seller, "The Uprising of the Twenty Thousand: Sex, Class, and Ethnicity in the Shirtwaist Makers' Strike of 1909," in *"Struggle a Hard Battle": Essays on Working-Class Immigrants*, ed. Dirk Hoerder, 254–79 (DeKalb: Northern Illinois University Press, 1986); Foner and Lewis, *Black Worker*, 108.

26. For example, Mari Jo Buhle sets the strike within the context of evolving socialist theory that struggled with the place of women as wage workers and of Socialist Party

women who were in the process of crafting a new sense of "socialist womanhood": Mari Jo Buhle, *Women and American Socialism, 1870–1920* (Urbana: University of Illinois Press, 1983), 179. Elizabeth Ewen argues that the Progressive coalition, including the radical strikers, made new demands on the "definition of civilization and Americanization" in which workers and others exercised their rights: Elizabeth Ewen, *Immigrant Women in the Land of Dollars: Life and Culture on the Lower East Side, 1890–1925* (New York: Monthly Review Press, 1985), 258. Nan Enstad focuses attention on ordinary strikers not active in the Socialist Party for whom the strike was an appropriation and reinvention of "working ladyhood": Enstad, *Ladies of Labor, Girls of Adventure*, 121.

27. Strunsky, "Strike of the Singers of the Shirt"; Avrahm Yarmolinsky, *Road to Revolution: A Century of Russian Radicalism* (Princeton: Princeton University Press, 1957), 236.

28. Louis Levine wrote that 80 percent of the strikers were women aged sixteen to twenty-five. Levine, *Women's Garment Workers*, 144. For an analysis of the Jewish women workers as members of an immigrant community whose cultural and ideological worldviews were shaped by experiences and political movements in the small towns of the Russian Pale of Settlement, see Susan A. Glenn, *Daughters of the Shtetl: Life and Labor in the Immigrant Generation* (Ithaca: Cornell University Press, 1990), 167–206.

29. *New York Call*, November 28, 1909, 2.

30. Alice Kessler-Harris, "Organizing the Unorganizable: Three Jewish Women and Their Union," *Labor History* 17, no. 1 (1976): 6.

31. Barbara Mayer Wertheimer, *We Were There: The Story of Working Women in America* (New York: Pantheon, 1977), 293–308.

32. Dye, *As Equals and as Sisters*, 94.

33. Orleck, *Common Sense and a Little Fire*, 37.

34. Ibid., 43.

35. Ibid., 45.

36. Ibid., 71, 106–7, 29.

37. *New York Call*, December 5, 1909, 2.

38. Dye, *As Equals and as Sisters*, 3.

39. *New York Call*, November 25, 1909, 2.

40. *New York Call*, November 26, 1909.

41. *New York Call*, November 19, 1909.

42. Guglielmo, "Negotiating Gender, Race, and Coalition," 2.

43. Tax, *Rising of the Women*, 223.

44. Guglielmo, "Negotiating Gender, Race, and Coalition," 43–44.

45. On the origins of the myth that Italians could not unionize or resisted organizing, see ibid., 55–63.

46. Levine, *Women's Garment Workers*, 149.

47. Tax, *Rising of the Women*, 207.

48. Charles Anthony Zappia, "Unionism and the Italian American Worker: A History of the New York City 'Italian Locals' in the International Ladies' Garment Workers' Union, 1900–1934" (Ph.D. diss., University of California, 1994), 166.

49. MacLean, "Culture of Resistance," 22.

50. ILGWU, "Report and Proceedings of the Tenth Convention of the International Ladies' Garment Workers' Union, Boston, Massachusetts, 1910," 76.

51. Ibid., 63.

52. Ibid., 75.

53. Ibid., 83, 89–90.

54. Zappia, "Unionism and the Italian American Worker," 173.

55. Kessler-Harris, "Organizing the Unorganizable," 6–7.

56. Tax, *Rising of the Women*, 210–11.

57. Daniel E. Bender, "Too Much of Distasteful Masculinity: Historicizing Sexual Harassment in the Garment Sweatshop and Factory," *Journal of Women's History* 15, no. 3 (2004): 91–116.

58. Levine, *Women's Garment Workers*, 156; MacLean, "Culture of Resistance," 19.

59. Tax, *Rising of the Women*, 211.

60. Levine, *Women's Garment Workers*, 197–98. For a discussion of the shirtwaist strike as the first moment in which garment workers acted in a progression of events that led to sweeping reforms, see Richard Greenwald, *The Triangle Fire, the Protocols of Peace, and Industrial Democracy in Progressive Era New York* (Philadelphia: Temple University Press, 2005), 26–34.

61. Levine, *Women's Garment Workers*, 168. Levine wrote fourteen years after the strikes during the most divisive period in the union's history. In the mid-1920s, the number of union members had fallen off sharply, and more women than men left the union. The socialist and anarchist leadership of the International was deeply suspicious of outside influences, especially from Communists, and suspicious of any quarter that the left wing used as a power base in the years after the strikes of 1909 and 1910. Levine's contrast between the women's and men's strikes likely reflects the anxiety male leaders in the 1920s felt about the ways in which the community organizing and social consciousness of women gave rise to education programs that in turn provided opportunities for left-wing activities. That anxiety also might help explain why the shirtwaist strike came to be known in the annals of the union as the Uprising of the *Twenty* Thousand, rather than Twenty-Five, Thirty, or even Forty Thousand, as some contemporary accounts put the number of strikers. The distinction union leaders drew between the behavior of women and that of men would have been blurred by using a higher number for the shirtwaist strike.

62. Nan Enstad makes a similar argument in her reading of the popular media coverage. Observers continually remarked on the clothing of the strikers and implicitly dismissed the rationality of the strike and the legitimacy of these women's public political expressions. See Enstad, *Ladies of Labor, Girls of Adventure*, 84–118.

63. Howe, *World of Our Fathers*, 300.

64. Levine, *Women's Garment Workers*, 122.

65. As quoted in Alpheus Thomas Mason, *Brandeis: A Free Man's Life* (New York: Viking, 1946), 303.

66. Greenwald, *Triangle Fire*, 73.

67. Laslett, *Labor and the Left*, 110.

68. Greenwald, *Triangle Fire*, 74.

69. Levine, *Women's Garment Workers*, 110. Joint Boards were created over time by the ILGWU when locals in the same industry or geographic area needed to cooperate in negotiations, grievances, and general strikes.

70. Greenwald, *Triangle Fire*, 82–83.

71. Levine, *Women's Garment Workers*, 273.

72. Before the Wagner Act was upheld by the U.S. Supreme Court in 1937, union organizing in many industries often took the form of strikes. Workers walked out until the employer recognized the union as the workers' representative.

73. Quoted in Laslett, *Labor and the Left*, 113.

74. Zappia, "Unionism and the Italian American Worker," 177.

75. Tax, *Rising of the Women*, 223.

76. Susan Stone Wong, "From Soul to Strawberries: The International Ladies' Garment Workers' Union and Workers' Education, 1914–1950," in *Sisterhood and Solidarity: Workers' Education for Women, 1914–1984*, ed. Joyce L. Kornbluh and Mary Frederickson (Philadelphia: Temple University Press, 1984), 40.

77. Levine, *Women's Garment Workers*, 485.

78. The convention was the union's highest policymaking body, composed of delegates from each local. The leadership of the International—the president, the secretary-treasurer, and the vice presidents who composed the GEB—often controlled the convention because each local, no matter how small, had an equal number of delegates. The GEB created locals, sometimes in geographically isolated places with a few dozen union members. These locals often had no exposure to other ILGWU union members and were connected only to the International leadership.

79. Levine, *Women's Garment Workers*, 273.

80. Laslett, *Labor and the Left*, 114–16.

81. Levine, *Women's Garment Workers*, 482.

82. Dorothy Swanson, "Rand School of Social Science," in *Encyclopedia of the American Left*, ed. Mari Jo Buhle, Paul Buhle, and Dan Georgakas (Urbana: University of Illinois Press, 1992), 640–42; Levine, *Women's Garment Workers*, 484.

83. Orleck, *Common Sense and a Little Fire*, 40.

84. Levine, *Women's Garment Workers*, 486–87.

85. Paula Hyman, "Culture and Gender: Women in the Immigrant Jewish Community," in *The Legacy of Jewish Migration: 1881 and Its Impact*, ed. David Berger (New York: Brooklyn College Press, 1983), 161.

86. Orleck, *Common Sense and a Little Fire*, 20.

87. Ricki Carole Meyers Cohen, "Fannia Cohn and the International Ladies' Garment Workers' Union" (Ph.D. diss., University of Southern California, 1976), 56.

88. Kessler-Harris, "Organizing the Unorganizable," 7.

89. MacLean, "Culture of Resistance," 60.

90. For a recitation of the ILGWU's achievements in workers' education in the 1920s, see Fannia M. Cohn, "Educational and Social Activities," *American Federationist*, December 1929, 1449–50. On the broad range of the Congress of Industrial Organizations' social and recreational programs inspired by the ILGWU in the 1930s, see Lizabeth Cohen, *Making a New Deal: Industrial Workers in Chicago, 1919–1939* (New York: Cambridge University Press, 1990), 340–43. Rose Pesotta writes about her itinerant organizing, in which she always employed broad educational activities, not only for the ILGWU but also with rubber workers in Akron and auto workers in Flint during the sit-down strikes that succeeded in founding permanent unions in those industries. See Rose Pesotta, *Bread upon the Waters* (1944; repr., Ithaca: Cornell University Press, 1987).

91. MacLean, "Culture of Resistance," 72.

92. Interview with Charles S. Zimmerman by Henoch Mendulsund, November 5, 1975, Kheel Center, ILGWU Records, collection 5780/118. Zimmerman was likely referring to *Tilim* or *Tehillim*, Hebrew for "Psalms."

93. Interview with Charles S. Zimmerman by Henoch Mendulsund, November 12, 1975.

94. Benjamin Stolberg, *Tailor's Progress: The Story of a Famous Union and the Men Who Made It* (Garden City, NY: Doubleday, Doran, 1944), 288.

95. Vice presidents were often, but not always, heads of their own local unions or joint boards (groupings of locals within an industry or geographic area). By the same token, the heads of local unions, usually called general managers, were not always vice presidents. See ibid., 287.

96. Orleck, *Common Sense and a Little Fire*, 175.

97. MacLean, "Culture of Resistance," 73.

98. Stolberg, *Tailor's Progress*, 287.

99. Orleck, *Common Sense and a Little Fire*, 176.

100. Stolberg, *Tailor's Progress*, 287. Charles Beard was an important influence on the Workers Education Movement and on Fannia Cohn. Beard was one of three Americans who founded Ruskin College, a workers' university, in England in 1899. Ruskin College was a model for the Brookwood Labor College that Fannia Cohn helped found in 1921 in Katonah, New York. See Jonathan D. Bloom, "Brookwood Labor College, 1921–1933: Training Ground for Union Organizers" (master's thesis, Rutgers University, 1979), 2, 47n. 2.

101. As quoted in Fannia M. Cohn, "The A.F. of L. Convention for Adult Labor Education," *Justice*, July 5, 1919, 3.

102. Orleck, *Common Sense and a Little Fire*, 179.

103. Guglielmo, "Negotiating Gender, Race, and Coalition," 119–20.

104. Zappia, "Unionism and the Italian American Worker," 184.

105. Stolberg, *Tailor's Progress*, 240.

106. Zappia, "Unionism and the Italian American Worker," 186.

107. Ibid., 180.

108. MacLean, "Culture of Resistance," 102.

109. Philip S. Foner, *Women and the American Labor Movement*, vol. 2, *From World War I to the Present* (New York: Free Press, 1980), 154.

110. Levine, *Women's Garment Workers*, 2–3, 35.

NOTES TO CHAPTER 3

1. ILGWU, "Report and Proceedings of the Fourteenth Convention of the ILGWU, 1918, Boston, Massachusetts," report, 42.

2. "A Pioneer of the Russian Revolution," *Ladies' Garment Worker*, July 1917, 28–29.

3. Philip S. Foner, *Women and the American Labor Movement*, vol. 2, *From World War I to the Present* (New York: Free Press, 1980), 154; Theodore Draper, *American Communism and Soviet Russia* (1960; repr., New York: Vintage, 1986), 19.

4. James R. Barrett, *William Z. Foster and the Tragedy of American Radicalism* (Urbana: University of Illinois Press, 1999), 105–10.

5. Nick Salvatore, *Eugene V. Debs: Citizen and Socialist* (Urbana: University of Illinois Press, 1982), 294–310.

6. Theodore Draper, *The Roots of American Communism* (New York: Viking, 1957), 204–7, 321, 323, 341–44, 390. The Communist Party nominally disbanded in 1923, as its entire membership had joined the Workers' Party. In 1925, the Workers' Party became the Workers' (Communist) Party of America, and in 1929 it became the Communist Party, U.S.A.

7. See Nancy MacLean, *Behind the Mask of Chivalry: The Making of the Second Ku Klux Klan* (New York: Oxford University Press, 1994), 23–24, 40, 96–97, 124.

8. Irving Bernstein, *The Lean Years: A History of the American Worker, 1920–1933* (Boston: Houghton Mifflin, 1960), 153–57.

9. Poyntz continued to contribute articles to *Justice* for a few years after she left. Her articles dealt with workers' education and the meaningful use of leisure time but also increasingly with the Russian Revolution.

10. "Dr. Friedland to Guide Educational Work of the International," *Justice*, September 27, 1919, 1.

11. Louis Friedland, "Our Educational Aims and Problems," *Justice*, November 21, 1919; Louis Friedland, "The Bases of Our Educational Work," *Justice*, February 2, 1920, 3.

12. Louis Levine, *The Women's Garment Workers: A History of the International Ladies' Garment Workers' Union* (New York: Huebsch, 1924), 488.

13. Friedland, "Our Educational Aims and Problems."

14. The number of ILGWU members who attended Rand School programs in 1920 is not clear. At the 1918 convention of the ILGWU, Algernon Lee, director of the Rand School, noted that "several hundred" ILGWU members had been among the four thousand students in the previous term. ILGWU, *Reports and Proceedings*, 1918 Convention, 82. But the Palmer Raids took a toll on the Rand School's staff and students. In 1920, Lee addressed the ILGWU convention asking for financial assistance due to the "unusual heavy deficit because of the persecution they had to undergo." ILGWU, *Reports and Proceedings*, 1920 Convention, 25.

15. Jonathan D. Bloom, "Brookwood Labor College and the Progressive Labor Network of the Interwar United States, 1921–1937" (Ph.D. diss., New York University, 1992), 1–5, 36.

16. Charles Howlett, *Brookwood Labor College and the Struggle for Peace and Social Justice in America* (Lewiston, NY: Mellen, 1993), vii.

17. Friedland, "Our Educational Aims and Problems." The Nebraska open-meeting law, for example, forbade public meetings held in any language other than English. This law, though eventually overturned by the U.S. Supreme Court, was only the latest in a series of Progressive Era laws that sought to force assimilation, often by suppressing foreign-language culture or denying citizenship rights to non-English speakers.

18. Friedland, "Bases of Our Educational Work."

19. Fannia M. Cohn, "The A.F. of L. Convention for Adult Labor Education," *Justice*, July 5, 1919, 3.

20. Irving Howe, *World of Our Fathers: The Journey of the East European Jews to America and the Life They Found and Made* (New York: Simon and Schuster, 1976), 460–96, quotation on 485.

21. David G. Ruskies, introduction to *The Dybbuk and Other Writings*, by S. Ansky, ed. David G. Ruskies, trans. Golda Werman, xi–xxxvi (New York: Schocken Books, 1992), xxv.

22. S. Ansky, *The Dybbuk: A Play in Four Acts*, trans. Henry G. Alsberg and Winnefred Katzin (New York: Liveright, 1926), 126.

23. Chaim Zhitlowsky, "A Note on Chassidism," in ibid., 16, 20.

24. See Mae M. Ngai, "The Architecture of Race in American Immigration Law: A Re-examination of the Immigration Act of 1924," *Journal of American History* 86 (1999): 67–92.

25. William Feigenbaum, "The Workmen's Circle of the Future," *Twentieth Anniversary Souvenir Journal*, 6–7, YIVO Library.

26. ILGWU, "Camp Report, Summer of 1926," 4, Cornell University, Martin P. Catherwood Library, Kheel Center for Labor-Management Documentation and Archives [hereafter Kheel Center], ILGWU Records, collection 5780/49, box 3, file 6.

27. Ibid.

28. Maximillian Hurwitz, *The Workmen's Circle: Its History, Ideals, Organization and Institutions* (New York: Workmen's Circle, 1936), 70–72.

29. Yankl Doroshkin, "In the Beginning . . . ," reprinted in Gedalia Sandler, *Kinderland: From Generation to Generation; Celebrating 75 Years of Camp Kinderland* (New York: Kinderland, 1998), 6.

30. New York State law required that Camp Kinderland be chartered, with a board and officers with specific responsibilities. As in many other institutions within the labor and socialist movements, the varying makeup of local organizations' boards meant that divisions provoked by differences in ideology and policy were possible within organizations that maintained multiple institutions. Most states' requirements created similar circumstances.

31. "Workmen's Circle Camp," 1930, 1, YIVO Institute for Jewish Research, Bund Archives, Workmen's Circle collection, file 323.

32. Theodore Kornweibel, Jr., *No Crystal Stair: Black Life and the Messenger, 1917–1928* (Westport, CT: Greenwood, 1975), 26, 30–32. Owen and Randolph edited the *Hotel Messenger* for eight months before their articles accusing their employers, the headwaiters, of exploiting the lower-status waiters resulted in their being fired. They then founded the *Messenger* as an organ to organize workers in various trades throughout the country.

33. *Justice*, August 6, 1920.

34. "Lectures on the Negro," *Justice*, July 23, 1920, 2.

35. *Justice*, June 18, 1920, 4–5.

36. ILGWU, "Report to the 1920 ILGWU Convention," 50.

37. ILGWU, "Report to the 1922 ILGWU Convention," 78.

38. John H. M. Laslett, *Labor and the Left: A Study of Socialist and Radical Influences in the American Labor Movement, 1881–1924* (New York: Basic Books, 1970), 121.

39. ILGWU, "Report to the 1924 ILGWU Convention," 107–8.

40. ILGWU, "Report to the 1928 ILGWU Convention," 266.

41. ILGWU, "Report to the 1925 ILGWU Convention," 137–38.

42. Benjamin Stolberg, *Tailor's Progress: The Story of a Famous Union and the Men Who Made It* (New York: Doubleday, Doran, 1944), 336.

43. Jennie Matyas, "The Violets Asked for You," *Justice*, June 4, 1920, 3. After a long hiatus, Jennie Matyas again became active in the ILGWU in the mid-1930s. The GEB hired her as a general organizer, and she helped to organize locals in the San Francisco area.

44. Nathan Shaviro, "A Visit to the Unity House," *Justice*, June 18, 1920, 5.

45. Charles Anthony Zappia, "Unionism and the Italian American Worker: A History of the New York City 'Italian Locals' in the International Ladies' Garment Workers' Union, 1900–1934" (Ph.D. diss., University of California, 1994), 219.

46. Ibid., 234–36.

47. Interview with Charles S. Zimmerman by Henoch Mendulsund, July 1, 1976, 228–29, Kheel Center, ILGWU Records, collection 5780/118. Zimmerman was elected to the office of secretary of the Workers' Council in Local 25 for the brief period it existed.

48. Interview with Charles S. Zimmerman by Henoch Mendulsund, December 11, 1975. ·

49. Levine, *Women's Garment Workers*, 354–55.

50. "The Reorganization of Local No. 25," *Justice*, October 8, 1920.

51. At the same time, the shirtwaist industry was in decline, as dresses became the dominant fashion in the early 1920s, and most of the shirtwaist makers migrated to the new local. See ILGWU, "Report to the 1925 ILGWU Convention, Philadelphia," 85.

52. Foner, *Women and the American Labor Movement*, 156; interview with Charles S. Zimmerman by Henoch Mendulsund, July 1, 1976, 239.

53. Interview with Charles S. Zimmerman by Henoch Mendulsund, December 23, 1975.

54. Barrett, *William Z. Foster*, 126.

55. Foner, *Women and the American Labor Movement*, 158.

56. Interview with Charles S. Zimmerman by Henoch Mendulsund, July 1, 1976, 239.

57. Interview with Charles S. Zimmerman by Henoch Mendulsund, October 14, 1976, 320–30.

58. Joseph Brandes, "From Sweatshop to Stability: Jewish Labor between Two World Wars," *YIVO Annual* 16 (1976): 50, 52.

59. Laslett, *Labor and the Left*, 128.

60. Stolberg, *Tailor's Progress*, 117.

61. Foner, *Women and the American Labor Movement*, 159–60; Nancy MacLean, "The Culture of Resistance: Female Institutional Building in the ILGWU, 1905–1925" (Michigan Occasional Papers in Women's Studies 21, Winter 1982), 104.

62. ILGWU, "Report to the 1922 ILGWU Convention," 77; ILGWU, "Report to the 1924 ILGWU Convention," 106.

63. ILGWU, "Report to the 1924 ILGWU Convention," 130.

64. ILGWU, "Proceedings of the 1924 ILGWU Convention," 53–54.

65. Ibid., 54.

66. Rose Pesotta, *Bread upon the Waters* (1944; repr., Ithaca: Cornell University Press, 1987), 16.

67. Laslett, *Labor and the Left*, 127.

68. ILGWU, "Proceedings of the 1924 ILGWU Convention," 29.

69. ILGWU, "Report to the 1925 ILGWU Convention," 91.

70. Interview with Charles S. Zimmerman by Henoch Mendulsund, July 28, 1976.

71. Melech Epstein, *Jewish Labor in the U.S.A.: An Industrial, Political, and Cultural History of the Jewish Labor Movement*, vol. 2, *1914–1952* (New York: Trade Union Sponsoring Committee, 1953), 128.

72. Ibid., 139.

73. Stolberg, *Tailor's Progress*; interview with Charles S. Zimmerman by Henoch Mendulsund, October 14, 1976.

74. Interview with Charles S. Zimmerman by Henoch Mendulsund, October 14, 1976.

75. Stolberg, *Tailor's Progress*, 139–41; interview with Charles S. Zimmerman by Henoch Mendulsund, November 8, 1976.

76. Epstein, *Jewish Labor in the U.S.A.*, 2:139.

77. Stolberg, *Tailor's Progress*, 130.

78. Ibid., 134–35.

79. John Holmes, "American Jewish Communism and Garment Unionism in the 1920s," *American Communist History* 6, no. 2 (2007): 126.

80. Quoted in ibid., 185.

81. Stolberg, *Tailor's Progress*, 139.

82. ILGWU, "Report to the 1928 ILGWU Convention," 90–135.

83. ILGWU, "Announcement of Courses Given in Workers' University, 1923–1924," 9, Tamiment Vertical File, TF ILGWU Educational Department.

84. Ibid., 11.

85. Ibid., 13.

86. See John F. Kasson, *Amusing the Million: Coney Island at the Turn of the Century* (New York: Hill and Wang, 1978); Kathy Peiss, *Cheap Amusements: Working Women and Leisure in Turn-of-the-Century New York* (Philadelphia: Temple University Press, 1986), 67–72; Lizabeth Cohen, *Making a New Deal: Industrial Workers in Chicago, 1919–1939* (New York: Cambridge University Press, 1990), 99–158; George Sanchez, *Becoming Mexican American: Ethnicity, Culture and Identity in Chicano Los Angeles, 1900–1945* (New York: Oxford University Press, 1993), 185–87.

87. ILGWU, "Report of the Educational Department to the Nineteenth Convention of the ILGWU, Boston, Monday May 7, 1928," 15.

88. ILGWU, "Report of the Educational Activities 1922–1924, Submitted by the Educational Committee to the General Executive Board," 8.

89. ILGWU, "Report to the 1925 Convention of the ILGWU," 153.

90. ILGWU, "Announcement of Courses, ILGWU Workers' University, 1924–1925," 8, Tamiment Vertical File, TF 1924.

91. ILGWU, "Report of the Educational Activities 1922–1924, Submitted by the Educational Committee to the General Executive Board," 9.

92. ILGWU Educational Department announcement, 1925–1926, 11, Tamiment Vertical File, TF 1925.

93. ILGWU, "Report to the 1925 Convention of the ILGWU," 92.

NOTES TO CHAPTER 4

1. "An Appeal to Public Opinion," May 1927, YIVO Institute for Jewish Research, Bund Archives, ILGWU collection, file 10.

2. Morris Sigman to Abraham Cahan, October 27, 1927, YIVO Institute for Jewish Research, Bund Archives, ILGWU collection, file 52. Sigman's casino was a summer guest house, not a gambling establishment. Sigman was born in Bessarabia in 1880 and went to New York in 1903 after a few years in London. He worked as a presser and, like a number of working-class Russian Jews who idealized the rural landscape, bought the land as soon as he accumulated the sum. See Benjamin Stolberg, *Tailor's Progress: The Story of a Famous Union and the Men Who Made It* (New York: Doubleday, Doran, 1944), 122.

3. Gus Tyler remembered that Sigman carried his rage at his ouster to his deathbed. "Sigman is dying, and he writes a will. And in the will he writes, 'The following people'—these were all leaders of the ILGWU who were on the other side—'The following people may not attend my funeral.'" Sigman appointed Harry Greenberg to enforce the provisions of his will that certain people not be allowed to attend. Interview with Gus Tyler, July 22, 1999.

4. Stolberg, *Tailor's Progress*, 148–50.

5. Harvey E. Klehr, *The Heyday of American Communism: The Depression Decade* (New York: Basic Books, 1984), 133, 163, 164.

6. Paul C. Mishler, *Raising Reds: The Young Pioneers, Radical Summer Camps, and Communist Political Culture in the United States* (New York: Columbia University Press, 1999), 5.

7. Randi Storch, *Red Chicago: American Communism at Its Grassroots, 1928–1935* (Urbana: University of Illinois Press, 2007), 25, 26, 76.

8. Mishler, *Raising Reds*, 5.

9. Storch, *Red Chicago*, 41.

10. Mishler, *Raising Reds*, 9, 37, 42–44, 50–55.

11. P. H. Geliebter, "Why a Yiddish Camp," 1930, 8, 9, YIVO Institute for Jewish Research, Bund Archives, Workmen's Circle collection, file 323.

12. Gedalia Sandler, *Kinderland: From Generation to Generation; Celebrating 75 Years of Camp Kinderland* (New York: Kinderland, 1998), 7.

13. Philip S. Foner, *The History of the Labor Movement in the United States*, vol. 10, *The T.U.E.L., 1925–1929* (New York: International Publishers, 1975), 266–67.

14. "A Call to All Women," Cornell University, Martin P. Catherwood Library, Kheel Center for Labor-Management Documentation and Archives [hereafter Kheel Center], ILGWU Records, collection 5780/14, box 18, file 11.

15. Storch, *Red Chicago*, 44–46.

16. Foner, *History of the Labor Movement*, 10:192–93.

17. Storch, *Red Chicago*, 44–46.

18. Klehr, *Heyday of American Communism*, 324–25.

19. Theodore Draper, *The Roots of American Communism* (New York: Viking, 1957), 387.

20. Klehr, *Heyday of American Communism*, 335. For one of the best scholarly narratives of the Scottsboro case, see James E. Goodman, *Stories of Scottsboro* (New York: Pantheon, 1994).

21. Klehr, *Heyday of American Communism*, 335.

22. Storch, *Red Chicago*, 111.

23. Ibid., 114–15.

24. ILGWU, "1927–1928 ILGWU Educational Department Bulletin," 6, Tamiment Vertical File, TF ILGWU Educational Department, 1928. Fannia M. Cohn repeated these ideas in various venues, including regular articles in the chief organ of the American Federation of Labor. See, for example, Fannia M. Cohn, "Twelve Years Educational Activities: International Ladies' Garment Workers' Union," *American Federationist*, January 1929, 110.

25. ILGWU, "1927–1928 ILGWU Educational Department Bulletin," 14–15.

26. ILGWU, "Report of the Educational Department to the Nineteenth Convention of the ILGWU, May 7, 1928," 14.

27. Walt Whitman, *Leaves of Grass: Comprehensive Reader's Edition*, ed. Harold W. Blodgett and Sculley Bradley (New York: NYU Press, 1965), 12.

28. David Reynolds, *Walt Whitman's America: A Cultural Biography* (New York: Knopf, 1995), 126.

29. Walt Whitman, "The Mystic Trumpeter," in *Leaves of Grass*.

30. See Ella Reeve "Mother" Bloor, *We Are Many* (New York: International Publishers, 1940), 19–24.

31. ILGWU, "1927–1928 ILGWU Educational Department Bulletin," 4.

32. Ibid., 5–6.

33. Ibid., 6.

34. ILGWU, "Report of the Educational Department to the Nineteenth Convention of the ILGWU, Boston, May 7, 1928," 27.

35. Fannia M. Cohn, "Educational and Social Activities," *American Federationist*, December 1929, 1448, 1449.

36. Ibid., 1449.

37. Sterling D. Spero and Abram L. Harris, *The Black Worker: The Negro and the Labor Movement* (New York: Columbia University Press, 1931), 87–115.

38. Ibid., 339–41.

39. Shiplacoff was a stalwart in the Socialist Party who had once been a New York State assemblyman. Melech Epstein, *Jewish Labor in the U.S.A.: An Industrial, Political, and Cultural History of the Jewish Labor Movement*, vol. 2, *1914–1952* (New York: Trade Union Sponsoring Committee, 1953), 77.

40. Abraham I. Shiplacoff to Fannia M. Cohn, July 18, 1927, New York Public Library, Fannia M. Cohn Papers, box 1, file 7.

41. Ibid.

42. ILGWU, "1928 Report to the ILGWU Convention," 286.

43. Ibid.

44. Kheel Center, ILGWU Records, collection 5780/15, box 3, file 16.

45. Kheel Center, ILGWU Records, collection 5780/16, box 2, file 14.

46. See Nathan Godfried, "Struggling over Politics and Culture: Organized Labor and Radio Station WEVD during the 1930s," *Labor History* 42, no. 4 (2001): 347–69; Elizabeth Fones-Wolf, *Waves of Opposition: Labor and the Struggle for Democratic Radio* (Urbana: University of Illinois Press, 2006), 21–22.

47. ILGWU, "Report to the 1929 ILGWU Convention," 85. The organizing campaign was moderately successful, but only for a short period. Local 22 jumped to a membership of twelve thousand for less than a year before falling to its lowest point in a decade.

48. Melinda Chateauvert, *Marching Together: Women of the Brotherhood of Sleeping Car Porters* (Urbana: University of Illinois Press, 1997), 44.

49. *Opportunity* (National Urban League) 4, no. 37 (January 1969): 197.

50. ILGWU, "ILGWU Graduates of Brookwood," 1936, Kheel Center, ILGWU Records, collection 5780/2, box 35, file 3B.

51. Nancy Marie Robertson, *Christian Sisterhood: Race Relations and the YWCA, 1906–1946* (Urbana: University of Illinois Press, 2007), 130.

52. ILGWU, "Report to the 1929 ILGWU Convention," 85–86.

53. ILGWU, "The 'Report of the Minority of the Committee on Officers' Report," May 1932, 11, Kheel Center, ILGWU Records, collection 5780/14, box 6, file 4.

54. ILGWU, "Financial Report, International Ladies' Garment Workers' Union, November 1, 1929–March 21, 1932, Twenty-First Convention, May 2, 1932, Elks Auditorium, Philadelphia, PA," 17.

55. Ibid., 11.

56. Annelise Orleck notes that Cohn solicited money from family members to support the Brookwood Labor College and the Workers Education Bureau, which she helped found. See Annelise Orleck, *Common Sense and a Little Fire: Women and Working-Class Politics in the United States, 1900–1965* (Chapel Hill: University of North Carolina Press, 1995), 185.

57. Dressmakers' Local 22 to Mr. A. L. Totten, June 15, 1931, Kheel Center, ILGWU Records, collection 5780/15, box 2, file 14.

58. Dressmakers' Local 22 to the *Amsterdam News*, August 11, 1931, Kheel Center, ILGWU Records, collection 5780/15, box 2, file 14.

59. ILGWU, "Report and Proceedings of the Twenty-First Convention of the International Ladies' Garment Workers' Union, Philadelphia, May 2 to May 14, 1932," 38.

60. Ibid., 42. Mendel Bailes, a Jew in Russian-controlled Poland, was accused in 1913 of killing a boy and using his blood for Passover matzo, a classic case of "blood libel." He was acquitted.

61. Ibid., 43.

62. Dressmakers Trade Union Circle to the Executive Board of Local 22, December 8, 1930, Kheel Center, ILGWU Records, collection 5780/15, box 2, file 11.

63. ILGWU, "Excerpts from the Minutes of the Executive Board and Joint Board Held since the Last Section Meetings—July 9, 1931," Kheel Center, ILGWU Records, collection 5780/15, box 2, file 11.

64. "Negro Choir Will Sing Old Plantation Songs," *Justice*, December 5, 1930, 7. The Hall Johnson Choir subsequently became one of the most recognizable groups in race musicals of the 1930s and 1940s, seen in such films as *Cabin in the Sky* (1943). Members of the choir also performed in Paul Peters's interracial labor play *Stevedore* and in the ILGWU production *Pins and Needles*.

65. See Donald Bogle, *Toms, Coons, Mulattoes, Mammies, and Bucks: An Interpretive History of Blacks in American Films* (New York: Continuum, 1991), 4–6.

66. ILGWU, "Manifesto Issued by the General Executive Board to the Cloakmakers and Dressmakers, December 12, 1928," YIVO Institute for Jewish Research, Bund Archives, ILGWU collection, folder 27.

67. Ibid.

68. Ibid.

69. Theodore Draper, *American Communism and Soviet Russia* (1960; repr., New York: Vintage, 1986), 131–33.

70. Ibid., 302–6.

71. Klehr, *Heyday of American Communism*, 12.

72. Ibid., 11.

73. James R. Barrett, *William Z. Foster and the Tragedy of American Radicalism* (Urbana: University of Illinois Press, 1999), 160.

74. Interview with Charles S. Zimmerman by Henoch Mendulsund, November 8, 1976, Kheel Center, ILGWU Records, collection 5780/118.

75. Draper, *American Communism and Soviet Russia*, 407–29; Barrett, *William Z. Foster*, 158.

76. Interview with Charles S. Zimmerman by Henoch Mendulsund, March 17, 1977.

77. Interview with Charles S. Zimmerman by Henoch Mendulsund, September 20, 1976, and March 17, 1977.

78. Interview with Charles S. Zimmerman by Henoch Mendulsund, April 14, 1977.

79. Yvette Richards, *Maida Springer: Pan-Africanist and International Labor Leader* (Pittsburgh: University of Pittsburgh Press, 2000), 38.

80. Kenneth C. Wolensky and Nicole H. Wolensky, *Fighting for the Union Label: The Women's Garment Industry and the ILGWU in Pennsylvania* (College Station: Penn State University Press, 2000), 47–49.

81. Interview with Charles S. Zimmerman by Henoch Mendulsund, March 24, 1977.

82. Ibid.

83. Interview with Charles S. Zimmerman by Henoch Mendulsund, March 30, 1977.

84. "Groups" in the ILGWU were caucuses that often organized around elections to support slates of candidates for local office and to the conventions of the union. Bluestein had been a supporter of Morris Sigman and as strongly opposed to some of the right-wing elements in the ILGWU as to the Communists. Bluestein formed an alliance with the Lovestoneites in part as a bulwark against the right-wing group in Local 22. Anarchists also formed a group, called the Dress Circle. See ibid.

85. Ibid.

86. Ibid. The term *pulled* refers to a method of organizing in which an outside organizer went into a targeted shop and pulled the shut-off switch to the electricity. The organizer would then announce that the shop was on strike and might blow a whistle or create some other diversion while workers poured out of the building. In ideal cases, workers expected the shop to be pulled, and shop leaders were prepared to lead workers on strike. But in other cases, workers were just as surprised as the employers were and followed organizers out of the shop without having had a say. Union activists through the 1930s never shied from rationalizing the tactic. In the worst shops, bosses were so tyrannical and controlling that workers were powerless to act initially on their own. If the union could not offer workers protection in the long run, there was no incentive for workers to remain in the union. Many of the garment workers involved in the August 1933 strike were organized using this method. Interview with Frank Stern, January 28, 2000.

87. "Editorial Notes," *Justice*, September 1, 1933, 2.

88. ILGWU, "Program of Local #22, I.L.G.W.U. 2/25/33," Kheel Center, ILGWU Records, collection 5780/15, box 2, file 14. Other language in this and other early literature from the Local 22 educational department is derived directly from Fannia Cohn's writings. See, for example, Cohn, "Twelve Years Educational Activities," 107.

89. ILGWU, "Entertainment and Dance, Dressmakers Union Local 22, Central Opera House, February 25, 1933," YIVO Institute for Jewish Research, Bund Archives, ILGWU collection, file 54.

90. Years later, Zimmerman accused Dubinsky of helping fix elections against him and other Communists during the 1920s and of creating paper locals to stack convention delegations. For a frank discussion between Zimmerman and Dubinsky of their early opposition and the tensions that carried over into their first years as secretary-manager and president, respectively, see David Dubinsky and A. H. Raskin, *David Dubinsky: A Life with Labor* (New York: Simon and Schuster, 1977), 84–117.

NOTES TO CHAPTER 5

1. Irving Bernstein, *The Turbulent Years: A History of the American Worker, 1933–1941* (Boston: Houghton Mifflin, 1970), 34.

2. The weaknesses of the NRA regarding unionization applied across most industries. On the lack of enforcement in the textile industry, see ibid., 303.

3. ILGWU, "Report of the General Executive Board to the Twenty-Second Convention of the International Ladies' Garment Workers' Union, May 28, 1934," 54.

4. David Dubinsky and A. H. Raskin, *David Dubinsky: A Life with Labor* (New York: Simon and Schuster, 1977), 112.

5. Interview with Maida Springer-Kemp, April 7, 1999.

6. Interview with Charles S. Zimmerman by Henoch Mendulsund, May 16, 1977, Cornell University, Martin P. Catherwood Library, Kheel Center for Labor-Management Documentation and Archives [hereafter Kheel Center], ILGWU Records, collection 5780/118.

7. "Editorial Notes," *Justice*, September 1, 1933, 2.

8. ILGWU, "Report and Proceedings to the Convention of the International Ladies' Garment Workers' Union, 1934." By 1937, the national Women's Trade Union League reported that the ILGWU represented between 5,517 and 6,122 Negroes. This range probably reflects midseason layoffs in the downturn year of 1937 in the garment industry. Kheel Center, ILGWU Records, collection 5780/2, box 12, folder 12A.

9. Many male leaders in the ILGWU held on to the myth that young women could not organize themselves or even be organized into the union. For the enduring myth that supported gender privilege in the trades and the union, see Alice Kessler-Harris, "Organizing the Unorganizable: Three Jewish Women and Their Union," *Labor History* 17, no. 1 (1976): 5–23; and Alice Kessler-Harris, "Where Are the Organized Women Workers?" in *A Heritage of Her Own: Toward a New Social History of American Women*, ed. Nancy Cott and Elizabeth Pleck, 343–66 (New York: Touchstone Books, 1979).

10. "Editorial Notes," *Justice*, September 1, 1933, 2.

11. Interview with Amelia Bucchieri, February 11, 1999. On Jewish employers that tried to undermine unionization through hiring across racial-ethnic lines, see Kessler-Harris, "Where Are the Organized Women Workers?" 358.

12. For methods of revolutionary and liberatory education that echo Fannia Cohn's sense of practical revolutionary education, see Paulo Freire, *Pedagogy of the Oppressed* (1970; repr., New York: Continuum, 2000), 87–124.

13. Fannia Cohn, "A New Era Opens for Labor Education," *Justice*, October 1, 1933, 9..

14. Susan Stone Wong, "From Soul to Strawberries: The International Ladies' Garment Workers' Union and Workers' Education, 1914–1950," in *Sisterhood and Solidarity: Workers' Education for Women, 1914–1984*, ed. Mary Frederickson (Philadelphia, 1984), 43.

15. ILGWU, "Suggestions for Social, Educational and Recreational Program for Our Local Unions, August, 1934," YIVO Institute for Jewish Research, unprocessed files, ILGWU—Educational Department.

16. ILGWU, "Financial Report, April 1, 1932 to April 30, 1934" (paper presented at the twenty-second convention of the International Ladies' Garment Workers' Union, Chicago, Illinois, May 28, 1934).

17. Will Herberg, "Educational Activities of Local 22," *Justice*, January 1934, 23.

18. Charles S. Zimmerman, "Local 22 Draws New Groups into Activity," *Justice*, December 1933, 11.

19. The AFL under Samuel Gompers first refused to admit unions that discriminated against Blacks in the 1890s. But by 1900, Gompers backpedaled and created a mechanism to grant AFL charters directly to Blacks barred from exclusively white unions. See Sterling D. Spero and Abram L. Harris, *The Black Worker: The Negro and the Labor Movement* (New York: Columbia University Press, 1931). A. Philip Randolph worked for years on behalf of the Brotherhood of Sleeping Car Porters to oblige the AFL to expel racist unions. At the

same moment that the Local 22 programs were formed in 1934, Randolph engineered a picket of the AFL's annual convention in San Francisco by Walter White and the National Association for the Advancement of Colored People to force the issue. See William H. Harris, *The Harder We Run: Black Workers since the Civil War* (New York: Oxford University Press, 1982), 89–92.

20. Eric Arnesen argues that this arrangement was at times beneficial to Blacks. In the case of New Orleans dockworkers, Blacks successfully built biracial union movements with white workers precisely because they had unions of their own from which they were able to assert their rights to work. See Eric Arnesen, *Waterfront Workers of New Orleans: Race, Class, and Politics, 1863–1923* (New York: Oxford University Press, 1990). Similarly, Dorothy Sue Cobble argues that separate women's local unions for waitresses offered a mechanism for women to assert a working-class feminist agenda in the workplace and in demanding protective legislation. See Dorothy Sue Cobble, *Dishing It Out: Waitresses and Their Unions in the Twentieth Century* (Urbana: University of Illinois Press, 1991). Sex segregation and racial segregation ensured the emergence of Black and female union leadership.

21. ILGWU, "Minutes of Local 22 Educational Committee, September 4, 1935," Kheel Center, ILGWU Records, collection 5780/36, box 1, vol. 7.

22. Nathan Glazer and Daniel P. Moynihan, *Beyond the Melting Pot: The Negroes, Puerto Ricans, Jews, Italians, and Irish of New York City* (Cambridge: MIT Press, 1963), 91.

23. ILGWU, "Minutes of the Executive Board of the Dressmakers Union Local 22, ILGWU, May 8, 1934," Kheel Center, ILGWU Records, collection 5780/36, box 1, vol. 7.

24. Virginia E. Sanchez Korrol, *From Colonia to Community: The History of Puerto Ricans in New York City* (Berkeley: University of California Press, 1994), 153–54, 158–59.

25. Interview with Louis Delgado by Celia Alvarez and Blanca Vasquez on August 15, 1984, Centro de Estudios Puertorriqueños, Hunter College of the City University of New York. Jesus Colon, prominent Puerto Rican community activist, spoke and wrote prolifically on the issue of tensions between Puerto Ricans and members of other ethnic groups. On Puerto Rican–Jewish relations, see the Jesus Colon Papers, Writings box 5, file 6, Centro de Estudios Puertorriqueños, Hunter College of the City University of New York.

26. Interview with Louise Delgado, August 15, 1984.

27. Rose Pesotta used education programs to organize new workers and to maintain organizations once they were established. See her discussions of organizing in Los Angeles and Puerto Rico in Rose Pesotta, *Bread upon the Waters* (1944; repr., Ithaca: Cornell University Press, 1987), 19–52, 103–34. See also Elizabeth Faue, "Paths of Unionization: Community, Bureaucracy, and Gender in the Minneapolis Labor Movement of the 1930s," in *Work Engendered: Toward a New History of American Labor*, ed. Ava Baron, 296–319 (Ithaca: Cornell University Press, 1991).

28. Interview with Gus Tyler, July 22, 1999; Benjamin Stolberg, *Tailor's Progress: The Story of a Famous Union and the Men Who Made It* (Garden City, NY: Doubleday, Doran, 1944), 234–36.

29. Interview with Gus Tyler, July 22, 1999.

30. Ibid.

31. Interview with Maida Springer-Kemp, April 7, 1999.

32. Interview with Anita Maurice, February 8, 1999.

33. Ibid.

34. ILGWU press release, November 26, 1934, Kheel Center, ILGWU Records, collection 5780/57, box 1, file 10.

35. The reference to "Spanish" reflects how members identified themselves as well as how the union referred to them. The Spanish members were mostly Puerto Ricans who lived in East Harlem. Union officials and Black representatives referred to the West Harlem branch of Local 22 variously as the West Harlem, English, or Colored section.

36. ILGWU, "September 13, 1935 Dressmakers Local 22 Press Release," Kheel Center, ILGWU Records, collection 5780/57, box 1, file 10; ILGWU, "Local 22 Education Committee Minutes," October 23, 1935, Kheel Center, ILGWU Records, collection 5780/14, box 8, file 5. Local 22 offered six dance groups—two modern, two ballroom, a dance group in the Harlem section, and a dance group in the Spanish section—and a drama group; *Justice*, June 1, 1936, 9.

37. ILGWU, "ILGWU Educational Department Annual Report for the Year Ending May 31, 1937." The 1938 publication *Growing Up: Twenty-One Years of Education with the I.L.G.W.U., 1917–1938* (by Ryllis Alexander Goslin and Omar Pancoast Goslin; New York: H. Wolff, 1938) claimed that over twenty-five thousand members joined classes in the 1937–1938 school year, but those numbers were likely projections written in advance of the year.

38. Michael Denning, *The Cultural Front: The Laboring of American Culture in the Twentieth Century* (New York: Verso, 1997).

39. Nora Lopez, "All in a Day," in *Labor Stuff* (New York: Educational Department, ILGWU Local 22, 1938), 6, Kheel Center, ILGWU Records, collection 5780/14, box 8, file 7.

40. ILGWU, "Minutes of the Educational Committee of Local 22, Wednesday, September 4, 1935," Kheel Center, ILGWU Records, collection 5780/15, box 2, file 11; ILGWU, "Local 22 Spring Course Guide, Spring 1935," Kheel Center, ILGWU Records, collection 5780/49, box 4, folder 4a.

41. Kheel Center, ILGWU Records, collection 5780/14, box 7, file 6.

42. *Justice*, January 1934, 24.

43. *Justice*, June 1934, 26–27.

44. Kheel Center, ILGWU Records, collection 5780/14, box 28, file 3.

45. ILGWU, "Minutes of the Executive Board Dressmakers Union Local 22, ILGWU, January 22, 1935," Kheel Center, ILGWU Records, collection 5780/36, box 1, vol. 7; *Labor Stuff* (New York: Educational Department, ILGWU Local 22, 1939), 35, Kheel Center, ILGWU Records, collection 5780/14, box 8, file 7.

46. *Labor Stuff*, 1938, 8, Kheel Center, ILGWU Records, collection 5780/14, box 8, file 7.

47. Educational Department of Dressmakers' Union, Local 22, ILGWU, "The Structure and Functioning of the ILGWU," 2, Kheel Center, ILGWU Records, collection 5780/14, box 8, file 6.

48. "N.Y. Dressmakers, Local 22, at Work," *Justice*, February 1934, 19.

49. "Who's Who in Local 91: Meet the Executive Board," *Our Aim*, September 1937, 3.

50. Karen Sacks uses the term "center women" to delineate gendered leadership roles among African American workers. She argues that in Black communities, center women work in concert with "spokesmen" to organize and represent their community, particularly in negotiating with whites. Karen Sacks, *Caring by the Hour: Women, Work, and Organizing at Duke Medical Center* (Urbana: University of Illinois Press, 1988), 120–21.

51. ILGWU, "November 26, 1934 Dressmakers Local 22 Press Release," Kheel Center, ILGWU Records, collection 5780/57, box 1, file 10; *Justice*, October 1934, 22.

52. ILGWU, "Dressmakers' International Ball," New York Public Library, Schomburg Center for Research in Black Culture, Manuscripts, Archives and Rare Books Division, collection MG100, box 2, folder 9.

53. Jay Williams, *Stage Left* (New York: Scribner's, 1974), 114, 118.

54. Paul Peters and George Sklar, *Stevedore: A Play in Three Acts* (New York: Covici, Friede, 1934).

55. Colette A. Hyman, *Staging Strikes: Workers' Theatre and the American Labor Movement* (Philadelphia: Temple University Press, 1997), 56–58, 74.

56. ILGWU Local 22, press release, November 10, 1934, YIVO Institute for Jewish Research, Bund Archives, ILGWU collection, file 49.

57. *Justice*, July 1934, 10.

58. ILGWU, "Organization Committee Report," April 28, 1934, Kheel Center, ILGWU Records, collection 5780/36, box 1.

59. "Educational Activities of Local 22," *Justice*, January 1934, 24.

60. Interview with Maida Springer-Kemp, April 7, 1999.

61. ILGWU, "Local 22 Education Committee Minutes Dec. 3, 1935," Kheel Center, ILGWU Records, collection 5780/14, box 8, file 5.

62. Kathy Peiss, *Cheap Amusements: Working Women and Leisure in Turn-of-the-Century New York* (Philadelphia: Temple University Press, 1986), 90–93.

63. Interview with Maida Springer-Kemp, April 7, 1999.

64. Interview with Celia Flores, September 13, 1999.

65. Ibid.

66. Rose Pesotta, "Singing in the Shop," *Justice*, July 1934.

67. Interview with Anita Maurice, February 8, 1999.

68. Interview with Amelia Bucchieri, February 11, 1999.

69. Interview with Maida Springer-Kemp, April 7, 1999.

70. "5,000 Italian Dressmakers Attend Dance in Brooklyn," *Justice*, March 1934, 25.

71. ILGWU, "Notice, Grand Solidarity Ball," Kheel Center, ILGWU Records, collection 5780/14, box 8, file 4.

72. ILGWU, "Minutes of Local 22 Executive Board, January 9, 1934," Kheel Center, ILGWU Records, collection 5780/36, box 1, vol. 7.

73. ILGWU Local 22 press release, Kheel Center, ILGWU Records, collection 5780/14, box 8, file 4.

74. Note that in the case of the one "Hindu," as with the many Jews, a religious designation replaced national origin.

75. Morris S. Novik to Charles Zimmerman, March 17, 1934, 3, Kheel Center, ILGWU Records, collection 5780/14, box 37, file 8. WEVD was named for Eugene Victor Debs, Socialist Party presidential candidate, who died in 1927, a year before the station was inaugurated.

76. *Unity House News* 1, no. 50 (August 26, 1935), Kheel Center, ILGWU Records, collection 5780/56, box 13, file 19.

77. *Unity House News* 1, no. 54 (September 1, 1935), Kheel Center, ILGWU Records, collection 5780/56, box 13, file 19. The Hall Johnson Choir was one of the best-known Black singing ensembles of the 1930s and 1940s. It performed in over a dozen Hollywood movies in that period, including *Green Pastures*, *Lost Horizon*, *Meet John Doe*, and *Cabin in the Sky*. The

ILGWU hired the Hall Johnson Choir to perform at least as early as 1929. Choir members later performed as part of the chorus in the union's Broadway play *Pins and Needles*.

78. Interview with Louise Delgado, August 15, 1984.

79. ILGWU, "Report on Spanish Activities Local 22, ILGWU, by Saby Nehama, Minutes of the Executive Board of the Dressmakers' Union Local 22, September 4, 1934," Kheel Center, ILGWU Records, collection 5780/36, box 1, vol. 7.

80. *Our Aim*, September 1937, 3.

81. For a similar scene in which local union members in Minneapolis greeted members of the General Executive Board as they were detraining for the 1938 ILGWU convention, see Elizabeth Faue, *Community of Suffering and Struggle: Women, Men, and the Labor Movement in Minneapolis, 1915–1945* (Chapel Hill: University of North Carolina Press, 1991), 126.

NOTES TO CHAPTER 6

1. ILGWU, "Report of the General Executive Board to the Twenty-Fourth Convention of the International Ladies' Garment Workers' Union, 1937," 43–44.

2. ILGWU, "Report and Record of the Twenty-Third Convention of the International Ladies' Garment Workers' Union, May 27, 1940," 55.

3. ILGWU, "Report and Proceedings of the Twenty-Second Convention of the International Ladies' Garment Workers' Union, May 28, 1934," 422.

4. Cornell University, Martin P. Catherwood Library, Kheel Center for Labor-Management Documentation and Archives [hereafter Kheel Center], ILGWU Records, collection 5780/49, box 4, folder 4a.

5. *It's Coming at Last*, Tamiment Vertical File.

6. Historians of the Communist Party USA disagree on numbers. As Harvey E. Klehr points out, the charge over the years by anti-Communists and anti-Semites that Jews and Bolsheviks were the same people have complicated the discussion. See Harvey E. Klehr, *Communist Cadre: The Social Background of the American Communist Party Elite* (Stanford, CA: Hoover Institution Press, 1978), 37–52; and Nathan Glazer, *The Social Basis of American Communism* (New York: Harcourt, Brace and World, 1961), 131.

7. Robin D. G. Kelley, *Hammer and Hoe: Alabama Communists during the Great Depression* (Chapel Hill: University of North Carolina Press, 1990), 94–96, 99, 105; Robbie Lieberman, *"My Song Is My Weapon": People's Songs, American Communism, and the Politics of Culture, 1930–1950* (Urbana: University of Illinois Press, 1995), 14–24. The Socialist Party camps were called Pioneer Youth.

8. The *Daily Worker* carried regular announcements of dances and athletic competitions sponsored by the Communist Party. For the Communist Party's focus on organizing Black workers during the 1930s, see Mark Naison, *Communists in Harlem during the Great Depression* (New York: Grove, 1983); Kelley, *Hammer and Hoe*.

9. Joel Seidman, *The Needle Trades* (New York: Farrar and Rinehart, 1942), 169.

10. Interview with Mary Boyer, February 12, 1999.

11. Ibid.

12. Unprocessed film in the Wagner Archives at the Tamiment Library, New York University. One veteran of the 1930s ILGWU told me, "We were the best-dressed workers in the whole city because, of course, we made our own clothes."

13. "A.F. of L. Protests Nazi Olympics," *Our Aim*, April 1936, 4.

14. For more on counter-Olympics, see Gail Malmgreen, "Labor and the Holocaust: The Jewish Labor Committee and the Anti-Nazi Struggle," *Labor's Heritage*, October 1991, 20–25.

15. "Mayor La Guardia Trophy Presented to 91 Athletes," *Our Aim*, August 1936, 6.

16. Quoted in Harry Merton Goldman, "Pins and Needles: An Oral History" (Ph.D. diss., New York University, 1977), 117.

17. Interview with Celia Flores, September 13, 1999.

18. Interview with Chencha Valdez, December 18, 1998.

19. Interview with Charles S. Zimmerman by Henoch Mendulsund, May 16, 1977, Kheel Center, ILGWU Records, collection 5780/118.

20. ILGWU, "Resolution Number 5, on Proportional Representation," *Resolutions of Dressmakers Union, Local 22 for the 22nd Biennial Convention of the ILGWU, May 1934,* Kheel Center, ILGWU Records, collection 5780/14, box 6, file 4.

21. Ibid. Member locals of the ILGWU located across the country were responsible for paying the delegates' way to the national conventions. For the details and Zimmerman's rationale, see ILGWU, "Preliminary Report: Dressmakers Union Local 22, ILGWU," April 15, 1933–April 1, 1934, 11, Kheel Center, ILGWU Records, collection 5780/36, box 1.

22. Joint boards are made up of locals in an industry or in a geographic area.

23. Charles S. Zimmerman, "Local 22 Draws New Groups into Activity," *Justice*, December 1933, 10.

24. Interview with Nettie Harari Shrog, May 22, 2000.

25. "Formation of Spanish Local Urged on President Dubinsky," *Justice*, January 1934, 29.

26. ILGWU, "Minutes of the Executive Board of the Dressmakers' Union Local #22, ILGWU, March 5, 1934, and May 8, 1934," Kheel Center, ILGWU Records, collection 5780/36, box 1, vol. 7.

27. Dubinsky held both positions beginning in 1932. See Benjamin Stolberg, *Tailor's Progress: The Story of a Famous Union and the Men Who Made It* (New York: Doubleday, Doran, 1944), 179–80.

28. ILGWU, "Report and Proceedings of the 21st Biennial Convention, 1932," 75.

29. "Election Marks New Chapter in Local 9," *Justice*, March 1934, 23.

30. Interview with Gus Tyler, July 22, 1999.

31. Interview with Maida Springer-Kemp, April 7, 1999.

32. "Impressions of Unity House Institute," *Our Aim*, June 1935, 6–7.

33. Ibid.

34. ILGWU, "Local 22 Executive Board Minutes, March 12, 1935," Kheel Center, ILGWU Records, collection 5780/36, box 1, vol. 7.

35. Lillian Gaskin to the members of the executive board, April 17, 1935, Kheel Center, ILGWU Records, collection 5780/14, box 13, file 8.

36. Lillian Gaskin, "A Report of My Work in Chicago, Ill.," n.d., 3, Kheel Center, ILGWU Records, collection 5780/14, box 13, file 8.

37. Lillian Gaskin to Charles Zimmerman, September 5, 1935, Kheel Center, ILGWU Records, collection 5780/14, box 13, file 8.

38. Lillian Gaskin to Charles Zimmerman, October 10, 1935, Kheel Center, ILGWU Records, collection 5780/14, box 13, file 8.

39. Lillian Gaskin to Charles Zimmerman, October 22, 1935, Kheel Center, ILGWU Records, collection 5780/14, box 13, file 8.

40. Charles S. Zimmerman to Lillian Gaskin, October 25, 1935, Kheel Center, ILGWU Records, collection 5780/14, box 13, file 8.

41. Lillian Gaskin to Charles S. Zimmerman, October 26, 1935, Kheel Center, ILGWU Records, collection 5780/14, box 13, file 8.

42. David Dubinsky to Charles Zimmerman, November 16, 1934, Kheel Center ILGWU Records, collection 5780/14, box 7, file 2.

43. John H. Seabrook, "Black and White United: The Career of Frank R. Crosswaith" (Ph.D. diss., Rutgers University, 1980), 6, 87, 14–15, 53, 94.

44. Nick Salvatore, *Eugene V. Debs: Citizen and Socialist* (Urbana: University of Illinois Press, 1982), 226.

45. Seabrook, "Black and White United," 29

46. Ibid., 106, 105.

47. Frank Crosswaith, "Some Vital Problems of Negro Labor," *Justice*, January 1, 1935, 5.

48. Frank Crosswaith, "Negro Dress Workers Ready for Battle," *Justice*, January 15, 1936, 1, 9.

49. "Sadie: A Presser," *Justice*, January 1, 1936, 5.

50. "Fay: An Examiner," *Justice*, January 15, 1936, 6; Crosswaith, "Negro Dress Workers Ready for Battle," 9. In a photomontage of voting for Local 22 officers, the picture of a Black woman exuberantly holding up her index finger in a victory sign is most prominent. *Justice*, April 15, 1935, 7. See also the biographical sketches in *Justice*, October 15, 1935, 6, and April 15, 1936, 5.

51. NLC, "Minutes of the Negro Labor Committee, January 29, 1937," New York Public Library, Schomburg Center for Research in Black Culture , Negro Labor Committee Papers, box 8, reel 14, file 82.

52. "The Negro Labor Committee," New York Public Library, Schomburg Center for Research in Black Culture, Negro Labor Committee Papers, box 8, reel 4.

53. According to John Seabrook, Crosswaith had a history of embellishing his accomplishments, and this tendency was noticed by potential supporters. Seabrook, "Black and White United," 70–71, 211, 227.

54. Roi Ottley and William J. Weatherby, *The Negro in New York: An Informed Social History* (Dobbs Ferry, NY: Oceana, 1967), 283–84.

55. Leyla Vural, "Unionism as a Way of Life" (Ph.D. diss., Rutgers University, 1994), 176–78.

56. Interview with Gus Tyler, July 22, 1999; Stolberg, *Tailor's Progress*, 296.

57. Interview with Gus Tyler, July 22, 1999.

58. *Our Aim*, February 1935, 6.

59. Interview with Gus Tyler, July 22, 1999.

60. Kenneth C. Wolensky, *Fighting for the Union Label: The Women's Garment Industry and the ILGWU in Pennsylvania* (University Park: Penn State University Press, 2002), 35.

61. Interview with Gus Tyler, July 22, 1999.

62. Ibid.

63. Ibid.

64. Vural, "Unionism as a Way of Life," 181.

65. Interview with Gus Tyler, July 22, 1999.

66. ILGWU Educational Department, "You and Your Union," YIVO Institute for Jewish Research, Bund Archives, ILGWU collection, file 15, 13–14.

67. "Can Women Lead?" reprinted from *Justice*, February 15, 1936, 2, YIVO Institute for Jewish Research, Bund Archives, ILGWU collection, file 13.

68. *Justice*, February 1, 1935, 6.

69. ILGWU, "Minutes of the Educational Committee of Local 22, Dec. 3, 1935," Kheel Center, ILGWU Records, collection 5780/14, box 8, file 5.

70. *Justice*, January 15, 1936, 7.

71. *Justice*, January 1, 1936, 5.

72. *Justice*, January 15, 1936, 1.

73. ILGWU, "Report and Proceedings of the Twenty-Third Convention of the International Ladies' Garment Workers' Union, 1937," 41.

74. ILGWU, "Negotiation and Enforcement Problems by David Dubinsky: Summary of a Talk Given March 2, 1936," Kheel Center, ILGWU Records, collection 5780/49, box 11, file folder 2.

75. Ibid.

76. ILGWU, "Report and Proceedings of the 1934 ILGWU Convention," 8–13. Irving Bernstein, *The Turbulent Years: A History of the American Worker, 1933–1941* (Boston: Houghton Mifflin, 1970), 30–36. Bernstein takes Dubinsky, John L. Lewis, William Green, and Dan Tobin at their word. But, as this chapter shows, Dubinsky had a philosophical and strategic interest in reinventing the narrative of labor's revival.

77. Bernstein, *Turbulent Years*, 34. Interestingly, Samuel Gompers had called the Clayton Anti-Trust Act of 1914 "Labor's Magna Carta."

78. "Editorial Notes," *Justice*, August 1, 1933, 2.

79. Rose Pesotta, "Address to the 13th Convention of the Free Federation of Labor at Mayaguez, Puerto Rico in September 1934," YIVO Institute for Jewish Research, Bund Archives, ILGWU collection, file 23. Rose Pesotta eloquently encapsulated the militant and feminist spirit of the 1933 generation.

80. *Organizer* 1, no. 1 (n.d.), Kheel Center, ILGWU Records, collection 5780/14, box 20, file 1.

81. Pesotta, "Address to the 13th Convention of the Free Federation of Labor at Mayaguez."

82. Rose Pesotta, "The Revolt of Los Angeles Dressmakers," *Justice*, January 1934, 21.

83. Ibid.

84. David Dubinsky and A. H. Raskin, *David Dubinsky: A Life with Labor* (New York: Simon and Schuster, 1977), 115.

85. Franklin Delano Roosevelt, "Sunday Radio Address," September 30, 1934.

86. Local 22 press release, October 3, 1934, YIVO Institute for Jewish Research, Bund Archives, ILGWU collection, file 49.

87. ILGWU, *Our Union at Work: A Survey of the Activities of Dressmakers Union Local 22, I.L.G.W.U., from April, 1935 to April, 1937*, 5, YIVO Institute for Jewish Research, Bund Archives, ILGWU collection, file 54.

88. Robert D. Parmet, *The Master of Seventh Avenue: David Dubinsky and the American Labor Movement* (New York: NYU Press, 2005), 128–32.

1. Brooks Atkinson, "Garment Specialty: 'Pins and Needles,' Being a Night Out for Thirty-Two I.L.G.W.U. Members," *New York Times*, January 23, 1938.

2. Ibid.

3. Julia L. Foulkes, "Angels 'Rewolt': Jewish Women in Modern Dance in the 1930s," *American Jewish History* 88, no. 2 (2000): 233–52.

4. Benjamin Stolberg, *Tailor's Progress: The Story of a Famous Union and the Men Who Made It* (New York: Doubleday, Doran, 1944), 296.

5. Ibid..

6. Ibid., 296–97.

7. Harry Merton Goldman, "Pins and Needles: An Oral History," (Ph.D. diss., New York University, 1977), 38.

8. According to several Internet websites, *Hellzapoppin* opened on September 22, 1938, and closed on December 17, 1941 after 1,404 performances. See, for example, Internet Broadway Database, "Hellzapoppin," www.ibdb.com/show.php?id=10069. Michael Denning reports that the *Pins and Needles* record stood until *Oklahoma*. See Michael Denning, *The Cultural Front: The Laboring of American Culture in the Twentieth Century* (New York: Verso, 1996), 295.

9. David Alan Rush, "A History and Evaluation of the ILGWU Labor Stage and Its Production of *Pins and Needles*, 1937–1940" (master's thesis, University of Iowa, 1965), 48–88.

10. Jay Williams, *Stage Left* (New York: Scribner's, 1974), 157, 160–64.

11. Denning, *Cultural Front*, 307.

12. Colette A. Hyman, *Staging Strikes: Workers' Theatre and the American Labor Movement* (Philadelphia: Temple University Press), 29, 37.

13. Williams, *Stage Left*, 203–6.

14. Rush, "History and Evaluation of the ILGWU Labor Stage," 41.

15. *Unity House News* 1, no. 51 (August 29, 1935), Cornell University, Martin P. Catherwood Library, Kheel Center for Labor-Management Documentation and Archives [hereafter Kheel Center], ILGWU Records, collection 5780/56, box 13, folder 19.

16. *Unity House News* 1, no. 54 (September 1, 1935), Kheel Center, ILGWU Records, collection 5780/56, box 13, folder 19; ILGWU, "Report to the Delegates of the Twenty-Third Convention of the International Ladies' Garment Workers' Union, 1937," 174.

17. Williams, *Stage Left*, 241.

18. Mari Jo Buhle, Paul Buhle, and Dan Georgakas, eds., *Encyclopedia of the American Left* (Urbana: University of Illinois Press, 1992), 99.

19. Williams, *Stage Left*, 225.

20. Goldman, "Pins and Needles," 27.

21. Quoted in ibid., 117.

22. Quoted in ibid., 116.

23. Liner notes, *Pins and Needles: Twenty-Fifth Anniversary Edition of the Hit Musical Revue*, music and lyrics by Harold Rome (Columbia Records, 1962).

24. Williams, *Stage Left*, 39; *Unity House News* 1, no. 48 (August 24, 1935), Kheel Center, ILGWU Records, collection 5780/56, box 13, folder 19.

25. Goldman, "Pins and Needles," 62.

26. Ibid., 63.

27. ILGWU, "Report to the Delegates of the Twenty-Third Convention of the International Ladies' Garment Workers' Union, 1937," 176.

28. Stolberg, *Tailor's Progress*, 297.

29. Goldman, "Pins and Needles," 63.

30. Ibid., 76.

31. Ibid., 164.

32. Ibid., 189. The *New York Post* reported on March 11, 1940, that the first company played fifty theaters in forty-one weeks.

33. Goldman, "Pins and Needles," 164, 175, 182.

34. Ibid., 5.

35. "'Pins & Needles': A Labor Union Goes into Show Business," *Life*, December 27, 1937, 52.

36. New York University, Tamiment Library, Department Store Organizing Committee Papers, box 1, folder: Department Store Employees Union (CIO)—Macy Chapter—"Macy Unionizer"; Gary M. Fink, ed., *The Greenwood Encyclopedia of American Institutions: Labor Unions* (Westport, CT: Greenwood, 1977), 331–32.

37. *Pins and Needles* brochure, YIVO Institute for Jewish Research, Bund Archives, ILGWU collection, file 11.

38. For a biography of Corey/Fraina that details his life in the Industrial Workers of the World, his participation in the founding of the American Communist Party, and his expulsion along with fellow Lovestoneites, see Paul M. Buhle, *A Dreamer's Paradise Lost: Louis C. Fraina/Lewis Corey (1892–1953) and the Decline of Radicalism in the United States* (Atlantic Highlands, NJ: Humanities Press International, 1995).

39. ILGWU, "Local 22 Executive Committee Minutes, October 20, 1937," Kheel Center, ILGWU Records, collection 5780/36, box 1, vol. 7.

40. Ibid..

41. Ibid.

42. Interview with Ruth Rubinstein Graeber, January 26, 2000.

43. Ethel Kushner, "Build a Labor Theater," in *Labor Stuff* (New York: Educational Department, ILGWU Local 22, 1939), 34, Kheel Center, ILGWU Records, collection 5780/14, box 8, file 7.

44. Ibid.

45. *Pins and Needles* program, n.d., New York University, Tamiment Vertical File, OF Labor Stage (New York, NY).

46. Ibid.

47. Goldman, "Pins and Needles," 114.

48. Interview with Irwin Corey, February 12, 2002; also see Goldman, "Pins and Needles," 34.

49. Quoted in Goldman, "Pins and Needles," 121.

50. Quoted in ibid., 122.

51. Interview with Ruth Rubinstein Graeber, January 26, 2000.

52. Ibid.

53. "'Pins & Needles': A Labor Union Goes into Show Business," 52.

54. Interview with Ruth Rubinstein Graeber, January 26, 2000.

55. *Unity House News* 1, no. 45 (August 24, 1935), Kheel Center, ILGWU Records, collection 5780/56, box 13, folder 19.

56. Interview with Ruth Rubinstein Graeber, January 26, 2000.

57. Interview with Irwin Corey, February 12, 2002.

58. Interview with Nettie Harari Shrog, May 22, 2000.

59. Interview with Ruth Rubinstein Graeber, January 26, 2000.

60. Quoted in Goldman, "Pins and Needles," 159.

61. Quoted in ibid., 155.

62. Allan Keiler, *Marian Anderson: A Singer's Journey* (New York: Scribner, 2000), 164. In 1939, Eleanor Roosevelt very publicly resigned from the Daughters of the American Revolution after the organization refused to rent its hall for a concert in which Marian Anderson was to sing. Roosevelt then arranged for a nationally broadcasted concern for Anderson at the Lincoln Memorial. Ibid., 207–15.

63. Interview with Olive Pearman Ashford, May 29, 2000.

64. Interview with Nettie Harari Shrog, May 22, 2000.

65. "Interviews Sepia Dancer in Big Labor Musical, 'Pins and Needles,'" *Philadelphia Independent*, May 8, 1938, 7.

66. Interview with Olive Pearman Ashford, May 29, 2000.

67. Ibid.

68. Pearman, who appeared in only a few numbers of the twenty or so skits in *Pins and Needles*, also worked as a seamstress for the company. She was enormously proud of her skill, and rightly so; it was quite an accomplishment to be recognized as a skilled seamstress among professional garment workers. She wrote, "We had a banquet given us by the ILGWU at the Roosevelt Hotel and I made a black cotton lace dress. At 2:00 pm it was 4 yards of material and I did a matinee and an evening performance and by the end of the show—10:45 pm it was a finished dress, all pressed and trimmed, snaps and all. I was at the banquet by 11:30 all dressed. And the main part is I made it all by hand, because the machine was out of order and in the shop getting fixed. What a dame, ha!" Olive Pearman to Mrs. A. A. Pearman, July 30, 1938, in the possession of Olive Pearman Ashford.

69. "Interviews Sepia Dancer in Big Labor Musical." Pearman and the other cast members did not always receive their full salaries. In one letter, Pearman noted, "I am sending 10 bucks. So sorry I can't send more this week but I have to send a lot to the union for back dues." Olive Pearman to Mrs. A. A. Pearman, July 30, 1938.

70. Olive Pearman to A. A. Pearman, from Ottawa, Canada, n.d., in the possession of Olive Pearman Ashford.

71. Interview with Olive Pearman Ashford, May 29, 2000.

72. Rosten, quoted in Goldman, "Pins and Needles," 195.

73. Ibid.

74. Interviews with Nettie Harari Shrog, May 22, 2000, and Ruth Rubinstein Graeber, January 26, 2000.

75. Tucker, quoted in Goldman, "Pins and Needles," 192–93.

76. Interview with Ruth Rubinstein Graeber, January 26, 2000.

77. Goldman, "Pins and Needles," 198–99.

78. Quoted in ibid., 149.

79. Quoted in ibid., 108.

80. Quoted in ibid., 107.

81. Ibid., 107–8.

82. Interview with Ruth Rubinstein Graeber, January 26, 2000.

83. Ibid.

84. Ibid.

85. Paul Seymour, quoted in Goldman, "Pins and Needles," 164.

86. Interview with Amelia Bucchieri, February 11, 1999.

87. Ibid.

88. *Justice*, May–June 1934, 9.

89. "Men, Awake!" words and music by Harold J. Rome, New York University, Tamiment Folder 86, Songbook Collection, The International.

90. Louis Yagoda, "Our English-Speaking Branches," *Call* (Workmen's Circle), May–June 1940, 51.

91. Ibid.

92. Goldberg, "Pins and Needles," 7.

93. YIVO Institute for Jewish Research, Bund Archives, ILGWU collection, file 11.

94. Ibid.

95. New York Public Library for the Performing Arts, Billy Rose Theatre collection, Pins and Needles Programme File.

96. Ibid.

97. Goldman, "Pins and Needles," 10.

98. *Call* (Workmen's Circle), January 1940, 3.

99. Morgan Himelstein, *Drama Was a Weapon* (New Brunswick: Rutgers University Press, 1963), 82.

100. *Call* (Workmen's Circle), August–September 1940, 4.

101. The idea of a cross-class Jewish alliance resonated well with Zionist ideology, which had, until this point, remained a subordinate political movement in the Jewish Diaspora. With the rise of Nazism, Zionism was gaining converts among former Yiddish socialists.

102. *Call* (Workmen's Circle), August–September 1940, 5.

103. *Call* (Workmen's Circle), January 1941, 9.

104. See Melech Epstein, *Jewish Labor in the U.S.A.: An Industrial, Political and Cultural History of the Jewish Labor Movement*, vol. 2, *1914–1952* (New York: Trade Union Sponsoring Committee, 1953), 84–85.

105. *Call* (Workmen's Circle), May 1941, 10.

106. Ibid.

NOTES TO THE EPILOGUE

1. Lizabeth Cohen, *Making a New Deal: Industrial Workers in Chicago, 1919–1939* (New York: Cambridge University Press, 1990), 324.

2. ILGWU, "Report of the Education Committee of Local 22," May 20, 1942, Cornell University, Martin P. Catherwood Library, Kheel Center for Labor Management Documentation and Archives [hereafter Kheel Center], ILGWU Records, collection 5780/14, box 8, file 5.

3. Franklin D. Roosevelt, *State of the Union Address to the Congress, January 6, 1941*.

4. Solomon Rabinowitz, "Socialists and the War," *Call* (Workmen's Circle), November 1942, 14.

5. Here, the "United Nations" refers not to the current UN, which was formed after the war's end, but to the twenty-six nations of the Atlantic Charter, led by the United States and Great Britain, that pledged to fight the war against Germany.

6. *Justice*, July 1, 1942, 6, 13.

7. Interview with Maida Springer-Kemp, April 7, 1999.

8. B. F. McLaurin, Chairman of the March on Washington Movement, to co-worker, May 6, 1942, Kheel Center, ILGWU Records, collection 5780/14-28-3.

9. Excerpts from keynote address to the Policy Conference of the March on Washington Movement, meeting in Detroit, Michigan, September 26, 1942, from the *Survey Graphic* 31 (November 1942): 488–89, available at http://www.bsos.umd.edu/aasp/chateauvert/mowmcall.htm.

10. Mark Starr to "Dear Colleague," May 1, 1946, New York Public Library, Schomburg Center for Research in Black Culture, Negro Labor Committee Papers, box 29, reel 14, F 23 FRC-ILGWU (1).

11. Ibid., 2.

Bibliography

MANUSCRIPT SOURCES

American Jewish Historical Society Archives, New York, NY
    Workmen's Circle collection
Centro de Estudios Puertorriqueños, Hunter College, New York, NY
Martin P. Catherwood Library, Cornell University, Ithaca, NY
    ILGWU Records, Kheel Center for Labor-Management Documentation and Archives
New York Public Library, New York, NY
    Fannia Cohn Papers, Rare Books and Manuscripts
    Frank Crosswaith Papers, Schomburg Center for Research in Black Culture
    Negro Labor Committee Papers, Schomburg Center for Research in Black Culture
    Rose Pesotta Papers, Rare Books and Manuscripts
    Programme File: *Pins and Needles*, Billy Rose Theatre Collection, Performing Arts
Tamiment Institute Archives, Bobst Library, New York University, New York, NY
    International Ladies' Garment Workers' Union Papers, Vertical Files
    Rand School Papers
YIVO Center for Jewish Research, New York, NY
    Bund Archives
    International Ladies' Garment Workers' Union collection

ORAL HISTORIES AND INTERVIEWS

Delgado, Louise. Interview by Celia Alvarez and Blanca Vasquez, August 15, 1984. Located
    at Centro de Estudios Puertorriqueños, Hunter College, New York, NY.
Harari Shrog, Nettie. Interview by Colette Hyman, July 14, 1991, New York, NY.
Pearman Ashford, Olive. Interview by Colette Hyman, June 29, 1991, Far Rockaway, NY.
Zimmerman, Charles Sasha. Interviews by Henoch Mendulsund, December 11, 1975,
    December 23, 1975, December 26, 1975, July 1, 1976, September 20, 1976, October 14,
    1976, November 8, 1976, March 17, 1977, March 24, 1977, March 30, 1977, April 14, 1977,
    May 16, 1977.

INTERVIEWS WITH AUTHOR

Andrade, Kathy. December 11, 1998, New York, NY
Boyer, Mary. February 12, 1999, Bronx, NY
Bucchieri, Amelia. February 11, 1999, New York, NY
Corey, Irwin. February 12, 2002, New York, NY

Cumberbatch, Marie. February 10, 1999, Queens, NY
Flores, Celia. September 13, 1999, New York, NY
Graeber, Ruth Rubinstein. January 26, 2000, New York, NY
Mankoff, Walter. December 29, 1998, New York, NY
Maurice, Anita. February 8, 1999, Brooklyn, NY
Novich, Shirley. January 1, 2001, New York, NY
Pearman Ashford, Olive. May 29, 2000, Long Island, NY
Shrog, Nettie Harari. May 22, 2000, New York, NY
Springer-Kemp, Maida. April 7, 1999, Pittsburgh, PA
Stern, Eli. January 21, 2000, Mayfield Heights, OH
Stern, Frank. January 28, 2000, New York, NY
Tyler, Gus. July 22, 1999, New York, NY
Valdez, Inocencia "Chencha." December 18, 1998, Bronx, NY

NEWSPAPERS, JOURNALS, AND CONVENTION PROCEEDINGS

American Federationist
Call (Socialist Party)
Call (Workmen's Circle)
Daily Worker (Communist Party)
ILGWU convention reports: 1918, 1920, 1922, 1924, 1925, 1928, 1932, 1934, 1937, 1940
Jewish Daily Forward
Justice
Ladies' Garment Worker
Life
New York Post
New York Times
Opportunity (National Urban League)
Our Aim
Philadelphia Independent
Pittsburgh Courier

BOOKS, ARTICLES, AND DISSERTATIONS

Anderson, Benedict. *Imagined Communities: Reflections on the Origin and Spread of Nationalism.* New York: Verso, 1991.
Ansky, S. *The Dybbuk: A Play in Four Acts by S. Ansky.* Trans. Henry G. Alsberg and Winnefred Katzin. New York: Liveright, 1926.
Arnesen, Eric. *Waterfront Workers of New Orleans: Race, Class, and Politics, 1863–1923.* New York: Oxford University Press, 1990.
Atkinson, Brooks. "Garment Specialty: 'Pins and Needles,' Being a Night Out for Thirty-Two I.L.G.W.U. Members," *New York Times,* January 23, 1938.
Barrett, James R. "Americanization from the Bottom Up: Immigration and the Remaking of the Working Class in the United States, 1880–1930," *Journal of American History* 79, no. 3 (1992): 996–1020.

———. *William Z. Foster and the Tragedy of American Radicalism*. Urbana: University of Illinois Press, 1999.

Barrett James R., and David Roediger. "Inbetween Peoples: Race, Nationality, and the 'New Immigrant' Working Class." *Journal of American Ethnic History* 16 (1997): 3–34.

Bauer, Otto. *The Question of Nationalities and Social Democracy*. Trans. Joseph O'Donnell. Minneapolis: University of Minnesota Press, 2000.

Baxandall, Rosalyn, Linda Gordon, and Susan Reverby, eds. *America's Working Women: A Documentary History, 1600 to the Present*. New York: Vintage Books, 1976.

Bender, Daniel E. "Too Much of Distasteful Masculinity: Historicizing Sexual Harassment in the Garment Sweatshop and Factory." *Journal of Women's History* 15, no. 3 (2004): 91–116.

Bernstein, Irving. *The Lean Years: A History of the American Worker, 1920–1933*. Boston: Houghton Mifflin, 1960.

———. *The Turbulent Years: A History of the American Worker, 1933–1941*. Boston: Houghton Mifflin, 1970.

Bloom, Jonathan D. "Brookwood Labor College, 1921–1933: Training Ground for Union Organizers." Master's thesis, Rutgers University, 1979.

———. "Brookwood Labor College and the Progressive Labor Network of the Interwar United States, 1921–1937. Ph.D. diss., New York University, 1992.

Bloor, Ella Reeve "Mother." *We Are Many*. New York: International Publishers, 1940.

Bogle, Donald. *Toms, Coons, Mulattoes, Mammies, and Bucks: An Interpretive History of Blacks in American Films*. New York: Continuum, 1991.

Bourne, Randolph. "Trans-national America." *Atlantic Monthly*, July 1916.

Brandes, Joseph. "From Sweatshop to Stability: Jewish Labor between Two World Wars." *YIVO Annual* 16 (1976): 1–149.

Brodkin, Karen. *How Jews Became White Folks and What That Says about Race in America*. New Brunswick: Rutgers University Press, 1994.

Buhle, Mari Jo. *Women and American Socialism, 1870–1920*. Urbana: University of Illinois Press, 1983.

Buhle, Mari Jo, Paul Buhle, and Dan Georgakas, eds. *Encyclopedia of the American Left*. Urbana: University of Illinois Press, 1992.

Buhle, Paul M. *A Dreamer's Paradise Lost: Louis C. Fraina/Lewis Corey (1892–1953) and the Decline of Radicalism in the United States*. Atlantic Highlands, NJ: Humanities Press International, 1995.

Buhle, Paul M., and Robin D. G. Kelley. "Allies of a Different Sort: Jews and Blacks in the American Left." In *Struggles in the Promised Land: Toward a History of Black-Jewish Relations in the United States*, ed. Jack Salzman and Cornel West, 197–229. New York: Oxford University Press, 1997.

Bus, Annette P. "Lower East Side, New York: Turn of the Century." In *Encyclopedia of the American Left*, ed. Mari Jo Buhle, Paul Buhle, and Dan Georgakas, 437–40. Urbana: University of Illinois Press, 1992.

Chateauvert, Melinda. *Marching Together: Women of the Brotherhood of Sleeping Car Porters*. Urbana: University of Illinois Press, 1997.

Cobble, Dorothy Sue. *Dishing It Out: Waitresses and Their Unions in the Twentieth Century*. Urbana: University of Illinois Press, 1991.

————. *The Other Women's Movement: Workplace Justice and Social Rights in Modern America*. Princeton: Princeton University Press, 2003.

Cohen, Lizabeth. *Making a New Deal: Industrial Workers in Chicago, 1919–1939*. New York: Cambridge University Press, 1990.

Cohen, Ricki Carole Meyers. "Fannia Cohn and the International Ladies' Garment Workers' Union." Ph.D. diss., University of Southern California, 1976.

Cohn, Fannia. "The A.F. of L. Convention for Adult Labor Education." *Justice*, July 5, 1919, 3.

————. "Educational and Social Activities." *American Federationist*, December 1929, 1446–52.

————. "A New Era Opens for Labor Education." *Justice*, October 1, 1933, 9.

————. "Twelve Years Educational Activities: International Ladies' Garment Workers' Union." *American Federationist*, January 1929, 110.

Conzen, Kathleen Neils, David A. Gerber, Ewa Morawska, George E. Pozzetta, and Rudolph J. Vecoli. "The Invention of Ethnicity: A Perspective from the USA." *Journal of American Ethnic History* 12 (Fall 1992): 3–41.

Crosswaith, Frank. "Negro Dress Workers Ready for Battle." *Justice*, January 15, 1936.

————. "Some Vital Problems of Negro Labor." *Justice*, January 1, 1935.

Danish, Max D. *The World of David Dubinsky*. Cleveland: World, 1957.

Denning, Michael. *The Cultural Front: The Laboring of American Culture in the Twentieth Century*. New York: Verso, 1997.

Dewey, John. *David Dubinsky: A Pictorial Biography*. New York: Inter-Allied, 1951.

Diner, Hasia. *In the Almost Promised Land: American Jews and Blacks, 1915–1935*. Baltimore: Johns Hopkins University Press, 1995.

Doroshkin, Yankl. "In the Beginning . . ." Reprinted in Gedalia Sandler, *Kinderland: From Generation to Generation; Celebrating 75 Years of Camp Kinderland*. New York: Kinderland, 1998.

Draper, Theodore. *American Communism and Soviet Russia*. 1960. Reprint, New York: Vintage, 1986.

————. *The Roots of American Communism*. New York: Viking, 1957.

Dubinsky, David, and A. H. Raskin. *David Dubinsky: A Life with Labor*. New York: Simon and Schuster, 1977.

Dye, Nancy Schrom. *As Equals and as Sisters: Feminism, the Labor Movement, and the Women's Trade Union League of New York*. Columbia: University of Missouri Press, 1980.

Encyclopedia Judaica. Vol. 4. New York: Macmillan, 1972.

Enstad, Nan. *Ladies of Labor, Girls of Adventure: Working Women, Popular Culture, and Labor Politics at the Turn of the Twentieth Century*. New York: Columbia University Press, 1999.

Epstein, Melech. *Jewish Labor in the U.S.A.: An Industrial, Political, and Cultural History of the Jewish Labor Movement*. Vol. 1, *1882–1914*. New York: Trade Union Sponsoring Committee, 1950.

————. *Jewish Labor in the U.S.A.: An Industrial, Political, and Cultural History of the Jewish Labor Movement*. Vol. 2, *1914–1952*. New York: Trade Union Sponsoring Committee, 1953.

————. *Profiles of Eleven: Profiles of Eleven Men Who Guided the Destiny of an Immigrant Society and Stimulated Social Consciousness among the American People*. Detroit: Wayne Sate University Press, 1965.

Ewen, Elizabeth. *Immigrant Women in the Land of Dollars: Life and Culture on the Lower East Side, 1890–1925*. New York: Monthly Review Press, 1985.

Faue, Elizabeth. *Community of Suffering and Struggle: Women, Men, and the Labor Movement in Minneapolis, 1915–1945*. Chapel Hill: University of North Carolina Press, 1991.

———. "Paths of Unionization: Community, Bureaucracy, and Gender in the Minneapolis Labor Movement of the 1930s." In *Work Engendered: Toward a New History of American Labor*, ed. Ava Baron, 296–319. Ithaca: Cornell University Press, 1991.

Fink, Gary M., ed. *The Greenwood Encyclopedia of American Institutions: Labor Unions*. Westport, CT: Greenwood, 1977.

Foner, Philip S. *American Socialism and Black Americans: From the Age of Jackson to World War II*. Westport, CT: Greenwood, 1977.

———. *The History of the Labor Movement in the United States*. Vol. 10, *The T.U.E.L., 1925–1929*. New York: International Publishers, 1975.

———. *Organized Labor and the Black Worker, 1619–1973*. New York: International Publishers, 1974.

———. *Women and the American Labor Movement*. Vol. 2, *From World War I to the Present*. New York: Free Press, 1980.

Foner, Philip S., and Ronald L. Lewis, eds. *The Black Worker: A Documentary History from Colonial Times to the Present*. Vol. 5, *The Black Worker from 1900 to 1919*. Philadelphia: Temple University Press, 1980.

———, eds. *The Black Worker: A Documentary History from Colonial Times to the Present*. Vol. 6, *The Era of Post-war Prosperity and the Great Depression, 1920–1936*. Philadelphia: Temple University Press, 1981.

Foner, Philip S., and Herbert Shapiro, eds. *American Communism and Black Americans: A Documentary History, 1930–1934*. Philadelphia: Temple University Press, 1991.

Fones-Wolf, Elizabeth. *Waves of Opposition: Labor and the Struggle for Democratic Radio*. Urbana: University of Illinois Press, 2006.

Foulkes, Julia L. "Angels 'Rewolt': Jewish Women in Modern Dance in the 1930s." *American Jewish History* 88, no. 2 (2000): 233–52.

Frankel, Jonathan. *Prophecy and Politics: Socialism, Nationalism, and the Russian Jews, 1862–1917*. Cambridge: Cambridge University Press, 1981.

Fraser, Steven. *Labor Will Rule: Sidney Hillman and the Rise of American Labor*. New York: Free Press, 1991.

Fraser, Steven, and Gary Gerstle, eds. *The Rise and Fall of the New Deal Order, 1930–1980*. Princeton: Princeton University Press, 1989.

Freeman, Joshua Benjamin. "Catholics, Communists, and Republicans: Irish Workers and the Organization of the Transport Workers Union." In *Working-Class America: Essays on Labor, Community, and American Society*, ed. Michael H. Frisch and Daniel J. Walkowitz, 256–83. Urbana: University of Illinois Press, 1983.

———. *In Transit: The Transport Workers Union in New York City, 1933–1966*. Philadelphia: Temple University Press, 2001.

Freire, Paulo. *Pedagogy of the Oppressed*. 1970. Reprint, New York: Continuum, 2000.

Friedland, Louis. "The Bases of Our Educational Work." *Justice*, February 2, 1920, 3.

———. "Our Educational Aims and Problems." *Justice*, November 21, 1919

Fuller, Paul W. "Miners' Educational Work." *American Federationist*, March 1926, 324–26.

Gabin, Nancy F. *Feminism in the Labor Movement: Women and the United Auto Workers, 1935–1975.* Ithaca: Cornell University Press, 1990.

Galenson, Walter. *The CIO Challenge to the AFL: A History of the American Labor Movement.* Cambridge: Harvard University Press, 1960.

Gechtman, Roni. "Socialist Mass Politics through Sport: The Bund's Morgnshtern in Poland, 1926–1939." *Journal of Sport History* 26, no. 2 (1999): 326–52.

———. "Yidisher Sotsializm: The Bund's National Program in the Context of the Second Polish Republic." Professor Bernard Choseed Memorial Lecture, YIVO Institute for Jewish Research, 2000.

Gerstle, Gary. *Working-Class Americanism: The Politics of Labor in a Textile City, 1914–1960.* New York: Cambridge University Press, 1989.

Glazer, Nathan. *The Social Basis of American Communism.* New York: Harcourt, Brace and World, 1961.

Glazer, Nathan, and Daniel P. Moynihan. *Beyond the Melting Pot: The Negroes, Puerto Ricans, Jews, Italians, and Irish of New York City.* Cambridge: MIT Press, 1963.

Glenn, Susan A. *Daughters of the Shtetl: Life and Labor in the Immigrant Generations.* Ithaca: Cornell University Press, 1990.

Godfried, Nathan. "Struggling over Politics and Culture: Organized Labor and Radio Station WEVD during the 1930s." *Labor History* 42, no. 4 (2001): 347–69.

———. *WCFL: Chicago's Voice of Labor, 1926–1978.* Urbana: University of Illinois Press, 1997.

Goldman, Harry Merton. "Pins and Needles: An Oral History." Ph.D. diss., New York University, 1977.

Goldsmith, Emmanuel S. *Architects of Yiddishism at the Beginning of the Twentieth Century: A Study in Jewish Cultural History.* Madison, NJ: Fairleigh Dickinson University Press, 1976.

———. *The Story of the Yiddish Language Movement.* New York: Shapolsky, 1987.

Goodman, James E. *Stories of Scottsboro.* New York: Pantheon, 1994.

Goslin, Ryllis Alexander, and Omar Pancoast Goslin. *Growing Up: Twenty-One Years of Education with the I.L.G.W.U., 1917–1938.* New York: H. Wolff, 1938.

Green, Nancy L. *Ready-to-Wear and Ready-to-Work: A Century of Industry and Immigrants in Paris and New York.* Durham: Duke University Press, 1997.

Greene, Julie. *Pure and Simple Politics: The American Federation of Labor and Political Action, 1881–1917.* New York: Cambridge University Press, 1998.

Greenwald, Richard. *The Triangle Fire, the Protocols of Peace, and Industrial Democracy in Progressive Era New York.* Philadelphia: Temple University Press, 2005.

Grossman, James R. *Land of Hope: Chicago, Black Southerners, and the Great Migration.* Chicago: University of Chicago Press, 1989.

Guglielmo, Jennifer. "Negotiating Gender, Race, and Coalition: Italian Women and Working-Class Politics in New York City, 1880–1945." Ph.D. diss., University of Minnesota, 2003.

Gutman, Herbert George. "The Negro and the United Mine Workers of America: The Career and Letters of Richard L. Davis and Something of Their Meaning." In *Work, Culture, and Society in Industrializing America: Essays in American Working-Class and Social History,* 121–208. New York: Vintage Books, 1976.

Harris, William H. *The Harder We Run: Black Workers since the Civil War.* New York: Oxford University Press, 1982.

Herberg, Will. "Educational Activities of Local 22." *Justice*, January 1934, 23.

Herzl, Theodor. *The Diaries of Theodor Herzl*. Ed. Marvin Lowenthal. New York: Grosset and Dunlap, 1962.

———. *The Jewish State*. 1896. Reprint, New York: Dover, 1988.

Himelstein, Morgan. *Drama Was a Weapon*. New Brunswick: Rutgers University Press, 1963.

Hollinger, David A. *Postethnic America: Beyond Multiculturalism*. New York: Basic Books, 1995.

Holmes, John. "American Jewish Communism and Garment Unionism in the 1920s." *American Communist History* 6, no. 2 (2007): 126.

Horowitz, Roger. *"Negro and White, Unite and Fight": A Social History of Industrial Unionism in Meatpacking, 1930–1980*. Urbana: University of Illinois Press, 1997.

Howe, Irving. *World of Our Fathers: The Journey of the East European Jews to America and the Life They Found and Made*. New York: Harcourt Brace Jovanovich, 1976.

Howlett, Charles. *Brookwood Labor College and the Struggle for Peace and Social Justice in America*. Lewiston, NY: Mellen, 1993.

Hurwitz, Maximillian. *The Workmen's Circle: Its History, Ideals, Organization and Institutions*. New York: Workmen's Circle, 1936.

Hyman, Colette A. *Staging Strikes: Workers' Theatre and the American Labor Movement*. Philadelphia: Temple University Press, 1997.

Hyman, Paula. "Culture and Gender: Women in the Immigrant Jewish Community." In *The Legacy of Jewish Migration: 1881 and Its Impact*, ed. David Berger, 157–68. New York: Brooklyn College Press, 1983.

———. "Immigrant Women and Consumer Protest: The New York Kosher Meat Boycott of 1902." *American Jewish History* 70 (1980): 91–105.

Jacobs, Joseph, ed. *The American Jewish Year Book, 5676*. Philadelphia: Jewish Publication Society of America, 1915.

Janiewski, Dolores. "Sisters under Their Skins: Southern Working Women, 1880–1950." In *Sex, Race, and the Role of Women in the South*, ed. Joanne Hawks and Sheila L. Skemp, 13–35. Jackson: University of Mississippi, 1983.

Kallen, Horace. *Culture and Democracy in the United States: Studies in the Group Psychology of the American People*. New York: Boni and Liveright, 1924.

———. "Democracy versus the Melting Pot." *Nation* 100 (February 19 and 25, 1915).

Kasson, John F. *Amusing the Million: Coney Island at the Turn of the Century*. New York: Hill and Wang, 1978.

Keiler, Allan. *Marian Anderson: A Singer's Journey*. New York: Scribner, 2000.

Kelley, Robin D. G. *Hammer and Hoe: Alabama Communists during the Great Depression*. Chapel Hill: University of North Carolina Press, 1990.

———. *Race Rebels: Culture, Politics, and the Black Working Class*. New York: Free Press, 1994.

Kelly, Brian. *Race, Class, and Power in the Alabama Coalfields, 1908–1921*. Urbana: University of Illinois Press, 2001.

Kessler-Harris, Alice. "Organizing the Unorganizable: Three Jewish Women and Their Union." *Labor History* 17, no. 1 (1976): 5–23.

———. *Out to Work: A History of Wage-Earning Women in the United States*. New York: Oxford University Press, 1982.

———. "Problems of Coalition-Building: Women and Trade Unions in the 1920s." In *Women, Work, and Protest: A Century of U.S. Women's Labor History*, ed. Ruth Milkman, 110–38. New York: Routledge, 1985.

———. "Where Are the Organized Women Workers?" In *A Heritage of Her Own: Toward a New Social History of American Women*, ed. Nancy Cott and Elizabeth Pleck, 343–66. New York: Touchstone Books, 1979.

Klehr, Harvey E. *Communist Cadre: The Social Background of the American Communist Party Elite*. Stanford, CA: Hoover Institution Press, 1978.

———. *The Heyday of American Communism: The Depression Decade*. New York: Basic Books, 1984.

Kornweibel, Theodore, Jr. *No Crystal Stair: Black Life and the Messenger, 1917–1928*. Westport, CT: Greenwood, 1975.

Korrol, Virginia E. Sanchez. *From Colonia to Community: The History of Puerto Ricans in New York City*. Berkeley: University of California Press, 1994.

Laidlaw, Walter. "Makes an Analysis of Census Figures: Federation of Churches Predicts That in Future Brooklyn Will Gain More than Manhattan." *New York Times*, September 4, 1910.

Laslett, John H. M. *Labor and the Left: A Study of Socialist and Radical Influences in the American Labor Movement, 1881–1924*. New York: Basic Books, 1970.

Letwin, Daniel. *The Challenge of Interracial Unionism: Alabama Coal Miners, 1878–1921*. Chapel Hill: University of North Carolina Press, 1998.

Levin, Nora. "The Influence of the Bund on the Jewish Socialist Movement in America." *Gratz College Journal*, 1971.

Levine, Louis. *The Women's Garment Workers: A History of the International Ladies' Garment Workers' Union*. New York: Huebsch, 1924.

Lewis, David Levering. "Parallels and Divergences: Assimilationist Strategies of Afro-American and Jewish Elites from 1910 to the Early 1930s." *Journal of American History* 71, no. 3 (1984): 543–64.

———. *Prisoners of Honor: The Dreyfus Affair*. New York: Holt, 1974.

———. *When Harlem Was in Vogue*. New York: Oxford University Press, 1981.

Lieberman, Robbie. *"My Song Is My Weapon": People's Songs, American Communism, and the Politics of Culture, 1930–1950*. Urbana: University of Illinois Press, 1995.

Lowenthal, Marvin. Introduction to *The Diaries of Theodor Herzl*, by Theodor Herzl. New York: Grosset and Dunlap, 1962.

MacLean, Nancy. *Behind the Mask of Chivalry: The Making of the Second Ku Klux Klan*. New York: Oxford University Press, 1994.

———. "The Culture of Resistance: Female Institutional Building in the International Ladies' Garment Workers' Union, 1905–1925." *Michigan Occasional Papers in Women's Studies*, Winter 1982.

Malmgreen, Gail. "Labor and the Holocaust: The Jewish Labor Committee and the Anti-Nazi Struggle." *Labor's Heritage*, October 1991, 20–25.

Marable, Manning. "A. Philip Randolph and the Foundations of Black American Socialism." In *Workers' Struggles, Past and Present: A "Radical America" Reader*, ed. James Green, 209–33. Philadelphia: Temple University Press, 1983.

Mason, Alpheus Thomas. *Brandeis: A Free Man's Life*. New York: Viking, 1946.

Matyas, Jennie. "The Violets Asked for You." *Justice*, June 4, 1920, 3.

Medem, Vladimir. *The Life and Soul of a Legendary Jewish Socialist: The Memoirs of Vladimir Medem*. Ed. Samuel A. Portnoy. New York: Ktav, 1979.

Michels, Tony. *A Fire in Their Hearts: Yiddish Socialists in New York*. Cambridge: Harvard University Press, 2005.

Mishler, Paul C. *Raising Reds: The Young Pioneers, Radical Summer Camps, and Communist Political Culture in the United States*. New York: Columbia University Press, 1999.

Morgan, Ted. *A Covert Life: Jay Lovestone—Communist, Anti-Communist, and Spymaster*. New York: Random House, 1999.

Nahshon, Edna. "*The Melting Pot*: Introductory Essay." In Israel Zangwill, *From the Ghetto to the Melting Pot: Israel Zangwill's Jewish Plays*, ed. Edna Nahshon, 211–63. Detroit: Wayne State University Press, 2006.

Naison, Mark. *Communists in Harlem during the Great Depression*. New York: Grove, 1983.

Nelson, Daniel. *Managers and Workers: Origins of the New Factory System in the United States, 1880–1920*. Madison: University of Wisconsin Press, 1975.

Ngai, Mae M. "The Architecture of Race in American Immigration Law: A Re-examination of the Immigration Act of 1924." *Journal of American History* 86 (1999): 67–92.

———. *Impossible Subjects: Illegal Aliens and the Making of Modern America*. Princeton: Princeton University Press, 2004.

O'Farrell, Brigid, and Joyce L. Kornbluh. *Rocking the Boat: Union Women's Voices, 1915–1975*. New Brunswick: Rutgers University Press, 1996.

———. "We Did Change Some Attitudes: Maida Springer-Kemp and the International Ladies' Garment Workers' Union." *Women's Studies Quarterly* 1–2 (1995): 41–70.

Orleck, Annelise. *Common Sense and a Little Fire: Women and Working-Class Politics in the United States, 1900–1965*. Chapel Hill: University of North Carolina Press, 1995.

Ottley, Roi, and William J. Weatherby. *The Negro in New York: An Informed Social History*. Dobbs Ferry, NY: Oceana, 1967.

Parmet, Robert D. *The Master of Seventh Avenue: David Dubinsky and the American Labor Movement*. New York: NYU Press, 2005.

Pastorello, Karen. *A Power among Them: Bessie Abromowitz Hillman and the Making of the Amalgamated Clothing Workers of America*. Urbana: University of Illinois Press, 2007.

Patkin, A. L. *The Origins of the Russian-Jewish Labour Movement*. Melbourne: F. W. Cheshire, 1947.

Peiss, Kathy. *Cheap Amusements: Working Women and Leisure in Turn-of-the-Century New York*. Philadelphia: Temple University Press, 1986.

Pesotta, Rose. *Bread upon the Waters*. 1944. Reprint, Ithaca: Cornell University Press, 1987.

———. *Days of Our Lives*. Boston: Excelsior, 1958.

———. "The Revolt of Los Angeles Dressmakers." *Justice*, January 1934, 21.

———. "Singing in the Shop." *Justice*, July 1934.

Peters, Paul, and George Sklar. *Stevedore: A Play in Three Acts*. New York: Covici, Friede, 1934.

Rabinowitz, Solomon. "Socialists and the War." *Call* (Workmen's Circle), November 1942, 14.

Renner, Karl. "State and Nation." In *National Cultural Autonomy and Its Contemporary Critics*, ed. Ephraim Nimni, 13–41. New York: Routledge, 2005.

Reynolds, David. *Walt Whitman's America: A Cultural Biography*. New York: Knopf, 1995.

Richards, Yevette. *Maida Springer: Pan-Africanist and International Labor Leader*. Pittsburgh: University of Pittsburgh Press, 2000.

Robertson, Nancy Marie. *Christian Sisterhood: Race Relations and the YWCA, 1906–1946.* Urbana: University of Illinois Press, 2007.

Roediger, David R. *The Wages of Whiteness: Race and the Making of the American Working Class.* New York: Verso, 1999.

———. *Working towards Whiteness: How America's Immigrants Became White; The Strange Journey from Ellis Island to the Suburbs.* New York: Basic Books, 2005.

Rush, David Alan. "A History and Evaluation of the ILGWU Labor Stage and Its Production of *Pins and Needles*, 1937–1940." Master's thesis, University of Iowa, 1965.

Ruskies, David G. Introduction to *The Dybbuk and Other Writings*, by S. Ansky, ed. David G. Ruskies, trans. Golda Werman, xi–xxxvi. New York: Schocken Books, 1992.

Sacks, Karen. *Caring by the Hour: Women, Work, and Organizing at Duke Medical Center.* Urbana: University of Illinois Press, 1988.

Salvatore, Nick. *Eugene V. Debs: Citizen and Socialist.* Urbana: University of Illinois Press, 1982.

Sanchez, George. *Becoming Mexican American: Ethnicity, Culture and Identity in Chicano Los Angeles, 1900–1945.* New York: Oxford University Press, 1993.

Seabrook, John H. "Black and White United: The Career of Frank R. Crosswaith." Ph.D. diss., Rutgers University, 1980.

Seidman, Joel. *The Needle Trades.* New York: Farrar and Rinehart, 1942.

Seller, Maxine Schwartz. "The Uprising of the Twenty Thousand: Sex, Class, and Ethnicity in the Shirtwaist Makers' Strike of 1909." In *"Struggle a Hard Battle": Essays on Working-Class Immigrants*, ed. Dirk Hoerder, 254–79. DeKalb: Northern Illinois University Press, 1986.

Shapiro, Judah Joseph. *The Friendly Society: A History of the Workmen's Circle.* New York: Media Judaica, 1970.

Shaviro, Nathan. "A Visit to the Unity House," *Justice*, June 18, 1920, 5.

Sollors, Werner. *The Invention of Ethnicity.* New York: Oxford University Press, 1988.

Spear, Allan H. *Black Chicago: The Making of a Negro Ghetto, 1890–1920.* Chicago: University of Chicago Press, 1967.

Spero, Sterling D., and Abram L. Harris. *The Black Worker: The Negro and the Labor Movement.* New York: Columbia University Press, 1931.

Stalin, Joseph V. "Marxism and the National Question." *Prosveshxhentye* 3–5 (March–May 1913). Transcribed and translated by Carl Cavanagh, Marxist.org, www.marxist.org/reference/archive/stalin/works/1913/03.htm.

Stein, Leon, ed. *Out of the Sweatshop: The Struggle for Industrial Democracy.* New York: Quadrangle, 1977.

———. *The Triangle Fire.* Philadelphia: Lippincott, 1962.

Stolberg, Benjamin. *Tailor's Progress: The Story of a Famous Union and the Men Who Made It.* Garden City, NY: Doubleday, Doran, 1944.

Storch, Randi. *Red Chicago: American Communism at Its Grassroots, 1928–1935.* Urbana: University of Illinois Press, 2007.

Strunsky, Rose. "The Strike of the Singers of the Shirt." *International Socialist Review* 10 (1909).

Susman, Warren I. *Culture as History: The Transformation of American Society in the Twentieth Century.* New York: Pantheon, 1984.

Taft, Philip. *The AF of L: From the Death of Gompers to the Merger.* New York: Harper and Brothers, 1959.

Tax, Meredith. *The Rising of the Women: Feminist Solidarity and Class Conflict, 1880–1917.* New York: Monthly Review Press, 1980.

Tobias, Henry J. *The Jewish Bund in Russia: From Its Origins to 1905.* Stanford: Stanford University Press, 1972.

Trotter, Joe William, Jr. *Coal, Class, and Color: Blacks in Southern West Virginia, 1915–1932.* Urbana: University of Illinois Press, 1990.

Trunk, Isaiah. "The Cultural Dimension of the American Jewish Labor Movement." In "Essays on the American Jewish Labor Movement," ed. Ezra Mendelsohn. *YIVO Annual of Jewish Social Science* 16 (1976).

Turner, Frederick Jackson. "The Significance of the Frontier in American History." In *Rereading Frederick Jackson Turner: "The Significance of the Frontier in American History" and Other Essays,* ed. John Mack Faragher, 31–60. New York: Holt, 1994.

Tyler, Gus. *Look for the Union Label: A History of the International Ladies' Garment Workers' Union.* Armonk, NY: Sharpe, 1995.

Vural, Leyla. "Unionism as a Way of Life." Ph.D. diss., Rutgers University, 1994.

Waldinger, Roger. "Another Look at the International Ladies' Garment Workers' Union: Women, Industry Structure and Collective Action." In *Women, Work, and Protest: A Century of U.S. Women's Labor History,* ed. Ruth Milkman, 86–109. Boston: Routledge and Kegan Paul, 1985.

Weinberg, David H. *Between Tradition and Modernity: Haim Zhitlowski, Simon Dubnow, Ahad Ha-Am, and the Shaping of Modern Jewish Identity.* New York: Holmes and Meier, 1996.

Wertheimer, Barbara Mayer. *We Were There: The Story of Working Women in America.* New York: Pantheon, 1977.

Whitman, Walt. *Leaves of Grass: Comprehensive Readers' Edition.* Ed. Harold W. Blodgett and Sculley Bradley. New York: NYU Press, 1965.

Williams, Jay. *Stage Left.* New York: Scribner's, 1974.

Williams, Raymond. "Base and Superstructure in Marxist Cultural Theory." *New Left Review* 82 (1973): 31–49.

Wolensky, Kenneth C., and Nicole H. Wolensky. *Fighting for the Union Label: The Women's Garment Industry and the ILGWU in Pennsylvania.* College Station: Penn State University Press, 2000.

Wong, Susan Stone. "From Soul to Strawberries: The International Ladies' Garment Workers' Union and Workers' Education, 1914–1950." In *Sisterhood and Solidarity: Workers' Education for Women, 1914–1984,* ed. Joyce L. Kornbluh and Mary Frederickson, 39–74. Philadelphia: Temple University Press, 1984.

Yagoda, Louis. "Our English-Speaking Branches." *Call* (Workmen's Circle), May–June 1940, 51.

Yarmolinsky, Avrahm. *Road to Revolution: A Century of Russian Radicalism.* Princeton: Princeton University Press, 1957.

Zappia, Charles Anthony. "Unionism and the Italian American Worker: A History of the New York City 'Italian Locals' in the International Ladies' Garment Workers' Union, 1900 1934." Ph.D. diss., University of California, 1994.

Zimmerman, Charles S. "Local 22 Draws New Groups into Activity." *Justice,* December 1933.

MISCELLANEOUS SOURCES

Boyer, Mary. Personal photographs.
Pearman Ashford, Olive. Personal letters in her possession.
Pins and Needles: Twenty-Fifth Anniversary Edition of the Hit Musical Revue. Music and lyrics by Harold Rome. Columbia Records, 1962. Recording. Liner notes.

Index

Page numbers in italics refer to illustrations

Dressmakers Local 22. See Local 22, ILGWU

Dressmakers Trade Union Circle, 113

Dreyfus Affair, 32–33, 247n47

Dubinsky, David, 91; and Fannia Cohn, 109, 119–20, 140, 184, 187–88; and liberal politicians, 192, 196, 197, 203, 207, 230; in Local 10, 91, 173; and NIRA, 123, 193, 195–96; and *Pins and Needles,* 207, 214, *215*; and racial issues, 113, 145, 177–79, 180, 214, 215, 237; rise of, in union, 91, 99, 115; and Socialist Party, 140, 175, 222; and union education, 184–88, 191–92, 234; and Charles Zimmerman, 91, 119–20, 140, 145, 172–75, 177–79, 192, 195–97, 262n90

Dubnow, Simon, 24

Dunham, Katherine, 204, 211–12, 218–19

Dutcher, Elizabeth, 54–55

Dybbuk, The, 77

Dyche, John A., 47, 60, 61–62, 63, 69

Dye, Nancy Schrom, 53

Eben, Al, 213

educational programs, 63–70; and ILGWU factional rivalries, 9, 87, 93, 96–97, 110; in Local 22, 129–31, 137–39, 140–41, 145, 146–49, 168–69, 208–10, 234; in Local 25, 66, 67–68, 69–70, 83–84; and Protocols of Peace, 62–63; and social unionism, 3–4, 8–9, 139–40; women's central role in, 6–7, 64–68, 83–84, 107–9, 143–44, 163; of Workmen's Circle, 38, 39–40, 42–43

—at International union level, 67–69, 187–88, 191, 210, 234; Fannia Cohn and, 67–68, 69, 75–77, 78–79, 97, 99, 105–10, 120, 127–29

Einstein, Albert, 40, 207, *209*

English classes, 158

ethnicity, 2, 7; Jewish, 219–20 (*see also* Yiddishism). *See also* multiculturalism; mutual culturalism

ethnicity (term), 11–12, 243n16

Eva Jessye Negro Choir, 156

family involvement, 79, 85, 146–48, 154–55, 156–57, *159*; and social unionism, 79, 156

Faue, Elizabeth, 13

Feigenbaum, Benjamin, 51

feminism, 12–13, 31, 53

Fichlandler, Alexander, 93

Fischer, Bruno, 141

Flores, Celia, 150–51, 172

Flynn, Elizabeth Gurley, 104

Forverts. See *Jewish Daily Forward*

Foster, William Z., 74, 86, 91–92, 116, 117

Four Freedoms, 235, 236

Fraina, Louis, 73. *See also* Corey, Lewis

Freiheit, 87, 98

Freire, Paulo, 128

Friedland, Louis, 75–76, 77

Friedman, Charles, 203–4, 221

Friedman, Mollie, 87, 92–93

fur industry, 100

gangsters, 91, 92

garment industry. *See* ladies' garment industry

garment strike of 1933, 123–25, 192–94, 197–98, 262n86; and ILGWU growth, 1, 123–24, 165, 184; and NIRA, 192–94

Gaskin, Lillian, 141, 177–80

Gaskins, Oretta, *142*

Geliebter, P. H., 102

Gelo, John, 154

gender stereotypes, 188–89; in *Pins and Needles,* 223–24

generational differences, 78, 94–95, 176

Gerber, David A., 12

Gerstle, Gary, 7

Gitlow, Benjamin, 73, 117

Glenn, Susan A., 31, 52

Gold, Benjamin, 92, 100

Goldman, Emma, 73, 74

Goldman, Harry Merton, 218, 223

Goldstein, Eugene, 219

Gompers, Samuel, 37, 50, 263n19

Gordon, Robert, 204, 217, 221

Graeber, Ruth Rubinstein, 207, 210, 213, 217, 219

Graham, Martha, 201, 204

Grand Solidarity Balls, 143

Great Depression, 136–37; and ILGWU membership, 112; and ladies' garment industry, 13, 99, 118–19, 136–37, 163

Johnson, Michael, 238–40
Joint Action Committee (JAC), 90–91
Justice, 76, 118, 126–27, 193; Fannia Cohn articles in, 108, 127–28, 188–89; on ILGWU multiculturalism, 189, 236; on racial issues, 81, 114, 182–83

Kallen, Horace, 5, 27
Kazan, Elia, 204
Keller, Helen, 104
Kinderland (Camp Kinderland), 79-80, 104, 256n30
Klehr, Harvey, 100
Kozakevich, Stefan, 119
Ku Klux Klan, 74, 97
Kushner, Ethel, 211, 212, 219

Labor Age, 108
Labor Stage Incorporated, 202, 204, 228, 234; and *Pins and Needles*, 202, 204, 206, 210, 211–12, 219
ladies' garment industry, 13–14, 36–37, 123, 164–65, 257n51; dispersal of, 118, 165, 186–87; gender differences in, 57–58; impact of Great Depression on, 13, 99, 118–19, 136–37, 163; jobbers in, 36, 117, 164, 191; New York City's role in, 13–14; privileging of men in, 57–58; seasonal employment in, 65–66; workforce composition in, 81, 82, 83, 99, 127; working conditions in, 36–37, 118–19
Ladies' Garment Worker, 56
La Guardia, Fiorello, 191, 192, 197, 207, 230
Lane, Lucille, *142*
Latinos. *See* Spanish-speaking workers
Lehman, Herbert H., 171, 192, 197, 207, 230
Lemlich, Clara (Clara Lemlich Shavelson), 48, 51, 53, 64, 65
Lenin, V. I., 74
Le Sueur, Meridel, 104
Levine, Louis, 55, 58–59, 63, 94, 176
Levy, Al, 219
liberalism, 197, 222–23, 227–28, 234, 240. *See also* New Deal
libraries, 137
Life magazine, 207, 212
Liga Puertorriqueña y Hispana, 132

Lilienthal, Max, 23
Local 22, ILGWU (Dressmakers' Local 22), 86–87, 112–14, 156–63, 165, 170, 205, 221, 260n47; Black workers in, 82, 112–14, 129–31, 141–42, 143–44, 145–46, 180, 237; diverse membership of, 9–11, 155; educational programs of, 129–31, 137–39, 140–41, 145, 146–49, 168–69, 208–10, 234; influence of, on other locals, 133; multiculturalism in, 161–63; residential sections of, 129, 141, 174; social and recreational events sponsored by, 143–45, 146–52, *159*, 166, 190, 208–11; social unionism in, 119, 130–33, 144–52, 154–55, 156–59, 160; Spanish-speaking workers in, 113–14, 130–33, 154–55, 156–59, 172; tension of, with International leadership, 86–87, 88, 90, 95, 96, 119–20, 173, 175; and Unity House, 80, 95, 96; women leaders in, 143–44, 146–47, 176; in World War II, 234, 237. *See also* Zimmerman, Charles "Sasha"
—residential sections of, 129, 141, 174; East Harlem, 130–31, 150, 154–55, *159*; Harlem (West Harlem), 130–31, 145 (*see also* Dressmakers' International Ball)
Local 25, ILGWU (Shirtwaist Makers' Local 25, later Waistcoat Makers' Local 25), 51, 63, 67, 85–87, 95; in 1909 shirtwaist strike, 50, 51; radicalism of, 63, 66, 70, 85–86, 87; splitting of Local 22 from, 86; union education in, 66, 67–68, 69–70, 83–84; women's leadership in, 66, 84
Local 91, ILGWU (Childrens' Dressmakers' Local 91), 129, 133–36, 143, 149, *157, 160, 167,* 170–71; choral group of, 185, *186*; diverse membership of, 129, 133–34; racial integration in, 143, *148,* 149, *157, 160*; Gus Tyler in, 135–36, *160*. See also *Our Aim*
Lopez, Nora, 138–39
Lore, Ludwig, 92
Los Angeles, 194–95
Lovestone, Jay, 73, 92, 114–15, 116–17
Lovestoneite faction, 114–18, 129, 133, 173, 208, 222
Lower East Side, 7, 37, 39, 46, 48–49
Lurye, Minnie, 117, 173

MacLean, Nancy, 47, 56
Mandel, Ida, 205
March on Washington Movement (MOWM), 237–38
Maskalim (Haskalah movement), 23, 34
Matyas, Jennie, 67, 83–84, 87, 256n43
Maurice, Anita Burke, 136–37, 153
May Day parades, 160–61, 169–70, 236
McKay, Claude, 105
"melting pot" metaphor, 27
"Men, Awake!," 221–22
Messenger, The, 80, 81, 82, 256n32
Mirsky, Bessy, 87
Mishler, Paul C., 100
Morrison, Lee, 211–12
multiculturalism, 2, 5–6, 97, 152–64, 189; Fannia Cohn and, 76–77, 84, 106–7; power of, in ILGWU, 7–9; variants of, 5–6, 27, 234; weakening of, in late 1930s, 165, 198, 237; and Yiddish socialism, 7, 9, 46–47, 56–57, 80, 83–84, 109. *See also* mutual culturalism
music, 119, 137, 153, 155, *159,* 185
Muste, A. J., 76
mutual culturalism, 5, 6, 144, 163, 232, 240; defined, 6; erosion of, in ILGWU, 165, 201, 219–20, 230, 232, 240; and Yiddish socialism, 5, 6, 28–29, 232

National Association for the Advancement of Colored People (NAACP), 105
National Industrial Recovery Act (NIRA), 123, 192–94, 195–98. *See also* National Recovery Administration
nationalism, 5, 27. *See also* Jewish nationalism
nationality (term), 9–10
National Labor Relations Act (Wagner Act), 8, 191, 197, 203, 232
National Recovery Administration (NRA), 192–94, 195–97
Nazism, 162–63, 168
Nearing, Scott, 76
Needle Trades Workers' Industrial Union (NTWIU), 93, 104, 110, 116, 117, 168, 173–74
Negro Labor Committee (NLC), 141, 183–84
Nehama, Saby, 132, 172
Nelson, Louis, 117, 118, 133, 173

New Deal, 230, 232. *See also* National Industrial Recovery Act; National Labor Relations Act
Newman, Pauline, 48, 53, 54, 64, 65, 66
New Masses, 105
New Workers School, 129
"New York at War" parade (1942), 235–37
New York Call, 51, 53, 54–55
New York Women's Trade Union League (NYWTUL), 50–51, 53–55
New York Workers School, 129
"1905 generation," 39, 44, 47, 49, 56–57, 70, 230
Ninfo, Salvatore, 55, 56, 69
Novik, Morris S., 155

Odets, Clifford, 204
open-shop campaign, 74, 186
O'Reilly, Leonora, 51
Orleck, Annelise, 13, 65
O'Sullivan, Mary Kenney, 53
Our Aim, 134–35, 158–59, *167,* 171, 177
Ovington, Mary White, 151–52
Owen, Chandler, 80–81, 104

pageants, 84, 106–7, 228
Pale of Settlement, 21, 22, 24, 31, 34
Palmer, A. Mitchell, 74
Palmer Raids, 74
parades, 235–37; May Day, 161, 169–70
Pearman, Olive (Olive Pearman Ashford), 177, 214–16, 217, 273n68n69
People's University, 40
People's Will (Narodnaia Volia), 24
Peretz, I. L., 24, 30, 78
Pesotta, Rose, 53, 67, 89, 153, 193; organizing tactics of, 178, 194–95, 264n27
Peters, Paul, 145
Philadelphia, 192–93
Pinkney, Floria, 111–12
Pins and Needles, 201–7, 226, 230; cast struggles in, 211–15, 217–18; and changing culture of ILGWU, 16, 207, 219–24, 230–31; gender stereotypes in, 223–24; popularity of, 202, 206–7; racial and ethnic issues in, *209,* 214–20; road performances of, 206, 207, 213–18. *See also* Schaffer, Louis: and *Pins and Needles*

34.00   12/6/11